WHS

WHS

A MANAGEMENT GUIDE | 3RD EDITION

RICHARD **ARCHER**   KERRY **BORTHWICK**   MICHELLE **TRAVERS**   LEO **RUSCHENA**

WHS: A Management Guide
3rd Edition
Richard Archer
Kerry Borthwick
Michelle Travers
Leo Ruschena

Publishing manager: Dorothy Chiu
Senior publishing editor: Dorothy Chiu
Senior project editor: Nathan Katz
Developmental editor: Meagan Carlsson
Text and cover design: Rina Gargaro
Proofreader: James Anderson
Editor: Gill Smith
Permissions research: Georgina Wober
Indexer: John Simkin
Cover: Image supplied by Photos.com
Typeset by Cenveo Publishing Services

Any URLs contained in this publication were checked for currency during the production process. Note, however, that the publisher cannot vouch for the ongoing currency of URLs.

First edition published in 2005
Second edition published in 2009

This third edition published in 2012

For product information and technology assistance,
in Australia call **1300 790 853**;
in New Zealand call **0800 449 725**

For permission to use material from this text or product, please email
aust.permissions@cengage.com

National Library of Australia Cataloguing-in-Publication Data
Title: WHS : a management guide / Richard Archer ... [et al.].
Edition: 3rd ed.
ISBN: 9780170196307 (pbk.)
Notes: Includes index.
Subjects: Industrial hygiene--Australia. Safety education, Industrial--Australia.
Other Authors/Contributors: Archer, Richard.
Dewey Number: 363.11071194

Cengage Learning Australia
Level 7, 80 Dorcas Street
South Melbourne, Victoria Australia 3205

Cengage Learning New Zealand
Unit 4B Rosedale Office Park
331 Rosedale Road, Albany, North Shore 0632, NZ

For learning solutions, visit **cengage.com.au**

Printed in China by RR Donnelley Asia Printing Solutions Limited.
1 2 3 4 5 6 7 15 14 13 12 11

CONTENTS

PREFACE

Workplace health and safety in Australia has undergone development since the publication of the last edition, the most significant being the harmonisation of health and safety Acts and regulations. Now there are identical Work Health and Safety Acts and regulations covering everyone in the major jurisdictions. (At the time of writing, early 2011, Western Australia indicated it would agree to harmonisation but with a few differences and NSW has allowed limited ability for unions to initiate prosecutions.) An initial set of codes of practice has also been developed. With the cooperation of everyone, harmonisation should enable greater fairness, effectiveness and efficiency in the management of health and safety. However, as long as the law governing workers compensation and injury management – an important driver of HS performance – stays 'un-harmonised', unfairness and confusion remain.

While coverage of the harmonisation of the laws represents the biggest change to this edition, we have added a new chapter on emerging issues in health and safety and undertaken considerable revision of the remainder of the text, making it a more practical, accessible and better book overall. However, the basic framework has been retained and the book remains as intended – a practical introduction to HS management for students and managers alike.

This edition also reflects the change in terminology from 'occupational health and safety' (OHS) to 'work' or 'workplace health and safety' (WHS). The change has been gradual over recent years and is reflected in the title of the principal Acts: 'Work Health and Safety Act'. It is also more accurate to talk in this way as the focus of health and safety is on work and the workplace, not on occupation.

Two other changes should be noted. Due to professional commitments, Susanne Tepe was unable to continue as co-author and is replaced by Leo Ruschena, also from RMIT. We thank Susanne for her help. We are also joined by Michelle Travers who brings her valuable VET experience to this text.

ACKNOWLEDGEMENTS

We thank the following reviewers for their constructive comments and criticisms, which were instrumental in making this textbook even better.

Deirdre Albrighton – Albrighton Consulting and Training Services
Maryann Davies – Holmesglen Institute
Greg Dickman – Swinburne University of Technology
Gun Dolva – Central Institute of Technology
Jenny Field – Australian College of Training & Employment
Patrick Lawrence – Australian Institute of Technology Transfer
Rebecca Loudoun – Griffith University
Grahame Lowe – Managed Corporate Outcomes
Ken Mattingley – Swinburne University of Technology
Barry Nicholls – Skills Tech Australia
Nimal Parawahera – Australian Centre for Work Safety
Bob Peoples – Swinburne University of Technology
Julie Quinlan – Wodonga Institute of TAFE

We are also obliged to Jenny Barron and Rod Hawkins, who provided important professional comment on chapters 13 and 16 respectively.

RESOURCES GUIDE

FOR THE STUDENT

As you read this text you will find a wealth of features in every chapter to enhance your study of work health and safety and help you understand its applications.

Learning objectives are listed at the start of every chapter to give you a clear sense of what will be covered.

Case studies appear in every chapter and are complemented by discussion questions to help you apply and test your understanding of key topics.

Did you know? boxes appear throughout each chapter and offer interesting facts on topical events and issues.

DID YOU KNOW?

An injury outcome is not required for there to be a contravention. The fact that a hazard exists, even in the absence of an injury, may be a contravention. Likewise, ignorance is no defence in WHS law. If information exists related to, say, toxicity of substances, or if research demonstrates safety problems with particular work practices, then there is a general presumption that the PCBU ought to be aware.

WHS in Practice boxes demonstrate how WHS theories can be applied to practical situations.

The **Glossary** provides a list of key terms and can be found at the back of the book.

You can also find an online version of the glossary, with flashcards and crosswords, on the book's companion website. To view this website visit http://login.cengagebrain.com/.

At the end of every chapter you'll find several tools to help you to review the key learning concepts, and also to help extend your learning.

The **In your workplace** activity provides a scenario-based activity that helps you apply key concepts to real-life situations.

Questions and **Activities** promote the application of theories and practices as well as encouraging group discussion.

The end-of-chapter **Summary** lists key points from the chapter, giving you a snapshot of the important concepts covered.

A 12 month subscription to **Search me! management** is provided with the text. This resource provides you with 24-hour access to full-text articles from hundreds of scholarly and popular journals, e-books, and newspapers, including *The Australian* and *The New York Times*, and is updated daily. Use the **Keywords** at the end of each chapter to explore topics further and find current references for assignments. These terms will get you started, and then try your own search terms to expand your knowledge of work health and safety.

FOR THE INSTRUCTOR

Cengage Learning is pleased to provide you with an extensive selection of online supplements to help prepare you for your course. These teaching tools are available on the companion website, accessible via **http://login.cengage.com**.

Instructor's Manual

The instructor's manual provides you with content to help you administer your course. It includes Learning Objectives, Teaching Tips and suggested solutions to the discussion questions and activities in the text.

PowerPoint Presentations

PowerPoint presentations cover the key concepts addressed within the text and can be edited to suit your specific teaching requirements. Use these slides to enhance your presentations and to reinforce key principles of each topic, or they can be provided as student handouts.

ABOUT THE AUTHORS

Richard Archer

Richard Archer is a WHS management consultant and president of Catalyst Australia. He was NSW Manager of Occupational Health and Safety for Comcare and, prior to that, a union WHS officer. Richard has also worked for PriceWaterhouseCoopers and the Hong Kong Jockey Club. His main interests lie in the areas of regulation and the effects of globalisation on workers. He holds a PhD from the University of Sydney and a Graduate Diploma in OHS from the University of Technology, Sydney.

Kerry Borthwick

Kerry Borthwick is a management consultant and director of Quality of Working Life. She is also a course author, coordinator and facilitator in health and safety management, as well as a co-author of enterprise risk management courses in the Master of Business & Technology program at the University of NSW. She has over 20 years' work experience in health and safety in the private and public sectors. Her main interests are WHS management-system development and effectiveness. She is a registered psychologist, a member of the Human Factors and Ergonomics Society of Australia, the Australian Epidemiological Association and the Australian Psychological Society.

Michelle Travers

Michelle Travers is a head teacher of Business Services (Human Resources & Management) at Western Sydney Institute of TAFE. She has held a number of human resource management, WHS and educational positions in both global and local organisations. Among her qualifications, Michelle holds a Masters of Human Resource Management and a Bachelor of Vocational Education and Training from Charles Sturt University, Wagga Wagga.

Leo Ruschena

Leo Ruschena is a consultant and senior lecturer in WHS at RMIT. He has held a number of senior management positions in human resources with organisations such as WorkSafe Victoria, ACTEW, Yallourn Energy and Generation Victoria. He has a Bachelor of Engineering (Chemical) and Bachelor of Economics from the University of Queensland; a Master of Science (Occupational Hygiene) from University of London; a Graduate Diploma in Organisational Behaviour, Swinburne University; and a Master of Industrial and Employee Relations from Monash University. Leo is a chartered fellow of the Safety Institute of Australia.

INTRODUCING HEALTH AND SAFETY

Learning Objectives

By the end of this chapter, the reader will be able to:

- define 'workplace health and safety'
- describe, in broad terms, the nature and size of Australia's health and safety problems
- provide the reasons for making health and safety a priority
- describe the factors affecting work and the implications for health and safety
- describe the institutional framework governing health and safety activity.

THE JAMES HARDIE STORY

Most people have heard of the dangers of asbestos, but not as many know that it is the cause of what is probably the biggest peacetime disaster in Australian history. The number of people diagnosed with asbestos-related **diseases** will not peak until 2020, when it is estimated upwards of 40 000 Australians will have died from mesothelioma and asbestos-related lung cancer.[1] This compares with the total of 40 500 military deaths suffered by Australia in World War II.

The mining and manufacture of asbestos and asbestos-related products took place in Australia for most of last century and was widespread until the 1980s. Deposits were mined in Tasmania, in Western Australia's Pilbara, and at Baryulgil in northern NSW, a mine owned by James Hardie, with a largely Aboriginal workforce. Australia was the highest per capita user of asbestos in the world from the 1950s to the 1970s.

Every third domestic dwelling built before 1982 is thought to contain asbestos. Asbestos was used in asbestos cement sheet or 'fibro' until the mid 1980s, potentially exposing every one of us now and into the future. It was finally banned in Australian workplaces in January 2004. In the meantime, asbestos miners, workers in asbestos plants, construction workers, installers and literally millions of others were exposed to asbestos, many acquiring fatal asbestos-related diseases such as mesothelioma.

ASBESTOS-RELATED DISEASES

Mesothelioma is a cancer caused by exposure to asbestos, commonly occurring in the lining of the lung. It results in extreme pain and breathlessness, as the lung is crushed by a tumour or tumours. It is fatal within about 9 to 12 months of diagnosis. The average time from initial exposure to the onset of mesothelioma is 37 years. There are currently no cures for mesothelioma.

In addition, asbestos also causes asbestosis and asbestos-related pleural disease. Both are severely disabling respiratory diseases for which there are currently no effective treatments or cure. Finally, lung cancer and other malignancies have been implicated in asbestos exposure.

JAMES HARDIE'S INVOLVEMENT

While not the only asbestos manufacturer, James Hardie was Australia's largest, producing goods containing asbestos throughout the twentieth century, including insulation products containing asbestos, asbestos cement sheet or 'fibro', and pipes and friction materials, particularly brake and clutch linings.[2]

Evidence presented at the 2004 Jackson Inquiry suggests that James Hardie had knowledge of the dangers of asbestos as early as the 1930s. No warnings or directions were placed on Hardie fibro until 1978, and the company continued to use asbestos in the manufacture of cement sheet until the mid 1980s.

DID YOU KNOW?

In 1899, a 33-year-old patient was admitted to a London hospital suffering from breathlessness; within 14 months he was dead. He had been the last survivor of a 10-man team that had worked in the carding room of an asbestos textile factory. The case of the unnamed patient, reported by Dr Montague Murray to the UK Parliament in 1906, was the first asbestos-related death to be officially documented; confirmation of the human health hazard posed by asbestos followed from France (1906), Italy (1908) and America (1918). And yet, a hundred years after European governments learned of this hazard, asbestos use is increasing in some Asian countries.

Source: Laurie Kazan-Allen, 2007, *Killing the Future – Asbestos use in Asia*, The International Ban Asbestos Secretariat: London, 2007, p. 6.

In what could only be described as the most cynical manoeuvre, the Hardie Group structured its operations so that the manufacture and supply of asbestos products was undertaken by subsidiary companies. In October 2001, the NSW Supreme Court approved an application from James Hardie to move to the Netherlands and set up as a Dutch company, taking with it $1.9 billion in assets from its former Australian companies. The court was assured these assets would be available if needed to meet the claims of Australian creditors, including asbestos victims. At the time, the Netherlands was one of only two countries with which Australia did not have a treaty enforcing civil court judgments.

In March 2003, the Dutch-based James Hardie severed its final links with its former Australian asbestos–producing entities and cancelled the capacity for them to call on the $1.9 billion to pay asbestos victims, should this be required. It did not advise the NSW Supreme Court, the NSW government or the Australian Stock Exchange of this.

It was only after a NSW Special Commission of Inquiry – the 2004 Jackson Inquiry – and the efforts of the ACTU, US and European unions, asbestos groups represented by Bernie Banton, the NSW government and council authorities that James Hardie finally agreed to settle and set up a special purpose fund to compensate victims. The first payment into the new fund of $184.3 million took place on 7 February 2007.

The estimated nominal value of compensation costs (after insurance and other recoveries) is $3.17 billion.

The lessons

A few of the many lessons that can be learned from this tragedy are:
* workplace health and safety affects us all – families and communities
* compensation comes too late and it is prevention that counts
* diseases often have long latency periods
* strong, effective institutions are needed to protect us
* people must come before profit.

The reader can add to this list.

Perhaps the most important lesson is that health and safety is not a thing of the past or limited to a small group of known high-risk industries – mining and construction, for example. The asbestos industry, including many workers, did not consider the fibres to be harmful until too late.

Today, materials, technologies and processes are used in the workplace often with little awareness or concern over the effects they have on our health and safety. New chemicals, new technologies such as nanotechnology, modern hazards such as electromagnetic radiation, work intensification involving extended working hours and non-standard employment using casual labour, telecommuting and mobile workforces are some examples. There is constant pressure for workers to adapt to the workplace and whatever is found there.

Nor is this pressure just found in organisations run for a profit like James Hardie. It applies to non-profit bodies such as government services and defence forces. Even charitable bodies are no exception to the rule. Ironically, working to help others can mean working under unhealthy conditions of extreme **stress** and long hours, using hazardous material and equipment.

While the pressure to put the objectives of the employer before the health and safety needs of its people varies from organisation to organisation, it is found everywhere. How to deal with this demand is the challenge set for all – managers, workers, unions and governments. This book examines ways to meet that challenge.

DEFINING WORKPLACE HEALTH AND SAFETY

The full definition of workplace, or occupational, health and safety (WHS), set jointly by the International Labour Organization and the World Health Organization, reads:

> Occupational health should aim at: the promotion and maintenance of the highest degree of physical, mental and social well-being of workers in all occupations; the prevention amongst workers of departures from health caused by their working conditions; the protection of workers in their employment from **risks** resulting from factors adverse to health; the placing and maintenance of the worker in an occupational environment adapted to his physiological and psychological capabilities; and, to summarize, the adaptation of work to man [*sic*] and of each man to his job.[3]

The key point is that the definition is positive – *promoting* and maintaining 'the highest degree of physical, mental and social well-being of workers in all occupations'. Such a definition presumes that workers must be safe from accident and injury. It is this definition that will be used throughout the text.

By contrast, some define health and safety slightly differently, and negatively, as activities preventing injuries or illness at work or removing or reducing the risk of such injuries or illness. The emphasis of such definitions is on being 'safe from'.

Using such definitions, complete success in health and safety terms would be an accident-free or risk-free workplace. Partial success would be a reduction in the frequency or incidence of accidents or a reduction in the degree of risk.[4]

HUMAN NEEDS

The main objection to such negative definitions is just that – they are negative. While prevention of injuries and reduction of risk are fundamental, these definitions do not look at health or wellbeing from the larger perspective of human needs. Such needs extend beyond physical safety and security to include psychological and social needs, such as having friends, enjoying respect, exercising a certain control over our lives, communicating openly, exploring our interests freely and so on. Without these, no one would describe their life as a vital or healthy one. We need much more than safety from danger, accident or disease to be healthy, thriving human beings. We must have quality of life.

Quality of life is reflected in our activities, and work, like it or not, makes up a good portion of our adult waking life – roughly half of it, if we add in preparing for, then travelling to and from work.[5] Organisations then should have among their business objectives the promotion of the highest degree of wellbeing for all who work in the organisation.

Finally, some see health and safety as a branch of risk management, dealing with the risk to employees of death, injury or disease. However, according to the positive definition used here – 'promoting the highest degree of wellbeing' – it is more accurate to say that health and safety begins with risk management. It does not end there. Health and safety uses risk management techniques to minimise human losses, but also seeks ways that the workplace can satisfy psychological and social needs essential to health and wellbeing.

Workplace health and safety then has a big job ahead of it. What precisely is its scope?

THE SCOPE OF HEALTH AND SAFETY

The definition says occupational health and safety covers workers in *all* occupations. However, in practice and under WHS law, it focuses on workers that are *paid* either with wages or fees for service. (See Section 7 of the Work Health and Safety Act ['the Act'].)

Because health and safety deals almost entirely with paid work, it excludes many unpaid workers – most importantly, housewives. This is odd, as housewives are exposed to the same hazards as paid workers doing the same tasks: they are cooks, childcare workers, drivers, gardeners, tutors, butlers and maids, counsellors, carers, handywomen and so on. Because they do not have an employment contract, housewives are not considered by health and safety. Instead, their health and safety concerns are treated primarily as personal health matters by doctors, counsellors and the like. Whether this is appropriate depends on how successful the current approach has been. It is difficult to assess, as we do not have a system of collecting health and safety data for unpaid workers that compares with the system used for paid workers (normally using workers' compensation statistics). Unpaid workers such as housewives are not covered by workers' compensation law. Hence, we have a dilemma that some might see as yet another example of the neglect and devaluation of work traditionally seen as women's work.

Workplace health and safety then focuses on work and is different from other forms of health- and safety-related activities, such as public health, environmental protection, traffic safety, consumer protection, fire safety and personal health. However, the boundaries are never clear-cut and there is often overlap. WHS legislation requires, for example, employers and workers to ensure that their work activities not only do not put third parties, such as visitors and contractors, at risk, but also do not endanger those to whom they supply their goods and services – customers, clients, the general public. Thus, there is an element of public safety in WHS. Similarly, the environment and health and safety are connected when, for example, production involves hazardous substances. Increasingly, health and safety managers have taken on environmental responsibilities and become HSE officers.

Nor is the boundary of the workplace clear-cut. It can vary from being a fixed, bounded location (factory, office, school or building site) where the employer can exert direct control, to virtually anywhere as is the case, for example, with reporters, sales representatives and police officers whereby control by the employer is indirect or shared. The workplace may be on the land, below the land (miners), in the sky (flight attendants) and below the sea (divers). The workplace may even be the home, as with telecommuters or self-employed people running businesses out of their house. (See Section 8 of the Act.)

Summing up, workplace health and safety is concerned with the promotion and maintenance of the highest degree of physical, mental and social wellbeing of workers in all (paid) occupations – wherever that work is carried out.

Workers' compensation and injury management

While health and safety is primarily about defending and promoting our wellbeing at the workplace, it has close links with workers' compensation and injury management – sometimes referred to as rehabilitation or 'return to work'. In fact, many measure health and safety performance simply by the size of the insurance premium covering injured workers. (We talk more about measuring health and safety later, in Chapters 4 and 13.) As a result, the functions of all three – health and safety, workers' compensation and injury management – are often the responsibility of the HS manager (see Chapter 16). Nevertheless, the focus of the book remains on the promotion of health and safety, not on when things go wrong.

Australia's performance

How does Australia fare in terms of health and safety performance? Are we winning or losing? Most government statistics on health and safety performance use compensation data: 'What is the number of new compensation claims – per 1000 employees – involving one working week off work or more, and have they increased or decreased from last financial year?'[6] Many governments, including Australia's, measure their performance using compensation claims and develop their health and safety strategy largely on this basis. Figure 1.1 gives the incidence rate of new claims over the five-year period to the end of the financial year of 2009/2010.

Figure 1.1	*Incidence rates (claims per 1000 employees) and percentage improvement of serious* compensated injury and musculoskeletal claims by jurisdiction*				
	2005–2006	**2006–2007**	**2007–2008**	**2008–2009 (PRELIMINARY)**	**2009–2010 (PROJECTED)**
Australia	12.9	12.3	12.0	11.3	11.6

*Includes accepted workers' compensation claims for temporary incapacity involving one or more weeks' compensation plus all claims for fatality and permanent incapacity.

Source: Safe Work Australia, 2010, *Comparative Performance Monitoring Report*, 12th edition, Commonwealth of Australia, p. 3.

According to these figures, we appear to be winning, despite a slight increase in incidence in 2009–2010 (projected). However, a reminder: we are using workers' compensation statistics. There are a number of reasons for this, the principal one being there is no other measure or comparable database that assesses workplace health and safety nationally. As soon as you think about it though, the shortcomings become clear.

Many accidents or diseases do not result in compensation being awarded. Research carried out for Safe Work Australia shows nearly half of legitimate claims are never made.[7] There are several reasons for this:

- Workers are not aware of their rights.
- They do not know if the injury or disease was work-related.
- It may be difficult or impossible to gather sufficient evidence to show that a work-related injury or disease was in fact work-related – however that may be judged. Some diseases only result from long-term exposure (industrial deafness), have long latency periods (asbestos-related) or involve other contributing factors, making claims too difficult, time-consuming or costly to establish.
- Even in relatively simple cases, the process seems to require too much effort.
- Workers are sometimes afraid of making a claim lest it affect their employment or chances of promotion.
- Some consider the injury too minor, although it resulted in time off work.
- Some work cultures treat compensation as 'sus' and discourage legitimate claims.

DID YOU KNOW?

An important feature of the growth and development of the labour market over the past 20 years that has influenced the development of workers' compensation schemes, in particular, has been the shift away from traditional employer–employee, full-time work arrangements as contract, casual and part-time work arrangements have increased. There is growing evidence that this has adversely affected OHS outcomes and reduced the likelihood of workers lodging claims.

Source: Productivity Commission, 2004, *National Workers' Compensation and Occupational Health and Safety Frameworks*, report no. 27, March, Canberra.

Furthermore, compensation law may only cover a restricted range of work-related injuries or diseases. Some self-employed people – many in the agricultural and construction sectors – are not covered under the law.

Add to this, changes in compensation law over time and differences between jurisdictions make comparisons difficult or near impossible.[8] For example, injuries and diseases occurring on a journey to or from work (commuting claims) are not covered by all compensation schemes.

However, the biggest criticism about using compensation data is that it is a negative indicator linked to the negative and minimal definition of health and safety – *preventing* death, injury and disease and not *promoting* wellbeing.

To appreciate this more clearly, imagine Australia to be a single workplace and you, a young worker, turn up at the door to see a sign saying that there has been a slight downward trend in compensated fatalities, injuries and diseases from previous years. This is hardly reassuring.

Even if you could be guaranteed a safe return home each day, you want conditions in the workplace that develop and support your mental and social wellbeing; factors such as respect, challenge, opportunity, autonomy, support, job satisfaction, friendship and so on. You want to know if these conditions are present, for without such positive ingredients your health will suffer, affecting your general quality of life.

Quality of working life index

Ideally, we should have a quality of working life index that uses a number of recognised indicators measuring the workplace's effect on our physical, mental and social wellbeing across the nation. This would involve standard surveys, interviews and tests administered regularly. It would reflect workplace culture, consultation and leadership, as well as risk management systems.[9]

Such an index would allow us to compare ourselves with others, and compare different industries and firms contemporaneously as well as over time. It would help us direct our efforts and learn more. In the meantime, we are forced to use the (clumsy) proxy of workers' compensation statistics for a picture of the national performance.[10]

MOST DANGEROUS INDUSTRIES AND OCCUPATIONS

In 2008–09, the most dangerous industries, as measured by incidence rates, were agriculture, forestry and fishing (25.2 claims per 1000 employees), followed by transport and storage (25.0), manufacturing (23.4) and construction (21.8).[11]

Labourers and related workers had the highest incidence rate: 37.7 serious claims per 1000 employees, nearly three times the national rate of 13.5 serious claims per 1000 employees. Intermediate production and transport workers, and tradespersons and related workers, had rates around double the national rate (28.2 and 24.8 serious claims per 1000 employees respectively).[12]

Among occupational subcategories, the highest incidence rate (70.4 serious claims per 1000 employees) occurred among skilled agricultural workers – more than five times the national rate. The next highest incidence rate (54.1 serious claims per 1000 employees) occurred among process workers – more than four times the national rate.[13]

The most dangerous industries and occupations offer few surprises, but they do remind us that certain sections of our society have significantly more chance of being killed, injured or made ill at work than others. Likewise, the fact that well-paid executives and senior management are not represented in the high incidence tables should startle no one. Just as the social distribution of income and wealth reveals much about the kind of society we live in, the social distribution of occupational or, more generally, 'premature' deaths, diseases and injuries presents its darkest shadow.

Whether our health and safety performance is improving or not, all workplace deaths, injuries and illnesses are unacceptable. One of the authors vividly remembers, as an inspector, the aftermath of his first industrial fatality and, as a union health and safety officer, watching a worker break down in tears recounting how she could no longer pick up and hold her baby because of occupational overuse syndrome. Reducing such experiences to numbers and rates may help us understand WHS professionally, but it does not alter the fact that we are dealing with an immense human tragedy.

Are all accidents avoidable?

While acknowledging that workplace accidents and deaths are a tragedy, many say that accidents are unavoidable. 'Accidents will happen', they say, and 'It's the nature of the business', or 'Wherever you have people, you will have accidents'.

If it is true that all accidents (unplanned, unwanted incidents) are unavoidable, then, strictly speaking, there is no point in prevention at all (or in reading any further). But this is nonsensical, as we all take steps to reduce risk at work, home and play. If all accidents were inevitable we wouldn't take risk into consideration. We would stop putting lights at intersections, we wouldn't bother with lift maintenance, hospitals wouldn't sterilise equipment and, as a result, we would all live shorter lives.

If some accidents are avoidable, which ones aren't? Focusing on the workplace, try pointing out which accident was unavoidable such that no steps could have been taken to reduce the likelihood (or the severity) of it occurring. If you can find ways that can reduce the chance of something occurring, it could have been avoided.

To illustrate this, look at the diagram of a chance dial in Figure 1.2. On the scale, '1' represents the certainty of an accident occurring within, say, the next 12 months, while '0' represents the certainty of an accident never occurring. The indicator represents the chance of a particular accident occurring.

Figure 1.2 *Chance Dial*

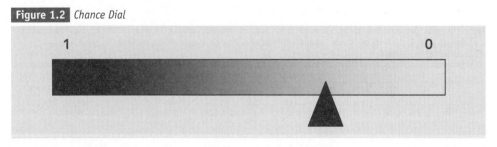

We all want to work in situations where the indicator is as close to 0 as possible. To say that an accident is unavoidable is to say that the indicator must stay at 1 and that there is nothing we can do to move it. However, if we can do something about reducing the chance of the accident happening, the indicator moves towards 0. As the indicator moves away from 1 to 0, the accident becomes more and more avoidable, until, at 0, it has become completely avoidable. An example would be removing asbestos from the workplace to make the chance of catching asbestosis (from the workplace) zero.

This book works on the basis that it is very difficult – if not impossible – to find unavoidable workplace accidents (those stuck at 1). There may be such things, but if unavoidable workplace accidents do exist, the authors haven't found any and, from what we know, neither have accident investigators.

Accident investigations, which we discuss in more detail later, usually point to a combination of factors that cause the accident to occur: the immediate or technical causes and the root or underlying causes. On that basis, they then make recommendations to deal with the causes and avoid a reoccurrence. Not one credible accident investigation the authors know of has ever concluded that the accident was completely unavoidable, even those involving the most complex situations. The language used in the investigations into the following two high-profile accidents is typical.

The following is an extract from the report of the Longford Royal Commission into the Esso Longford gas plant accident on 25 September 1998, in which an explosion and fire killed two, injured others and broke off all gas supply from the plant.

LONGFORD GAS PLANT ACCIDENT

Notwithstanding the matters mentioned above, the conclusion is inevitable that the accident on 25 September 1998 would not have occurred had appropriate steps been taken following the tripping of the GP1210 pumps. When efforts to restart those pumps proved unsuccessful, it should have been realised immediately that cold temperatures would ensue downstream from the absorbers and render vessels not designed to operate at low temperatures dangerous. Had this been realised, steps could and should have been taken to isolate the outlets of both rich oil and condensate from the absorbers in order to prevent those cold temperatures from developing in the ROD/ROF area. Those who were operating GP1 on 25 September 1998 did not have the knowledge of the dangers associated with loss of lean oil flow and did not take the steps necessary to avert those dangers. Nor did those charged with the supervision of the operations have the necessary knowledge and the steps taken by them were inappropriate. The lack of knowledge on the part of both the operators and supervisors was directly attributable to a deficiency in their initial or subsequent training. Not only was their training inadequate, but there were no current operating procedures to guide them in dealing with the problem they encountered on 25 September 1998.

Source: Excerpts from legislation of the Parliament of the State of Victoria, Australia, are reproduced with the permission of the Crown in right of the State of Victoria, Australia. The State of Victoria accepts no responsibility for the accuracy and completeness of any legislation contained in this publication

The following is from the executive summary of the NSW Ministry of Transport's final report into the rail accident at Waterfall.

WATERFALL RAIL ACCIDENT

On 31 January 2003 at approximately 7:14 am, a four car Outer Suburban Tangara passenger train, designated G7 and travelling from Sydney Central railway station to Port Kembla, left the track at high speed [nearly twice the safe speed] and overturned approximately 1.9 kilometres south of Waterfall railway station. The train driver and six passengers were killed. The train guard and the remaining 41 passengers suffered injuries ranging from minor to severe ...

Expert evidence before the Special Commission indicated that an incapacitated driver weighing more than 110 kilograms could, by the static weight of his legs, hold the foot pedal in the set position whilst G7 was in motion, preventing an emergency brake application. Mr Zeides weighed 118 kilograms at autopsy.

The Commissioner was satisfied that Mr Zeides was using the foot pedal when he had a heart attack and that the foot pedal failed to operate as intended.

It became apparent that the SRA had information for approximately 15 years that the deadman foot pedal in Tangara trains had the inherent deficiency that train drivers over a certain weight could set the pedal inadvertently if they became incapacitated. In attempting to determine why such a dangerous state of affairs had been allowed to exist for such a long period, the Commissioner concluded there were serious deficiencies in the way in which safety was managed by the SRA over that period of time.

Source: © State of New South Wales through ITSR. Special Commission of Inquiry into the Waterfall Rail Accident, Final Report, Volume 1, January 2005, (McInerney Inquiry), pp. i, iv.

The accidents were not inevitable, chance or random – 'acts of God', to use that quaint and curious phrase from insurance. They resulted from human activity or, more often, inactivity. They mark a failure to take the right preventive steps.

Clearly, some accidents are more avoidable than others in the sense that some steps may be difficult, time-consuming or costly. Nevertheless, they could have been taken, but they weren't. Too often, other organisational motives or agendas intervene, putting ourselves and others at risk. It is a question of priorities. This book is about making health and safety a priority.

MAKING HEALTH AND SAFETY A PRIORITY

Apart from the powerful instinctive human concern for our own health and safety and that of others, there are many other reasons for making it a priority. They include:
- community standards or expectations that organisations have a responsibility for those that work for them
- the loss of staff morale and potential industrial relations problems in the event of death, injury or disease
- legal obligations that require workplaces be safe and healthy for employees as well as for contractors and visitors
- insurable costs, predominantly workers' compensation premiums, that are related to the claims experience of the organisation and, to a large extent, controllable by the organisation

- non–insurable costs associated with workplace injury, such as lost time, reduced productivity, staff replacement and retraining costs, as well as loss of business reputation
- costs to the community, such as health services, rehabilitation and loss of skilled labour
- costs to employees through reduced quality of life as a result of workplace injury and disease, reduced income for the injured and their family, and the grief endured by everyone involved.

DID YOU KNOW?

TOTAL COST OF WORK-RELATED INJURIES TO AUSTRALIAN SOCIETY

A 2009 report into the costs of work-related injury to employers, employees and the community, indicates that the total cost of workplace injury and illness to the Australian economy between 2005 and 2006 was a staggering $57.5 billion, with workers bearing 49 per cent of this cost.

The report revealed that employers bore only 3 per cent of the total cost and the community, 47 per cent of the cost. The cost to the worker was up by 5 per cent from the 2000–2001 financial year report.

The total cost to the nation's economy is the equivalent of 5.9 per cent in forgone GDP for the 2005–2006 financial year. Of the cost to the economy as a whole, 67 per cent was attributed to injury as opposed to disease. For workers, 63 per cent of their costs were attributed to injury.

The average cost to the worker for each work-related injury was $52 400, while the average cost of work-related disease per individual was significantly higher at $87 800. Costs for the worker took the form of a loss of current and future income and non-compensated medical expenses.

The report notes that the cost borne by workers rises with the severity of the incident, with workers who are permanently incapacitated estimated to incur, on average, $650 000 in economic costs (including estimates of future income lost). In comparison, workers who suffer from minor injuries or diseases are estimated to only incur between $150 and $270 in total costs. Cases involving permanent incapacity account for the bulk of total costs to the economy.

Source: Australian Safety and Compensation Council, 2009, *The Cost of Work-related Injury and Illness for Australian Employers, Workers and the Community: 2005-2006*, Commonwealth of Australia.[14]

BENEFITS OF HEALTH AND SAFETY

Just as important are the positive benefits to everyone if the funds spent on workplace accidents and diseases were reallocated to improve life on all fronts. Imagine what could be done if the $57.5 billion could be retained each year by the community and instead used to improve education, public health, transport, housing or the environment. Our standard of living would improve incrementally each year. You don't need a degree in economics to appreciate that health and safety makes good investment sense.

Above all, the workplace plays a key role in developing our human potential and providing that quality of life. Work impacts on our health profoundly.

DID YOU KNOW?

RAMAZZINI FOUNDS INDUSTRIAL MEDICINE

> When a doctor visits a working-class home he should be content to sit on a three-legged stool, if there isn't a gilded chair, and he should take time for examination; and to the questions recommended by Hippocrates, he should add one more – What is your occupation?
>
> Source: Bernardo Ramazzini, 1700, *De Morbis Artificum Diatriba* (*The Diseases of Workmen*), Italy.

Ramazzini, considered to be the father of industrial medicine, insisted that occupational diseases should be studied in the workplace rather than in hospitals. His comprehensive book also included one of the earliest references to women's WHS when he recommended precautions against syphilitic infections, as well as cleanliness among midwives.

It falls to the workplace to play a role in promoting our health and wellbeing as humans while providing protection as well. To do this, the workplace must fit the worker.

Most employers recognise this. Increasingly, many look to health and safety to identify factors such as proper work organisation and training to promote human development as well as furthering corporate objectives. In other words, work should satisfy human needs as much as organisational goals. The two are closely related.

Health and safety that simply looks at reducing the negative factors misses the opportunity to contribute fully to business performance. Linking a positive conception of health and safety with organisational goals makes WHS mainstream in a way that reducing insurance costs or complying with the law doesn't. Using this broader positive definition, the signs of success could include matters such as reduced absenteeism and staff turnover, improved skills and job satisfaction levels, increased participation in decision making, and other indicators of greater quality of working life and organisational productivity.

FACTORS AFFECTING WORK AND WHS

If health and safety focuses on (paid) work, then performance will be affected for good or ill by several factors: first, by the type of work that organisations carry out and how they manage it; and second, by the changing conditions those organisations operate in, such as the economy, the level of technology available, political developments, changes within the community, the level of research and information, environmental influences and developments in WHS law. To be truly effective, the health and safety manager not only needs to know all about the organisation, but also much about the conditions in which it operates.

Figure 1.3 *Factors that influence an organisation*

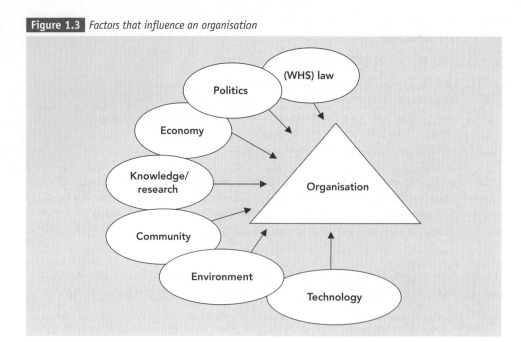

To illustrate this, we briefly highlight some of the recent changes to work caused largely by Australia's exposure to international competition and integration into the global market – so-called globalisation. Then, we summarise the fallout for health and safety and its management.

Figure 1.4 *Changes and their effects on health and safety*

FACTOR	CHANGE TO WORKPLACE	HEALTH AND SAFETY IMPLICATIONS
Economy	More employment in the services sector – such as finance, insurance, property and business services, retailing, hospitality and education – rather than traditionally more dangerous sectors, such as manufacturing, rail transport and utilities; decline in union membership; more low-paid, part-time and casual jobs; longer working hours and work-intensification	Overall decline in reported industrial injuries; less support for WHS; more fatigue, stress; less balance between work and life for some
Technology	Increased reliance on information and communication technology rationalising work processes and workforce, and leading to different jobs and new workplaces, such as call centres	Reduction in boring, repetitive work and associated hazards in some areas; greater flexibility to balance work–life for some; lack of job control and increased job demand in other areas
Politics	Greater deregulation of the economy; privatisation of public sector and decentralisation of industrial relations, leading to productivity gains and greater job flexibility but also increased income inequality and job insecurity, as well as blurring of employment relation (labour hire and contractors)	Increased levels of stress, fatigue; potential decline in overall health and wellbeing; confusion over WHS responsibility

FACTOR	CHANGE TO WORKPLACE	HEALTH AND SAFETY IMPLICATIONS
Community	Increased migration from non-European areas leading to a more diverse workplace; women seeking an identity outside of the family leading to increased presence in the workplace; ageing population and skill shortages putting pressure on government and industry to retain older workers	Outsourcing of work to homes and potentially hazardous locations; discrimination hiding behind health and safety issues; greater demand to balance work–life; older workforce presenting different risk profile
(WHS) law	Increased self-regulation and less prescriptive legislation; more emphasis on general duty of care; larger penalties in civil cases; introduction of industrial manslaughter legislation	Greater flexibility in applying the law to the workplace but uncertainty about compliance; greater concern over personal liability; increase in administration
Knowledge/ research	Greater amount of material dealing with hazards and wellbeing; more online access; expansion of education and training	Increased capacity to exercise duty of care and improve health and safety performance; increased responsibility; information overload

Some examples of changes affecting health and safety

LOSS OF PERMANENT FULL-TIME JOBS

Casual, part-time and contract work is gradually overtaking permanent full-time employment as the standard type of job for the majority of working Australians. The massive rise in precarious forms of employment is exposing working families to greater financial risk and is part of a push by businesses to drive down costs and regain profits lost during the global financial crisis.

The ACTU is today releasing a major new report into work and working life in Australia before and after the global financial crisis.

The report *Shifting Risk – Work and Working Life in Australia* by Mike Rafferty and Serena Yu at Sydney University's Workplace Research Centre identifies a series of major transformations, including:

- **Growing inequality in Australia**. Despite strong increases in the productivity of Australian workers since the 1980s, returns to labour as measured by real wages growth has lagged significantly. Conversely, the returns to capital have grown markedly and profit share is at record levels.
- **Casual, contract and precarious employment is now the norm**. The increase in precarious jobs and in particular the rise in the casual workforce to 2 million Australians is proof of what is happening in Australian workplaces today. Growth in non-standard forms of employment is outstripping standard full-time employment, defined as a working week in excess of 35 hours attracting paid leave benefits. The greatest growth has been in full-time casual and part-time jobs.
- **Massive increase in financial risk among working families**. The period of excessive credit and leverage preceding the GFC saw working families take on more and more debt. While household indebtedness has eased since the GFC, it is still at levels above 150% and the likelihood of interest rate rises in the near future poses further risks for families.
- **Growing fixed costs are adding to financial pressure**. As a proportion of the family's budget, spending on non-food fixed costs has risen from 37% to 42%, driven by increases in housing, health, and education expenses – the traditional domain of governments. This rise in fixed costs means many families are now more sensitive to shocks from rises in price or the loss of wages.
- **High household debt makes the economy vulnerable**. As the sub-prime experience in the US showed, a highly leverage economy cannot cope when the system comes under stress. The GFC was precipitated by extreme and irresponsible risks caused by seemingly inexorable rises in asset values and accessibility to credit.

ACTU President Ged Kearney said: 'This major new report is a wake up call for Australia. As a nation we survived the global financial crisis better than most but that doesn't mean it should be business as usual for the big corporations. Australians are among the hardest workers in the world. We work long hours and we are highly productive but wages are not keeping pace with company profits and families are exposed to high levels of debt and greater financial risk. Families deserve more secure jobs and less financial pressure. This will also deliver greater stability to our economy, making it less prone to shocks that could cause another financial crisis. It is time for businesses and government and unions to work together on these major challenges,' said Ms Kearney.

Source: ACTU, 2010, 'Loss of permanent full-time jobs is putting families at greater financial risk: new report', ACTU media release, 4 October, http://www.actu.org.au.

OUTSOURCING: WINNIE'S STORY – MAKING THE SUSSAN LABEL

I came from China twelve years ago and I have two children. First I worked in a sweatshop. After I had my second child I started working from home.

At home, the boss just gives me overlocking work [stitching the edges of garments to prevent them from fraying] for part of the garment, so I don't make whole garments. Because of this I am not always busy as I have to wait for someone else to finish the rest of the garment. I only work about 6 hours a day. The boss gave me the machine to use, so I am not able to get other work from other contractors to increase my income. Even though the boss gave me the machine I have to pay for any repairs if it is broken.

I am very fast at sewing, but my rate of pay is still very low as the piece rate is low. I usually can get about $6 an hour. When I first started working at home I was actually getting $8–9 an hour because I was fast. The boss was surprised that I was so fast, so he reduced the rate he paid me for future orders of the same style.

Because my husband's income is very low it is not enough for our family to survive, so I must keep this job. Sometimes the sewing work gets busy with large, urgent orders, and then I don't have time to look after my children properly. At these times I get a lot of pain in my back and neck. There is also a lot of dust in the house from the material, so my children and I often get sick from this.

All these things make me really upset and I want to give up sewing, but I don't have any choice about getting another job. Even if I can only make $100–200 in a week, that is very important income for my family.

The labels I make for include Sussan, Suzanne Grae and Sportsgirl. One of the dresses I made for Sussan I later saw in the shop for $50. I received $1 for doing the overlock sewing on that garment, which was about half the total sewing. In Sportsgirl I saw a top I had made selling for nearly $30 and I only received 60 cents per garment for overlocking, which was most of the sewing for that garment.

In addition to these low rates of pay, I did not receive any superannuation, holiday pay, sick pay, overtime pay and I am not covered for workers' compensation.

I am telling my story because I want people to understand the outworkers' situation and the bad conditions in which your clothes are made. I want the government to take steps to stop this exploitation. They must force the retailers to take responsibility for the clothes they sell. I don't want my children to experience the same injustice I have suffered.

Source: © Fair Wear Australia. Fair Wear Campaign, Sussan Outworkers' Stories, 1999. *This article was first published in 1999. Information about the labels named here is based on outworkers experience at the time of initial publication.*

AGEING WORKFORCE

Dr Lynette Guy, senior research officer at the University of Newcastle, noted that the process of ageing may make some employees more vulnerable to injury. Examples include physical strength and muscular changes over time, cardiovascular and aerobic powers decline with age, reduced work pace, and mental and cognitive changes at the age of 60+.

Factors that are predictive of a decline in work capacity are:

- work content – work demands, physical load, cumulative body stress
- work environment – stress, noise, fumes, heat, humidity, etc.
- organisational environment – role conflicts, poor supervision, lack of freedom of choice, lack of acknowledgement, lack of personal development.

Despite the above, data from Comcare and the former WorkSafe Australia suggests that the highest rates of injury and illness occur among employees aged 35–44, and the lowest rates of injury occurred among those aged 55 and over. However, the greatest duration of time lost due to injury/illness occurred in the age groups 45–49 and 55–64.

Guy therefore posed the question of why injuries/illness do not increase with age. Are older employees more aware of OHS issues and take fewer risks, or do they develop their own coping strategies? Are there selection factors, such as older employees moving out of 'risky' jobs into safer (e.g. less physical) ones, or do early or phased retirement affect the data?

Results

Guy outlined the results of a case study of a local government organisation that sought to compare OHS incident rates and claims costs by age group, compare attitudes to OHS among different age groups and clarify the perceptions of different age groups towards 'ageing'.

Overall the study found a general increase in OHS commitment among employees. Older employees were using their experience to train others, younger employees were tending to respond to OHS-related media coverage, and a combination of better OHS systems and awareness of the need for compliance were also having a positive impact.

Note, however, that these trends were across the workforce, not related to age.

In summary, 'safety doesn't relate to age, it depends on the individual'. Therefore, management of an ageing workforce requires assessment and management of the needs of each individual employee.

Some new OHS risks are emerging, however; for example, due to new technology, more females taking on 'traditional male' jobs, changing ways of performing work, dealing with difficult customers and information overload. For some older employees, having to learn to use computers may add to stress levels, as noted above.

Source: Ageing workforce doesn't mean worse OHS: research, *Workplace OHS*, 16 November 2007

THE INSTITUTIONAL FRAMEWORK

To address developments in health and safety, Australia has created an institutional framework involving key players, often with differing interests.

In addition to these immediate players are the associations representing workers, such as unions, trade associations, state and territory trades and labour councils, the Australian Council of Trade Unions (ACTU), employers' peak bodies, such as the Australian Chamber of Commerce and Industry (ACCI) and specific industry associations, and, finally, insurer and health professional bodies. Other players include

Figure 1.5 *Key players and their interests*

KEY PLAYERS	INTERESTS
Workers	• avoid risks to health and safety • have good quality of working life • be adequately compensated for any injury or illness
Employers	• meet organisational objectives • reduce costs • comply with the law
Governments	• protect the community • build the economy and employment • reduce costs
Insurers	• expand business • be competitive
Health and safety professionals: nurses; ergonomists; occupational physicians, hygienists, psychologists, therapists; safety engineers and rehabilitation providers	• assist workers and employers • build professional capacity

the courts, lawyers dealing with health and safety and compensation law, standards bodies, scientists carrying out research into hazards and health and safety consultants.

There are also international bodies active in health and safety that governments and others recognise as having a role to play, such as the International Labour Organization (ILO) and the World Health Organization (WHO). Australia has ratified the ILO's Convention on Occupational Safety and Health (No. 155), which requires countries to implement a national policy on occupational health and safety in the workplace.

CONSULTATION AND COOPERATION

The improvement of health and safety depends on a variety of participants cooperating at times when their interests do not always point them in the same direction.

Australia has tried to build consensus among these participants and direct activities towards agreed goals using health and safety legislation and commissions – government-supported bodies in which players meet to determine policy and strategy.

Under Australia's federal system, there are three levels at which players are brought together.

FEDERAL LEVEL

In 2009, Safe Work Australia (SWA) was created to take over from the Australian Safety and Compensation Council (ASCC), which was the successor to the National Occupational Health and Safety Commission (NOHSC).

Safe Work Australia

Safe Work Australia is an Australian Government statutory agency set up to
• 'achieve significant and continual reductions in the incidence of death, injury and disease in the workplace

- 'achieve national uniformity of the work health and safety legislative framework complemented by a nationally consistent approach to compliance policy and enforcement policy
- 'improve national workers' compensation arrangements.'

It is tripartite and comprises 15 members, including an independent chair, nine members representing the Commonwealth and each state and territory, two representing the interests of workers, two representing the interests of employers and the CEO of Safe Work Australia.

Safe Work Australia overlooks the National OHS Strategy 2002–2012 and was instrumental in harmonising law using the Model WHS Act. SWA collects national health and safety statistics. Its annual report, *Compendium of Workers' Compensation Statistics Australia*, gives an overview of health and safety in Australia, showing trends based on accepted workers' compensation claims. A National Online Statistics Interactive (NOSI) system can be found on the SWA website as well.

The SWA is not a regulatory authority and does not make or enforce laws. Health and safety laws in Australia operate in each of the state, territory and commonwealth jurisdictions, and are administered by jurisdictions' regulators.

Two other bodies need mentioning – NICNAS and the Federal Safety Commissioner.

NICNAS

The Australian Government's industrial chemical safety regulator, the National Industrial Chemicals Notification and Assessment Scheme (NICNAS), was established in 1990. NICNAS provides a national notification and assessment scheme to protect the health of the public, workers and the environment from the harmful effect of industrial chemicals. It assesses all chemicals new to Australia and assesses those chemicals already used (existing chemicals) on a priority basis, in response to concerns about their safety on health and environmental grounds.

NICNAS produces assessment reports that contain safety recommendations for the handling and labelling of the chemical. It also publishes the *Chemical Gazette* electronically every month and the *Australian Inventory of Chemical Substances* (AICS), which lists more than 38 000 chemicals. The latter is a very useful free online database.

Federal Safety Commissioner

In 2005, a Federal Safety Commissioner (FSC) was appointed to the then Department of Employment and Workplace Relations. The functions of the FSC include:

- promotion of best-practice health and safety on Australian Government building and construction projects
- development and administration of the Australian Government Building and Construction OHS Accreditation Scheme (now mandatory)
- promotion of the adoption of safe design on Australian Government construction projects with the aim to eliminate and/or minimise health and safety risk during the construction phase

- work with industry stakeholders to identify initiatives that will lead to an improved health and safety performance in the industry.

JURISDICTIONAL LEVEL

Because the Constitution does not give the Commonwealth general power to legislate for health and safety, there are nine principal jurisdictions in Australia – eight state and territory and one Commonwealth (see Chapter 2). Here, we find WHS acts and government regulators whose role it is to administer their legislation; for example, collect incident data, provide information and carry out inspections and prosecutions.

In addition, governments also support the commissions that oversee health and safety matters, including compensation and rehabilitation. Here, policy and strategy are debated. At this jurisdictional level, insurers and others involved in the commissions, including the government, employers and unions are to be found.

WORKPLACE LEVEL

Finally, at the workplace or organisation level, there are employers, workers and, sometimes, union representatives and health and safety professionals meeting on workplace health and safety issues. In larger workplaces or organisations, this also involves health and safety committees. We will talk in more detail of this important phenomenon later. Needless to say, it is at the workplace level where we see whether health and safety is successful. It is here we see the final outcome.

The experience of working in this framework over many years has led to a consensus that the critical elements within an organisation determining WHS performance are as follows.

Figure 1.6 *Critical elements within an organisation in determining WHS*

Commitment	Does senior management make health and safety a priority – planning, funding, training, reporting, etc.? How is this communicated?
Consultation	Are workers and their representatives involved in WHS decision making at the earliest stages? Do the consultative arrangements have support? Is WHS communication between managers and workers open and two-way?
System	Are there policies and procedures? Is there an effective WHS organisation and program for the systematic identification of hazards and management of risk? Is performance monitored, measured, audited and reviewed to ensure continuous improvement?
Culture	Is everyone aware of and sensitive to hazards and risk? Do people talk about health and safety? Are they empowered to report hazards?

All four elements are necessary, as set out in the model in Figure 1.7.

The health and safety system of policies, procedures and practices – the machinery – lies at the core; however, it must be fuelled by active management commitment, a spirit of genuine consultation and a robust health and safety culture. In the following chapters, we explain the importance of those elements and how the health and safety manager can help to build them. First, though, we examine the law covering health and safety.

Figure 1.7 *The four elements of health and safety performance*

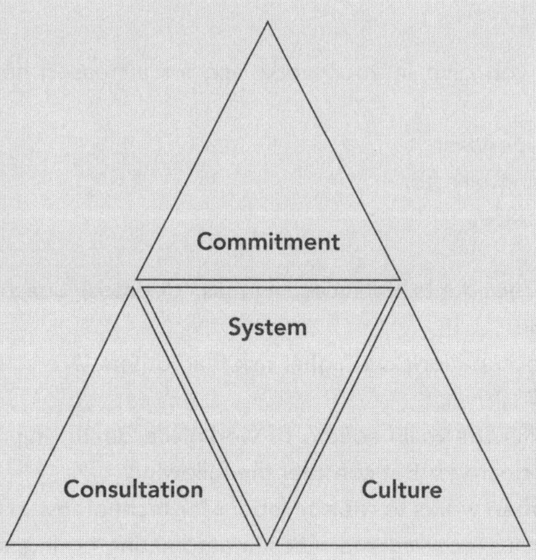

Summary

- Health and safety in the workplace remains a significant widespread problem costing workers, the community and the economy alike.
- Instead of just preventing death, injury and disease, organisations need to focus on promoting health and safety to fulfil the basic human needs of workers, while at the same time improving organisational performance.
- Workplaces are changing in response to a number of factors such as developments in the economy, technology, research, politics, law and society. New threats to our health and safety are emerging as others are removed.
- Health and safety managers need to understand not only how their own organisation works, but also the factors influencing it, such as the law and the institutional framework in which WHS has developed.
- Within the organisation, health and safety performance can be strengthened with active management commitment by creating an effective health and safety management system, with genuine consultation among workers, their representatives, managers and supervisors, and growing a health and safety culture.

Questions

1 What does your employer (or college) mean by 'workplace health and safety'? Examine your health and safety policy or interview the management. Is this term understood positively or negatively?
2 Go to page 6 of Safe Work Australia's 2010 *Comparative Performance Monitoring Report*, 12th edition, at www.safeworkaustralia.gov.au. How would you account for the different performance outcomes for the different jurisdictions?
3 List the direct and indirect costs of workplace accidents to
   a the injured
   b the organisation

    c the family

    d the community

    e the economy.

4 What reasons would you give in your workplace for increased health and safety activity? Consider

    a your manager or supervisor

    b the CEO or managing director

    c the chief financial officer

    d your workmates.

5 Are some workplace accidents (fatalities, injuries, diseases) unavoidable? Explain what is meant by (un)avoidable.

6 Some industries and occupations are higher risk than others. Are some individuals higher risk as well? If so, why?

7 Is the search for profits the main source of workplace death, injury and disease? In many cases, the answer is a clear yes. But consider the following:

- The profit motive often works to replace labour for technology. In many cases this means substituting dangerous jobs with machines or automating boring, stressful work.
- Profits can also be made from safe workplaces. Accidents increase downtime and associated costs such as lost sales, replacement and repair. They also bump up insurance costs and cripple morale.
- Other factors such as labour market supply, industrial relations (unionisation), workplace culture, education, WHS and compensation law mean that profit is not the only driver for good or ill.
- Many employers in the capitalist economy have cooperated to make significant efforts to reduce risk while others have been less responsible even in the same industry.
- If profit is *the* cause of workplace risk, we could expect the public sector and other not-for-profit employers to provide safe or at least safer workplaces. However, consider railways and nursing, for example. Is the picture in the public sector significantly different from the private sector? And if it is, is the difference due to the drive for profit? The results of privatisation may provide some answers.
- Finally, it is far from clear that countries embracing socialism of one form or the other are better at health and safety than economies like Australia's. It is very difficult making worthwhile comparisons and drawing conclusions.

    Is there a final answer or solution?

8 What we don't get from compensation-based data is a breakdown in terms of ethnicity, income grouping or educational background. Where, for example, are Indigenous people in the picture? What other categories would you consider significant that are missing? Where/how do you think the data for these categories might be collected?

Activities

1 In your organisation or college, who is the health and safety officer? Interview them. In which section or department are they located? What are their responsibilities? Compare your organisation's arrangements with those found in other organisations. What are the main issues?

2 Find out if your employer (or college) uses workers' compensation statistics as a measure of health and safety performance? If so, in what form (e.g., insurance costs, incidence rate, frequency rate)? Is it (a) the only measure, (b) the main measure or (c) simply one among others?

Search me!

| ▶ | Search me! 🖑 |

Explore **Search me! management** for relevant articles on workplace health and safety. Search me! is an online library of world-class journals, ebooks and newspapers, including *The Australian* and the *New York Times*, and is updated daily. Log in to Search me! through www.cengage.com/sso using the access card in the front of this book.

KEYWORDS

Try searching for the following terms:
- ▶ modern industrial hazards
- ▶ precarious employment
- ▶ women and health and safety
- ▶ measuring national health and safety performance
- ▶ asbestos
- ▶ nanotechnology

Search tip: **Search me! management** contains information from both local and international sources. To get the greatest number of search results, try using both Australian and American spellings in your searches, e.g. 'globalisation' and 'globalization'; 'organisation' and 'organization'.

Additional resources

- The websites of Safe Work Australia (www.safeworkaustralia.gov.au) and the International Labour Organization (www.ilo.org) provide information on the big picture of WHS in Australia and the world.
- A helpful summary of Australia's WHS performance can be found in the Safe Work Australia booklet *Key Work Health and Safety Statistics Booklet Australia*, updated annually: http://www.safeworkaustralia.gov.au/AboutSafeWorkAustralia/WhatWeDo/Publications/Pages/KeyWHSStat2011.aspx.
- Safe Work Australia's *Compendium of Workers' Compensation Statistics* is published annually (see SWA website). It provides a picture of our national performance and how it has been developing over the years. The National Strategy on OHS, also found on the SWA website, is based in large part on the Compendium.
- The various jurisdictional websites contain more specific information relating to health and safety performance in the states, the territories and the Commonwealth. A complete list can be found at http://www.safeworkaustralia.gov.au/AboutSafeWorkAustralia/WhoWeWorkWith/StateAndTerritoryAuthorities/Pages/StateAndTerritoryAuthorities.aspx.
- See the ILO *Encyclopaedia of Workplace Health and Safety Information* and the CISDOC databases at www.ilocis.org/en/contilo.html and www.ilo.org/public/english/protection/safework/cis/products/dbs.htm respectively. There may be a charge to access these databases.
- In addition to the ILO, it is useful to visit other overseas websites to follow developments from different perspectives. The ones most relevant to Australia are:
  - USA: Occupational Health and Safety Administration (OSHA), www.osha.gov
  - National Institute for Occupational Safety and Health (NIOSH), www.cdc.gov/niosh. OSHA is the regulator and NIOSH does the research.
  - UK: Health and Safety Executive (HSE), www.hse.gov.uk, which also has many useful links
  - Canada: Canadian Centre for Occupational Health and Safety, www.ccohs.ca
  - New Zealand: the Occupational Safety and Health Service (OSH), at www.osh.dol.govt.nz.
- *Workplace OHS* is a subscription service, providing daily updates on WHS matters while containing a useful database. It can be found at www.workplaceohs.com.au.
- *Planning Occupational Health and Safety*, 8th edn, 2009, CCH, Sydney.
- Quinlan, M., Bohle, P. & Lamm, F., 2010, *Managing Occupational Health Safety in Australia: A Multidisciplinary Approach*, 3rd edn, Macmillan, Melbourne; this is the leading comprehensive text on WHS.

Endnotes

1   From the Asbestos Diseases Society of Australia (from research in WA) at www.asbestosdiseases.org.au/asbestosinfo/medical_research.htm: 'Owing to the long latency period from the exposure to asbestos fibres and manifestation of asbestos disease (often up to 30 years or more), the epidemic of asbestos diseases is yet to peak in Australia (around 2023). It is believed that as many as 45 000 persons may die in Australia over the next two decades if effective medical treatments are not found. About 2500 persons are annually diagnosed with diseases caused by asbestos, and the numbers are rising.'

2   See Haigh, G., 2006, *Asbestos House – The Secret History of James Hardie Industries*, Scribe: Carlton North, and Peacock, M. 2009, *Killer Company*, Harper: Sydney.

3   This definition was prepared by the Joint ILO/WHO Committee on Occupational Health at its first session in 1950 and revised at its 12th session in 1995. Alas, the terminology ignores 50 per cent of the world's population.

4   'Frequency' as used here is the ratio of incidents to the number of hours worked and 'incidence' the ratio of incidents to the number of workers. This is explained in more detail when we discuss measuring WHS performance.

5   As one of the authors was reminded once by a manager, 'Look around you. This is your real family. You will spend more of your waking life with us than with those at home … We had better learn to get along together.'

6   Incidence rates need to be used, as the number of workers changes over time.

7   Safe Work Australia, 2009, Work-Related Injuries in Australia, 2005–06: Factors Affecting Applications for Workers' Compensation, Commonwealth of Australia.

8   Changes in the nature of Australia's industry may account for changes in performance; for example, where higher-risk industries such as manufacturing move offshore.

9   Such an index could be created from the tools referred to in Chapters 13 and 17. See Considine, G. & Callus, R., 2001, The Quality of Work Life of Australian Employees: The Development of an Index, Working Paper 73, ACCIRT, University of Sydney: Sydney, NSW.

10 For a defence of workers' compensation data, see Foley, G., 2006, The Role of Workers Compensation-based Data in the Development of Effective Occupational Health and Safety Interventions, Statistics Unit, Worksafe Australia. This can be found at the Safe Work Australia website (http://www.safeworkaustralia.gov.au) under 'Publications'.

11 Safe Work Australia, 2010, *Comparative Performance Monitoring Report*, 12th edition, Commonwealth of Australia, p. 40.

12 Safe Work Australia, *Compendium of Workers' Compensation Statistics Australia* 2007–08, Commonwealth of Australia, p. 7.

13 Safe Work Australia, *Compendium of Workers' Compensation Statistics Australia* 2007–08, Commonwealth of Australia, pp. 7, 8.

14 See Safe Work Australia, http://www.safeworkaustralia.gov.au/AboutSafeWorkAustralia/WhatWeDo/Publications/Documents/178/CostsofWorkRelatedInjuryAndDisease_Mar2009.pdf.

UNDERSTANDING THE LEGAL FRAMEWORK

Learning Objectives

By the end of this chapter, the reader will have a general understanding of how to:

- determine the legal framework of health and safety in the workplace
- provide advice on WHS compliance
- comply with legal requirements
- explain the purpose and use of Australian standards
- explain the purpose and use of WHS codes of practice.

INTRODUCTION

Health and safety law has evolved in response to the failure of employers to provide safe working conditions for workers. While there have always been employers who have been sufficiently concerned about the health and safety of their workers, it is a sad fact that some are not. The evidence for this can be found in the statistics at the beginning of this book, in the media and in the history of the struggle for legal protection. This chapter provides a general introduction to health and safety law, focusing on the key elements affecting compliance.

In general, law is made up of two types: **common law** and **statute law**, or legislation passed by parliaments. Common law is made by judges in court decisions. To help make judgments, courts use statutory law together with significant decisions by judges, or 'precedents' as they are called.

Common law covers civil actions, when one party, believing another has wronged them, takes the other party to court looking to be compensated, usually with money.

In this chapter, we are dealing with statute law or legislation, not common law, because we are concerned with preventing accidents and promoting health, not obtaining money for death, injury or disease (see Chapter 16).

Under common law, there is a **duty of care** to provide a healthy and safe workplace and guard against reasonably foreseeable risks. Statutory law makes clear what your duty of care is and how to meet it.

EARLY LAWS

Coal was discovered in Australia near Newcastle; export began as early as 1800. In 1854, New South Wales legislated for inspections of coalmines. In 1862, children under 13 were banned from working in the pits. Mining remained extremely dangerous, with disasters occurring in 1889 at Bulli, in 1905 in Mt Kembla and in 1921 at Mt Mulligan, where 75 miners died in a methane explosion.

Victoria was among the first states to pass factory health and safety legislation (1873), although this early legislation was principally aimed at restricting female workers. Eventually, in most states, a patchwork of WHS laws emerged, covering different industries and hazards, most of which were confusing, administered by different authorities, left out certain workers and hazards, were reviewed irregularly, held only minimal standards, were poorly enforced and left workers with little or no say in their development. This state of affairs lasted until the 1980s, when a second wave of reform occurred.

ROBENS LEGISLATION

Modern WHS legislation is often referred to as Robens legislation, after Lord Robens, who led a major review of UK health and safety law in 1972. The main features of this type of legislation are
- the placing of a general duty of care, principally on employers, for the health and safety of their workers
- the right of workers to be consulted on health and safety matters affecting their workplace

- a Principal Act, which enables further specific **regulation** and guidance
- so-called performance-based regulation focused on outcomes rather than detailed specification of what to do with particular hazards.

Robens legislation has been described as self-regulatory, whereby the responsibility for health and safety lies primarily with the employer and not with others, such as the government and its inspectors. It is this model that is used in Australia. The NSW *Occupational Health and Safety Act 1983* was the first modern version of this model in Australia. Others followed: *Occupational Health and Safety Act 1985* (Vic.), *Occupational Safety, Health and Welfare Act 1986* (SA) and *Workplace Health and Safety Act 1995* (Qld).

MODERN WHS LAW

Health and safety legislation is law passed by parliament (state, territory or Commonwealth) and includes Acts (statutes) and their supporting regulations.

Regulations are part of legislation. They prescribe how to comply with an Act. Mandatory standards referred to in an Act also form part of the legislation and they must be followed as well.

Non-mandatory standards and codes of practice provide important guidance but are not part of the law. We discuss their role later in this chapter.

Figure 2.1 *Pyramid of WHS legislation*

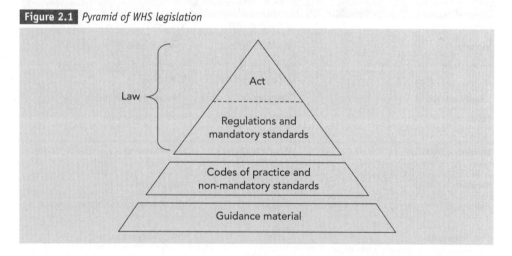

Workers' compensation and injury management (rehabilitation) legislation, like WHS legislation, is found in Acts and regulations. These are discussed in Chapter 16.[1]

The Constitution does not give the Commonwealth the general power to legislate in the area of WHS. As a result, there are nine principal WHS Acts: six state Acts, two territory Acts and a Commonwealth Act covering, mostly, Commonwealth employees.

HARMONISATION OF HEALTH AND SAFETY ACTS

Until recently, the Commonwealth and each state and territory government had differing health and safety laws, making it unfair for workers and inefficient for employers working in different jurisdictions with different standards. In 2008, everyone agreed to harmonise their work health and safety laws (including regulations and codes of practice underpinning them) so that the laws are similar in each jurisdiction.[2] A Model Work Health and Safety Act was used by the various governments for this purpose.

The Commonwealth, states and territories remain responsible for making and enforcing their own health and safety laws but now provide the same legal protection to all Australians. Whether the jurisdictions are equally *effective* will depend on other matters such as the resourcing and training of inspectors, enforcement policies and the court systems, as well as cooperation from other stakeholders. It is expected that all laws will take effect on 1 January 2012.

Some model WHS regulations and codes of practice have been developed and will be implemented as part of the harmonisation process.

The principal Acts are each called the Work Health and Safety Act sometimes with the name of the jurisdiction attached – for example, *South Australian Work Health and Safety Act* – and followed by the year it was passed (2011). They are administered by different government agencies referred to as 'regulators', such as Workplace Health and Safety Queensland and WorkSafe Victoria. A complete list of those regulators is found in Figure 2.2 together with their website addresses.

Figure 2.2 *State, territory and Commonwealth WHS jurisdictions, regulators and websites*

JURISDICTION	REGULATOR	WEBSITE
NSW	WorkCover NSW	www.workcover.nsw.gov.au
Victoria	WorkSafe Victoria	www.worksafe.vic.gov.au
Queensland	Workplace Health and Safety Queensland	www.deir.qld.gov.au/workplace/index.htm
South Australia	SafeWork SA	www.safework.sa.gov.au
Tasmania	Workplace Standards Tasmania	www.wst.tas.gov.au
Western Australia	WorkSafe Western Australia	www.commerce.wa.gov.au/WorkSafe
Northern Territory	NT WorkSafe	www.worksafe.nt.gov.au
ACT	WorkSafe ACT	http://www.worksafety.act.gov.au/health_safety
Commonwealth (Commonwealth employers authorities licensed to self-insure under the *Safety, Rehabilitation and Compensation Act 1988*)	Comcare	www.comcare.gov.au

As we have said, the Acts have been harmonised and mirror one another. The structure and the content are the same for all jurisdictions with minor technical variations.[3] The Acts may be found online at the government websites.

RELATED ACTS

In addition to these nine principal Acts is legislation addressing WHS in specific industries such as seafaring and the offshore petroleum industry, as well as stevedoring, air and rail transport. Some laws deal with specific hazardous activities such as transporting dangerous goods.

Health and safety managers should be aware that other pieces of legislation, such as federal, state and territory anti-discrimination, equal employment opportunity and privacy Acts,[4] contract law, trade practices law, criminal law, common law as well as industrial relations law can have a bearing on WHS activity. Policies and practices should not, for example, discriminate unfairly against certain groups of people, explicitly or implicitly. For example, pre-employment medical screening should not be used to continue hazardous work practices by excluding, say, pregnant women or people with disabilities. Record keeping must also protect the privacy of workers.

Some workplaces may be subject to enterprise bargaining agreements that contain references to required WHS activity. While not legislation, these agreements do have the force of law, so health and safety managers need to be aware of any such agreements and their implications.

Where possible, it is recommended that organisations subscribe to a legal service in order to keep abreast of developments in the law and that the health and safety manager receives copies of the latest updates. Your company secretary or counsel, if you have one, may be able to assist. Government WHS regulators normally provide email updates or feeds on changes to the law.

KEY ELEMENTS OF THE WHS ACT

The remainder of this chapter looks at the various parts of the Work Health and Safety Act, summarising and explaining key features. However, it is no substitute for close reading of the Act, which is written in plain English and, in general, easy to understand.

Figure 2.3 *Parts of the WHS Act*

1	Preliminary	What are the objects of the Act? What do some terms mean? What does the Act cover or exclude?
2	Health and safety duties	What is expected of duty-holders?
3	Incident notification	What are the requirements for notifying incidents, keeping records?
4	Authorisations	What work or equipment must be licensed?
5	Consultation, participation and representation	What are the provisions for WHS committees and representatives?
6	Discriminatory, coercive and misleading conduct	What is discriminatory, coercive and misleading conduct?
7	Workplace entry by WHS entry permit holders	What are the conditions for union right of entry into the workplace?
8	The regulator	Which government agency administers the Act and what is it required to do?
9	Securing compliance	What powers do inspectors have?
10	Enforcement measures	What notices can be served by inspectors?
11	Enforceable undertakings	How are work health and safety undertakings by offenders dealt with?
12	Review of decisions	Which decisions by inspectors are reviewable and how?
13	Legal proceedings	What are the legal processes for dealing with contraventions?
14	General	What are the provisions for making codes of practice and regulations?

PART 1: PRELIMINARY

Objectives

The object of the Act is set out in Section 3(1)[5]: 'to provide for a balanced and nationally consistent framework to secure the health and safety of workers and workplaces'. The paragraphs following show how the Act aims to achieve that object; namely, by

- protecting workers and others from harm to their health, safety and welfare through the elimination or minimisation of risks
- providing for workplace consultation, cooperation and issue resolution
- encouraging unions and employer organisations to promote improvements in work health and safety practices, and assisting duty-holders to achieve a healthier and safer working environment
- promoting the provision of advice, information, education and training
- securing compliance
- reviewing persons exercising powers and performing functions under the Act
- providing for continuous improvement and progressively higher standards
- maintaining and strengthening the national harmonisation of work health and safety laws, and facilitating a consistent national approach to work health and safety.

    Subsection 2 states 'that workers … should be given the highest level of protection … as is **reasonably practicable**'. We discuss the term 'reasonably practicable' shortly.

    Such wide-ranging objectives enable the government to be flexible and adopt legislative and administrative strategies in the face of changes inside and outside the workplace.

    Importantly, the Act deals not only with protecting people from injuries and fatalities, but also with illnesses and diseases, physical and psychological. If, for example, a worker or group of workers is being harassed, the stress associated with such harassment may lead to health problems. More obvious psychological aspects of work health may include the effects of armed hold-ups or assaults on workers, as well as organisational factors such as inappropriate shift or roster arrangements and excessive workloads.

Definitions

The most significant definitions are 'person conducting a business or undertaking' (PCBU), 'worker' and 'workplace'. Before explaining those, a number of important terms not defined in the Act need mentioning here.[6]

- 'Welfare' refers to the provision of proper workplace facilities, such as first aid rooms, toilets and washrooms.
- 'Risk' is the potential of a hazard to cause harm, injury or damage.
- 'Business' and 'undertaking' are defined in corporate law and by the courts, not in the Act.

- 'Officer' is defined in the *Corporations Act 2001*. It refers to directors and senior managers who exercise decision-making responsibilities.
- A 'system of work' is the way in which work is carried out in normal and abnormal situations such as breakdowns and maintenance.
- 'Plant' is the general term used for machinery, equipment, tools and appliances.

Person conducting a business or undertaking

Significantly, the WHS Act does not use the terms 'employer' and 'employee' but instead uses 'person conducting a business or undertaking' (PCBU) (s. 5) and 'worker' (s. 7). This provides a better understanding of who these duty-holders are by using terms with wider, more accurate meanings than 'employer' and 'employee'. As these terms are critical, and the person conducting a business or undertaking holds the primary duty of care, it is worth being clear about whom we are talking.

While 'person' suggests an individual, a person conducting a business or undertaking (a task or assignment) may be either an individual or a company ('body corporate') employing workers – an employer in either form. So, a PCBU may simply be an individual tradesperson employing an offsider or a corporation such as Telstra. A PCBU could be a self-employed person, municipal corporation, subcontractor or franchisor. The business or undertaking may be conducted by a partnership or an unincorporated association. If the business or undertaking is conducted by a partnership, then PCBU refers to each of the partners. Furthermore, a person conducts a business or undertaking whether alone or with others and whether for profit or not. So long as it is a business or undertaking, whoever or whatever is conducting it is a PCBU.

A person engaged solely as a worker or as an officer (a senior manager with decision-making responsibilities) is not a PCBU. Nor is an elected member of a government authority, nor a volunteer association. The regulations may specify the circumstances in which a person is not a person who conducts a business or undertaking. (s. 5)

The important lesson is that 'PCBU' is a wider ranging term than 'employer', though this will be what most people understand by it. Because 'person conducting a business or undertaking' is a cumbersome, uncommon term, we will only use it or 'PCBU' in a legal context. Elsewhere, we use the term 'employer'. Readers, however, should be aware that 'employer' is not equivalent to 'person conducting a business or undertaking'.

Finally, it is important to note that the Act says conduct by an employee, agent or officer of the body corporate acting within the scope of his or her employment or authority is deemed conduct also engaged in by the body corporate. (s. 244) So, for example, if as a company supervisor you are acting within the scope of your employment or authority, those activities are also activities of the company you work for.

Worker

A person is a worker if he or she carries out work in any capacity for a person conducting a business or undertaking; for example as

- an employee
- a contractor or subcontractor, or an employee of a contractor or subcontractor
- an employee of a labour-hire company assigned to work in the person's business or undertaking
- an outworker
- an apprentice, trainee or student gaining work experience
- a volunteer
- anyone of a class prescribed by the law to be a worker. (s. 7)

Similarly, 'worker' means more than 'employee'. Moreover, the 'person conducting the business or undertaking is also a worker if the person is an individual who carries out work in that business or undertaking'. (s. 7(3)) So the tradesperson working with their offsider is a worker as well as a PCBU.

Workplace

A workplace is a place where work is carried out for a business or undertaking and includes any place where a worker goes, or is likely to be, while at work. (s. 8) A workplace then can be anywhere, including at home providing a worker is working for a business or undertaking.

Application of the Act

In the preliminary part of the Act and elsewhere, you may find exclusions or provisions such as those applying to mining, defence force personnel, national security, federal police and other special categories. Under certain circumstances, the law could apply to work overseas.

The rest of this chapter outlines everyone's duties and how they are enforced. The rest of this book tells you how to comply with those duties in the spirit of the Act.

PART 2: HEALTH AND SAFETY DUTIES

A number of principles apply to duties. A person cannot transfer health and safety duties *laid down in the Act* to others. For example, you or the organisation cannot transfer the PCBU's duty to provide a safe and healthy workplace to someone in the company, to a contractor or the health and safety committee. That duty stays with the PCBU. Managers may, of course, transfer specific *operational* duties associated with health and safety – say, site inspections or training – from one person or position to another person or position so long as it complies with the duties set down in the Act.

Note also that there is no requirement to appoint someone with specific WHS responsibility (as there was in Queensland, South Australia, Tasmania and Victoria). Whether this is necessary will depend on the nature of the business, its size and hazard profile.

A person could have more than one duty under the law; for example, providing information and securing a safe workplace. And persons can share duties with others; for example, a PCBU and contractor, also a PCBU, can share the duty to prevent harm to third parties such as visitors to a workplace. The sharing of duties is a new requirement and will mean closer consultation among those who share the same duties. (ss. 13–15)

PCBUs must eliminate risks as far as reasonably practicable and if it is not reasonably practicable to eliminate risks, to minimise those risks so far as is reasonably practicable. (s. 17)

'Reasonably practicable' means taking into account and weighing up all relevant matters including
- the likelihood of the hazard or the risk concerned occurring
- the degree of harm that might result
- what the person concerned knows, or ought reasonably to know, about
  - the hazard or the risk
  - ways of eliminating or minimising the risk
  - the availability and suitability of ways to eliminate or minimise the risk
  - after assessing the extent of the risk and the available ways of eliminating or minimising the risk, the cost associated with available ways of eliminating or minimising the risk, including whether the cost is grossly disproportionate to the risk. (s. 18)

These are tricky waters. Once you think you have taken everything into account, how do you weigh up these factors? The standard of reasonably practicable is discussed in more detail in Chapter 6.

Role of PCBUs

The Act places the primary duty of care on the person conducting a business or undertaking. (s. 19) A person conducting a business or undertaking must ensure the health and safety so far as reasonably practicable of
- workers engaged, or caused to be engaged by the person
- workers whose activities in carrying out work are influenced or directed by the person
- other persons (visitors, customers). (s. 19)
  The person must also provide
- a work environment without risks to health and safety
- safe **plant** (machinery, equipment, tools) and structures
- safe **systems of work**
- the safe use, handling, storage and transport of plant, structures and substances
- adequate facilities for the welfare of workers
- necessary information, training, instruction or supervision
- monitoring of workers' health and workplace conditions. (s. 19(3))

These duties should shape the general headings for planning WHS (see Chapter 4) and any compliance checklist.

Elsewhere in the Act, it says that a PCBU 'must not impose a levy or charge on a worker … for anything done, or provided, in relation to work health and safety'. (s. 273)

Further, if a worker occupies accommodation owned, managed or controlled by the PCBU, and this is necessary for the worker's engagement, the PCBU must maintain the premises so that there are no risks to health and safety. (s. 19(4))

Finally, a self-employed person must ensure their own health and safety while at work. (s. 19(5)) This may appear odd, but we do have legislation prescribing the wearing of seatbelts.

Controllers of workplaces, designers, manufacturers, importers, suppliers and installers

The person with management or control of a workplace must ensure that the means of entering and exiting the workplace and anything arising from the workplace are without risks to the health and safety of any person. (s 20(2))

The person with management or control of fixtures, fittings or plant at a workplace must ensure that they are without risks to the health and safety of any person. (s. 21) (See Chapter 7 for further discussion of this duty.)

Designers of plant, substances or structures must ensure they are without risks to health and safety. (s. 22) (For more details on this requirement, see Chapter 12.)

Similarly, manufacturers, importers, suppliers and installers of plant, substances or structures must take necessary steps to eliminate or minimise any associated risks. (ss. 23–26)

Officers

Officers of the person conducting the business or undertaking – directors and senior managers with decision-making responsibilities – must exercise *due diligence*; that is, take reasonable steps to

- acquire and keep up-to-date knowledge of work health and safety matters
- gain an understanding of the nature of the operations of the business or undertaking and generally of the hazards and risks associated with those operations
- ensure the PCBU has and uses appropriate resources and processes to eliminate or minimise risks; receives, considers and responds to information regarding incidents, hazards and risks; and implements processes for complying with any duty or obligation such as
  - reporting notifiable incidents
  - consulting with workers
  - ensuring compliance with notices
  - training and instructing workers about health and safety
  - training health and safety representatives
  - verifying the provision and use of the required resources and processes. (s. 27)

In light of the requirement to exercise due diligence, businesses may need to review who are officers.

Workers

Workers must

- take *reasonable care* of their health and safety and that of those affected by their activity
- comply with any reasonable instruction that is given by the PCBU to allow the person to comply with the Act
- cooperate with any reasonable policy or procedure set by the PCBU that has been notified to workers. (s. 28)

Other persons at the workplace

Similarly, other persons – for example, visitors or customers – must take reasonable care of their health and safety and those affected by their activity while complying with any reasonable instruction by the PCBU. (s. 29)

Note that the standard changes from *reasonably practicable* (PCBUs) to *due diligence* (officers) to *reasonable care* (workers and other persons).

Penalties for contraventions

Penalties for contraventions vary and are detailed throughout the Act. The maximum penalties for duty offences by individuals as a PCBU or officer are $600 000 or five years' imprisonment or both; in the case of a body corporate the maximum penalty is $3 000 000.

DID YOU KNOW?

An injury outcome is not required for there to be a contravention. The fact that a hazard exists, even in the absence of an injury, may be a contravention. Likewise, ignorance is no defence in WHS law. If information exists related to, say, toxicity of substances, or if research demonstrates safety problems with particular work practices, then there is a general presumption that the PCBU ought to be aware.

PART 3: INCIDENT NOTIFICATION

PCBUs must notify the regulator of certain types of incidents – 'notifiable incidents' – immediately after becoming aware of them. They include fatalities, serious injuries and illnesses, and dangerous incidents – 'near-misses'. These are defined in the law, as is the method of notification. Records must be kept for five years. Subject to certain conditions set out in the Act, the PCBU must ensure, so far as is reasonably practicable, that the site where the incident occurred is not disturbed. (ss. 35–39) In Chapter 15, we deal with reporting and recording as well as other matters associated with incidents.

PART 4: AUTHORISATIONS

The regulations specify what type of work needs to be 'authorised': for example, where licences, permits or registrations are required, such as for removing asbestos, or operating cranes or forklifts. PCBUs must be aware of those requirements. (ss. 40–45)

PART 5: CONSULTATION, PARTICIPATION AND REPRESENTATION

The Act specifies how PCBUs must consult with workers on health and safety matters. This includes not only formal consultation with health and safety representatives and in committees but also consultation on a day-to-day basis. This part of the Act is extensive (ss. 46–103) and is dealt with in the next chapter, where we also discuss the important issue of dispute resolution.

PART 6: DISCRIMINATORY, COERCIVE AND MISLEADING CONDUCT

The Act prohibits discriminatory, coercive and misleading conduct. This part is aimed principally at protecting workers and their representatives when they exercise their powers or functions under the Act.

'A person must not engage in discriminatory conduct for a prohibited reason', where that reason was the dominant reason for the conduct. (s. 104(1–2)) The Act goes on to define 'discriminatory conduct' and 'prohibited reason'. (ss. 105–106)

Likewise the Act prohibits coercion or inducement against another to exercise or not to exercise their powers or functions. (s. 108)

PART 7: WORKPLACE ENTRY BY WHS ENTRY PERMIT HOLDERS

Under certain conditions, union officers may enter workplaces for health and safety purposes providing they are suitably trained and hold an entry permit from the authorising authority, as specified in each jurisdiction. The permit holder must also hold an entry permit under the federal *Fair Work Act 2009* or the relevant state or territory industrial law. (s. 124) This part sets out the conditions for such union right of entry.

A permit holder may enter a workplace for the purpose of inquiring into a suspected contravention of the Act affecting a relevant worker; that is a worker
- who is a member, or eligible to be a member, of the union represented by the permit holder
- whose industrial interests the union is entitled to represent
- who works at that workplace. (s. 117(1))

The entry permit holder must reasonably suspect before entering the workplace that the contravention has occurred or is occurring. (s. 117(2))

The permit holder may
- inspect any work system, plant, substance, structure or other thing relevant to the suspected contravention
- consult with the relevant workers in relation to the suspected contravention
- consult with the relevant person conducting a business or undertaking about the suspected contravention

- require the relevant person conducting a business or undertaking to allow the WHS entry permit holder to inspect, and make copies of, any document that is directly relevant to the suspected contravention and that is kept at the workplace
- warn any person whom the WHS entry permit holder reasonably believes to be exposed to a serious risk from an immediate or imminent exposure to a hazard. (s. 118(1))

Notice of entry

A WHS entry permit holder must, as soon as is reasonably practicable after entering a workplace, give notice of the entry and the suspected contravention, in accordance with the regulations, to the relevant person conducting a business or undertaking, and the person with management or control of the workplace. (s. 119)

Inspecting and copying documents

The permit holder may inspect or make copies of employee records directly relevant to a suspected contravention or other directly relevant documents. The permit holder must give prior notice to the person from whom the documents are requested and the relevant person conducting a business or undertaking. That notice must comply with the regulations and must be given during usual working hours at that workplace at least 24 hours, but not more than 14 days, before the entry. (s. 120) But note that the use or disclosure of personal information obtained under this section is regulated under the Commonwealth *Privacy Act 1988*.

A permit holder may also enter a workplace to consult and advise on work health and safety matters with one or more relevant workers who wish to participate in the discussions. Similar prior notice must be given. (ss. 121–122)

The regulator may deal with a dispute about the exercise by a permit holder of a right of entry. (ss. 142–143)

PART 8: THE REGULATOR

The regulator is the government agency that administers and enforces the WHS Act; for example, NSW WorkCover or WorkSafe WA. This part of the Act sets out the functions and powers of the regulator.

The regulator has the following *functions*:
- to advise and make recommendations to the minister, and report on the operation and effectiveness of the Act
- to monitor and enforce compliance
- to provide advice and information on work health and safety to duty-holders and to the community
- to collect, analyse and publish statistics relating to work health and safety
- to foster a cooperative, consultative relationship between duty-holders and the persons to whom they owe duties and their representatives
- to promote and support education and training on matters relating to work health and safety

- to engage in, promote and coordinate the sharing of information, including the sharing of information with a corresponding regulator
- to conduct and defend proceedings before a court or tribunal
- any other function conferred on the regulator by the Act. (s. 152)

The regulator has the *power* to do what is required to perform its functions and all the powers that an inspector has under the Act. (s. 153) If the regulator has reasonable grounds to believe that a person has information regarding a possible contravention or information that would assist the regulator to monitor or enforce compliance then the regulator may ask for that information and the person must provide it. (s. 155)

A quick visit to your regulator's website should confirm these functions and powers. These can range to the licensing of amusement devices such as merry-go-rounds and big dippers!

The WHS regulator often sits in the same agency that administers workers' compensation, with the one agency governed by a board or council accountable to the government. Annual reports from the regulators provide useful details of their activities and some, like WorkSafe Victoria, list the year's prosecutions (successful and unsuccessful) together with the fines.

PART 9: SECURING COMPLIANCE

Inspectors, usually employees of the regulator, have a number of important functions and powers. They include:

- to provide information and advice about compliance
- to assist in the resolution of work health and safety issues at workplaces
- to review disputed provisional improvement notices issued by health and safety representatives
- to issue notices
- to investigate contraventions and assist with prosecutions
- to attend coronial inquests in respect of work-related deaths and examine witnesses. (s. 160)

Right of entry

An inspector may at any time enter a place that is, or that the inspector reasonably suspects is, a workplace without the consent of the person with management or control of the workplace and without prior notice. An inspector may enter any place if the entry is authorised by a search warrant. (ss. 163–164)

Investigation

An inspector may then

- inspect, examine and make inquiries at the workplace
- inspect and examine any thing (including a document) at the workplace

- bring to the workplace and use any equipment or materials that may be required
- take measurements, conduct tests and make sketches or recordings (including photographs, films, audio, video, digital or other recordings)
- take and remove for analysis a sample of any substance or thing without paying for it
- require a person at the workplace to give the inspector reasonable help to exercise the inspector's powers
- exercise any compliance power or other power that is reasonably necessary to be exercised by the inspector for the purposes of the Act. (s. 165)

The inspector has the power to require production of documents and interview persons. (s. 171) A person is not excused from answering a question or providing information or a document on the ground that the answer to the question, or the information or document, may tend to incriminate the person or expose the person to a penalty. However, the answer to a question or information or a document provided by an individual is not admissible as evidence against that individual in civil or criminal proceedings. The inspector must warn the person of this requirement beforehand. (ss. 172–173)

The inspector also has the power to

- copy and retain documents, seize evidence and things for, say, testing, as well as to secure workplaces (ss. 174–176)
- require names and addresses from persons (s. 185)
- take affidavits (s. 186)
- examine witnesses at coronial inquests. (s. 187)

There are hefty penalties for threatening or obstructing inspectors: for individuals, up to $50 000 or two years' imprisonment or both, and in the case of a body corporate up to $250 000. (s. 190)

PART 10: ENFORCEMENT MEASURES

In addition to being able to enter workplaces and investigate, inspectors have the power to enforce measures with notices to the PCBU. These include:

- improvement notices (ss. 191–192)
- prohibition notices (ss. 195–196)
- non-disturbance notices. (ss. 198–199)

If a notice is issued to you, you must, as soon as possible, display a copy of the notice in a prominent place at or near the workplace at which work is being carried out that is affected by the notice (s. 210) and comply with it within the timeframe.

Under certain circumstances, failure to comply may be met with remedial action by the regulator – at your expense – and with court injunctions. (ss. 211–214)

The ability to review an inspector's decision is set out in Part 12 of the Act.

WHS IN PRACTICE

CRUSH INJURIES CAUSED BY FORKLIFT: OPERATOR'S VISION OBSCURED[7]

An employee of a labour-hire firm was working as a production supervisor and safety officer at the plant of a host employer who was manufacturing concrete blocks and pavers.

On 30 April 2008, he heard a noise from a moveable conveyor rack and found that a guard had been bent out of shape and was coming into contact with the conveyor chain. While he tried to repair the guard, another labour-hire employee was operating a forklift to transfer pavers in racks towards the conveyor. His sight line was blocked and when he put down the pavers in front of the conveyor he could not see the supervisor working on the faulty guard. The supervisor was struck by the rack of pavers and sustained crush injuries to his abdomen, a lacerated liver and fractured vertebrae.

The labour-hire firm was prosecuted for breach of s 8(1) of the NSW *Occupational Health and Safety Act 2000* and pleaded guilty. It had failed to conduct a comprehensive workplace assessment, implement a safe work procedure for the operation of forklifts, restrict pedestrian access to the loading area, provide adequate signage and clearly mark pedestrian exclusion zones, and ensure its employees received site-specific induction training, forklift operation training and supervision.

Obvious steps could have been taken to eliminate or reduce the risk. This was demonstrated by measures taken after the incident. They included holding a toolbox safety meeting, carrying out a risk assessment on the guard and replacing it with a new guard made from thicker metal, installing a mirror to provide a clear view of the loading area, implementing a forklift/pedestrian traffic management plan, and providing new signage and clear marking for pedestrian exclusion zones.

After the incident, the firm's employees engaged in forklift operations had been issued with new training logbooks and instructed in how to fill them out. Trainee forklift operators had received special attention and the firm had sought to accelerate their opportunities to gain their forklift licence.

The court acknowledged that the labour-hire firm had instituted some safety procedures before the incident. For example, the firm's manager had walked around the premises in an informal worksite assessment. However, it had not been documented, so there was no indication of what risks had been identified or if any corrective action had been taken.

In sentencing, the court took into account the guilty plea and allowed a 25% discount in the penalty assessment.

Other mitigating factors included the labour-hire firm's expression of remorse and contrition for the offence and the fact that it had made reparation for the injuries, loss and damage caused. The court noted that the firm was a non-profit organisation and also took into account its limited financial means. The firm was convicted and fined $20,000.

Source: www.workplaceohs.com.au

PART 11: ENFORCEABLE UNDERTAKINGS

To avoid court action in all but the most serious cases, offenders may, with the regulator's approval, carry out an enforceable undertaking, usually some substantial health and safety initiative that will benefit the workplace, industry and society – a type of community service. Part 11 sets out the processes for such enforceable undertakings.

WHS IN PRACTICE

Examples of enforceable undertakings can be found on the websites of the regulators. This is just one example.

– BOEING TRAINING & FLIGHT SERVICES

In October 2010, Workplace Health and Safety Queensland, accepted an enforceable undertaking by Boeing Training & Flight Services Australia Pty Limited for an alleged breach of s. 24 and s. 28(1) of the *Workplace Health and Safety Act 1995*.

In May 2008, at Eagle Farm Queensland, an employee was standing on a steel service pit cover when the pit cover suddenly fell. This resulted in the employee falling approximately 1.8 metres into the service pit. As a result, the employee suffered lacerations to the shoulder and tendon damage.

The undertakings included
- conducting a series of third-party audits of the company's occupational health and safety management system using AS/NZS 4801:2001, and then implementing any audit recommendations
- providing specified health and safety training to employees on issues such as risk assessment, confined spaces and hazardous materials
- providing all employees with free health and wellbeing assessments
- publishing a case study and article, in an industry journal, on the safe management of risks associated with hydraulic services pits
- providing agreed services in kind to the Royal Flying Doctor Service
- providing agreed services in kind and training to students of Aviation High, a high school for students considering careers in the aviation and aerospace industries.

In total the undertaking had a total minimum expenditure of $104,000 which included any recoverable government costs.

Source: Workplace Health and Safety Queensland, 2010, http://www.deir.qld.gov.au/workplace/law/
enforceable-undertakings/2010/boeing/index.htm.

PART 12: REVIEW OF DECISIONS

Decisions by the inspector may be reviewed internally; that is, by someone appointed by the regulator. Section 223 identifies which decisions are reviewable and who is eligible to apply for the review. Sections 224 to 227 outline the processes for such internal reviews. Sections 228 and 229 set out the processes for an external review of a decision either made by the regulator or by an internal review.

PART 13: LEGAL PROCEEDINGS

Legal proceedings under the Act can be complex and require professional advice. A few key points are listed here.

Proceedings may only be brought by the regulator, an inspector with authorisation from the regulator or the Director of Public Prosecutions. (s. 230)[8] If no prosecution has been brought for an alleged offence under the Act and someone believes there should be, there is a procedure for pursuing this. (s. 231)

Any prosecution brought under the Act may not prevent separate common law action being taken against a person – individual or company – for the same matter. (s. 267)

In addition to any penalty that may be imposed, the court may make a number of orders: adverse publicity order (s. 236), restoration order (s. 237) and project order (s. 238). Injunctions (s. 240) and training orders (s. 241) are also available to the courts.

If the Crown – Commonwealth, state or territory government – is guilty of an offence against the Act, the penalty to be imposed on the Crown is the penalty applying to a body corporate. (s. 245)

PART 14: GENERAL

This Part covers mainly regulations and codes of practice.

Regulations

Unlike codes that are approved by the minister, regulations as part of the law must be approved by parliament. (s. 276(1)) Regulations set out what *must* be done in relation to certain WHS matters. They are not simply pieces of good advice.

The regulations are consolidated, unlike the codes, which are set out in separate documents. Altogether they are, currently, almost three times the length of the Act. Your regulator's website has the regulations online.

Regulations cover a very wide range of detailed health and safety matters. (See Schedule 3 to the Act as well as the preliminary Chapter 1 of the regulations.) They need to be read together with the related parts of the Act. For example, to understand exactly what is required by law to deal with safe handling of substances such as inorganic lead or asbestos you would also need to read the regulations covering those substances (parts 7.2 and 7.3).

Regulations may refer to standards such as **Australian standards** produced by Standards Australia and mandate them for use in the workplace. Another source may be the National Standards produced by Safe Work Australia. Wherever they come from, these mandatory standards form part of the 'regs' and must be followed.

Regulations have changed over time from prescribing details of the procedures, equipment and substances to be used (*prescriptive* regulations) to setting the outcomes and letting you devise the best means of achieving them. Setting maximum noise levels is one example of the more flexible outcome or *performance-based* regulations. Once set, it is up to you to see that you don't go over the limit. Regulations can also specify general processes or procedures (*process* regulations) to achieve safe outcomes such as the risk management methodology to control hazards associated with manual handling. The focus of the different types of regulations is outlined below.

REGULATION	FOCUS	EXAMPLES
Prescriptive	Activities, plant, facilities, materials	working at heights, signage, safety boots, hard hat, guarding, no asbestos
Performance-based	outcomes	noise, heat, vibration levels
Process	method	risk assessment, consultation

All three types of regulation have their pluses and minuses. As a result, what we have today is a mixture of types to meet the health and safety issues of rapidly changing workplaces.

Codes of practice

Following consultation with stakeholders, **codes of practice** may be approved by the minister responsible. (s. 274(1)) Codes provide advice on how to apply the law with respect to specific WHS matters. The initial codes include:
*   How to Manage Work Health and Safety Risks
*   How to Consult on Work Health and Safety
*   Managing the Work Environment and Facilities
*   Facilities for Construction Sites
*   Managing Noise and Preventing Hearing Loss at Work
*   Hazardous Manual Tasks
*   Confined Spaces
*   How to Manage and Control Asbestos in the Workplace
*   How to Prevent Falls at Workplaces
*   How to Safely Remove Asbestos
*   Labelling of Workplace Hazardous Chemicals
*   Preparation of Safety Data Sheets for Hazardous Chemicals.

Codes can also be used in court to determine whether or not a duty has been complied with. The court may use the code as evidence of what is known about a hazard and how to control it so far as reasonably practicable. At the same time, other evidence may show there to be a better standard than that found in the code. (s. 275)

Because of their role in court proceedings, codes of practice are sometimes referred to as 'evidentiary standards'.

You can find the codes on your regulator's or Safe Work Australia's website.

Guidance material

Regulators provide **guidance notes** that do not form part of the law. This material covers basic introductions to WHS law as well as specific information on hazards. The breadth of information is impressive. For example, NSW WorkCover, together with other authorities, has, to its credit, produced health and safety guidelines for brothels.

Finally, it is important to remember that the law requires duty-holders to consider all risks associated with work, not only those for which regulations and codes of practice exist. You may find hazardous situations in your workplace that are not addressed by specific regulations, standards or codes of practice. In which case, guidance may be needed from others such as WHS professionals, government workplace inspectors or other experts such as engineers, scientists, ergonomic experts or doctors. Failure to seek and use such guidance may contravene the law, resulting in fines or imprisonment.

This completes our overview of the law but leaves open the question of whether or not it is effective in improving health and safety performance.

DOES THE LAW WORK?

As we have seen in the previous chapter, compensation data indicates a gradual improvement in our national performance. How much of that improvement, if any, can be attributed to WHS law or improvements to it is difficult to answer with any accuracy as it is not the only factor at play – as we saw in Chapter 1. For example, independent of any considerations of WHS law, there have been changes to technology that have made jobs safer and some riskier industries have moved offshore.

Nevertheless, there is reason for thinking that the law can bring greater awareness of health and safety and help to build a culture less tolerant of risky behaviour and more mindful of health. Simply knowing that it is the law is enough for many to comply even if they never expect to see an inspector on their doorstep or worry about penalties. Taking those steps to comply with good law should mean a safer and healthier workplace.

We may assume then that the law and other activity by regulators does have some effect but how much is hard to judge. A lot will depend on the nature of the individual workplaces themselves as well as the range of other factors affecting those workplaces. WHS law is just one important factor in the mix.

One thing is certain. Fines for contraventions that result in death, serious injury and disease are weak weapons. When measured by the devastation of workplace death, injury and disease, fines are trifling penalties, particularly for larger firms. In the case study below, Australand Holdings, the principal contractor, made a profit of $163.2 million on revenue of $1.5 billion for the 2007 financial year preceding the fine. The fine of $178 500 was then equivalent to one-tenth of one per cent of their profit.

JOEL EXNER'S DEATH

The principal contractor at the site where 16-year-old labourer Joel Exner died was fined $178 500 by the NSW Industrial Court. The young Sydney labourer died in 2003 when he lost his balance and fell through safety mesh, approximately 11 metres to the floor below. He suffered extensive internal and other injuries as a result of the fall and died a short time later in hospital. It was later discovered that the safety mesh had been incorrectly installed, leaving gaps for workers to fall through.

JB Metal Roofing Pty Ltd, which installed the safety mesh, and its directors were fined a total of $255 700 over the labourer's death.

The court heard that Australand Holdings' general practice was to require the subcontractor to complete a subcontractor safety pack. That pack included a Safe Work Method Statement (SWMS) and a Job Safety Analysis (JSA) relevant to the work to be undertaken. The JSA was to specify how the work was to be done and the measures taken to eliminate the hazards associated with the work. The safety pack was then reviewed and approved by Australand's site safety coordinator.

An initial JSA provided by JB Metal Roofing was found to be inadequate, and the site safety coordinator directed it to be amended with changes he specified, which included that the safety mesh installation be altered. Although the document was amended, JB Metal Roofing did not implement the changes and Australand did not check that the documented measures were being carried out.

For further details, see *WorkCover Authority of New South Wales (Inspector Dubois) v. Australand Holdings Limited* [2007] NSWIRComm 156 (5 July 2007).

Questions

1 Under the WHS Act what are the maximum and minimum fines that can apply to the PCBU (Australand Holdings, in this case)?
2 On what basis was the subcontractor (JB Metal Roofing) fined?
3 What do you think the appropriate fine would have been if the WHS Act had been in place at the time?

Whether heavier fines or sentences would improve compliance is a matter of debate. What is critical is the probability of being caught and punished, which in turn raises questions about resourcing of the inspectorate and the efficiency of the court system. (Note the time lag between the death and the fine in the Exner case.)

Given very limited resources, regulatory strategies have become more inventive. For example, many carry out proactive interventions and workplace visits that have not resulted from a complaint or workplace incident. These include all planned interventions, routine workplace visits, inspections/audits and industry forums/ presentations (at which an inspector delivers educational advice or information as well as conducts a field inspection). There are also media campaigns.

Enforcement policies and practices also vary among jurisdictions. Although the law allows for the prosecution of individual managers and directors of corporations, most prosecutions are conducted against corporate employers – that is, the company – particularly when injuries or fatalities involving machinery occur. Actions against manufacturers, designers and suppliers of plant, equipment and substances are rare.

Recently, public prosecutors began considering bringing manslaughter prosecutions under the general criminal law in situations when gross negligence causes workplace deaths. There have been a few successful manslaughter prosecutions in the past. However, proving negligence by a corporation can be a complicated, lengthy and expensive exercise. As a consequence, unions and others have called for specific industrial manslaughter legislation that would expedite cases involving workplace fatalities.

DID YOU KNOW?

INDUSTRIAL MANSLAUGHTER LAW IN THE AUSTRALIAN CAPITAL TERRITORY

On 1 March 2004, the *Crimes (Industrial Manslaughter) Amendment Act 2003* (ACT) came into force, creating the offence of industrial manslaughter. A senior officer of a corporation commits the offence of industrial manslaughter if the officer's negligent or reckless conduct is a substantial cause of a worker's death at the workplace. For an individual, this offence attracts a maximum fine of $200 000, imprisonment for 20 years, or both.

While laws can provide the important framework for successful WHS, it is activity in the workplace that is critical. As we saw, meaningful consultation is recognised by the law as essential and it is this topic we turn to next.

Summary

- WHS legislation comprises the principal Act and regulations or mandatory standards. In Australia, there are nine such Acts covering the Commonwealth, states and territories.
- The PCBU has a legal duty of care to provide a safe and healthy workplace to all workers as well as to third parties. Managers and supervisors, as representatives of the PCBU, need to be aware of the law and act in accordance with it. In addition, manufacturers, suppliers and others specified under the legislation have a duty of care to ensure that their activities do not create a risk.
- Workers have a right to enjoy a safe and healthy workplace as well as a duty to cooperate with PCBUs in exercising their duty of care.
- Workers also have a right to be consulted on workplace health and safety matters.
- To administer the Act, government agencies, regulators, have been created to appoint inspectors, collect data, undertake research, provide information and advice, and certify certain tradespeople. These agencies are an important source of information on the law and WHS matters in your jurisdiction.
- Inspectors have the right to enter workplaces, conduct inspections, gather evidence, issue improvement or prohibition notices, and initiate prosecutions. In addition to reactive investigations into incidents, inspectorates also target high-risk industries and activities in a systematic, proactive manner.
- The principal Act enables regulations, standards and codes of practice to be called up. Regulations and mandatory standards form part of the law and breaches may result in penalties. Codes of practice, on the other hand, advise on the best methods of dealing with risks in the workplace. The codes should be followed, unless there are equally effective or better ways of dealing with the particular risk.
- It is important to remember that the duty of care requires the PCBU to provide a safe and healthy workplace, not just to comply with the existing regulations or mandatory standards. Some hazardous situations may require additional information and advice if there is to be effective compliance.

In your workplace

The management of your company, a furniture retail firm with franchise operations in all states and territories, has heard of the new legislation covering WHS and has an interest in ensuring that all the franchisees know of their duties and where they can get practical information on compliance. The firm carries out some manufacturing, and supplies offices as well as homes.

1 How would you as health and safety manager devise a strategy to deal with compliance?
2 What sort of issues would you highlight?
3 How would you ensure that everyone is informed and that the message is getting through?
    Consider the relevant regulations as well as codes, addresses, training. You may wish to change the example to your own workplace.

Questions

1 Referring to the WHS Act, answer the following questions:
   a What does the PCBU's duty of care cover?
   b What are the responsibilities of the manufacturer or supplier?
   c What are the duties *and* rights of the worker?
2 What are the advantages and disadvantages of
   a prescriptive standards?
   b performance-based standards?
   c process standards?
3 There has been a serious accident involving a worker in your workplace. Does a relevant union official have the right to enter your workplace? If so, under what conditions?
4 Does your jurisdiction make available its enforcement policy? If so, what are the key principles?

Activities

1 Using a significant hazard from your workplace, prepare advice to managers and supervisors on
   a the regulation(s) or mandatory standard(s) that covers the hazard
   b the penalty for breach
   c any code of practice, Australian Standard or suitable guidance material that would advise you on how to comply with the regulation or standard.
   Outline the main steps to be taken to control the hazard, as set out in the information. Gather feedback from your workplace on the effectiveness of the information.
2 Interview (or invite) an inspector to discuss their experience. Report on the main issues and their view of the most difficult and rewarding aspects of their job.
3 Attend a court hearing on a WHS case and report back.

Search me!

Search me! Explore **Search me! management** for relevant articles on health and safety law. Search me! is an online library of world-class journals, ebooks and newspapers, including *The Australian* and the *New York Times*, and is updated daily. Log in to Search me! through www.cengage.com/sso using the access card in the front of this book.

KEYWORDS

Try searching for the following terms:

▶ duty of care
▶ Robens
▶ health and safety regulations

▶ health and safety codes of practice
▶ industrial manslaughter

Search tip: **Search me! management** contains information from both local and international sources. To get the greatest number of search results, try using both Australian and American spellings in your searches; e.g. 'globalisation' and 'globalization'; 'organisation' and 'organization'.

Additional resources

For students wishing to know more about WHS law, the simplest and easiest place to start is with the regulators whose websites contain the Act and regulations and also provide explanatory material. WHS authorities notify changes through the websites and many provide free email updates. See page 28 for the relevant websites.

* Bluff, E., Gunningham, N. & Johnstone, R. (eds), 2004, *OHS Regulation for a Changing World of Work*, Federation Press: Sydney. Published 30 years after the Robens Report, the authors explore new models of WHS regulation that take account of gaps and deficiencies.
* Quinlan, M., Bohle P. & Lamm, F., 2010, *Managing Occupational Health and Safety: A Multidisciplinary Approach*, 3rd edn, Palgrave Macmillan: Melbourne. This is the standard academic text on WHS; see Chapter 7 'Law and prevention' for a discussion of the law pre-harmonisation.
* CCH and the Law Book Company provide legal update services aimed at legal practitioners and WHS managers.

Endnotes

1 Industrial agreements may contain WHS provisions enforceable under industrial relations legislation.
2 At the time of writing, the Commonwealth maritime industry jurisdiction is not committed to the harmonisation process but will consider it later in 2011.
3 At the time of writing, WA indicated that it was unable to support the following recommendations contained in the Model WHS Act:
   a the introduction of a conciliation concept for resolution of issues
   b power for health and safety representatives to stop work
   c reverse onus of proof for discrimination issues
   d level of penalties
   e right of entry.
4 The Office of the Australian Information Commissioner provides information on the federal Privacy Act.

5 Note that pinpoint references to Acts – for example, s. 3(1)(a) – follow the rule of listing the section number (3), followed by any subsection number (1) and paragraph letter (a) in brackets. Pinpoint references to the regulations refer similarly to the sections, then any subsections and paragraphs.
6 A glossary can be found at the end of the book.
7 Full details of the case, *Inspector Walker v Great Lakes Community Resources Incorporated, t-as Workplace Services* [2010] NSWIRComm 182 (2 *December* 2010), are available at http://www.lawlink.nsw.gov.au/ircjudgments/2010nswirc.nsf/c1b955f60eecc5fcca2570e60013ad15/a624ed9d06d0127cca2577f5000b67e9?OpenDocument.
8 At the time of writing, early 2011, NSW allowed restricted provision for unions to prosecute.

CONSULTING ON WHS

Learning Objectives

By the end of this chapter, the reader will be able to assist in:
- identifying the need for WHS consultative arrangements
- designing WHS consultative arrangements
- developing WHS consultative arrangements
- supporting the implementation of consultative arrangements
- evaluating the design and development of consultative arrangements.

INTRODUCTION

Consultation with workers is critical to the success of workplace health and safety, building understanding and commitment. Governments and employers have run hot and cold on consultation as it appears to challenge managerial prerogatives. But many have also recognised the clear dividends that come from WHS consultation and so, on health and safety issues, it has become a legal requirement under the Work Health and Safety Act for employers ('PCBU's') to consult with their workers. (s. 47(1))

Formal consultation, using health and safety representatives (HSRs) and health and safety committees (HSCs), is only part of the picture. Informal day-to-day consultation in its broadest form should be standard management practice. In fact, you may not need to establish formal consultation arrangements in a small business with few workers if, for example, you have weekly team meetings or you have discussions with them as part of everyday work.

Informal consultation can include

- holding floor meetings
- gathering input for safety audits
- carrying out **hazard identification** and risk assessment processes
- communicating hazard alerts
- carrying out surveys using checklists
- holding toolbox meetings
- sending Intranet emails
- requesting feedback on procedures (see example on Danum Engineering below).

A key feature of the success of all such informal consultation is the inclusion of positive feedback – congratulating particular individuals and groups whenever possible, especially when it comes from senior management.

In an important sense, formal consultative arrangements are there to ensure that information-sharing and proper communication are genuine and two-way so that decision making in general is improved. Consultation outside formal requirements ought to occur as part of day-to-day operations, provided everyone is trained to deal with the issue and has sufficient information, proper supervision and equipment to do so.

Formal consultation ensures such day-to-day operations promote health and safety and do not endanger workers. Formal consultation especially, in larger organisations, can overcome the shortcomings of a suggestion-box approach and an open-door policy. It reinforces a systematic approach to health and safety.

Finally, consultation over WHS is an important step towards broader workplace democracy, giving workers a say over matters that affect their lives and the community. Why should democracy stop when work starts? Involving workers in this way provides a model for reviewing how organisations and society can be managed in a more accountable and effective way.

In this chapter, we explain what formal consultation requires, its benefits and how to implement it effectively using three basic steps.

DANUM ENGINEERING

Danum Engineering is a Geelong-based firm that shows how informal consultation such as toolbox meetings can be used to improve performance.

Strategy

Danum's safety strategies are based on a comprehensive safety management plan. This, together with Danum's commitment to safety and close monitoring and communication with work groups, has been instrumental in maintaining an excellent safety track record.

Approach

All company work groups attend a daily job start meeting to discuss the day's activities and any special precautions that may be required on the job. Any incidents from the previous day are discussed and recorded.

Weekly toolbox meetings address issues relating to safety in the workplace and are held throughout the entire company. The toolbox meetings are also used as a forum for employees to air any concerns or put forward any new initiatives for review. The meetings also provide an information channel for clients to communicate with Danum about safety standards and the process of reviewing safety.

Training

Work groups conduct job safety analyses in which potential safety or environmental hazards are identified and actions to prevent their occurrence are discussed and implemented. Periodic safety audits are conducted on procedures, providing management with statistical data to identify any trends that may require action. Regular safety training courses are conducted by qualified instructors to increase employee awareness to potential hazards.

This successful Danum Occupational Health & Safety (OH&S) program has been recognised at both national and state levels. Danum Engineering was one of Work Safe Australia's OH&S Best Practice case studies. Danum also won an award for 'Innovation in Occupational Health & Safety' from the Victorian OH&S Authority.

Source: Danum Engineering Pty Ltd, Commitment to Safety, http://www.danum.com.au/cgi-bin/site/wrapper.pl?c1=safety, © Copyright 2009. Danum Engineering Pty Ltd

WHAT IS CONSULTATION?

Consultation is information-sharing and discussion with the objective of gaining greater understanding and agreement between all parties involved in an issue. The underlying assumption of the requirement to consult is that WHS issues are best resolved through meaningful and effective consultation within the organisation.

In contrast, some consider consultation to be merely informing people in advance about, for example, an upcoming change to the workplace without letting all the people affected by the decision have a say in how that change is to be implemented. However, if there is no real intention or effort to reach agreement among all the parties concerned, this is not real consultation at all; rather, it is a warning or a notice. Consultation must be a two-way street in which workers are given the opportunity to consider the issues and have their opinions heard and valued.

Consultation then requires that

- relevant information about health and safety matters is shared with workers
- workers have a reasonable opportunity to
  - express their views and raise work health or safety issues
  - contribute to the decision-making process
- the views of workers are taken into account by the employer
- workers are advised of the outcome of the consultation in a timely manner. (s. 48(1))

Finally, if workers are represented by a health and safety representative, consultation must involve that representative. (s. 48(2))

Consultation is often contrasted with negotiation, whereby negotiation is understood as a formal and often adversarial bargaining process involving representatives from management and, in the case of workers, normally their union representatives. Any agreement resulting from the negotiation is then signed by both parties and lodged with an industrial court. While there is usually some form of negotiation during consultation, the consultation under discussion here is not negotiation in the strict sense outlined above. Although union representatives may be involved and the agreements must be binding, there is no use of the formal industrial process.

Where consultation over health and safety does not result in consensus, any resulting dispute may have to be resolved in other ways, usually by submission to a third party, an expert, an inspector or an industrial court. A consultation policy statement should make clear how disputes are to be resolved and incorporate any legal requirements or industrial agreements.

Employers (persons conducting businesses or undertakings, PCBUs) have a duty to consult as far as reasonably practicable and so this will depend on factors such as the

- size and structure of the business
- nature of the work
- type of decisions or actions to be consulted on as well as their urgency
- work arrangements (shiftwork, part-time and remote work)
- workers' languages and literacy levels.

Consultation should not be seen as shifting management's legal responsibilities to the HS committee or other consultative framework. Rather, consultation enables the parties to better exercise their duty of care. Those legal duties of care stay unchanged irrespective of any consulting, successful or otherwise.

Consultation is not restricted to employees, but applies to contractors and labour hire also – that is, all workers. (s. 47(1)) A firm using contractors must consult on the WHS issues contractors may face; for example, on the most appropriate way to remove toxic materials from the workplace or how best (and safest) to maintain hazardous plant or equipment.

There are often situations in which more than one business or undertaking operates at a workplace and in which people share responsibility for health and safety to varying degrees; for example, at shopping centres, on construction projects, and in multi-tenanted office buildings.

In general, if more than one person shares the same duty to consult, everyone must consult, cooperate on and coordinate activities with all other persons who have a duty in relation to the same matter. Everyone involved must cooperate to ensure appropriate consultation takes place. (s. 46)

Section 5 of the code of practice *How to Consult on Work Health and Safety* provides advice, and Appendix C gives two examples of how this might work in practice.

WHAT ARE THE BENEFITS OF CONSULTATION?

Consultation improves decision making and, as a result, health and safety.

1 Consultation provides an opportunity for finding better solutions to health and safety issues using the experience and knowledge of the entire workforce. It is almost a certainty that after every investigation into a major industrial accident, poor communication and consultation with workers is identified as a factor leading to the incident.

2 With the improved understanding brought about by consultation comes a greater commitment to WHS. As a result, implementation becomes easier.

3 Consulting improves morale and industrial relations by showing concern for all parties involved in the process.

4 Consulting provides a model and the skills for addressing other operational and industrial matters.

5 With better health and safety and improved industrial relations, there is real potential for increases in productivity.

6 There is an improved awareness and involvement of WHS activities and strategies.

There are costs, such as time and energy, and some usually minor financial costs involved in consultation, which are clearly offset by the benefits of well-managed consultation.

2010 WORKSAFE VICTORIA AWARDS

Finalist Keni Navusolo, HSR, Health and Safety Representative of the Year

Overview

Located in northeast Victoria, Woolstar Pty Ltd, Wodonga Regional Distribution Centre (RDC) also known as 'the Shed', is a large regional distribution centre supplying supermarkets.

Keni Navusolo has been a health and safety representative (HSR) in the Shed since December 2008. There are 14 HSRs in the Shed representing 471 members of the designated work group (DWG) and covering all shifts.

Achievements

Keni has worked hard to achieve several key health and safety improvements for the shed:

- Negotiating with management for regular HSR meetings, monthly Wodonga RDC Health and Safety Committee meetings and twice-weekly DWG meetings
- Campaigning to highlight to management the problem of bullying and harassment in the workplace. This resulted in the provision of an awareness-raising education program for workers
- Working with other HSRs to negotiate a maximum of five-and-a-half hours picking activity per 10-hour shift to reduce the risk of musculoskeletal injuries through excessive manual handling
- Changing the way incoming pallets arrive in the warehouse by limiting their height to 1.6 metres so workers do not have to pick above shoulder height. This included the design and development of a picking platform to enable pallets to be broken down to a suitable size before entering the warehouse.

Source: WorkSafe Victoria, WorkSafe Awards 2010. Access www.worksafe.vic.gov.au for more information and future updates.

INTRODUCING CONSULTATION INTO THE WORKPLACE

Once consultation and its benefits have been understood, it must be built on and maintained. The following steps assume that you are starting from scratch in a medium-to-large organisation involving health and safety representatives and committees. Of course, in a small organisation, you may not need to follow all steps but the principles still apply. The requirement to consult with workers *may be* demonstrated by other methods such as are agreed with by workers and comply with the duty to consult as set out in the Act.

The steps are based on the Work Health and Safety Act and regulations and incorporate lessons on how to consult effectively. Further information can be found on government websites, in codes of practice and in other official guidance material. If still unclear, you can ask your government WHS agency directly or seek further legal advice from a lawyer or consultant.

Key questions are:

- What must the employer do?
- When do you consult?
- Who do you consult with?
- How is consultation organised?
- What are the procedures for consulting?
- How are disputes resolved?
- How can a consultative culture be built?

STEP 1: DRAFT A CONSULTATION STATEMENT

Draft a summary statement for discussion and agreement that indicates the commitment to consultation and that contains matters such as:

- a simple definition or understanding of what consultation is
- the purpose and principles of consultation on WHS
- when it should occur
- how, in general, consultation will occur
- a commitment to review.

The consultation statement flows from the WHS policy (see next chapter). It is important to remember that the statement and the policy should reflect the drivers: the workers, the employer and the law. If WHS sounds like it is only driven by the need to comply with the law, then it is not being approached in the spirit that will make it totally effective.

As a general framework, the statement should not go into the specific procedures of consultation, but it should have enough detail for everyone to understand the implications. It should be signed by the head of the organisation to indicate management's commitment to the statement. Normally, the signed policy is displayed in an appropriate location at the worksite or placed on the Intranet. The statement ought to be reviewed by the HS committee annually.

Note that consultation might cover commercially sensitive information; for example, new product lines or proposed acquisitions. Management must have the trust and agreement of everyone that such matters remain confidential. Specific agreements may need to be struck to cover commercial-in-confidence or other sensitive matters, such as individual privacy. The policy statement may refer to the need for such confidentiality.

SAMPLE WHS CONSULTATION STATEMENT

Commitment

(*Facility name*) fosters open and effective communication and recognizes its vital role for good industrial relations, quality management and effective management of Health and Safety.

Consultation and Communication enables (*Facility name*) to meet organizational and legal requirements on Consultation and ensure all employees / residents have a genuine opportunity to effectively participate in decision making on matters with potential to affect their environment.

Establishment of Consultation Arrangements

The management discussed establishing consultation arrangements with staff in (*insert date*). After feedback from department meetings and discussion with staff, it was agreed to establish an HS Committee (other Consultation mechanism) will be/ has been established with representatives from both management and employees. Major objectives are:

1. Facilitate co-operation between (*Facility name*) and its employees in developing and carrying out measures designed to ensure a safe and healthy working environment.
2. Formulate, review and disseminate to employees of (*Facility name*) and where appropriate to residents and their relatives, the standards, rules and procedures relating to HS.

3. Facilitate communication between employees of non-English speaking backgrounds and Managers and other employees, to ensure that the HS needs for **all** employees are met.

Staff Consultation and Communication

HS will be included on the agenda of all staff meetings held at the facility. It is the responsibility of the meeting coordinator to refer issues raised to the HS Committee and to ensure that action is noted in the minutes of the meeting.

Minutes will be posted on noticeboards.

Residents, visitors and contractors will be encouraged to use the Hazard Report Form to notify the HS Committee of issues needing to be addressed. The Hazard Report Form will be available at the front office and information about this form will be included in the facility newsletter.

Review of Consultation Arrangements

It has been agreed by the management and staff that these HS consultation arrangements will be monitored and reviewed biannual basis. This will ensure that consultation with all members of staff is effective and that all safety issues are being addressed.

Source: Adapted from agedcareOHS.info

STEP 2: DRAFT AN AGREEMENT SETTING OUT PROCEDURES

Flesh out the consultation statement in the form of a detailed agreement that sets out the procedures for consultation, dispute resolution and review for discussion with workers and/or their union reps.[1] The agreement should

- include goals of consultation and when it should occur
- describe how consultation is organised – work groups, HSRs/deputies, HS committee
- outline procedures for dealing with HS issues and any disputes
- outline procedures for monitoring, reviewing and evaluating consultation.

It does not need to repeat what is found in the legislation but must reflect the requirements.

What is the purpose of the consultation?

How the consultation is organised and the procedures governing it should be first set by the goals of WHS consultation: What, precisely, do you want to achieve through consultation? This should be reflected in your WHS policy and could cover such considerations as

- greater mutual understanding and cooperation
- the safest and healthiest workplace possible
- continuous improvements in productivity
- full compliance with the law and community expectations.

It is important to be clear about the objects as you will need to monitor and review consultation against them. Are you going forwards, backwards or standing still as a result? How are you going to measure this?

What are the critical features of the employer?

The consultation will need to take into consideration the nature of the employer and such factors as the

- size and structure of the organisation – is it national, multinational, state-based? Some organisations work across two or more jurisdictions and have a peak WHS consultative structure to cover the entire organisation.
- ownership of the organisation – public, private, not-for-profit?
- industry or industries involved
- work carried out – what kind of processes, products and services are involved and, hence, what are the issues?
- work organisation – nine-to-five, shift, central office, depots, warehouses?
- nature of the workforce – what is the male:female ratio, blue-collar:white-collar ratio, high:low literacy level? Is the workplace unionised?

When is consultation required?

Consultation is typically required in the following instances:

- when identifying hazards and assessing risks to health and safety
- when making decisions about ways to eliminate or minimise those risks
- when making decisions about facilities for the welfare of workers
- when proposing changes that may affect the health or safety of workers
- when making decisions about the procedures for consultation
- when resolving health or safety issues
- when monitoring the health of workers
- when monitoring workplace conditions
- when providing information and training. (s. 49)

The next step is to set out in the agreement how consultation is organised, the powers and duties of those involved and the procedures for resolving issues.

How is consultation to be organised?

The basic structure for a system of workplace consultation uses health and safety representatives (HSRs), one elected representative – and, preferably, a deputy – for a work group. The HSRs usually are also HS committee members, but we deal with HS committees later. Figure 3.1 shows a typical structure for consultation, subject to agreement by all parties.

 **Figure 3.1** *Typical consultative organisation*

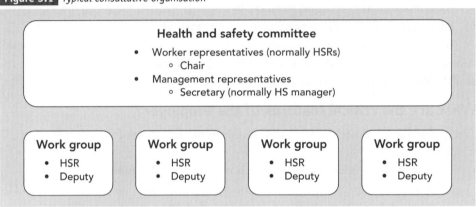

Formally, the process begins with a request by a worker for the employer to 'facilitate the conduct of an election' for one or more health and safety representatives. (s. 50) Once the request has been made, the employer must start the process of determining one or more work groups of workers. (s. 51)

Within 14 days of the request, the employer must negotiate with workers on the nature of the work group or work groups. (s. 52(2)) Usually this is done with a union representative or organiser. Unions, where they are present, normally insist. If a worker asks for union representation, that must be accepted. (s. 52(4))

Negotiation would include
- the number and composition of work groups to be represented by health and safety representatives
- the number of health and safety representatives and deputies (if any) to be elected
- the workplace or workplaces which the work groups cover
- the businesses that the work groups will cover. (s. 52(3))

The nature of the work group is determined by the need of the HSR and the work group to communicate with each other. So, factors such as size and location of the work group are important considerations, as well as function and shift. A work group may include workers at one or more workplaces. (s. 52(5)) See also the regulations (Part 2.1) specifying the considerations that must be taken into account in forming work groups. There is also provision under the Act for determining work groups for workers carrying out work for two or more PCBUs at one or more workplaces (see subdivision 3 of the Act).

A large retail 'box' company operates across the state, specialising in white goods imported from Asia. It has a state administrative headquarters, 35 outlets (large stores almost entirely located in malls or complexes), three warehouses (central, north and south), supplied from the main port by an independent transport firm that also supplies the outlets. With the exception of the state HQ, it is largely an 8 am to 6 pm operation, except in the warehouses where it is 24/7. There is modest union density, mostly in the warehouses and some of the outlets. The majority of the workforce is 'Anglo' but there are concentrations of different migrant groups in the warehouses. There are very few university graduates and the median age is 30, with regular turnover. The outlets employ many women part time, who have children either at school or in care. Cleaning, maintenance and security in the outlets are dealt with under the lease arrangements with the shopping centre management. In the warehouses, cleaning is done by contractors.

Discussion questions

1 In developing an agreement with the workers, what would be the key considerations for identifying work groups?
2 How many work groups would you propose and why?

The outcome of the negotiations must be recognised in the consultation agreement and publicised. (s. 53) If there is a failure to reach agreement, an inspector can be called in to determine the matter. (s. 54)

The following section sets out the details of HSRs and HSCs. As they can be found in the law, they needn't be put down in the agreement. However, the agreement should refer to the commitment to training and administrative support.

HSRs

Eligibility, election and disqualification

A worker is eligible to be elected as a health and safety representative for a work group only if they are a member of that work group and have not been disqualified under the Act. (s. 60)

The workers in a work group may determine how an election of a health and safety representative and deputy for the work group is run, provided it complies with the regulations. If a majority of the workers in a work group agree, the election may be conducted with the assistance of a union or other person or organisation. The employer must provide the needed resources, facilities and assistance for the elections to be held. (See Section 61 and Division 2 of the regulations.)

All workers in the work group and only those workers are entitled to vote in the election of a health and safety representative for that work group. (s. 62) When only one candidate stands for election in the work group – as is almost always the case – that candidate is elected. (s. 63)

DID YOU KNOW?

There are an estimated 30 000 HSRs in Australia.

Source: Quinlan, M., Bohle P. & Lamm, F., 2010, *Managing Occupational Health and Safety – A Multidisciplinary Approach*, 3rd edn, Macmillan: Melbourne, p. 473.

The term is for three years unless the person resigns as HSR, stops being a worker in the work group, is disqualified under the Act from acting as a health and safety representative or is removed from that position by a majority of the members of the work group in accordance with the regulations. (s. 64) A health and safety representative can stand for re-election. (s. 64(3))

An application may be made to disqualify a health and safety representative if the representative has:

- exercised a power or performed a function as a health and safety representative for an improper purpose or
- used or disclosed any information they acquired as a health and safety representative for a purpose other than in connection with their role as an HSR.

The procedures for disqualification are set out in the legislation. (s. 65)

Note that HSRs are not personally liable for anything done or omitted to be done in good faith while exercising their legal powers. (s. 66)

Deputies are elected in the same way. (s. 67)

The employer must then

- prepare and keep up to date a list of each health and safety representative and deputy health and safety representative (if any) for each work group
- display a copy of this list at the principal place of business and at any other workplace that is appropriate, in a manner that is readily accessible to workers
- provide a copy of the up-to-date list to the regulator as soon as practicable after it is prepared. (s. 74)

Note that neither HSRs nor HSC members have special legal duties or responsibilities as HSRs or HSC members for which they can be held personally liable. For example, they can't be fined for not carrying out expected functions.

Note also that HSRs and HSC members who raise a complaint in relation to health or safety are protected from discrimination or dismissal arising from their activities as representatives or committee members.

Finally, persons must not mislead others about their rights, obligations or powers. (s. 109)

COURT RULING SENDS MESSAGE TO EMPLOYERS TO RESPECT THE ROLE OHS REPS PLAY IN KEEPING WORKPLACES SAFE

A court ruling against Patrick Stevedores this week sends a clear message to employers not to discriminate against workers who raise legitimate health and safety issues, say unions.

Patrick will be sentenced in Melbourne Magistrates Court today (Friday) after being found guilty earlier this week of three charges of discriminating against an Occupational Health and Safety representative for raising safety issues on the job.

ACTU President Ged Kearney said the ruling was a warning to all employers that health and safety representatives (HSRs) have a legitimate role and should not be intimidated or discriminated against for raising concerns.

In a landmark decision on Monday, the Melbourne Magistrates Court found in favour of WorkSafe Victoria on three of five charges under section 76 of the *Victorian Occupational Health and Safety Act 2004*.

More than 12 months ago, a former Patrick employee and Maritime Union of Australia safety representative at Geelong Port was suspended, reprimanded and threatened with the sack for raising safety breaches where workers' lives were at risk.

Ms Kearney said safety issues are a key point of dispute in current enterprise bargaining negotiations between the MUA and Patrick, including lack of training and high casualisation at bulk and general operations.

'Health and safety reps are democratically elected volunteers who play an essential role in protecting their workmates,' Ms Kearney said.

'Their presence is often a key factor in the OHS performance of a workplace. They are often the first to raise the alarm about unsafe practices and they must in turn be protected from intimidation or discrimination by their employers.

'They have a hard enough time representing the rights of workers without also facing discrimination. That's why we need to empower OHS reps and give them legal protection to keep their workplaces safe.

'At Patrick, an HSR raised legitimate concerns about safety in Geelong and was hounded out of a job by a management culture that puts profits ahead of the health and safety of workers. The wharves are dangerous places, and three waterside workers were killed on Australian docks last year.

'This ruling against Patrick should be a wake-up call to all Australian employers, who often behave with impunity, and we call on all regulators around Australia to more vigorously prosecute employers who discriminate against HSRs.'

Ms Kearney said existing rights and protections must be maintained in new model national health and safety laws due to commence next year. She said Safe Work Australia should examine this decision and confirm that the new laws would deliver the same outcome.

Patrick will be sentenced in Melbourne Magistrates Court at 2 pm today (Friday). It faces a fine of up to $250,000 for each offence.

Source: ACTU, http://www.actu.org.au/Media/Mediareleases/CourtrulingsendsmessagetoemployerstorespecttheroleOHS repsplayinkeepingworkplacessafe.aspx

Powers and rights

In relation to their work group, HSRs (or deputies in their absence) can

- represent the work group on health and safety matters
- monitor the measures taken by the employer to provide a healthy and safe workplace
- investigate complaints from members of the work group
- inquire into anything that appears to be a risk to the health or safety of workers. (s. 68(1))

  This means that the HSR may

- inspect the workplace at which a worker in the work group works at any time after giving reasonable notice or at any time, without notice, in the event of a serious incident
- accompany an inspector during an inspection of the workplace
- with the consent of a worker or group of workers that the HSR represents, be present at an interview between them and an inspector or the employer
- request the establishment of a health and safety committee

- receive information concerning the health and safety of workers in the work group
- whenever necessary, request the assistance of any person. (s. 68(2))

In relation to the receipt of information about the health and safety of workers, an HSR is not entitled to have access to any personal or medical information concerning a worker without the worker's consent unless the information is in a form that does not identify the worker directly or indirectly. (s. 68(3))

The HSR may exercise their rights with respect to another work group only when the HSR for that work group is not available and only if there is a serious risk to workers in that work group or if the workers in that work group request help. (s. 69)

Cease-work orders

Sections 83 to 89 deal with the right of HSRs to issue cease-work orders. An HSR may direct a worker in their work group to cease work if the HSR has a reasonable concern that the worker is exposed to a serious risk from an immediate or imminent exposure to a hazard. However, the HSR must first consult with the employer and attempt to resolve the issue, unless, of course, the risk is so serious and immediate that it is not reasonable to consult beforehand. In such a case, the HSR must consult as soon as practicable after giving the direction. (s. 85(1–4))

The HSR cannot direct work to cease unless the representative has been appropriately trained. (s. 85(5))

A worker who ceases work in this case must notify the employer and be available to carry out suitable alternative work until it is safe to resume normal duties. (s 85(6–8))

The HSR or the employer may ask for an inspector to resolve any issue arising out of a cessation of work. (s. 89)

Provisional improvement notices

Another powerful right of the HSR is the ability to issue a provisional improvement notice (PINs). This is covered in Division 7 of the Act. If an HSR reasonably believes a person – for example, the employer or a third party such as a contractor or supplier – is contravening the Act or has contravened the Act, and it likely that the contravention will continue or be repeated, then the HSR may issue – *in writing* – a provisional improvement notice. (ss. 90(1–2), 91)

The PIN may require the person to remedy the contravention or prevent a likely contravention from occurring or remedy the things causing the contravention or likely contravention. (s. 90(2)) However, the HSR must first consult the person on the matter. (s. 90(3))

An HSR cannot issue a PIN unless they have been given appropriate HSR training. (s. 90(4)) Nor can they issue a PIN if an inspector has already issued (or decided not to issue) an improvement notice or prohibition notice in respect of the same matter. (s. 90(5))

Contents of a provisional improvement notice

A PIN must state

- that the HSR believes the person is contravening a provision of the Act or has contravened a provision of this Act in circumstances that make it likely that the contravention will continue or be repeated

- the specific provision of the Act the HSR believes is being, or has been, contravened
- briefly, how the provision is being or has been contravened
- the day, at least eight days after the notice is issued, by which the person is required to remedy the contravention or likely contravention. (s. 92)

A PIN may specify the measures to be taken to remedy the contravention or prevent the likely contravention. It may refer to a code of practice and offer a choice of ways to remedy the contravention. (s. 93)

A notice may be issued by delivering it personally; sending it by post, facsimile or electronic transmission to the person's place of residence or business; leaving it for the person with an adult at the person's residence or business; leaving it at the person's workplace with a person in charge of the workplace; or delivering it in a manner prescribed in the regulations. (s. 209)

The HSR may at any time cancel a PIN issued to a person by written notice to that person. (s. 96)

The person to whom the PIN is issued must as soon as practicable display a copy of the notice in a prominent place at or near the workplace affected. (s. 97(1))

Unless an inspector has been required to attend the workplace to review the PIN, the person must comply with the PIN within the time specified. (s. 99(2))

Review of PIN

Within seven days after a PIN is issued to a person, that person may ask for an inspector to review the notice, in which case the PIN is not in operation until the inspector makes a decision on the review. (s. 100) The inspector must review the PIN and inquire into the circumstances. (s. 101(2)) An inspector may review a PIN even if the period for compliance has expired. (s. 101(3))

After reviewing the PIN, the inspector must confirm the PIN, confirm the PIN with changes, or cancel it. A copy of the decision must be given to the person applying for the review and the HSR who issued the PIN. A PIN confirmed (with or without changes) by an inspector is taken to be an improvement notice issued by the inspector. (s. 102)

Employer's duties

In order for HSRs to exercise their powers and rights, the employer must
- consult and confer on health and safety matters with HSRs
- provide HSRs access to information on hazards and the health and safety of the workers in the work group
- with the consent of the worker(s), allow the HSR to be present at an interview between the worker and an inspector or the employer
- provide any necessary resources, facilities and assistance to an HSR to enable the representative to exercise their rights
- allow a person assisting an HSR to have access to the workplace if required
- permit an HSR to accompany an inspector during an inspection

- provide any other assistance that may be required by the regulations. (s. 70(1))
- allow an HSR to spend such time as is 'reasonably necessary to exercise his or her powers and perform his or her functions under this Act'. (s. 70(2))

Any time that an HSR spends for the purposes of exercising their rights must be with 'such pay as he or she would otherwise be entitled to receive for performing his or her normal duties during that period'. (s. 70(3))

How are HSRs and deputies to be trained?

The employer must, if requested by an HSR, allow them to attend a training course in health and safety that is

- approved by the regulator
- a course that the HSR is entitled to attend under the regulations
- chosen by the HSR in consultation with the employer. (s. 72(1))

As soon as practicable within the period of three months after the request is made, the employer must allow the HSR time off work to attend the course of training and pay the course fees and any other reasonable costs associated with the training. (s. 72(2))

Note that if an HSR represents a work group of more than one business or undertaking and any of the employers has complied with the training requirement, then the other employers are to be taken to have complied as well. (s. 72(3))

Again, any time that an HSR is given time off work to attend the course of training 'must be with such pay as he or she would otherwise be entitled to receive for performing his or her normal duties during that period'. (s. 72(4))

Consultation training focuses on

- how to ensure effective and meaningful consultation
- how to systematically manage health and safety.

When deciding whether workers who have previously undertaken approved training need to undertake training again, you should consider

- how long ago the training was undertaken
- any legislative changes that have occurred since the original training
- differences between the learning outcomes of the original training course and the current required outcomes.

HS committees

What is their purpose?

The principal objectives of an HSC are to promote cooperation between the employer and workers on health and safety and to help develop workplace standards, rules and procedures. (s. 77)

While other objectives may be added, it is important that they be clear so that you know whether the committee is successful or not. In this way the committee can keep its shape and not 'morph' into something else. We will talk more of the success criteria after we first look at how committees are set up. Again, we are focusing on medium to large organisations to establish the principles of formal consultation.

How are they to be established and constituted?

The employer must establish a health and safety committee within two months after being requested to do so by

- an HSR for a group of workers carrying out work at that workplace
- five or more workers at that workplace
- within the time prescribed by any regulations.

Alternatively, the employer may establish an HSC on their own initiative. (s. 75(1–2))

If an HSC is not required to be established, other consultation procedures can be established for a workplace provided they are consistent with the duty to consult set out under the Act.

It is important to note that consultative decision making aims at consensus and not, for example, majority voting. Further, if consensus cannot be achieved, then procedures for resolving matters such as referring to third parties needs to be agreed on. Finally, remember also that the legal duty of care stays in place all the time. So, for example, if there is a lack of consensus over what to do, the employer, or person in control, and workers still have legal duties and must act accordingly.

The constitution of an HSC is usually agreed on between the employer and the workers – the HSR or their union representative. As a guide, the total number of committee members – workers and management representatives – should not exceed 12: otherwise it becomes unwieldy. The composition of the HSC should be contained in the agreement.

Normally, the HSRs become the workers' representatives on the committee. This will depend on the nature of the agreed constitution and the size of the workplace. At least half of the members of the committee must be workers not nominated by the employer. (s. 76(4))

As far as possible, committee composition ought to reflect the broad workforce – males and females, white-collar and blue-collar – with management representatives being in the minority. In this way, the committee hears as much as possible of the issues affecting everyone. People can see their faces at the committee level and broad consensus can be better achieved.

To enable everyone to feel that this is a genuine form of consultation the chair of the committee should be a worker representative. Provided there are volunteers, the chair ought to be rotated regularly.

If agreement cannot be reached on the constitution within a reasonable time, any party may ask the regulator to appoint an inspector to decide on the matter, which is then binding on everyone. (s. 76(5))

The committee must meet at least once every three months and at any reasonable time at the request of at least half of the members of the committee. (s. 78)

Employer's duties

The employer must allow each member of the HSC to spend as much time as is reasonably necessary to attend meetings or to carry out functions as a committee member. (s. 79(1)) Committee members must be paid with 'such pay as he or she would otherwise be entitled to receive for performing his or her normal duties during that period'. (s. 79(2))

The employer must provide committee members access to information that the employer has relating to hazards (including associated risks) at the workplace and the health and safety of the workers at the workplace. (s. 79(3)) This does not include access to any personal or medical information concerning a worker without the worker's consent, unless the information is in a form that does not identify the worker directly or indirectly. (s. 79(4))

Procedures such as the scheduling of meetings, due notification periods, leave arrangements, training and resourcing may also be spelt out. If there are other consultative or negotiating forums, then the relation of the HSC to these organisations must be made clear.

The health and safety manager is usually the main administrative support for the formal consultation, organising the meetings, calling for agenda items and drafting the agenda, providing background papers, taking minutes and reporting to the senior management team.

The effectiveness of a committee will depend on the support it receives from the employer. Indicators of support would include
- demonstrated commitment and support from senior and middle management
- consultative arrangements being established and budgeted for
- management representatives having the power to make decisions as well as the skills to communicate them, and valuing the opinions of others
- provision of administrative support
- sharing of information in a timely fashion
- provision of appropriate time off and support to representatives in order that they may carry out their functions as representatives and responsibilities as employees
- availability of requisite training for consultation and specific HS matters; for example, hazard identification and risk assessment
- prompt implementation of decisions and as agreed
- promotion of the committee's activities throughout the organisation
- access to facilities, such as meeting rooms and support resources.

Barriers to information-sharing and consultation
Special attention needs to be paid to any barriers to individuals or groups seeking health and safety information and data or to raising identified issues. These may include
- language, literacy and numeracy
- employees' special needs
- shiftwork and rostering arrangements
- contractual arrangements
- timing of information provision
- workplace organisational structures (for example, geographic, hierarchical)
- workplace culture related to health and safety.

Management should be prepared to make recommendations that will address any identified barriers, such as choice of the timing and venue of meetings, tailored training and adoption of culturally sensitive protocols (see also, Chapter 5).

The HSC should be marketed internally, and the procedures necessary to raise health and safety issues or request information be communicated to stakeholders and other interested parties and then implemented.

The committee must identify exactly what it needs to achieve its goals – what kind of information, data, reports, records and documents are needed and in what format. Nowadays, in most organisations, much of this information – policies and procedures, the WHS program, health and safety information, safe operating procedures, hazard reports, risk analyses, controls, manufacturers' manuals and specifications – can be put on the local Intranet.

If Intranet is not available, alternative methods of communicating on WHS would be suitable, including regular face-to-face meetings, interviews, noticeboards, signs, posters, brochures, letters, memos, reports, photographs, maps, plans, audiovisual methods (such as videos, CDs and DVDs) and newsletters. The value of the content and method of communicating on WHS will need to be reviewed on a regular basis. Clearly, the amount of consultation will need to be measured against other job requirements.

Above all, a sense of trust and mutual respect must be produced through the consultative process.

WHS IN PRACTICE

A CHECKLIST FOR HS COMMITTEE MEETINGS

1 What is the agenda?
   The agenda should be standard but may need to be reviewed to ensure the meeting does not run over time and is dealing with the most important issues first. A sample agenda includes
   - carry out welcome and call to order[2]
   - note absences and apologies
   - introduce visitors
   - review last meeting's minutes for additions or corrections
   - review items for discussion.
   To ensure that all relevant issues are covered, the committee should agree on some standing items for the agenda and allow for other items to be added as necessary. Consider standing items such as
   - safety policies and programs
   - statistics on incident records, ill health, sickness absences
   - incident investigations and subsequent action
   - inspections of the workplace by management or employee representatives

- risk assessments
- health and safety training
- emergency procedures
- changes in the workplace affecting the health, safety and welfare of employees
- old business (items not covered or resolved during the last meeting)
- new business (items the committee needs to discuss and resolve)
- reports (incidents and inspections)
- recommendations to management
- next meeting date, location and time.

2 Have the minutes of the previous meeting been circulated and read beforehand?
   The agenda, minutes and any written reports should have been circulated earlier for the representatives to discuss with the workers. The minutes can be displayed or placed on the Intranet.

3 Are the minutes correct?
   Make sure someone is recording or minuting the meeting. This is usually the person in management with responsibility for health and safety. Everyone should be making their own notes as well. The minutes should not go into great detail but just record decisions taken. The minutes should record who attended and chaired and any apologies.

4 Are there any matters arising from the minutes that need to be dealt with?
   This is a critical stage of the meeting. If action has been promised but not taken, the mood for the remainder of the meeting is set.

5 Are reports heard on elements of the WHS plan?
   Go to the plan! How are we performing against the key performance indicators?

6 What action needs to be taken? By whom? When?
   Whether you are a worker representative or management representative, you will be asked to report back on these key outcomes. Make sure the committee is absolutely clear and you have notes. The chair may wish to summarise.

7 When is the next meeting? Where?

8 Reflect on the meeting to see how it might be improved.
   - The key to the meeting will be whether the chair conducts it in a focused, business-like manner without being overly formal. It is a difficult task and the chair should be supported. Everyone should try to ensure that all participants are given the opportunity to talk and that limits are observed.
   - The meeting should not have to deal with matters that ought to be handled in the daily course of events. Instead focus on monitoring the implementation of the WHS plan.
   - It is hard to maintain attention for over an hour, especially after lunch. If the meeting tends to be longer than that, consider using subcommittees. It is possible to enliven meetings by designating monthly safety topics (e.g. manual handling, vehicle safety, personal protective equipment) or inviting a guest speaker.
   - Success will be judged by the progress made against the objectives of the committee and the plan.

- Committee meetings – health and safety or not – can become routine and dull unless there is something different, like a story. We never get tired of stories of what went wrong or right here in the workplace or somewhere else in Australia or the world. Reports of incidents or research break the routine and show a concern for local health and safety by looking at matters beyond the immediate workplace.

How are issues to be resolved in the case of any disputes?

The role of committees and representatives in resolving disputes is especially useful. A dispute resolution procedure, or 'issue resolution' as the Act terms it, is critical and should be made part of the agreement. Apart from reducing the potential workload, it is the most effective way of resolving problems at the earliest stage; that is, as long as everyone is properly trained, skilled and committed to the procedures.

A sample dispute resolution procedure is outlined in the following diagram in which the role of the committee and the HSR are identified. In addition to making clear the steps to be taken, such a procedure enables problems to be solved at the workplace level as far as possible, freeing the HSC to focus on the bigger picture and larger problems.

The agreement should cover the issues covered in Step 2 without repeating what is said in the legislation. One final important step needs to be settled on as part of the agreement.

STEP 3: MONITOR, REVIEW AND EVALUATE CONSULTATION

A method of monitoring, reviewing and evaluating the consultative arrangements needs to be agreed on and set against the goals of consultation, as laid out in the policy or constitution for the committee. Criteria could include

- active participation by all
- level of informed discussion
- quality of information-sharing
- timely implementation of decisions, which could be used as indicators.

Input could include anecdotal and structured feedback from the workplace and management. A survey of a representative portion of management and workers could be used. A half-yearly review and an end-of-year review may be conducted, perhaps using an external facilitator or consultant for the purpose.

Having drafted an agreement and received approval from management and workers, the next step is to put the arrangements in place and watch how they develop. An important aspect of this is to publicise the agreement and the activities together with the outcomes. Representatives and committees need to be made visible in the workplace. Successes – and failures – should be recognised. Individuals and sections need to be congratulated for their participation and the results achieved. Story-formats are the best method of achieving some recognition. How was the plan and how were the issues dealt with using the consultative methods and what were the outcomes?

Figure 3.2 *Sample dispute resolution procedure*

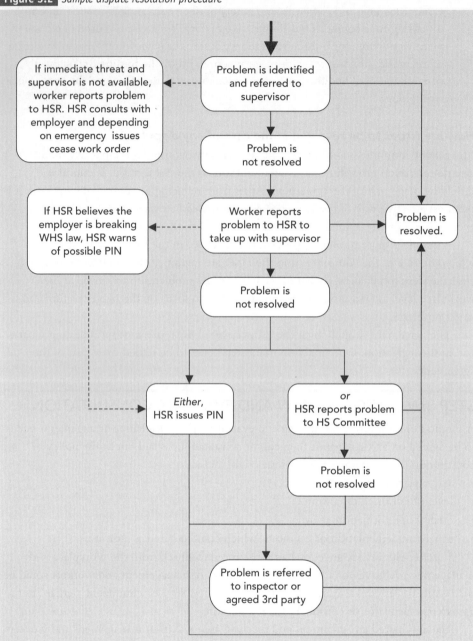

The review process as agreed to in the documentation is particularly important. It would be exceptional if everything went perfectly the first time or when the organisation and personnel change. The continued ability to achieve clear positive outcomes from WHS consultation depends on the effectiveness of the review. Special effort needs to be spent on ensuring its success, as the quality of consultation is one of the clearest indicators of the quality of management in general. The results of the review should be communicated to the workforce together with any recommended changes designed to improve performance. They should also be highlighted in the company annual report (see Chapter 18).

With an effective system of consultation, building and maintaining a WHS management system is made much easier. It is that topic we turn our attention to next.

Summary

- Consultation is information-sharing and discussion carried out with the objective of achieving greater understanding and agreement. Consultation over health and safety is, then, critical to success as decisions must be built on the experience, knowledge and commitment of everyone involved.
- The law requires employers to consult on WHS and specifies when such consultation should occur.
- The law sets out the arrangements for consultation and the procedures for setting them up, such as the election of health and safety representatives.
- Rights and duties for health and safety representatives are specified in the law.
- The effectiveness of consultation relies heavily on the commitment of management to its success.
- Careful attention must be paid to the effectiveness of consultative arrangements if they are not to slide into time-wasting talk-shops. Training is especially critical.
- High-quality monitoring, evaluating and review processes are essential to continued success.

In your workplace

Using the retail company case study on page 59 as an example, you find that the managers or workers failed to meet or agree on consultative arrangements.
1   How would you as health and safety manager proceed?
2   You have an agreed set of dispute procedures but find that (i) a manager or (ii) a worker refuse to abide by them. What would you do?
3   The health and safety committee has finally been established but it has turned into a clash of personalities between a worker representative and one or two of the management representatives. How would you as HS manager deal with it?

Questions

1   What is consultation and how does it differ from negotiation and information-sharing?
2   What are the benefits of consultation and what are the costs?
3   Under the law, when must employers consult with employees and when must a health and safety committee be formed?
4   What are the powers of an HSR?

5   'The requirement to consult undermines management's appointed right and duty to manage in the best interests of everyone involved.' Discuss.

6   Is health and safety a matter for industrial relations?

Activities

1   Focus on your organisation or college. Work in small teams where possible.

   a   What are the HS consultative arrangements: formal and informal?

   b   Are they effective? Construct a brief checklist of, say, 12 to 20 items to evaluate the consultative arrangements.

   c   What are the dispute settling procedures?

   d   Who has been trained?

   e   How may the arrangements be improved?

2   *Role play:* Pretend that you work in a small metal recycling firm with a lot of young apprentices and you want to enable people to raise issues of safety. In a group, run a toolbox meeting and try different methods of promoting discussion of any safety problems. Spend five to ten minutes and then let someone else try the same exercise. When everyone in the group has had a turn, review the outcomes to find out what worked and what didn't.

3   There are many providers of consultative and/or communication training. Find five providers and assess their services and suitability for your workplace. Finally after consideration of their cost, make a (hypothetical) recommendation.

Search me!

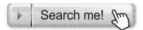

Explore **Search me! management** for relevant articles on health and safety consultation. Search me! is an online library of world-class journals, ebooks and newspapers, including *The Australian* and the *New York Times*, and is updated daily. Log in to Search me! through www.cengage.com/sso using the access card in the front of this book.

KEYWORDS

Try searching for the following terms:

▶ effective workplace consultation   ▶ industrial democracy

▶ health and safety representatives   ▶ health and safety dispute procedures

▶ health and safety committees   ▶ health and safety training

Search tip: **Search me! management** contains information from both local and international sources. To get the greatest number of search results, try using both Australian and American spellings in your searches, e.g. 'globalisation' and 'globalization'; 'organisation' and 'organization'.

Additional resources

• The code of practice *How to Consult on Work Health and Safety* on the Safe Work Australia website at www.safeworkaustralia.gov.au/Legislation/PublicComment is a good introduction to workplace consultation, with a number of examples of consultative options.

• Also worth looking at are the annual Safe Work Australia Awards, which include those for health and safety representatives, at http://www.safeworkaustralia.gov.au/AboutSafeWork Australia/NationalActivities/AnnualSafeWorkAustraliaAwards/6thAnnualSafeWorkAustralia Awards/Pages/4Cat_6thAwards.aspx.

• Quinlan, M., Bohle P. & Lamm, F., 2010, *Managing Occupational Health and Safety: A Multidisciplinary Approach*, 3rd edn, Palgrave Macmillan: Melbourne, Chapter 9.

- Sheriff, B. & Dunn, G., 2007, 'Workplace OHS consultation: legal and practical issues', in *Australian Master OHS and Environmental Guide,* 2nd edn, CCH: Sydney. The list of 'tips and common barriers' is especially useful.

Endnotes

1 The Australian experience shows that unions play a positive influence by encouraging involvement in WHS. However, union density is relatively low in recent times, especially in the private sector. Where their presence can be found, they should be involved.

2 Increasingly, the opening of meetings involves recognising the Indigenous landowners in an 'acknowledgement of country'.

DEVELOPING A SYSTEMATIC APPROACH

Learning Objectives

At the end of this chapter, the reader should be able to effectively design and develop a systematic approach to managing WHS, and:

- analyse the workplace to identify needs
- design integrated approaches to managing WHS
- plan and develop integrated approaches to managing WHS
- support planning and implementation of integrated approaches to managing WHS
- evaluate the design and development of integrated approaches to managing WHS.

INTRODUCTION

In this chapter we show how you may build an integrated, systematic approach to WHS. This is in contrast to workplaces in which WHS activity is sidelined, minimalist, or a reaction to work–related accidents as they occur. Systematic approaches have widespread support with industry, labour, government and WHS professionals. Not only do they offer the best way of promoting health and safety, but also they contribute to improved productivity and a competitive economy.

Many organisations now use what is called a 'workplace health and safety management system' (**WHSMS**) for this purpose. A WHSMS is the name given to a system of linked management activities designed to continuously improve WHS and comply with the law. In a sense, a WHSMS is like a carefully designed machine that, once set in motion, properly maintained and regularly upgraded, methodically works its way through an organisation, making it healthier and safer for people to work in.

WHSMSs became popular following modern WHS legislation, whereby a duty of care was placed on the employer. Employers needed a documented *system* to exercise their duty of care; hence, WHSMSs. A certified and independently audited WHSMS may also assist an organisation to market itself, particularly when contract requirements require such systems to be in place.

It is not necessary to have a WHSMS in place to have a systematic approach towards WHS. Nevertheless, the principles underlying a WHSMS represent a systematic approach. Since many organisations these days increasingly insist on having a WHSMS, we approach the development of a systematic approach using a WHSMS.

There are a number of different models of WHSMSs developed by industry, health and safety authorities and others. The Australian and New Zealand standard AS/NZS 4804:2001 *Occupational health and safety management systems – General guidelines on principles, systems and supporting techniques*, and AS/NZS 4801:2001 *Occupational health and safety management systems – Specifications with guidance for use* together provide a framework for implementing and auditing WHSMSs. This chapter uses these standards. However, just as there is no best dress or suit, there is no best WHSMS. The 'best' WHSMS is the one that fits your organisation, the particular WHS issues facing the organisation and the laws governing it. If you don't already have one, your industry association may be able to provide you with a model system you can tailor (see 'Additional resources' at the end of this chapter for further assistance).

Some confuse WHSMSs with audit tools. Audit tools are a form of checklist used to assess aspects of health and safety practice against specified criteria, such as legal requirements or good management practice. We discuss audit tools in Chapter 13.

DEVELOPMENT PROCESS AND RATIONALE

Adopting and developing a systematic approach requires consultation with managers, workers and their representatives, as well as any other possible stakeholders such as contractors. For this to be effective, WHS training is critical. Plainly, those managers and workers directly involved must have a certain minimum level of WHS knowledge if they are to assist. A committee could be used to develop a WHSMS with the assistance of a WHS consultant. Again, a suitable industry model would be a good starting place, which could then be adapted to local circumstances.

It is important to make sure the reasons for adopting a systematic approach are made explicit. These may be moral concerns, legal and customer requirements or brand and image considerations. Such reasons will be expressed in the WHS policy, which, in turn, identifies what the specific requirements or standards for the system will be. These reasons will be used when monitoring, evaluating and reviewing the WHSMS.

The factors influencing the design of a particular system also need to be discussed. They would include
- the benefits of any resulting certification
- the organisational structure
- the level of management commitment to WHS
- the suitability of management style
- the degree of WHS knowledge and skills
- workplace (safety) culture
- industrial relations considerations
- the capacity of current consultation and communication processes
- the interface and overlap with existing management systems; for example, quality, environment, performance management, finances, operations
- the resources and organisational capacity available to make it work
- the nature of work processes, hazards and level of risk
- the abilities and constraints of the workforce to participate and make a systematic approach effective; for example, literacy, numeracy, diversity, special needs.

INTEGRATED SYSTEMS

Whichever WHSMS you eventually develop and use, it should be part of the overall management system of the organisation and sit comfortably alongside other systems. Like other systems, it should form part of the planning, goal setting, budgeting, organising, implementing, monitoring, measuring and reviewing processes undertaken to continually improve performance. Putting the 'management' in a WHSMS is achieved by identifying the WHS responsibilities, accountabilities and authority of each and every person in the organisation, from the CEO to the receptionist. For more information on this, see the section on 'Organising' below.

Often a WHSMS is linked closely with quality or risk management systems and may have environmental concerns attached to it. Whatever the links, WHS becomes a seamless part of business activity by being organised as an important business system alongside others.

DYNAMIC SYSTEM

Like other management systems, a WHSMS should not be mechanical but dynamic, involving the workplace in continuously improving its health and safety and responding to changes. Continuous monitoring and regular reviews of the WHS program by the HS committee can ensure that the WHSMS is dynamic and responsive.

The remainder of this chapter deals with the elements of a WHSMS in more detail and how they may be integrated into the overall management system.

ELEMENTS OF THE WORKPLACE HEALTH AND SAFETY MANAGEMENT SYSTEM

WHSMSs contain the six basic elements shown in Figure 4.1.

Figure 4.1 *The basic elements of WHSMSs*

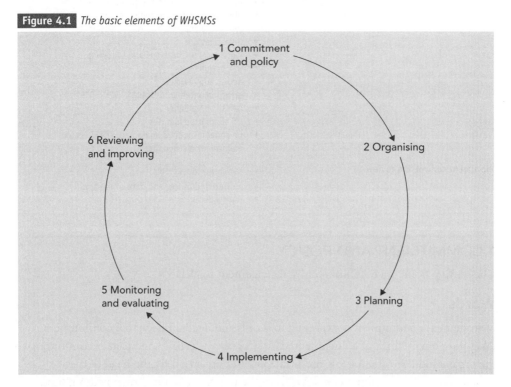

As you might imagine, WHSMSs are not usually found in very small organisations, in which the administration would involve too many resources and more scaled-down solutions are appropriate.

You will need to document your system. Figure 4.2 lists the basic elements of documentation, which should be made available online.

Figure 4.2 *System documents*

DOCUMENT TYPES	DETAIL
WHS policies and procedures	• company WHS policy • training • consultation • emergencies • inspections • investigations • purchasing, etc.
Roles, responsibilities, accountabilities, authority	for each position specific to WHS
Safe work procedures	based on job safety analyses and risk assessments
Registers and records	• current and past WHS annual plans • first aid and injury register • notifications to regulator • training – induction, safe operating procedures, consultation, refresher • certificates, licences and permits • plant and equipment registrations • job safety analyses and risk assessments • investigations • workplace notifications and follow-up • inspections • audits and reviews • environmental monitoring • health surveillance • HS committee minutes • personal protective equipment (PPE) issued • maintenance schedules, etc.
Document control and review	• register of documents • authorising officer and date of release • review dates

1 COMMITMENT AND POLICY

The starting point is a commitment by management to WHS.

Words

Management commitment is expressed in words and deeds. The verbal commitment takes the primary form of a documented WHS policy – usually one page – committing the organisation to certain goals and principles and signed off by the head of the organisation.[1] As everything else flows from the policy – planning, organisation, funding and activity – the wording is significant, and careful attention should be paid to its content. It should be remembered that it will be displayed throughout the organisation and could be submitted as evidence in court.

Aspects to consider in a WHS policy include
* a reflection of the relevant objective from the organisation's overall mission, vision and core values – how does WHS fit in?

- a commitment to
  - provide a healthy and safe workplace and effective return-to-work programs for the injured
  - measurable objectives and ongoing improvement
  - compliance with relevant WHS law and the highest standards in WHS
  - consultation with staff at all levels to achieve policy goals
  - consistent identification, evaluation and control of hazards
- an expression of the WHS responsibilities of all key stakeholders; for example, workers, supervisors, managers.

Importantly, the policy should be endorsed by employees (normally through the HS committee), as cooperation is needed for implementation. The policy also needs to be reviewed periodically to ensure it is relevant and up to date. The date of last review should be indicated on the policy itself. Finally, it should be displayed prominently and headlined in training and induction. Below is an example of a WHS policy by Sydney Power House, an electrical and communications contracting business.

OHS POLICY STATEMENT – SYDNEY POWER HOUSE

The management of Sydney Power House Pty Ltd is committed to providing a safe and healthy workplace for all that work on or visit our worksites.

This company recognises that our people are our most valuable asset and as such we strive to provide them with a safe and productive environment.

Sydney Power House Pty Ltd will achieve our health and safety requirements by:

- Identifying hazards, assessing risks and implementing controls which prevent injury or illness to our employees or subcontractors
- Consulting with all employees, subcontractors and key stakeholders in OH&S matters
- Planning, implementing and maintaining an effective occupational health and safety system that takes into account all relevant OH&S Legislation and meeting or exceeding requirements
- Establishing safety rules, policies and procedures which all employees, subcontractors and visitors will be required to adhere to on our worksites
- Investigating promptly any accident or incident in order to implement corrective actions as soon as possible
- Ensuring our company actively participates in OH&S issues, including the identification and provision of training requirements
- Providing effective rehabilitation to injured workers and supporting them as required
- Continually monitoring compliance and performance of our OH&S program
- Supporting OH&S Representatives and/or Committees established on our worksites.

Sydney Power House Pty Ltd requires all employees and subcontractors to work in a safe manner and report any hazards so that they can be dealt with as soon as possible. Remember safety is everyone's responsibility. Sydney Power House ensure that each employee has completed a 'Construction Industry General Induction Training' course and has been inducted into our company safety plan.

Source: Sydney Power House, 2010, OHS Policy Statement, http://sydneypowerhouse.com.au/about-sph/ohs-policystatement. Copyright © 2010 Sydney Power House

Deeds

To demonstrate real commitment, the organisation needs to implement the policy through **WHS management** activities such as planning and reviewing, consulting, communicating, resourcing, recognising and rewarding good WHS performance. Apart from living up to the policy, commitment can be shown by management 'walking the talk'; for example, taking part in inspections, participating in fire and emergency drills, discussing health and safety at regular meetings, following up promised corrective activity and modelling appropriate behaviour in the workplace. Finally, each activity needs to be reported and communicated to staff as part of marketing WHS to them. People need to be aware and reminded of the priority management attaches to WHS by deeds more comprehensive than simply putting up safety posters.

DID YOU KNOW?

GAINING MANAGEMENT COMMITMENT

An individual approach by the health and safety manager is a useful way of developing wider management commitment.

First understand what the issues are for the managers you are addressing. Different managers have various agendas and a different understanding of what WHS is about. Don't assume that the managing director, the financial officer, the marketing manager, the human resource director and the chief operations officer all have the same issues or understanding. Break down your audience to individuals and listen to what their problems are – WHS or non-WHS – remembering that all the while they are working under time and resource constraints.

It may be WHS issues they are directly concerned about: a rash of incidents, a near miss, increased compensation costs or a compliance issue. Other problems may be related to WHS, such as productivity lags, absenteeism (including unpunctuality) or corporate culture. Many will be issues that bear no relation to WHS: a supply problem, dysfunctional staff member or forthcoming merger, for example. Listen to the managers and respect their experience and understanding, even if you don't agree.

Where you have the skills and resources – and the manager is amenable – prepare a proposal to help them with a significant WHS or WHS-related problem that you are confident will be successful. In the first instance, work with those individuals who have the most influence in the organisation – normally the CEO or managing director. Otherwise, build up your credibility with others on the management team. Above all, only pick those problems that you can be sure of solving; do not add to the manager's workload and make sure the improvement can be clearly identified. With their support, market the project as the manager's initiative. 'I have been asked by JB to …' Having consulted and gained endorsement, then deliver. Document the project and, where appropriate, publicise it internally and possibly externally. The managing director may wish to use it as a marketing tool.

Commitment to WHS by managers grows incrementally with each successful project. With that commitment, senior management is more comfortable with WHS and will make sure that line management makes it their responsibility too. In this way, the health and safety manager does not become the 'WHS sheriff'.

2 ORGANISING

To implement policy and demonstrate commitment, WHS activity first needs to be organised and people need to know their roles within it.

WHS responsibility, accountability and authority

With any job, we all need to know
- what our responsibilities or duties are
- to whom we are accountable and what we are accountable for; that is, what are the standards by which we are measured
- what authority we have to carry out our responsibilities.

These need to be written down somewhere, such as in a job description or contract, and fully understood. So it is with WHS. Our health and safety responsibility, accountability and authority must also be documented.

Identifying responsibilities, accountabilities and authority will depend on
- the position held and the tasks carried out
- what corporate WHS policy and the law requires
- the hazards associated with the job.[2]

These case studies are brief examples of WHS specifications.

EXAMPLE 1

The head of the purchasing department is responsible for the purchase of all goods and services. The head is accountable to the chief financial officer for ensuring that all supplies or contracts are checked to make sure they meet the relevant health and safety standards and those receiving or using the goods or services have been informed of any associated hazards and know how to control them. The purchasing head will need the authority to cancel services, return products or refuse delivery.

EXAMPLE 2

The fleet manager is responsible for the leasing, maintenance and allocation of company vehicles. The manager is accountable to the chief administrative officer for ensuring that all the vehicles meet the latest safety standards and are properly maintained, that drivers are licensed and trained in safe loading procedures and that accident/incident notification procedures are in place. The fleet manager must have the right to take any action to make sure all of this happens, such as taking the vehicle off the road or suspending a driver from further use of company vehicles.

Discussion questions

1 Examine your own job statement (or someone else's). Have the WHS specifications been detailed sufficiently?
2 If not prepare a statement that does fully detail your WHS specifications.

Responsibility, accountability and authority begin with the managing director or CEO and cascade down throughout the organisation, including to contractors. Everyone then knows what they are supposed to do as part of their WHS responsibility, to whom they report, to what standard, and what action they may take to ensure that their WHS duties are fulfilled. This needs to be documented, regularly reviewed and checked to see that everyone complies with corporate WHS policy and the law.

As a good test, imagine an accident has occurred and the case has reached court. Can it be demonstrated clearly that everything has been done to ensure everyone knows what their WHS responsibilities are, to whom they are responsible, what standards must be met and what power they have to carry out their responsibilities?

Safe working procedures

Underneath the description of responsibilities, accountabilities and authorities, every job should have a set of procedures – the specific tasks and steps to be followed by the job-holder. These should include or refer to **safe working procedures** – a set of written instructions that identifies the health and safety issues that may arise from the jobs and tasks that make up a system of work. The procedures are based on a job safety analysis (JSA) (see Chapter 6).

A safe working procedure should be written when

- designing a new job or task
- changing a job or task
- introducing new equipment or substances
- reviewing a procedure when problems have been identified; for example, from an accident or incident investigation

The safe working procedure should identify

- the supervisor for the task or job and the workers who will undertake the task
- the tasks that are to be undertaken that pose risks
- the equipment and substances that are used in these tasks
- the control measures that have been built into these tasks
- any training or qualification needed to undertake the task
- the personal protective equipment to be worn
- action to be undertaken to address safety issues that may arise during the task.

Safe working procedures should be referred to when advertising and selecting workers; for example, when certain skill levels are required to implement procedures. Pre-employment medicals may be required. At the same time, the requirements must not violate human rights and anti-discrimination or equal opportunity legislation.

These procedures must be read, understood and acknowledged (signed) by the job-holder before starting work, as they set the standard for work to which the job-holder is held accountable. As with all documentation, they need to be reviewed and upgraded to meet new situations and requirements. Workers should know how to use the procedures and be provided with necessary training and supervision. Again, in the case of an accident, a court will almost certainly ask for a copy of these procedures, together with evidence to show that the worker knew how to apply the procedures before starting work and was trained and supervised in their application. In short, safe working procedures form an important basis for organising health and safety systematically, while at the same time fulfilling the duty of care.

The role of the health and safety manager

The principal role of the health and safety manager is to assist the organisation, its managers and its employees to promote health and safety in the workplace in line with corporate policy and the law. This normally includes

- reporting to the senior management team on WHS matters
- conducting safety inspections
- providing administrative support for consultative arrangements
- preparing the WHS program
- developing risk management strategies and monitoring their progress
- establishing appropriate information and training programs
- reporting and assisting in the investigation of incidents
- administering workers' compensation and rehabilitation.

As part of the management team, the HS manager also has obligations to inform other managers and the CEO of changes to WHS legislation and codes of practice, and to contribute to the reporting of WHS matters to senior managers. Health and safety managers ought to participate in benchmarking their approach to the management of WHS and in sharing information within their industries.

Whatever the duties of the HS manager, the responsibility for health and safety lies with the organisation and all its workers – CEO, managers, supervisors and staff – not just with the HS manager. This is made clear in the law and should be made clear in the policy. From time to time, HS managers need to remind themselves and others of this fact. Otherwise, they may be identified with health and safety responsibility and the (impossible) task of implementing it by themselves. Health and safety activity must be owned by the line managers involved and not be seen to be owned by the HS manager or anyone else. For example, the development of safe working procedures mentioned above ought to be the responsibility of the managers and supervisors with, of course, any required help from the HS manager or suitable expert.

Similarly, the arrangements by which employees and management consult on WHS should not lessen the responsibilities of everyone. Consultative arrangements are there to assist and not to take over WHS responsibilities.

3 PLANNING

With everyone's WHS role specified, you can begin to plan the implementation of the WHS policy. A plan or program is needed to direct implementation based on an understanding of what is required. At the end of the day, you want two things: a documented WHS system (Figure 4.2), if you don't already have one, and a plan to implement it.

A basic planning tool is represented in Figure 4.3, using the example of a partially successful organisation. It only deals with a few aspects of the WHS program. Whether you are starting from scratch or not, the general steps remain the same.

Figure 4.3 A basic planning tool

WHAT WE NEED TO DO (I.E. LEGAL REQUIREMENTS, POLICIES AND PROCEDURES, STANDARDS)	WHERE WE ARE	WHAT WE NEED TO DO TO FILL ANY GAP	PRIORITY (CRITICAL, MAJOR, MINOR)	WHAT ARE OUR OBJECTIVES, TARGETS, PERFORMANCE INDICATORS[3]	WHO IS GOING TO DO WHAT, WHEN AND WITH WHICH RESOURCES
Identify hazards, assess and control risks in all workplaces (ref: Company WHS handbook s. 5)	Hazards have been identified in the last six months, risks assessed and controls put in place for head office and four depots. Three depots are regularly non-compliant.	Have relevant depot supervisors complete hazard identification and risk assessments. Train depot supervisors in risk management (RM).	Major	Completed documentation by end of December 2012. RM training completed by end of November.	Logistics Manager and depot supervisors – week commencing 15/11/12. HS Manager to conduct RM workshop – week commencing 1/11/12. HS Manager to check with Logistics Manager – 7/1/13. HS Manager to check with all sites to ensure activity occurs regularly.
Provide safe access and egress (ref: Building Code of Australia)	All passageways, exits and entries compliant, except two emergency doors in dispatch area open inwards.	Arrange with landlord for alteration of doors.	Major	100% compliant by end of November.	Facilities Manager – week commencing 1/11/12. HS Manager to check with Facilities Manager – 3/12/12.
Put in place an alcohol policy (ref: WorkSafe Vic. – 'Alcohol in the Workplace')	No policy and procedures in place. Two related incidents reported 2009.	Have WHS medical provider prepare policy for discussion by HS committee.	Minor	Policy prepared and endorsed at next February's WHS Committee meeting and placed on Intranet.	HS Manager to contact offsite medical provider – first week Nov. 2012, and liaise with Communications Manager.

Step 1: Identify what is required by policy

Everything flows from the WHS policy. The policy should state what the *general* requirements are. These can include

- compliance with the law
- any company-specific standards
- enterprise agreements with unions
- Australian standards
- industry-best practice.

Regulations, codes and guidance material explain in greater detail what is required. Industry or Australian standards will have specific requirements. Corporate policy may have even more stringent standards. It is then a matter of listing the specific program requirements in headline form (in the first column). You don't need to repeat the detail, but refer instead to the documentation used.

Typical requirements

In addition to having a WHS policy and organising HS responsibilities and consultation, which we have discussed, the following detailed requirements should be found in WHSMSs and in audit tools such as SafetyMAP:

- training management and workers in WHS
- gathering WHS information, collecting data, analysing data and managing records
- identifying hazards and managing risk
- health and safety policies and procedures (P&Ps) to deal with hazards particular to the workplace; for example, manual handling, stress, alcohol, motor vehicles, confined spaces
- inspecting workplaces
- promoting health
- preparing for emergencies
- notifying, reporting and investigating incidents
- auditing health and safety
- providing medical and first aid
- compensating and rehabilitating injured workers.

These requirements should be documented for reference so that everyone is clear about what needs to be done. For example, what is meant by 'preparing for emergencies'? What are the policies and procedures to deal with manual handling? What standards do they refer to?

In the vast majority of cases, documentation of regulations and codes of practice can be found online or purchased, as in the case of Australian standards. If this documentation hasn't already been assembled for the organisation, it needs to be. And where it has been, it needs to be checked to see if it is up to date and relevant.

Once you have identified the requirements, you can begin to prepare the (annual) WHS plan with the input of trained managers and supervisors.

Step 2: Assess where the organisation is

The next step is to assess how far current organisational arrangements and activities match the requirements. Information can be gathered from the previous review of the annual plan, records, interviews, inspections, surveys and databases. If your managers and supervisors have been trained, they can do much of this assessment with your assistance; otherwise, it falls entirely in your lap. This checking should form part of general management duties throughout the year. For the purpose of preparing a yearly plan or program a deadline for reporting needs to be made.

Step 3: Identify what activities are required

There are the requirements that are being met and the requirements that need further attention. *Both* sorts of activities – ongoing and gap-filling – make up the WHS plan.

You can expect to find gaps between what should be and what is. The size of the gap will vary, with some gaps being able to be fixed relatively easily. Others may suggest that a program is failing seriously and needs special attention. The review of last year's plan should tell a lot about what needs to be done.

In discussion with those affected, identify how the gap can best be closed and if WHS specialists or technical advisers are required. If this involves significant costs, set out all the options, their comparative effectiveness and full costing to provide reasons for the preferred option.

Step 4: Prioritise activities

All the activities that make up a WHSMS are important to health and safety. Attending to the gaps without neglecting the other activities is tricky. In terms of the consequences for the organisation and employees, some gaps will appear more serious or basic than others. Establish some priorities based on an estimate of the likelihood and consequences for everyone if the activity does not take place. A simple triage – critical, major and minor – is used by most to order and schedule gap-filling activities while fulfilling ongoing requirements.

Step 5: Set objectives, targets and key performance indicators

Before setting objectives, targets and indicators, we must ask *why* we measure performance in the first place, as this will tell us *how* to measure.

The three main reasons for measuring performance are shown below.

1 To identify the level of existing performance	to help set goals and strategy
2 To identify progress against goals	to see how we are going, and possibly review strategy and, sometimes, goals
3 To identify outcomes against goals	to see how we went, identify areas for improvement and, often, reward (or punish) those involved

By measuring, we are able to manage our performance. We are able to make clear our goals and plan to achieve them. We can then see how we are going and make any necessary changes. Finally, we can see if we achieved our goals and how we could improve next time around. And, if we did well enough, we would hope to be rewarded. Measurement, then, motivates us.

The link between measurement and motivation is worth stressing. Measuring effectiveness not only highlights areas for attention but it also can be a boost if we are doing well (or a source of sleepless nights if we aren't). By being linked to pay incentives, awards or, more often than not, personal achievement and professional recognition, measurement drives performance.

Dimensions of performance

If measurement is 'good for us', how do we measure? To understand how to measure HS performance, we need to understand the dimensions of performance.

Figure 4.4 *Dimensions of performance*

EXAMPLE: SAFETY TRAINING COURSE		
TERM	DEFINITION	EXAMPLE
Goals (or 'objectives',[4] 'aims', 'purposes', 'ends')	What you want to achieve	Safer handling of hazardous substances
Targets	What you want to achieve in measurable terms	20% improvement in safety audit rating by the end of the year
Inputs (money, time, energy, people, facilities, material, information)	What you use in trying to achieve your goals	8 weeks of my time, $10 000 of my budget, 150 supervisor days ...
Outputs (products, services)	What you produce or provide in order to achieve your goals	Provided five two-day courses on hazardous substances to 75 supervisors together with 75 handbooks
Outcomes ('results', 'effects', 'consequences')	What you achieve through your outputs	Safer handling of hazardous substances; 30% improvement in safety audit rating at the end of the year

The distinction some people have difficulty with is the difference between 'outputs' and 'outcomes'. When you think about the goal or purpose of your activity, an outcome may be better. Your output – what you *put out* into the world – may not be what is needed. In this example, training courses and handbooks may not have been what was needed, but instead better labelling or use of non-hazardous substitutes. The outputs – the training and handbooks – may not have been effective in achieving the goal. Seen in this way, outputs and outcomes, then, are very different.

Effectiveness, efficiency, economy

In general, we measure performance in three ways.
1 **Effectiveness**: Did you achieve your goals? Were you successful?
2 **Efficiency**: Did you get maximum use of the time and resources provided to you? Did you avoid waste?
3 **Economy**: Did you use the least amount of time and resources necessary?

Figure 4.5 puts together the two sets of terms.

Figure 4.5 *Evaluating the performance of a training program*

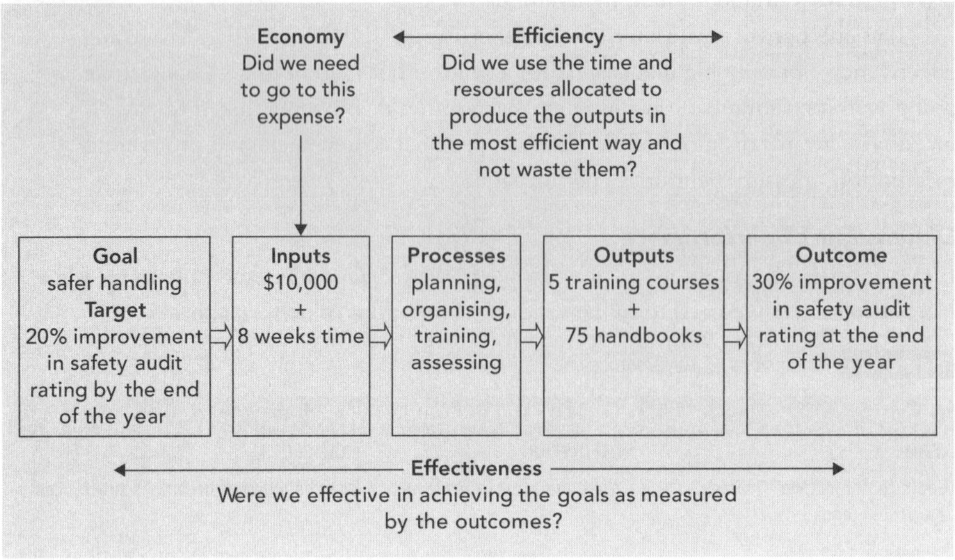

Indicators

To measure things, we use indicators or measures. To measure our weight, we use kilograms; for distance, we use metres or kilometres.

Economy indicators are used to measure the amount of the *inputs*: the amount of money, time, material, people and resources used. As a health and safety manager, your economy indicators would include your WHS budget, the number of full-time-employee days used in the WHS program or the cost of your suppliers; for example, your workers' compensation premium.

Efficiency indicators are used to measure the *processes* of converting the inputs into outputs. The more output per unit of input means greater efficiency. These indicators are usually expressed as a ratio or equation; for example, X kilometres per 1 litre of petrol. Your WHS efficiency indicators could include the number of people trained per $1000 of your budget.

Economy and efficiency indicators are usually not difficult to understand or use. You need to live within your budget and make best use of your time and money. On the other hand, measuring the *effectiveness* of an organisation's WHS performance can be tricky.

We begin by looking at three commonly used *effectiveness* indicators, based on lost time injuries:

- lost time injury frequency rate (LTIFR)
- lost time injury incidence rate (LTIIR)
- average lost time rate (ALTR)

As the first two are based on incidents, we need to understand them. Workplace incidents are broadly categorised according to their severity. Australian Standard AS 1885.1:1990 – *Workplace injury and disease recording* uses the following definitions:

- **Lost time injuries/diseases** – those occurrences that resulted in a fatality, permanent disability or time lost from work of one day/shift or more.
- **No lost time injuries/diseases** – those occurrences that were not lost time injuries and for which first aid and/or medical treatment was administered.
- **Near-misses** – any unplanned incidents that occurred at the workplace that, although not resulting in any injury or disease, had the potential to do so.

Following these definitions, workplace incidents can be categorised as the following, shown in Figure 4.6.

Figure 4.6 *Categorisation of workplace incidents*

Major (accidents)	Incidents resulting in lost time injuries/ diseases	LTIs
Minor (accidents)	Incidents resulting in no lost time injuries/ diseases	IWLTs (injuries without lost time)
Near-misses (dangerous occurrences)		NMs or DOs

Some organisations measure their performance by the *number* of lost time injuries or illnesses over a set period – usually, a year. Others also use the number of working days lost over a period. However, because the number of workers employed or hours worked during a period may vary, many prefer to use *rates* such as lost time injury frequency rates, lost time injury incidence rates or average lost time rates. The standard way of calculating them is as follows.

Lost time injury frequency rate	$\dfrac{\text{Number of lost time injuries or illnesses in the period} \times 1\,000\,000}{\text{Number of hours worked in the period}}$
Lost time injury incidence rate	$\dfrac{\text{Number of lost time injuries or illnesses in the period} \times 1000}{\text{Number of workers employed}}$
Average lost time rate	$\dfrac{\text{Number of working days lost in the period}}{\text{Number of lost time injuries or illnesses in the period}}$

DID YOU KNOW?

Some large organisations such as BHP Billiton and Lihir Gold use other rates such as the 'classified injury frequency rate' (CIFR) whereby classified injury is any workplace injury that results in the person not returning to their unrestricted normal duties after the day on which the injury was received. The CIFR is the number of classified injuries per million work hours.

Another, the 'total recordable injury frequency rate' (TRIFR), represents the total number of fatalities and injuries resulting in lost time, restricted work duties or medical treatment per million work hours.

To make this easier to understand consider the following hierarchy of incidents.

Figure 4.7 *Hierarchy of incidents*

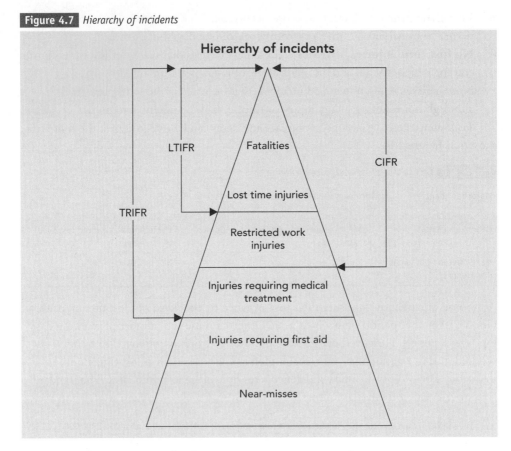

Keeping the rates standard To keep the rates standard for comparison purposes, the number of cases of injury/disease includes those resulting in lost time of one day/ shift or more during the specified period. The 'number of workers' is defined as the average number of workers who worked in the recording period. Persons who were absent from work on paid or unpaid leave for the entire period should be excluded from this calculation. In the case of incidence rates, it may be useful to break down the category of 'workers' into employees and contractors, full-time and casuals, male and female, blue-collar and white-collar, or other categories, in order to get more information. Otherwise, frequency rates are more commonly used.

The 'number of hours worked in the period' refers to the total number of hours worked by all workers in the recording unit including, for example, overtime and extra shifts. Where incidence rates can be influenced by the number of full-time, part-time or casual workers, the frequency rate focuses on the hours exposed to hazards however many are actually employed.

The 'average lost time rate' measures the severity of the incidents being experienced by workplaces over time. The 'number of working days lost' refers to the total number of working days, irrespective of the number of hours that would normally have been worked each day, that were lost as a result of the injury or disease up to a maximum of 12 months for any individual incident. For the purposes of calculating the average time lost rate, occurrences that result in a fatality should be assigned a time lost of 12 months

(220 standard working days). The focus here is not on the number of incidents, but on the severity of their impact.

Measurement intervals Rates can be calculated at intervals that best meet the individual organisation's needs. Medium to large employers (that is, those who have 200 or more employees) may benefit from calculating rates on both a monthly and a cumulative monthly basis. Individual monthly totals and rates can be derived from counting those incidents that occurred in a particular month and the corresponding time lost in respect of those cases in that month. Cumulative monthly data can be derived by adding the total number of incidents for a specific period, such as 12 months, and the total time lost that corresponds to those cases for that period. Smaller employers need only calculate totals or rates on a six monthly or annual basis as rates calculated more frequently are likely to be meaningless due to the influence of random factors.

Analysis Measurement rates are of limited value when used in isolation. Analysing the rates in conjunction with each other provides workplaces with more complete information. This is particularly so for frequency and average time lost rates, which, when examined together, give a more accurate measure of the number of incidents and time lost as they relate to the level of exposure to risk.

Large organisations will need to keep data to compare rates over time and identify seasonal trends. For small businesses that generally experience few incidences of injury or disease, time series analysis will be largely meaningless due to the random nature of events. Data may also be aggregated to cover all the operations of a firm or broken down to check performance of individual units.

Analysis using external data can be useful. Comparing your organisation's rate with government-produced industry rates or with information from your insurer may be able to tell you how well you are going in comparison with others and how *comparatively* serious your WHS problems are. This may motivate management. However, the aim of continually improving is only really helped by measuring your own performance and setting realistic goals and strategies. Rates measuring incidence, frequency and average cost, together with other indicators, should be directed towards self-improvement and not just finding your position on a league table.

Because they directly measure failure these indicators are called *negative* indicators. And because they focus on performance outcomes – the end results of everyone's efforts – they are called *outcome* indicators. Combining the two, we call these rates *negative outcome* indicators.

Such indicators are straightforward, relatively easy to apply and widely accepted. Used internally, they can help identify hot spots. Rates can be tracked over time as well as benchmarked against comparable industry or occupation rates.[5] You can use them to set targets; for example, 'reduce the LTIFR by 30 per cent for the next calendar year'.

Problems with outcome indicators While such indicators make good sense and should be used, they are not *sufficient* on a number of scores:

• Such indicators tend to encourage under-reporting, either by supervisors trying to make their sections look good or by employees trying to protect their continued employment and career prospects.

- The indicators don't tell you whether your strategy or management system is responsible or not for the outcome. For example, you may have a low rate of LTIs but there may have been a lot of fortunate escapes. The workplace could still be an 'accident waiting to happen'. In this way, outcome indicators are almost useless in small- and medium-sized businesses as the rates may vary wildly from one period to another. Outcome data tells you very little.
- Even where accidents occur and are reported, such goals and indicators focus on the injury and not necessarily the potential seriousness of the accident. For example, had others been nearby at the time, the impact could have been much worse. Again, you are not given enough information.
- Similarly, negative indicators don't capture all incidents; that is, when no time or money is lost, but when the consequences could have been enormous. Near-misses provide the some of the best pieces of information one could hope for.
- Outcome indicators don't always pick up occupational diseases when there is a prolonged latency period. The statistics may show a decline in time off work for a period, but much later the figures may raise and suddenly spike as a disease takes hold; for example, with occupational cancer.
- Outcome indicators tend to reinforce reactive rather than preventative action. Action focuses on dealing with yesterday's problems and not what may lie ahead.
- As most outcome indicators are negative, they focus on the downside of WHS activity. The fact that you didn't have as many accidents this year as last year is good, but it doesn't necessarily make you feel inspired.
- Importantly, such indicators focus on only one aspect of human concern: the need to be safe and secure. They do not tell whether the workplace is satisfying the wider range of psychological and social needs that contribute to our wellbeing.

For such reasons, we need to supplement the negative outcome indicators with others that point to a safe and healthy workplace.[6]

You need indicators that tell you whether the system you have put in place is actually working and likely to achieve immediate and final goals. You must go 'upstream' from outcomes and look at the *inputs* and *processes* you are using to promote health and safety (see Figure 4.8). For this, you require *input* and *process indicators*, or what are called *positive performance indicators (PPIs)*.

An analogy may help. To arrive home safely, you must have a safe car and drive safely. The use of a regularly serviced car (input) and driving to the rules of the road (process) indicate that you are likely to arrive home safely. The same applies to WHS.

Fortunately, finding WHS input and process indicators is not too hard. You have already done the hard work. They are in your system requirements: policy, organisation, training, consultation, risk assessment, inspections and so on. The presence and quality of these indicate whether you are performing well now and can be expected to continue to do so. They are *lead* indicators, indicators of where you are *leading* to. By contrast, an LFITR is an outcome or *lag* indicator.

Figure 4.8 *Lead indicators: inputs and processes*

INPUTS	PROCESSES, ACTIVITIES
<ul><li>updated WHS policy</li><li>proper resourcing of WHS</li><li>purchasing policy incorporates WHS matters</li><li>latest personal protective equipment</li><li>complete material safety data sheets (**MSDSs**)</li><li>safe working procedures online</li></ul>	<ul><li>WHS placed on the agenda of business meetings regularly</li><li>induction includes WHS awareness</li><li>contractors screened for WHS performance</li><li>effective WHS committee meetings</li><li>regular inspections</li><li>annual WHS audits</li><li>JSAs reviewed when jobs change</li></ul>

If you saw these in place and being done well, then you would have reason to expect the workplace to be a safe and healthy one. These are indicators that WHS is alive and well.

Key performance indicators

The problem is not so much finding performance indicators, but settling on which are your *key performance indicators (KPIs)*. These would be based on the goals found in your WHS policy and any further specific goals set out for the WHSMS.

Having reviewed your goals, a useful principle for assembling your KPIs is to think in terms of a (car) dashboard.

WHS IN PRACTICE

THE DASHBOARD PRINCIPLE

Ask yourself

- What sort of 'gauges', 'meters' or 'warning lights' do you need to assist you to manage?
- Is the information provided relevant to the objective (WHS), accurate, reliable and up to date? Do you have confidence in those gauges, meters and warning lights?
- Have you enough? Have you too many – a flight deck?
- Which are essential? Which are used most?

    Once identified, then see if the indicators can be represented graphically on one side of a single sheet of A4 (landscape) and arranged to reflect priorities and associations.

- Are the gauges designed appropriately? For example, which of bar charts, pie charts, dials or other graphic representations are more suitable?
- Are they self-explanatory, requiring the absolute minimum of words and numbers?
- Are priorities reflected, for example, in the size or position?
- Are they arranged together logically, reflecting associations?

    If the number of indicators makes the page too crowded, cut back. Keep working at it, testing it with other 'drivers' until you are satisfied.

    Such a dashboard not only functions as a simple presentation tool, it serves to help you remember key performance information – and sound as if you have the material under control. Most of all, it is an important test of your management focus, remembering that we measure to help us manage.

Targets Once you have decided on your key performance indicators – outcome, input and process – you need to devise targets using them. In assigning targets, use the SMARTA principle: targets should be **s**pecific, **m**easurable, **a**chievable, **r**elevant, given a **t**imeframe and **a**greed upon.

A sample set of indicators with targets and mid-year progress report might look like the following.

TYPE OF INDICATOR	INDICATOR	TARGET AT END OF YEAR	YEAR TO DATE	ON TARGET?
Outcome	Frequency rate (LTIFR)	30% reduction	31%	Y
	Incidence rate (LTIIR)	30% reduction	35%	Y
	Medical and rehabilitation costs	30% reduction	32%	Y
Process	All senior management team meetings receive and discuss WHS reports and act on issues arising	100% of all meetings	100%	Y
	Committee members attend meetings	90% attendance over the year	95%	Y
	Managers/supervisor WHS training	95% by end of year	60%	Y
	Workplace hazard inspections	55 as set out in WHS program	35	Y
Input	Contractors screened for WHS performance	100%	85%	N
	WHS policy reviewed regularly	by end of year	N	N/A
	MSDSs updated regularly	quarterly	twice	Y

It is important to keep the list of KPIs and targets manageable and to review them to see if they are indeed effective indicators of meeting your WHS policy goals. You may have to tweak them and their targets using the SMARTA principle.

Step 6: Assign Responsibility, Schedule and Resource

Once the objectives have been identified, it is a matter of management assigning responsibilities, scheduling the activities and providing resources according to any priorities. This is the point at which the *system* produces a *plan* that needs to be consolidated by management into a draft for discussion and implementation. Management and workers, usually within the framework of the HS committee or its equivalent, need to read, discuss, possibly amend and, finally, endorse the plan. They need to be clear how it was drafted, the thought processes involved and the evidence underlying it. They have to be confident of achieving the objectives. If possible, a subcommittee should be involved in preparing the plan. Often this will mean taking last year's plan as the base document and amending it in the light of its review. In any case, buy-in would be helped by prior subcommittee discussion.

Resourcing or budgeting for the WHS program should be prepared by management on a careful estimate of the required inputs for activities to be successful (people, money, WHS information, training, equipment and so on) and their costs. The health and safety manager should be involved! Among the bigger upfront costs will be

- workers' compensation insurance
- salaries and administrative costs for the health and safety unit (manager, support staff, superannuation, payroll tax, office, furniture, equipment, travel)
- training.

The finance officer or cost accountant may be needed to help, depending on the size of the total activity required, particularly if it involves capital purchases. Estimates of any downtime may need to be made if significant amounts of training are required. Where the money comes from will depend on the financial management system used by the firm.

The important points are that there should be the sufficient resources as pledged in the WHS policy and that WHS is specifically budgeted for. So, for example, the WHS training budget should form an identifiable part of the total training budget along with other items, such as human resource training for managers and supervisors, professional development and so forth.

4 IMPLEMENTING

Having developed the plan, it is a matter of everyone implementing it. For effective implementation the health and safety management plan should be integrated into the organisation's business plan as one section of it.

An obvious way of ensuring this is to combine some or all of the WHS KPIs with the organisation's other KPIs such as for staff turnover, new customers, repeat sales, financial ratios and so on. When management has its regular meetings to see reports against the KPIs and gather an estimate of how the firm is 'travelling', WHS is then seen as part of the business and a contributor to its success.

The HS manager should report on the implementation of the plan at regular management meetings and to the HS committee, if you have one. A standard format can assist understanding by both audiences. When activities – for example, training, inspections and risk assessments – are reported, it is especially important to add what the outcomes of those activities were.

Although the ultimate responsibility lies with senior management, everyone in the organisation has an active role to play in the management of WHS. While the HS manager will advise and provide support, it is the responsibility of the workers, supervisors, line management, senior management and the managing director to implement the plan. Implementation should not be the responsibility of the HS manager, nor should it be seen to be so.

5 MONITORING AND EVALUATING

The monitoring and evaluation of the effectiveness of all the activities is a form of pulse-taking. You are checking to see, first of all, if such activities are happening at all and whether they are achieving their targets or are likely to achieve them. What is the performance level? Do we need to make changes? Is the pulse there? Is it strong? If it is weak, what do we prescribe?

It is worth emphasising that the monitoring and evaluation process applies to *all* activities comprising the WHSMS, not simply hazard identification and risk management activities. So, for example, the policy needs to be checked to see if it is properly communicated to all staff. The HS committee should monitor how well information is shared among members and decisions acted upon. The allocation of WHS responsibilities, accountabilities and authority should be monitored to see that it is appropriate and reflects changes to the work and law. And so it goes throughout the entire WHSMS.

The method of monitoring and evaluating will vary according to the nature of the activities and the associated objectives, targets and performance indicators. Those methods need to be discussed, agreed on and documented.

The main considerations are as follows.
- Who will do the monitoring? (Technical assistance may be required.)
- What equipment, data, information or procedures are required?
- When will it be done and how often?[7]
- How will it be reported, by whom and to whom?

Monitoring and evaluation reports are then made directly up the line to senior management for any comment and to the health and safety manager and the HS committee.

The point of such procedures should be clear – to ensure WHS remains, ultimately, the responsibility of management. Having the monitoring and evaluation carried out by the HS manager in other than an assisting role or having the reports delivered immediately to the HS manager would, in many cases, undermine management's responsibility for WHS.

6 REVIEWING AND IMPROVING

Developing an improvement strategy means identifying the specific actions that need to be taken to meet any system shortcomings (for example, ineffectiveness, unsuitability) and realistic ways of improving upon current levels of performance.

The review will need the attention of the WHS committee. If possible, it should spend time away from the workplace to hear activity performance reports and discuss ways of improving. The CEO should be invited to open any workshop to show commitment to WHS and the review, and indicate what changes or challenges face the organisation that will impact on WHS. They should be invited back to hear the outcomes. The health and safety manager can assist by gathering information on 'best practice' in similar firms or industries, while managers and workers can be encouraged to come up with their own recommendations. Providing they are done professionally, techniques such as brainstorming and using de Bono's 'six hats' can be useful.[8] The use of external third-party facilitators can also be effective in opening people's imagination to possible improvements.

Whatever process is used, it needs to have input from management and workers before recommended changes are adopted. In many organisations these days, this would occur using the Intranet.

The most important point is that there should be no performance complacency as that is precisely when things go wrong. It is important to continually question the way things are done and find ways to do them better. The process of change never stops.

As this chapter has demonstrated, managing WHS information is critical to a systematic approach. The next chapter outlines the principles of WHS information management.

Summary

- Planned systematic approaches to WHS pay dividends to workers and employers and enjoy widespread support from labour, industry and the government.
- Workplace health and safety management systems (WHSMSs) are used to provide a systematic approach to HS in many organisations. A WHSMS is made up of linked management practices aimed at improving health and safety and complying with the law. WHSMS models should be tailored to the specific needs of the organisation.
- A WHSMS contains certain basic elements:
  - WHS policy that commits management
  - organisation of WHS responsibility, accountability and authority
  - planning to implement the WHS policy – its requirements and the activities needed to fulfil them
  - implementation of the plan by management and workers as part of their responsibilities
  - monitoring and evaluation of the system
  - regular review and improvement.
- Measuring WHS performance requires a combination of negative outcome indicators and positive process indicators.

In your workplace

You have begun work as the health and safety officer in a company that manufactures paint, mostly for the local market. The company has around 80 workers and although it has not had an accident in the last six months, you can tell from an initial inspection, they are very lucky they have not had more. The WHS system, such that it is, is minimal. The CEO knows and that is why you have been given the job, but the operational managers and supervisors are reluctant to change: 'If it isn't broken, why fix it?'

1 How would you go about gaining commitment to building the WHSMS to a satisfactory level?
2 How could you demonstrate its usefulness?
3 Where would you start?

Questions

1 What is a 'systematic approach to WHS' and what are the benefits to
   a employers?
   b workers?

2   How is commitment to WHS expressed in your organisation? Provide evidence. How could it be improved?

3   In your organisation, what are your chief responsibilities, your accountabilities and your authority? Are these written down and, if so, are they accurate? Do they contain reference to WHS?

4   When measuring WHS performance, what are the pros and cons of
    a   outcome indicators?
    b   process indicators?

Activities

1   Locate a copy of your organisation's strategic plan and analyse it to determine whether the organisation's WHS planning is explicit or implicit (or non-existent) in this document. If it is only implicit or non-existent, list the ways that WHS could be included. If WHS is incorporated in your organisation's strategic plan, list the ways the plan could be improved.

2   Locate a copy of your organisation's WHS policy and mission/value statement and consider the following.
    a   Are these policies/statements readily available to all staff?
    b   Are they routinely referred to in WHS training?
    c   Does the WHS policy fit with the principles outlined in the mission/values statement?

3   Using the planning format provided, identify three legal requirements applicable to your workplace; identify any shortfall; specify the activity or activities required to meet the requirement; allocate a suitable priority; identify the relevant objectives, targets and performance indicators; and, hypothetically, assign responsibilities, schedules and resources.

Search me!

 Explore **Search me! management** for relevant articles on managing health and safety systematically. Search me! is an online library of world-class journals, ebooks and newspapers, including *The Australian* and the *New York Times*, and is updated daily. Log in to Search me! through www.cengage.com/sso using the access card in the front of this book.

KEYWORDS

Try searching for the following terms:
▶ health and safety management systems
▶ planning health and safety
▶ lead and lag indicators
▶ performance measurement
▶ key performance indicators

Search tip: **Search me! management** contains information from both local and international sources. To get the greatest number of search results, try using both Australian and American spellings in your searches, e.g. 'globalisation' and 'globalization'; 'organisation' and 'organization'.

Additional resources

• See Laurie Stiller's article Three steps to take control, in *Australian Master OHS & Environment Guide*, 2nd edn, 2007, CCH: Sydney, Chapter 1, pp. 3–13, provides a simple three-step process to take control of WHS management.

• The Australian/New Zealand standard and guidelines on health and safety should be referred to when developing a systematic approach to WHS: AS/NZS 4804:2001, *Occupational health and safety systems – General guidelines on principles, systems and supporting techniques*; AS/NZS 4801:2001 *Occupational health and safety management systems – Specification with guidance for use.* AS/NZS 4804 provides a model and standards by which you may audit your system.

- Although audit tools are not WHSMSs, they imply a model upon which the tool is built and may provide assistance in building a WHSMS (see 'Additional resources' in Chapter 13). SafetyMAP's five elements follow the framework of AS/NZS 4801:2001 and also link neatly with AS/NZS ISO 14001:1996 *Environmental management systems – Specification with guidance for use* and AS/NZS ISO 9001:2000 *Quality management systems – Requirements.*
- For a review of WHSMSs, see http://www.worksafe.vic.gov.au/wps/wcm/connect/wsinternet/WorkSafe/Home/Forms+and+Publications/Publications/import_SafetyMAP_+Measuring+Health+_+Safety+Management.
- For more discussion of positive performance indicators, see M. Tranter, 'Positive performance indicators for OHS', in *Australian Master OHS & Environment Guide*, 2nd edn, 2007, CCH: Sydney, and an overview by Safe Work Australia at http://www.safeworkaustralia.gov.au/AboutSafeWorkAustralia/WhatWeDo/Publications/Documents/127/OHSManagementSystems_ReviewOfEffectiveness_NOHSC_2001_ArchivePDF.pdf
- Your regulator's website will also contain information on building systematic approaches to WHS.
- Many HS software programs are available that can provide assistance as well as, of course, WHS consultants, the National Safety Council being only one of these. See http://www.nsca.org.au/Programs__Products_Directory/OHS_Programs__Products/FiveStar.aspx.

Endnotes

1 Some companies also have the chair of the board of directors or a director appointed as the WHS champion sign the policy. Leighton Holdings, the construction company, sees commitment to safety starting at the board level and has a board subcommittee overviewing its WHS responsibilities.

2 Job safety analyses should identify such hazards, the risks associated and the controls needed to deal with the risks.

3 These terms are explained later.

4 'Objective', for some, means the same as 'target', not 'goal'. For others, it means both. In this book, we reserve the word 'target' to mean the measurable state of affairs that tells you the goal/objective has been achieved.

5 See the *Compendium of Workers' Compensation Statistics*, Australia, produced annually by SWA.

6 It is not just negative indicators that are the problem, it is outcome indicators of any sort,

positive or negative. For example, we could measure the outcome of our WHS activities positively, such as the number of accident-free days per person per year or the number of hours free of work-related injury or disease per person per week (without including overtime). An increase would signify an improvement and a drop the reverse. However, positive outcome indicators only go some way to solving the problems of negative indicators. Most importantly, they don't overcome the problem of ensuring that you are making progress to achieving your desired outcomes, your goals.

7 Incidents will often reinforce the monitoring of activities such as hazard identification and control.

8 Edward de Bono's 'six hats' framework is designed to encourage creative thinking. See E. de Bono, 2001, *Six Thinking Hats*, Penguin: Harmondsworth, UK.

MANAGING WHS INFORMATION

Learning Objectives

By the end of this chapter, the reader will be able to understand the principles required to:

- identify requirements for WHS information and data
- make recommendations for the design of the WHS information and data processes
- develop the WHS information and data process, and the reporting and recording process
- monitor and evaluate the effectiveness of information and data collection and analysis processes.

INTRODUCTION

It should go without saying that information and data are required to design and make the WHS system work. You not only need to know about the legal and corporate requirements, but you also need information about the organisation itself, the hazards associated with the work and the measures available to control those hazards and to monitor and evaluate them. You will also need to assess the performance of the system. It is not only the person responsible for health and safety management who requires WHS information, but also the rest of the organisation. The information must be reliable, up to date, readily accessible and in a form people can use. Some information, such as that identifying trends and hot spots, will require development.

There are also record-keeping issues. Certain information, such as medical and rehabilitation records, must be kept in a secure fashion in order to respect the privacy of those involved. Some information, such as the register of injuries, must be kept for a set period.

With all these factors to consider, the prospect of managing WHS information and data looks overwhelming. Without a strategy it can be. In this chapter, we outline how you can manage information in an ordered and effective way.

A word of warning first: there are many WHS software programs available. Too often, however, the one-size-fits-all aspect of many of them can restrict you. First find out what you need and not what the brochures tell you that you need. This chapter tells you how to find out what you require. Then approach your networks or ask your insurer to suggest the software that may suit your requirements. Good software can save you a lot of headaches; inappropriate software can create them.

WHAT IS INFORMATION MANAGEMENT?

'Information management' describes the measures required for the effective collection, storage, distribution/access, use, maintenance and disposal of information to support business processes. Figure 5.1 is a model of managing information.

This process includes such considerations as the following.

- To what level of detail will information be defined?
- Who should be made responsible for it?
- How will its sensitivity be protected and its quality preserved?
- How can it be made more accessible?

In most cases, your organisation has already addressed these issues in the context of general business information management and so has an established system that will assist you managing HS information. The likely situation is that you already have a WHS information system and want to know whether it works and could be improved. If you have an information officer or equivalent, contact that person to ensure the smooth development or review of a WHS information management system, one that is integrated with other service systems your company might have, such as records management, data administration, library services and publishing.

Figure 5.1 *Information management model*

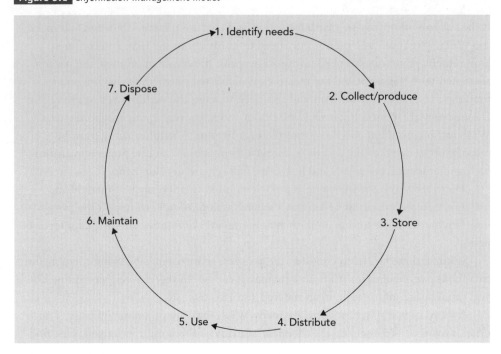

Range of information

To begin with, it is important to recognise the range of information. HS information exists in many forms – textual, numerical, graphic, spatial or audiovisual – and can be found in internal sources and those external to the organisation.

Figure 5.2 *External and internal sources of HS information*

EXTERNAL	INTERNAL
• WHS legislation, codes of practice and guidance material • Australian and industry standards • Australian Bureau of Statistics (ABS) data • Information provided by regulator and Safe Work Australia • Union and industry bodies • WHS professional bodies • Technical information and data • Research literature • Manufacturers' manuals and specifications • Internet, blogs, YouTube • Books, journals and magazines • Social networks (e.g. Facebook, Twitter)	• Workers • WHS policies and procedures • Work instructions, job and work system analyses • Risk assessments (past and present) • Material safety data sheets (MSDSs) and registers • Manufacturers' manuals • WHS positive performance indicators • Insurance and incident investigation records • Workers' compensation data • Safety handbooks • Employee information papers, brochures, notes and newsletters • WHS reports, including workplace inspections, hazard and incident reports, technical reports, consultations and observations

Some useful sources of information for the health and safety manager can be found in the 'Additional resources' section at the end of this chapter. The following is an alert sent out by NT WorkSafe, a division of the Northern Territory Department of Justice,[1] and represents one form of information that may need to be circulated in your workplace.

HEALTH AND SAFETY ALERT

Asbestos Gaskets in Imported Plant

Purpose

A Safety Alert has been issued by WorkSafe WA after items of plant were recently imported into Western Australia and found to contain bonded asbestos gaskets. The plant was imported from New Zealand and Thailand for installation at a major industrial site in that state. Workers at the site were unaware that any gaskets contained asbestos.

Contributing Factors

- All forms of asbestos-containing materials have been prohibited imports in Australia since 31 December 2003.
- Gaskets containing-asbestos are still manufactured in some other countries.
- Plant was imported that included temporary shipping gaskets containing asbestos.
- Gaskets containing asbestos may have a similar appearance to non-asbestos gaskets.

Recommendations

1 Importers should ensure that imported plant does not contain asbestos-containing materials.
2 Suspect material should be analysed by a National Association of Testing Authorities (NATA) accredited laboratory.
3 Any removal work must be carried out by a competent person such as a licensed asbestos removalist.
4 Removal methods for asbestos gaskets and other asbestos containing materials are found in the Code of Practice for the Safe Removal of Asbestos.
5 Asbestos waste must be disposed of at a licensed asbestos disposal site.

Further Information

Code of Practice for the Management and Control of Asbestos in Workplaces [NOHSC:2018(2005)]
Code of Practice for the Safe Removal of Asbestos, 2nd edition [NOHSC:2002(2005)]
Australian Customs Service website: www.customs.gov.au

Information on workplace safety matters is available at NT WorkSafe:
GPO Box 1722 Darwin NT 0801
Telephone: 1800 019 115
Facsimile: (08) 8999 5141
Email: ntworksafe@nt.gov.au
Website: www.worksafe.nt.gov.au

Source: Reproduced courtesy of WorkSafe, Department of Commerce, Western Australia (www.worksafe.wa.gov.au).

So, with all this information, where do you start? The following case study is a useful introduction.

In each of the capital cities, a major pharmaceutical producer operates warehouses in which imported over-the-counter drugs are stored for pick-up and distribution by the pharmacy chains. Forklifts and pallets are used to store goods in bays. Each warehouse has a manager and supervisor and a small number of warehouse workers, who store the incoming supplies and load the distributors' trucks and vans. A significant number of Cambodian immigrants work in the two largest warehouses. The warehouse managers report to the chief operations officer. The major HS hazards are fire, manual handling and plant (forklifts).

Questions

1 What do you think are the main information requirements of the warehouse manager?
2 What format would be most appropriate for them?

In this chapter we refer to this hypothetical example to illustrate how you can best manage information.

The first step in managing information involves two parts: *identifying needs* and then *designing and developing the processes* to meet the needs. After that comes implementation – actually collecting and producing the information, storing it (much of it online), distributing or making sure it is available, using the information in the workplace, maintaining and disposing it. Finally, there is ongoing monitoring, evaluating and reviewing the WHS information system.

This chapter deals with the first step of identifying information needs and designing the processes. The implementation is up to you and your organisation. General monitoring, evaluating and reviewing of your WHSMS activities should reveal whether there any faults in the information system. The specific informational requirements of the HS manager are looked at – what information you must have and what you must produce – and then we look at some of the standards and pitfalls associated with managing information.

IDENTIFYING NEEDS

To learn what information on specifications or requirements you require, begin by going to the WHS program of activities – the requirements set out in your WHSMS, if you are using one – to see what information is necessary to make each of the activities listed in the program successful. This is your starting point. (Figure 4.2 in Chapter 4 gives you a good picture of what sort of documents are needed.)

Some common program headings would be

- training
- consultation
- identifying hazards and managing risk
- developing and maintaining health and safety policies and procedures
- inspecting workplaces
- promoting health
- preparing for emergencies
- notifying, reporting and investigating incidents
- auditing health and safety

- providing medical aid and first aid
- compensating and rehabilitating injured workers.

From there, the information needs should be settled during the course of developing the WHS program, often with those responsible for implementing the program activities, but in some cases, it will be just you, the health and safety manager.

KEY QUESTIONS

The first three questions deal with identifying the specifications or needs.

1 What information is needed to make the WHS activity successful?
2 Who will use it?
3 What format is needed?

The remaining questions deal with designing and developing the processes to meet the specifications or needs.

4 How is the information to be collected, produced or amended?
5 Where and how will it be stored?
6 How will it be distributed?
7 How is to be maintained?
8 How will it be disposed of when it is no longer needed?

Sometimes the information required will be an *input* – information already produced. Information on potential hazards, for example, is required to identify and control such hazards. This information may come from a number of internal and external sources. Other information needs will be *products* or *outputs*; for example, reports produced regarding the results of identifying hazards and managing their risk. These, in turn, may require report training.

The role of the health and safety officer or manager is to help those responsible for each of the activities to be aware of the information needs and provide assistance in obtaining and using the information. In the case study, the warehouse manager will need to know what the policy and procedures are for manual handling in order to manage the risk, and will need to prepare information in a specified form as well; for example, reports on workplace inspections and incidents. The health and safety manager will also need to know what those requirements are if they are to assist.

In the course of going through each of the health and safety program activities, the health and safety manager will also identify information requirements they have; for example, the latest information on health and safety standards, changes in the law, proposed changes to work processes, reports to senior management and so on.

Remember that everyone is both an information user – one who needs information to decide and act – and an information provider – one who provides information to others who need to decide and act. Managers, supervisors, HS committee members, HS managers, contractors and staff have differing situations and needs as information users and providers.

Figure 5.3 *The flow of information*

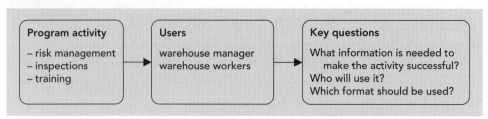

In any case, the key questions listed in Figure 5.4 should be asked after selecting the activity. The case study of the warehouse manager is used as an illustration.

Figure 5.4 *Information requirements*

KEY QUESTION	PROGRAM ACTIVITY: RISK MANAGEMENT
1 What are the main information requirements (inputs or outputs) to make the activity successful?	Knowledge of appropriate controls: principally, the fire brigade requirements (sprinklers, extinguishers, alarms, exits and drills); safe manual handling practices; safe working procedures for use of the forklifts; driver certification requirements; maintenance procedures
2 Who will use this information?	All workers in the warehouse should know the controls as everyone is called on to work at various tasks throughout the day. However, the manager and supervisor should know the detailed requirements in order to plan and supervise the implementation of the controls. The manager and supervisor need the information to induct and instruct all employees.
3 What format is required?	Text, videos, maps (access and egress, written emergency exits, assembly points), graphics (signage). Summary procedures and signage will need to be in Khmer as well as English.

Here we have looked only at one small example of how you would identify information needs. When compiling such details from each of the program activities, the requirements of a WHS information system will be fleshed out. Database requirements for ensuring the information is accessible and up to date, for example, will become clearer. It is only after working through the WHS program activities that the bigger picture is put together.

There are three considerations – internal workplace factors, technical considerations and legal requirements – when asking and answering the key questions.

Internal workplace factors

Internal workplace factors must be considered. These include the

- size of the organisation and industry type
- organisational structure
- management style and WHS knowledge and skills found within the organisation
- workplace culture, industrial relations and safety culture
- other management systems requiring interface or integration with the information and data processes for WHS
- resources available
- nature of the hazards and level of risk from each
- staff profile, including language, literacy and numeracy, and cultural diversity.

Technical considerations

Specific technical considerations that your systems or information officer may be able to help you with are

- the required level of security for the WHSMS, including prevention of theft and fraud
- access security
- prevention of interruption of services
- inadvertent release of sensitive material
- information data destruction, corruption and alteration.

Legal requirements

Finally, are there any specific legal requirements related to the activity? Such requirements could include

- the WHS Act and regulations
- workers' compensation
- equity and workplace diversity
- privacy
- freedom of information
- trade practices
- standards: national, international, industry.

DID YOU KNOW?

The regulators' websites offer free subscriptions to newsletters containing up-to-date information. For example, WorkCover NSW offers the following.

> WorkCover News, a quarterly workplace safety and injury management magazine containing case studies, practical information and coverage of important safety matters. WorkCover eNews regularly provides small to medium sized businesses with practical tools to address workplace health and safety concerns as well as topical information on upcoming WorkCover events. Construction eNews has been introduced to help keep you informed with the latest on workplace safety and workers' compensation specifically for the construction industry. This includes safety alerts, new programs, rebates, forthcoming workshops and other events.

WorkCover News is available from the WorkCover NSW website at http://www.workcover .nsw.gov.au/FORMSPUBLICATIONS/Pages/default.aspx?Category=WorkCover+Information& SubCategory=WorkCover+News.

Depending on the nature of the activity, policies and procedures may need to be developed to deal with information. The use of pre-placement medical information or ongoing health surveillance, for example, often requires policies to be developed so that people can be assured of their rights to privacy and fair treatment. The need for policy and procedures must be made clear and agreed upon, as will the nature of the policy and procedures themselves.

Keeping these considerations in mind is made easier by consulting directly with those affected in the course of developing the WHS program activities. These people will have operational knowledge that can be drawn on to check that the information specifications are all there. You can draw, too, on the specialist knowledge others have. If, for example, you have a company secretary or counsel, ask them to provide you with help on the legal details. Human resource managers, industrial relations officers, IT officers and website managers can also assist.

Specifying information needs can be the biggest task of designing and implementing successful WHS program activities. Once that has been done, the next task is to design the processes.

DESIGNING AND DEVELOPING INFORMATION PROCESSES

The design of the required information and data processes will be peculiar to each of the activities. However, there will be experience within the organisation, and the communication or information officers should be able to help. Otherwise, draw on the experience of other health and safety managers, preferably in your industry, or perhaps use an information consultant. You will need to investigate the format for and the availability of databases to identify the most suitable form of presentation – electronic or paper-based. Remember, it has all been done before.

People who could be consulted are

- ergonomic experts
- occupational hygienists
- health professionals (for example, doctors, occupational health nurses, psychologists, physiotherapists, occupational therapists)
- legal practitioners
- injury management advisers
- emergency services personnel who may need to access your company's hazardous substances and **dangerous goods** information and data, or relevant medical records, such as
    - medical and first aid personnel
    - information and data technology, and database management support.

Fire services or a suitably qualified professional can tell you where information can be found on controls needed to manage any fire risk. Professional assistance (for example, interpreters) may also be needed to deal with language constraints.

DEVELOPING THE PROCESSES

Once the requirements have been identified and the design of the processes have been discussed and recommended, tools to record and collate information are needed. These days, such tools are mostly electronic-based. The financial, IT and human resources for the successful collection, analysis, reporting and recording of data must be set out. Tools could include registers, software for information and data recording and analysis, performance monitoring charts and checklists and handbooks. Arrangements also should be made for the establishment of a system of backup or archiving and storage or disposal of the information and data.

The questions listed in Figure 5.5 deal with processes, referring again to the case study. These questions should be asked during consultation over the WHS program.

Figure 5.5 *Design requirements*

KEY QUESTION	PROGRAM ACTIVITY: RISK MANAGEMENT
4 How is the information to be collected or produced?	The health and safety manager will need to collect some of the information – for example, latest standards – and inform the division where to collect the remainder – for example, information on fire safety.
5 Where will it be stored?	Text-based information will be put on the firm's Intranet for downloading. The warehouse manager will have hard copy of the rest.
6 How will it be distributed?	The warehouse manager will distribute summary policy, procedures and standards to all workers in the course of special instruction and induction of new employees. Summary policy and procedures need to be posted in the warehouse, together with signage in English and Khmer. Videos demonstrating the controls will be used for induction training. Maps identifying exits and assembly points are to be posted, as are internal and external contact details.
7 How will it be maintained?	The information on the Intranet is the responsibility of the health and safety manager, who has a subscription service to assist in the updating. They will also need to determine who has the authority to amend and/or update the information. Only authorised personnel will be given 'write' access to the information on the Intranet. A fire safety consultant will keep the firm abreast of fire safety developments.
8 How will it be disposed of?	Out-of-date information is to be disposed of (recycled wherever possible) on receipt of current information. There are no archival requirements.

The warehouse manager in the case study must have a system of collecting the risk management information. The information may simply be provided on the Intranet. Some of the information needed would be data relating to when the information was provided, where and to whom.

Links with other functional areas and management systems may be required to ensure that the information requirements are being met. Details on information collection and delivery should be monitored in reports by the warehouse manager to the chief operations officer and possibly copied to the health and safety manager.

Throughout this process, everyone needs to know their roles and responsibilities. It should not, for example, be the responsibility – normally – of the warehouse manager alone to develop the process of collecting information or devising tools. The manager should be assisted by the health and safety manager. However, once the process has been set up, it is up to the warehouse manager, with the help of the HS manager, to collect and use the information and, again with the possible assistance of the HS manager, monitor and evaluate its effectiveness.

MONITOR, EVALUATE AND REVIEW EFFECTIVENESS

The central question is does the information and data enable the activities to be successful? This could be asked at any time while monitoring the activities themselves. If, say, the WHS training activities did not meet their objectives, could it have been as a result of poor information provided at the courses? Did any incident point to a lack of appropriate or timely information? Were the processes up to the task? Are there better ways of meeting the information requirements of the program?

While the frequency, method and scope of review should be discussed and agreed upon by employees and other stakeholders, holding such a discussion should not be left for more than a year. Recommendations for improvement should be made and implemented whenever the monitoring and reviewing processes reveal any opportunities. A subcommittee of the HS committee could be used for this purpose. Sometimes the use of consultants or internal expertise from other areas with similar information issues can assist by bringing fresh eyes to the system.

Managing HS information is critical to the success of the WHS program and its evaluation, as discussed in the previous chapter. It is of special importance to the core activity of identifying hazards and assessing risk, as we shall see in the next chapter.

THE INFORMATION NEEDS OF THE HS MANAGER

We began with the information needs of the WHS program and worked from there. In so doing, we have created an ordered way of answering all the questions relating to WHS information management in the organisation. You should now have an understanding of what you, as the person responsible for health and safety management, should have and do in order to fulfil your information management responsibilities.

In general terms, you require the following key inputs, as well as analytical and reporting skills, to carry out your duties (see Figure 5.6).

In Chapter 4, in the section 'Step 5: Setting objectives, targets and key performance indicators', we discussed how HS performance should be measured – the importance of having a range of outcome indicators, determining key performance indicators and defining targets. We also touched on analysis. Chapter 10 offers information on analysis of trends, which deals with terms such as 'median', 'mode' and 'mean'. In this chapter we look at some of what is involved in ensuring the quality of that process.

| Figure 5.6 | *Information needs of the HS manager* |

Inputs	• *Performance data*: for example, incident reports, environmental and health monitoring, compensation statistics, rehabilitation data, absenteeism statistics, information relating to process indicators (for example, inspection statistics, HS committee meeting data, induction and training output data)
	• *Reports and records*: for example, inspection reports, investigation reports, HS committee minutes, risk assessments, job safety analyses, medical records, certificates, registrations, licences, general correspondence
	• *Information on hazards and controls*: for example, MSDSs, WHS manuals, computer databases, hazard registers, codes of practice
	• *Information on requirements*: for example, legal databases and subscription services, company policy manuals, standard operating procedures, reporting forms and schedules

RECORDING AND ANALYSING INFORMATION

A major purpose of any WHS information system is to record, monitor and evaluate HS performance. Can we identify associations between workplace hazards and adverse effects on exposed workers? Are there trends or hot spots? Are we going forwards, backwards or staying put?

To answer such questions, performance data should be gathered and assembled. Data can then be keyed into spreadsheets, where it can be analysed and updated. Many off-the-shelf software programs will suit organisations such as smaller businesses. After some instruction, spreadsheets are, generally, relatively easy to use and are adaptable to particular management reporting formats.

Most importantly, you need to be aware of the limitations of the input data you are using and the different ways of interpreting it. Figure 5.7 shows the example of incident reporting.

| Figure 5.7 | *Factors involved in incident reporting* |

Error	The person making the report may have written down wrong information.
Unreliable	People may be under-reporting, thereby making the reporting system unreliable.
Error	The administrative clerk may have encoded the incident inaccurately.
Irrelevant	The fact that the incident occurred in the Easter period may be irrelevant.
Invalid	The conclusion that the incident was due to poor instruction may be affected by limited information or data, bias or bad logic.

Clearly, information and analysis need to be tested for accuracy, reliability, relevance and validity. In particular, data analysis and the drawing of conclusions should not be affected by forms of bias; otherwise, you have only invalid conclusions. Some of the more common biases are described in Figure 5.8.

While skill and experience may help you overcome bias, review by others is the very best check.

Ethics

Records may need to be made of any patterns of occupational injury and disease within particular areas, which must be done ethically to take into consideration requirements for privacy, confidentiality and access to personal records. The outcomes of such analyses

Figure 5.8	*Forms of bias*	
Information bias	The information or data used to draw conclusions is limited or one-sided.
Selection bias	The sample population chosen is not representative of the population (at risk).
Measurement bias	How you measure can affect outcomes as it affects the scope of the data collected.
Confounding bias	Confounding bias occurs when two factors are closely associated and the effects of one confuse or distort the effects of the other factor on the outcome. The distorting factor is a confounding variable.
Recall bias	The recall of exposures or events may differ.
Attention bias (Hawthorne effect)	Attention bias occurs when subjects systematically alter their behaviour when they are being observed.
'Referee' bias	The investigator is predisposed to deriving certain outcomes, even after a full investigation.

should then be suitably formatted and disseminated, considering the target audience and respecting legal and ethical requirements.

In the next chapter, which deals with hazard identification and managing risk, assistance from the health and safety manager with information gathering and information production should be appreciated by everyone in the organisation.

Summary

- 'Information management' describes the measures required for the effective collection, storage, distribution, access, use, maintenance and disposal of information to support business processes.
- To find out your information requirements, simply go to the WHS program to see what information is needed to make each of the activities listed in the program successful.
- The main questions are:
  - What information is needed to make the WHS activity successful?
  - Who will use it?
  - What format is needed?
  - How is it to be collected or produced?
  - Where will it be stored?
  - How will it be distributed?
  - How is to be maintained?
  - How will it be disposed of?
- Everyone is an information user – one who needs information to decide and act – and an information provider – one who provides information to others who need to decide and act.
- The identification of requirements, design, development, implementation, monitoring and review depend heavily on effective consultation with all users and stakeholders. The use of specialist advice, both internal and external, will assist greatly.
- Information and data and their analysis must be checked for accuracy, reliability, relevance and validity.

In your workplace

You are the principal of a small state primary school in an outback regional centre. The school employs eight full-time teachers and four support staff and cleaners. The main WHS issues are heat (air-conditioning), communicable diseases and manual handling.

1 How would you determine the WHS information needs?
2 Who will use it?
3 What format is needed?
4 How is it to be collected or produced?
5 Where will it be stored?
6 How will it be distributed?
7 How is to be maintained?
8 How will it be disposed of when it is no longer needed?

Questions

1 What are the eight steps of WHS information management?
2 What are the key questions to be asked when identifying needs?
3 Using the example of a workplace inspection
   a How would you define 'accuracy', 'reliability' and 'validity'?
   b How would you check for bias in the report and its conclusions?
4 Identify the information requirements in your workplace for effective emergency procedures. How are those requirements being met? How may the information management be improved?
5 In your organisation, how is information on hazards managed? Is there a hazards register? Could it be improved?

Activities

1 Using a search engine, type 'OHS software', 'safety management software', 'safety reporting software'. Examine the products and, if you can, assess their suitability for your workplace.
2 Examine Safe Work Australia's *Key Work Health and Safety Statistics* on their website and note the different types of graphs used to explain the statistics. Then look at the statistics from your workplace. What graphs, if any, does your workplace use? How would you improve them? What is the range of suitable graphs available?

Search me!

 Explore **Search me! management** for relevant articles on health and safety information. Search me! is an online library of world-class journals, ebooks and newspapers, including *The Australian* and the *New York Times*, and is updated daily. Log in to Search me! through www.cengage.com/sso using the access card in the front of this book.

KEYWORDS

Try searching for the following terms:
▶ health and safety statistics
▶ health and safety reporting
▶ health and safety software programs

Search tip: **Search me! management** contains information from both local and international sources. To get the greatest number of search results, try using both Australian and American spellings in your searches, e.g. 'globalisation' and 'globalization'; 'organisation' and 'organization'.

Additional resources

For the WHS manager, some basic information management may be bought in the form of software packages that enable requirements and activities to be tracked, workplaces and compensation cases to be monitored, data collected and analysed, and reports generated. However, spreadsheets are easy to use and apply to local circumstances. It is worth visiting the jurisdiction websites to see how their statistics units deal with the collection and analysis of WHS performance information.

- The *Compendium of Workers' Compensation Statistics Australia*, produced annually by Safe Work Australia, discusses the problems of WHS information gathering. It can be found at http://safeworkaustralia.gov.au/AboutSafeWorkAustralia/WhatWeDo/Statistics/Pages/CompendiumOfWorkersCompensationStatistics.aspx.
- Articles and books about information management tend to focus on IT solutions and technical applications. In this chapter we have looked at information management as a process of all WHS activity whether IT-based or not.
- Information on WHS performance measurement can be found in the 'Additional resources' in Chapter 4. There are a number of good introductory books on statistics and the pitfalls associated with using them. The following is one of the best in terms of WHS: Janicak, C., 2009, *Safety Metrics: Tools and Techniques for Measuring Safety Performance*, 2nd edn, Government Institutes: Maryland, USA.

Endnotes

1   NT WorkSafe administers the Workplace Health and Safety Act, Dangerous Goods (Road and Rail Transport) Act, Dangerous Goods Act, Radioactive Ores and Concentrates (Packaging and Transport) Act, and the Electricity Reform Act on behalf of the Northern Territory Government.

IDENTIFYING HAZARDS AND MANAGING RISK

Learning Objectives

By the end of this chapter, the reader will be able to understand the principles required to:

- establish the context and define the parameters of a WHS risk study
- analyse the WHS risk of a task or process
- evaluate the WHS risk of a task or process
- identify appropriate risk controls
- monitor and review the effectiveness of risk management activities.

INTRODUCTION

Employers must make sure – as far as reasonably practical – that their workplaces are free from hazards that could cause injury or illness to their workers or to other people in the workplace, such as customers or visitors. The law requires employers to use a **risk management** approach to ensure that their workplaces are safe for everyone who enters there.[1]

A 'hazard' is a dangerous action, situation or occurrence. A 'risk' is the likelihood and consequence of the hazard affecting people or property. 'Risk management' is the term given to the systematic identification of hazards, the assessment (analysis and evaluation) of risks posed by the hazards, and the control of those risks, either by eliminating the hazard entirely or by minimising the risk.[2]

Managing risk is proactive in that it tries to prevent injury from occurring by dealing with hazards before they can cause any harm. It also applies to future as well as current arrangements. Whenever changes to the workplace are proposed or new information on work processes comes to light, the risks to health and safety must be identified and managed. It is an approach that is used widely in WHS law.

RISK MANAGEMENT

LEGISLATIVE BACKGROUND

Section 19 of the Work Health and Safety Act states that:

> (1) A person conducting a business or undertaking must ensure, so far as is reasonably practicable, the health and safety of:
> (a) workers engaged, or caused to be engaged by the person
> (b) workers whose activities in carrying out work are influenced or directed by the person, while the workers are at work in the business or undertaking.

Section 18 states:

> In this Act, *reasonably practicable*, in relation to a duty to ensure health and safety, means that which is, or was at a particular time, reasonably able to be done in relation to ensuring health and safety, taking into account and weighing up all relevant matters including:
> (a) the likelihood of the hazard or the risk concerned occurring
> (b) the degree of harm that might result from the hazard or the risk
> (c) what the person concerned knows, or ought reasonably to know, about:
> (i) the hazard or the risk
> (ii) ways of eliminating or minimising the risk
> (d) the availability and suitability of ways to eliminate or minimise the risk
> (e) after assessing the extent of the risk and the available ways of eliminating or minimising the risk, the cost associated with available ways of eliminating or minimising the risk, including whether the cost is grossly disproportionate to the risk.

Risk management, then, is a core element of any WHS program, together with other programs such as training, health promotion and injury management. It forms a central element of the larger WHS management system.[3] Health and safety risk management should be part of the day-to-day risk management that organisations use to deal with potential deviations from planned activities, such as IT backup, preventive maintenance, plant and equipment testing and business continuity planning.

DID YOU KNOW?

Young males (20–24 years) are at the highest risk of workplace injury. In Australia in 2005–06, male workers aged 20–24 years experienced the highest injury rate of all workers; that is, 98 injuries per 1000 workers compared to female workers of the same age whose injury rate was 51 per 1000 workers. In contrast, older workers, aged 55 years and over, experienced the lowest work-related injury rates – 50 per 1000 employed. Unlike all of the younger age groups, the injury rates for men and women in this age group were similar.

Source: Australian Bureau of Statistics, *4102.0 – Australian Social Trends*, 2007

Managing WHS risk is made up of five basic steps, as shown in Figure 6.1.

Figure 6.1 *The risk management process*

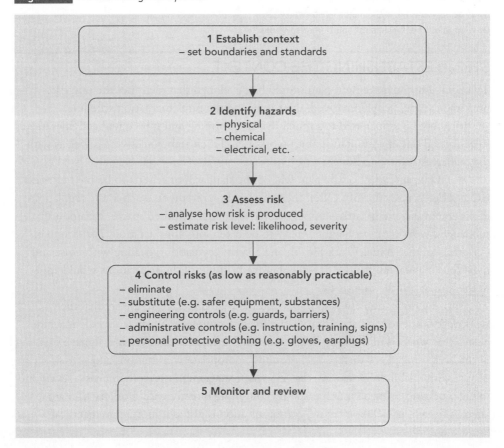

In this chapter we look at these five basic steps in more detail, using Australian standard AS/NZS ISO 31000:2009 *Risk Management principles and guidelines* as the basis.[4] The following fictitious case study is used to illustrate the steps and how to deal with the risks associated with plant.

HANDY FOUNDRY

Handy Foundry has been operating as a family business since 1974. The business employs approximately 80 people in the manufacturing and marketing of ferrous castings, the bulk of which are for automotive and transmission use. All the workers in manufacturing are labour hire.

At the dressing room or shotblast area, a labourer is required to load, by hand only, a ball mill with ferrous castings, principally disc brakes, for discharge to a cleaner where they are deburred, removed of sand and sorted into bins.

This is done from a standing position but requires some reaching, bending over into the container to pick up the disc brakes and carrying to the ball mill where they are thrown into the input feed of the mill. The disc brakes are loaded individually in loads of 40 at a time over approximately 12-minute cycles. The minimum weight is 4 kilograms, the maximum 13.5 kilograms. There are approximately three to four loads per hour. The standard day is eight hours and overtime is worked from time to time.

The process is batch operated, while the system of work and plant layout are open-ended, thereby allowing a variation in duties and the capacity to split into rest periods and share responsibilities.

Discussion questions

1 What do you think is the major risk to workers?
2 What might be the simplest solution or solutions?

STEP 1: ESTABLISHING THE CONTEXT

To begin, a risk management plan should be developed that identifies the purpose, principles, scope, people involved, their roles and the implementation schedule.

It cannot be emphasised too much that the planning and subsequent activities need to be carried out in consultation with workers and their representatives, as well as with the managers and supervisors.

An important aspect of the plan will be the standards or criteria to be used to assess risk and determine controls. Often there are legal requirements, such as the regulations dealing with specific hazards – noise, manual handling, confined spaces, hazardous substances, working from heights, etc. – to be taken into consideration. For example, Chapter 4 of the Model Work Health and Safety Regulations, dealing with noise and hazardous manual tasks and Part 4.6 (Abrasive blasting) of the regulations would apply to the foundry in the case study.

Anti-discrimination law and policy must also be respected to ensure that the workplace is safe for and accommodating to all. Examples of practice include machine guards that workers of differing height and size are capable of operating, signage that is suitable for people of various backgrounds, appropriate workstations and access for people with disabilities. Ensuring that HS risk management meets the needs of everyone in the workplace is made much easier by consulting directly with workers who are affected. Again, in WHS, effective communication is just as important as technical knowledge.

There may also be corporate requirements that set higher standards or address operational hazards in more detail than the law does. This may occur, for example, in a factory using good manufacturing practice standards. If you have a quality assurance program, consult the program directors to see whether the standards or criteria are going to have an impact on WHS.

Finally, judgements about high, medium and low risk and tolerable risk should be guided by criteria. Definitions and examples of what each level of risk means should be agreed upon by all parties and clearly set out in the documentation. Some suggestions are found below.

Once these judgements are made, the organisation should then be grouped into workplaces for risk management purposes, usually as locations or functional groups; for example, purchasing, maintenance. This provides boundaries and a scope to the individual activities. Some workplaces (say, a quarry) will be more risky than others (say, the accounts department), so establishing context is important before planning and setting priorities.

As part of the planning process for implementing risk management, managers, supervisors and health and safety representatives will need to be trained beforehand in the risk management process and the use of a hazard register. SafeWork South Australia defines a hazard register as 'a summarised record of the hazards identified in a business, where the hazards occur, and the tasks, machinery or situations with which they are associated'.[5] A basic blank hazard register format is set out in Figure 6.2.

A spreadsheet format is useful for data collection and analysis. More detailed hazard registers can be developed.

STEP 2: IDENTIFYING HAZARDS

Before the level of risk can be determined and reduced it is necessary to identify what are the risks in your workplace. A hazard is simply a situation that has the potential to harm people physically or psychologically. The hazards in each workplace, then, need to be located and identified. The risk is the possible outcome – the likelihood and consequence – of a person being exposed to the hazard. Risks are analysed and evaluated after the hazards have been first identified. Hazards can be grouped to assist checking, as shown in Figure 6.3.

In the sample hazard register in Figure 6.2, these general categories have been further subdivided.

There are two ways of identifying hazards: desktop information collection and onsite inspection. These methods can include systematic (formal) and incidental (informal) identification of hazards. Systematic identification can be achieved through both desktop information collection and onsite inspection, whereas incidental hazard identification may arise from complaints, or informal observation. Both desktop information collection and onsite inspections are necessary.

Figure 6.2 Blank sample page from a hazard register

WORKPLACE:						INSP. DATE:		INSPECTOR:		
PROCESS	HAZARDS	POTENTIAL INJURY	SEVERITY	PROBABILITY	RISK	CONTROL	RESP. PERSON	IMP. DATE	CHECK DATE

Report reviewed by manager: _____ Date: _____.

Report reviewed by HS rep. _____ Date: _____.

Hazard code: PE (plant and equipment), E (electrical), C (chemical), MT (manual tasks), OOS (occupational overuse syndrome), B (biological), P (psychological), (N) noise, WE (working environment)

Consequence: 1 = Insignificant; 2 = Minor; 3 = Moderate; 4 = Major; 5 = Severe

Likelihood: A = Almost certain; B = Likely; C = Possible; D = Unlikely; E = Rare

Risk: Low = 1C, 1D, 1E, 2D, 2E; Medium = 1A, 1B, 2B, 2C, 3D, 3E, 4D, 4E, 5E; High = 2A, 3A, 3B, 3C, 4B, 4C, 5D; Very High = 4A, 5A, 5B, 5C

Figure 6.4 *Handy Foundry hazard and risk register*

WORKPLACE: FOUNDRY						INSP. DATE: 4/10/10	INSPECTOR: R. ATKINS		
PROCESS	HAZARDS	POTENTIAL INJURY	SEVERITY	PROBABILITY	RISK	CONTROL	RESP. PERSON	IMP. DATE	CHECK DATE
shotblast	PE – guard damaged								
grinders	WE – dust								
grinders	E – extension cords								
pattern and core making	MT – manual tasks								
etc.									

Figure 6.5 *Handy Foundry hazard and risk register (identifying potential injuries)*

WORKPLACE: FOUNDRY						INSP. DATE: 4/10/10	INSPECTOR: R. ATKINS		
PROCESS	HAZARDS	POTENTIAL INJURY	SEVERITY	PROBABILITY	RISK	CONTROL	RESP. PERSON	IMP. DATE	CHECK DATE
shotblast	PE – guard damaged	knock/abrasion							
grinders	WE – dust	damaged lungs							
grinders	E – extension cords	fall/abrasion							
pattern and core making	manual tasks	sprains/strains							
etc.									

STEP 3: ASSESSING THE RISK

Figure 6.6 *Foundry pattern-making shop*

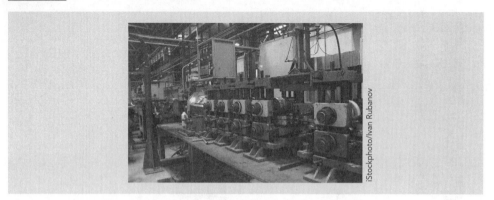

Having identified the hazards in the workplace, the next step is to assess the risk they pose to people.

This means *analysing the risk*, seeing how the hazard could lead to injury or disease; for example, monitoring atmospheric contaminants to see how they could lead to illness, or identifying the movements or postures that could lead to back problems. In the foundry, workers involved in pattern and core making can be required to lift loads, perform repetitive movements and work in a fixed position, which can lead to sprain and strain damage to upper back and shoulders.

By analysing the risk, you are assessing the effectiveness of any controls put in place to control the hazard. Among the factors affecting the risk of injury in the case study is the position of the disc brakes in the container, which forces the worker to bend over and pick them up. There are no controls to prevent injury.

Estimate how big the risk is, given any existing precautions or what are termed 'controls'; for example, which people may be affected, how many people, how likely they are to be affected and how badly affected.

A very high-risk workplace is one where things are certain to go wrong and have the severest consequences for everyone involved. A very low-risk workplace is one where things rarely go wrong and, if they did, only one or two people would require some minor first aid.

In estimating the size of the risk, estimates of severity (impact) and probability (likelihood) are made on the basis of

- the experience of those involved
- data from the organisation's experience
- information obtained from the insurer, government agencies or industry bodies.

Consideration needs to be given to the numbers of people expected to be exposed to the hazard, together with the frequency and duration of exposure to the hazard. As numbers, frequency and duration increase, so too does risk. At Handy Foundry there are five people working on pattern and core making, so there are five people who are at risk of injury from the manual tasks hazard involved in the pattern-and core-making process.

Consider the types of people likely to be exposed – experienced and inexperienced employees, contractors, cleaners and visitors – as this will affect the risk assessment.

Finally, the law and codes of practice may require you to consider factors specific to certain hazards. With excavation, for example, consideration should be made of

- the fall or dislodging of earth and rock
- instability of the excavation or any adjoining structure
- inrush or seepage of water
- unplanned contact with utility services; for example, electricity cables and gas mains
- placement of excavated material
- falls into excavations
- movement and positioning of heavy plant and equipment affecting the excavation
- ground vibration affecting the stability of the excavation and nearby built structures
- vehicle movement
- excessive noise from the operation of machinery and plant
- manual handling injuries
- changes to excavation conditions.

The point of estimating the level of risk is not to make precise scientific calculations, but to determine priorities and assess the time, money and effort needed to manage the risk. The risk level is determined by assessment of the consequences (severity of the injury) and the likelihood (a probability on the estimate of how soon) that an injury of that severity might occur.

The tables below show one method used to classify the severity, likelihood and risk level.[7] Use Figure 6.7 to estimate consequences (severity).

Use Figure 6.8 to estimate likelihood (probability).

Figure 6.7 *Estimating consequences*

CONSEQUENCES		
LEVEL	DESCRIPTOR	EXAMPLES
1	Insignificant	Injuries not requiring first aid
2	Minor	First aid required
3	Moderate	Medical treatment required
4	Major	Hospital admission required
5	Severe	Death or permanent disability to one or more persons

The consequences and likelihood ratings assigned to the incident or injuries are then multiplied to provide a total risk rating and ranked as 'high', 'medium' or 'low'. Many HS managers like to represent the calculation in the form of a matrix with axes of likelihood and consequences.

The method in the example is applied by the University of New South Wales to determine risk levels and is similar to that used in many other workplaces. More

Figure 6.8 *Estimating likelihood*

LIKELIHOOD		
LEVEL	DESCRIPTOR	EXAMPLES
A	Almost certain	Is expected to occur in most circumstances
B	Likely	Will probably occur in most circumstances
C	Possible	Could occur at some time
D	Unlikely	Not likely to occur in normal circumstances
E	Rare	May occur only in exceptional circumstances

Figure 6.9 *Risk level matrix*

LIKELIHOOD	CONSEQUENCES				
	INSIGNIFICANT 1	MINOR 2	MODERATE 3	MAJOR 4	SEVERE 5
Almost certain A	Medium	High	High	Very high	Very high
Likely B	Medium	Medium	High	High	Very high
Possible C	Low	Medium	High	High	Very high
Unlikely D	Low	Low	Medium	Medium	High
Rare E	Low	Low	Medium	Medium	Medium

sophisticated versions may be used to help assess risk and determine priorities, especially in high-risk industries.

In the Handy Foundry case study, the risk of musculoskeletal (sprain/strain) injury from pattern and core making would be likely (B), meaning that it will probably occur in most circumstances and the impact will be severe but not fatal (B), making the overall risk rating very high and, based on normal criteria, an urgent priority.

At the end of the risk assessment, you have a list of those hazards that, according to your criteria or standards, require action in some order of priority. Logically, you would give priority to those with the highest rating and look at how you could treat (control) the associated risk.

STEP 4: CONTROLLING THE RISK

The next step is to control the risk. There is a **hierarchy of controls** and the controls are ranked according to their effectiveness in controlling hazards at their source:

* elimination
* substitution; for example, less hazardous substances, better-designed equipment and workstations, job redesign
* isolation; for example, barriers, enclosures, remote handling, protective gates
* **engineering controls**; for example, guards, ventilation

Figure 6.10 *Handy Foundry hazard and risk register and risk rating*

WORKPLACE: FOUNDRY					INSP. DATE: 4/10/10		INSPECTOR: R. ATKINS			
PROCESS	HAZARDS	POTENTIAL INJURY	SEVERITY	PROBABILITY	RISK	CONTROL	RESP. PERSON	IMP. DATE	CHECK DATE
Pattern and core making	Manual tasks	Sprain/strain to upper back and shoulders	5	B	Very high				
etc.									

- administrative controls; for example, reducing exposure by rotating jobs or limiting access, training, policies and procedures
- personal protective clothing and equipment; for example, hard hats, safety boots, goggles, earmuffs, gloves.

The preference is always for elimination. However, if that is not practical because alternatives are unavailable or prohibitively expensive, then other methods of reducing the risk need to be explored, beginning with substitution and following on down the hierarchy. **Personal protective equipment (PPE)** is the last resort and is, by itself, the least effective method. Among other reasons for this is that people find this type of equipment difficult or awkward to wear and maintain.

Specific hazards, such as lead, noise and manual handling, may have regulations governing the methods of **risk control**. Check with authorities. Controls can then include

- physical devices, such as guards, barriers, earmuffs, alarms
- policies and procedures
- processes that are safer than those currently used.

Hazard controls should not impose unnecessary limitations on the employment of women (including pregnant women), people from non-English-speaking backgrounds and those with disabilities. Rather, they should widen employment opportunities. The process of identifying hazards, assessing the risk and settling on controls should take into consideration the whole range of potential employees. Raising the issue and consulting with workers is the key here. If the job is not safe for one person, it is probably not safe for anyone else to do either.

While the effectiveness of the control is a key consideration, the control should be commensurate with the risk, which is where cost comes in. If the risk is high, then the expense of controlling the risk is easier to justify. But as the risk reduces, then the cost in money, time and effort must suit the level of risk. There is no precise formula operating here but instead an understanding of what is tolerable. Industry standards tend to have a large part to play in determining whether a proposed control is insufficient, appropriate or excessive. Importantly, courts look to those standards if specific regulations do not apply. The point is that people and organisations are willing to tolerate some risk for the benefits that may be produced – productivity, comfort and enjoyment. People are willing to strike a balance and tolerate risk, but only if everything has been done to reduce the risk to as low as reasonably practicable.

ALARP

To understand the balance between risk and cost – money, time and effort – some have used the **ALARP** principle. ALARP is an acronym for 'as low as reasonably practicable'. An equivalent term, **ALARA**, 'as low as reasonably achievable', is more commonly used in North America.

As mentioned earlier in this book and chapter, 'reasonably practicable' is the term used to describe the standard to which persons conducting businesses and undertakings are to exercise their duty of care. The ALARP principle, illustrated in Figure 6.11, attempts to show how that standard is to be applied when managing risks. You will see that the width of the cone indicates the size of risk and the cone is divided into bands. When risk is close to intolerable, the expectation is that the risk will be reduced unless the cost is grossly disproportionate to the benefits gained. When risks are close to the negligible level then action may only be taken to reduce risk when benefits exceed the costs of reduction.

Figure 6.11 *The ALARP principle*

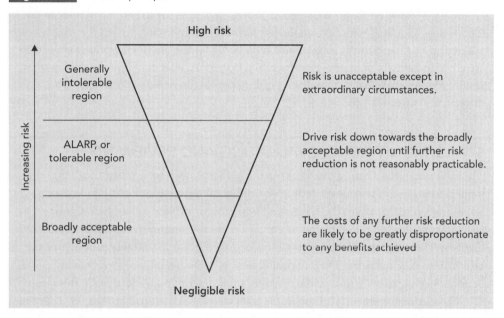

WHS IN PRACTICE

In the Handy Foundry case study changes designed to reduce the risk of injury from the pattern- and core-making process to as low as reasonably practicable might include

- redesigning the work processes or the physical work area
- using mechanical lifting devices
- providing task-specific training
- using personal protective equipment
- ensuring tools and equipment are regularly maintained
- ensuring adequate numbers of workers to do the work
- giving workers adequate rest breaks and work variety.

However, the preferred option is elimination by using an overhead crane that would feed steel bins of castings directly to the ball mill. Individual handling would therefore be removed entirely.

In the meantime, there may be the option of hiring a conveyor but the castings would still have to be loaded and the conveyor may not be of the required strength or size. Such an option would be described as altering or substituting the original process.

Another temporary measure is to reduce the exposure. Workers could be rotated through the job, possibly with two labourers working in tandem to take care of heavier castings. Rest breaks would be enforced and overtime allocated only to those who had not worked in the area in the previous 24 hours. Manual handling training would be given to all workers in the interim period. These would be considered administrative controls.

Having decided on the best course of action, any changes to controls – interim or long-term – should be written into the standard operating procedures.

Finally, and importantly, implementation dates for the control measures should be specified, as should the person responsible. Dates to check the implementation also should be recorded so that monitoring and reviewing to ensure continuous improvement can take place.

STEP 5: MONITORING, EVALUATING AND REVIEWING

The final step is monitoring the workplace and the controls to see, first of all, that the implementation of the controls took place and were effective and if any follow-up action is required. Second, there is a need with any workplace to conduct regular checking and ongoing monitoring to ensure continuous improvement. It is important that both these tasks be identified as a local management responsibility, not that of the health and safety manager. The responsibilities and accountabilities, as well as any performance measures found in the manager's job description, should make this clear.

The risk management plan should be reviewed at least annually to see whether the context needs changing, the hazards have all been identified, the risk assessment is accurate and the controls are effective. Regular reviews should occur as workplaces, jobs and personnel change. This can be done internally.

A third form of monitoring and reviewing is auditing the risk management program. This may be carried out as an external audit by contracting with professional health and safety auditors or internally using a team of trained auditors seconded from elsewhere within the organisation to look with fresh eyes at a different section of the business. Such audits normally focus on assessing whether the risk management system complies with corporate and legal requirements (see Chapter 13).

This last step of monitoring, evaluating and reviewing is often underdone, putting the original investment of time, money and energy at risk. Records should be kept not only for monitor and review reasons but also for reporting to senior management and publicising the lessons learned within the organisation. Where WHS targets have been set for managers, such stories send a powerful message and increase commitment to effective risk management.

When reviewing risk management measures, it is useful to select some – or all – and cost them to identify the net benefit (or loss) over a certain timeframe (one or two years). Benefits could include improved productivity, reduced insurance costs, less turnover, less administration and so on. The company financial officer or accountant may be able to help. Some benefits may not be able to be quantified but as long as they can be confirmed, use them to market health and safety.

The general principles of risk management apply to a wide variety of hazards; however, each hazard has its own peculiarities. As one example, we look in the following chapter at managing risk associated with plant.

Summary

- Systematically managing risks in the workplace is a fundamental part of any WHS program and general organisational risk management.
- Risk management forms the basis for modern WHS law. Codes of practice use a risk management framework to deal with specific hazards.
- Risk management critically depends on effective consultation and communication with managers and workers at every step.
- The basic steps involved in risk management are
  - identifying the context for risk management activities – the scope and standards to be used
  - identifying the hazards associated with each of the work processes
  - assessing the level of risk by analysing the risk and estimating the likelihood and severity of any injury or illness
  - treating (controlling) the risk either by eliminating it entirely or minimising it to as low as reasonably practicable using the hierarchy of controls
  - monitoring and reviewing the activities to continuously improve HS performance and successfully market WHS.

In your workplace

Surfboard Manufacture

A former Australian international board-riding champion has recently started a surfboard-making business in a beachside suburb of Geelong. The work is undertaken in a single-storey unit of an industrial complex. He employs five assistants, only one of whom is a qualified tradesperson (a carpenter). The surfboards are made of polyurethane foam cores, wooden stringers and layers of fibreglass and resin. All the work is carried out using handheld machine tools. Although the use of hand tools and noise levels are hazardous, the major hazard is exposure to hazardous substances such as fibreglass, resins, solvents and paints used in the manufacture. Disposable facemasks are provided as well as plastic goggles; however, some of the employees have expressed concern that these are not sufficient or appropriate controls to ensure their health and safety.

1   What controls are required to reduce the risk from exposure to hazardous substances in the surfboard factory?

Hint: make sure you consider the control hierarchy when preparing your answer. Refer to the regulations and the code of practice *Managing the Work Environment and Facilities*, as well as other codes of practice referred to earlier, available at http://safeworkaustralia .gov.au.

Aircraft Noise

A regional airport has attached to it an open plan maintenance workshop in a disused hangar that maintains DASH 8s for two airlines. There are 30 licensed aircraft maintenance engineers and a small number of apprentices, who are being taught by the local TAFE. The airport is also the location for training of RAAF pilots, and a number of jet trainers use the adjacent runway, as well as commercial and private planes of various sorts. The noise inside the workshop can be very high, regularly exceeding the limit of 85 decibels, and on the runway when a fighter is taking off noise can easily exceed the recommended peak levels of 140 decibels. The manager and supervisor of the workshop are very aware of the noise problem and the potential for noise-induced hearing loss and tinnitus. They are also aware of their obligations to the workforce, students, visitors and customers. However, so far, controls have been limited to the issuing of earmuffs to workers and apprentices.

1   Assess the risk to workers from the aircraft noise. Use the risk level matrix (Figure 6.9) to determine the risk rating when no controls are used and then reassess the risk rating when earmuffs are worn to see if the risk is reduced.

   Hint: Refer to the code of practice *Managing Noise and Preventing Hearing Loss at Work*, available at http://safeworkaustralia.gov.au.

Questions

1   What do the terms 'risk management', 'hazard' and 'risk' mean?
2   What are the main hazard groups?
3   What are the control categories in the hierarchy of control?
4   Identify the hazards in your workplace. What sort of information would you look for? Where would you look for it?

Activities

1   Using an example of a workplace you know, describe how you would plan risk management activities.
2   Develop a simple hazard register for your workplace and complete it. Make sure you give reasons for your risk assessment and selection of controls.
3   Using the following example, first individually and then in a group decide how would you apply the ALARP principle. Use the code of practice *Hazardous Manual Tasks*, available at http://safeworkaustralia.gov.au. Then compare results and discuss.

A large city hotel is being refurbished and updated. The dining room and its equipment can be improved to be more efficient and to reduce injury risk to staff. Some of the issues are that the waiting staff carry large, heavy trays; the crockery is thick and heavy; the sideboard unit where most of the clean crockery and glassware is kept is located at one end of the dining room and has shelves from waist height to floor level; and, in busy periods, staff carry more plates and are quickly and constantly moving between tables, the kitchen and the sideboard.

Search me!

Explore **Search me! management** for relevant articles on WHS risk management. Search me! is an online library of world-class journals, ebooks and newspapers, including *The Australian* and the *New York Times*, and is updated daily. Log in to Search me! through www.cengage.com/sso using the access card in the front of this book.

KEYWORDS

Try searching for the following terms:

▶ OHS risk management   ▶ hierarchy of controls
▶ tolerable risk   ▶ best manufacturing practice
▶ acceptable risk   ▶ hazardous substances
▶ ALARP   ▶ noise limits

Search tip: **Search me! management** contains information from both local and international sources. To get the greatest number of search results, try using both Australian and American spellings in your searches, e.g. 'globalisation' and 'globalization'; 'organisation' and 'organization'.

Additional resources

- Safe Work Australia's website, www.safeworkaustralia.gov.au, offers codes of practice and guidance material that illustrates proper risk management.
- The UK Health and Safety Executive's 'Five steps to risk assessment' puts risk management in simple terms. It can be found at www.hse.gov.uk/risk.
- The Standards Australia (SAI Global) website, www.saiglobal.com/search-publications/, can be searched to locate useful standards and guidelines such as AS 4801 *OHS management systems* and ISO 31000 *Risk management*.
- Each of the state and territory jurisdictions has a wealth of relevant and useful material available for downloading. Their websites are listed in Figure 2.2, Chapter 2.
- *Hazpak – Making Your Workplace Safer: Guide* by WorkCover NSW is one example of a popular guide to basic risk management, written to assist with compliance with basic risk management. It can be downloaded from the WorkCover NSW website at http://www.workcover.nsw.gov.au/Pages/default.aspx. Other government health and safety authorities have also produced valuable guides on applying risk management to WHS.
- Standard AS/NZS ISO 31000:2009 *Risk management* is the recognised framework for risk management and is readily applicable to WHS. However, it is not a WHS standard.

Endnotes

1 New Zealanders talk of 'hazard management' rather than 'risk management'. While the terminology is different, the principles are the same.

2 Terms such as 'risk assessment','risk analysis' and 'risk evaluation' are sometimes used slightly differently by individuals, organisations and jurisdictions. The use of different terms does not appear to affect the practice of risk management, which is what we are concerned with here.

3 In this book, risk management is a system of identifying hazards and assessing and controlling risk. The application of the system by an organisation is called 'a risk management program' and makes up part of the WHS program. The WHS program, the review of which is usually an annual event, is the active core of the WHS management system. Some identify WHS systems and programs as types of risk

management systems and programs. By contrast, this book treats risk management as a part of WHS, albeit a very important part.

4 The terminology has been changed slightly – for example, 'hazard identification' has been used instead of 'risk identification' – however, the principles are the same.

5 http://www.safework.sa.gov.au/contentPages/docs/swiY1A3T2HazardRegisterSample.pdf.

6 A JSA focuses on the individual job and involves analysing each basic task of a job to identify potential hazards and to determine the safest way of doing the job. In this chapter, we focus on processes, rather than on jobs, though, obviously, the two overlap.

7 Figures 6.7, 6.8 and 6.9 are available on the Internet at http://www.hr.unsw.edu.au/ohswc/ohs/pdf/pro_risk_rating.pdf or http://www.ohs.unsw.edu.au/ohs_forms_checklists/forms/frm_risk_assessment.doc.

MANAGING HAZARDS ASSOCIATED WITH PLANT

Learning Objectives

By the end of this chapter, the reader will have a general understanding of how to:

- monitor and facilitate the management of hazards associated with plant
- identify hazards arising from the use of plant and associated systems of work
- analyse WHS risk associated with plant
- control risks associated with plant hazards
- identify and recommend controls for hazards associated with maintenance activities and continued safe use of plant and equipment
- identify and advise on licensing and certification issues associated with plant and equipment
- review and evaluate risk control measures for plant.

INTRODUCTION

'Plant' covers a wide range of things including any machinery, equipment (including scaffolding), appliance, implement or tool, and any other component, fitting or accessory.[1] In other words, you are likely to find plant in practically every workplace not just in factories or workshops – computers and staplers, for example, are plant, as are sewing machines and kitchen and bar equipment.

Consequently, the associated hazards are also wide-ranging and include manual tasks, noise, electrical shock, moving parts, fire and explosion, heat, slips, trips and falls. Each year, there are over 200 fatalities and thousands of injuries involving plant.[2]

DID YOU KNOW?

Goodman Fielder (a breakfast cereal manufacturer) was prosecuted for an incident at their Wahgunyah premises in which a casual plant operator sustained multiple arm fractures when her left arm became entrapped in an unguarded oven out-feed conveyor. The company was found guilty and fined a total of $80 000 under the Victorian *Occupational Health and Safety Act 1985*. The fine comprised a $70 000 fine under Section 21(1) and (2)(a) – 'Employer failed to provide and maintain so far as was practicable for employees a safe working environment – plant and systems of work' – together with a $10 000 loading under Section 53: 'Prohibition on coercion' of the Act.

Source: Prosecutions 2006, WorkSafe Victoria media release, 2 April 2004.

In this chapter, we use the general approach outlined in the previous chapter to identify hazards and manage risk, highlighting the particular issues associated with plant. To begin with we look at our legal obligations.

DUTIES ASSOCIATED WITH PLANT

The law defines the duty-holders, who they are and what their duties are, many of which relate to plant.

THE WHS ACT

Section 19 of the WHS Act sets out the primary duty of care for persons conducting businesses and undertakings (PCBUs) and the ways this must be carried out (see Chapter 2). This is a general duty and covers the use of plant.

There are further duties in sections 20–26 of the Act relating to PCBUs involving:
- the management or control of workplaces
- the management or control of fixtures, fittings or plant at workplaces
- the design, manufacture, import, supply of plant, substances or structures as well as the installation, construction or commissioning of plant and structures.

These duties cover the requirement that plant, substances and structures do not pose a risk to the health and safety of persons at work and that adequate information is provided for their safe use.

The Act does not specify any further duties for officers, workers and other persons in relation to plant or structures apart from the general duties spelt out in sections 27, 28 and 29.

REGULATIONS

Chapter 4 of the Model Work Health and Safety Regulations deals with the regulation and registration of plant and structures such as scaffolding, forklifts, tractors, boilers, gas cylinders, lifting equipment (cranes, hoists, escalators, etc.) and amusement machines. The regulations are detailed and cover 60 pages.

As well as the Act and regulations, Australian standards, codes of practice and guidance material should also be referred to for help with compliance.

In the remainder of this chapter we outline how the duties of the employer (PCBU) are to be carried out. We assume a review of the organisation's exposure to plant hazards is being carried out.

DID YOU KNOW?

That in the 2007/2008 financial year there were 11 work-related fatalities caused by being trapped by moving machinery or equipment (that is, plant).

Source: Safe Work Australia, 2009, *Work-related Traumatic Injury Fatalities, Australia 2006–2007*, SWA: Canberra.

PURCHASING

The first step in mitigating plant hazards is informed selection of the plant item to be purchased. This requires development of policy guidelines for purchasing plant and equipment. Many organisations use a pre- and post-purchasing checklist that covers the following items.

Pre-purchase

Requirements include:
- a list of the safety information (for example, equipment manuals, specifications, Australian standards, etc.) obtained from the manufacturer or supplier
- identification of the hazards associated with the plant
- assessment of the risk
- identification of control measures in place or required to be put in place (for example: Is a safe working procedure required and, if so, who will write it and when?; Are modifications required and, if so, what is required, how will it be done, by whom, etc.?)
- details of the training necessary (that is, who should be trained, what training is necessary and who will carry it out)
- review of supplied information to determine whether the plant meets Australian standards, whether it requires licensing and whether any hazards associated with the

plant are able to be controlled so that the risk is tolerable (the ALARP principle mentioned in the previous chapter).

Post-purchase

After the plant has been delivered, checks include:

*   if all the necessary safety information has been provided by the manufacturer or supplier
*   that the plant is in good order
*   that equipment is electrically tested and tagged
*   that the safe working procedure (if required) is written
*   that risk controls have been implemented
*   that appropriate training has been carried out.

RISK MANAGEMENT ASSOCIATED WITH PLANT

STEP 1: PLANNING A REVIEW OF PLANT HAZARDS

If you are carrying out a thorough review of plant hazards, you will need a plan. In the previous chapter, in which we dealt with hazard identification and risk management, we recommended the use of a hazard register as a useful way of organising activity. One way of planning a review of plant hazards would be to see what is required to complete such a register. Once completed for all sections of the organisation, the hazard register will form a central part of the documented output.

The following basic template in Figure 7.1 is one example. The template may be expanded and upgraded to gather more detail as required.[3]

Organising a review team

As part of your review of plant hazards, you will need a team representing management and workers. People with experience and qualifications – such as ergonomists, occupational hygienists, engineers (design, acoustic, safety, mechanical, maintenance) and workplace injury management personnel – could be called upon. Of course, the team will need to be small and well qualified. The team must:

*   know the law and any codes of practice governing plant
*   have the authority and the support of management to carry out their work
*   be able to read and understand information found in manuals and other relevant documentation
*   be able to inspect, analyse and report on findings.

A plan for consultation will need to be drafted and cover the objectives, the standards to be used, the scope of the review, and cite the workplaces to be visited, the resources required, the activities to be conducted and the schedules and

Figure 7.1 Plant hazards check template

WORKPLACE:			INSPECTION DATE:		INSPECTOR:				
PROCESS	HAZARDS	POTENTIAL INJURY	SEVERITY	PROBABILITY	RISK	CONTROL	RESP. PERSON	IMP. DATE	CHECK DATE

Report reviewed by manager: _____ Date: _____
Report reviewed by HS representative: _____ Date: _____

Hazard code: PE (plant and equipment), E (electrical), C (chemical), MH (manual handling), OOS (occupational overuse syndrome), B (biological), P (psychological), N (noise), WE (working environment)

Severity: 1 – first aid only; 2 – reversible health effects; 3 – irreversible health effects; 4 – fatality
Probability: 1 – not within next 30 years; 2 – within next 5–30 years; 3 – within next 1–5 years; 4 – within 12 months
Risk = severity × probability: High = 9–16; Medium = 6–8; Low = 1–4

reporting arrangements. Equipment and techniques for assessing any risk should be identified.

Identifying the workplace

As set out before, we use the framework in the hazard register, beginning with the workplace – normally, the site or operational unit – and then look to the processes or activities to identify the exposure to plant hazards. In large organisations, for example, where depots involve similar units and processes, the hazard identification and risk assessment process may only involve one representative workplace. Site plans would normally be required.

It is then a process of completing the hazard register for each of the workplaces by identifying the processes and the hazards associated with the plant used in each of the processes. The other way round would be to list all the plant used and, by identifying the associated processes, identify the hazards.

Identifying hazards associated with plant

Preferably, identification of hazards should be done:
- before any decision is made to purchase
- before and during the introduction of plant into the workplace
- before and during any alteration or change to the system of work associated with the plant
- whenever new or additional health and safety information becomes available.

Systems of work

When identifying hazards associated with plant, systems of work should be considered as sources of potential hazards as much as the physical machinery or equipment itself. The machine may be safe in itself, but not the system of work in which it is used. This requires looking at factors such as:
- policy and procedures for purchasing plant
- staff roles, accountabilities, authorities
- instruction and supervision
- work organisation
- skills and experience of the employees
- work practices and procedures
- emergency procedures
- training needs.

Hazards may also be posed by the layout and condition of the related work environment and any reasonably foreseeable abnormal conditions such as power failures, breakdowns or, in the case of outdoor work, changes to the weather.

Sources of information

To assist in identifying such hazards (and their controls) there are a number of sources of information available. The first and perhaps most important source will be the information that comes from consultation with relevant managers, supervisors, employees, and health and safety representatives.

Other sources of information will include:

- regulatory material, such as
  - relevant legislation, regulations, associated standards and codes of practice
  - Australian standards
  - plant and certification standards and associated guidance material
- assistance from bodies such as
  - state and territory WHS regulatory bodies
  - professional associations, such as the Institute of Engineers Australia, the Design Institute of Australia and Building Design Professionals
  - employer groups, unions and industry bodies
- WHS professionals, including those working in safety engineering, **occupational hygiene**, occupational health, injury management, toxicology, human factors/ **ergonomics** (including cognitive ergonomics) and epidemiology
- manufacturers' manuals and specifications
- internal documentation, such as
  - hazard, incident and investigation reports
  - workplace inspections
  - minutes of meetings
  - reports
  - audits
  - questionnaires and surveys.

Not only would you be looking for hazards associated with everyday use of plant, but you would also be taking into account any hazards in the installation, commissioning, maintenance, testing, dismantling, storage and disposal of plant.

In trying to find out exactly what the hazards are with any systems of work associated with plant, as noted above, you would look at:

- organisation policies and procedures dealing with operations, maintenance, and purchasing management systems, such as fleet management, procurement, design and quality assurance
- manufacturers' operations manuals
- standard operating procedures
- documents describing how tasks, projects, inspections, jobs and processes are to be undertaken.

These sources would also be able to provide you with information on existing work environments that may contribute to risk. Computer manuals and sewing machinery, for example, point to the need for proper lighting.

So that the hazard identification process is conducted methodically, it is useful to always develop checklists and worksheets when it comes to physically inspecting the workplace. Such worksheets will save a lot of work later and can be used in training and demonstrating duty of care.

After using the sources, we may have identified the following hazards associated with items of plant.

Figure 7.2 *Hazards associated with items of plant*

WORKPLACE	
PROCESS	**HAZARDS**
Lifting drums with forklift	Items falling Mast hitting fittings dislodging items Overturning
Slicing food	Contact with blade or electricity
Forming panels with power press	Caught in machinery

STEP 2: ASSESSING RISK

The next step is assessing what risk there is of injury occurring by identifying the risk factors – the factors that could lead to an injury, the likelihood of an injury occurring and severity of any injury, given the effectiveness of existing controls. Those closely involved with operations, together with any specialists, would be able to help, as would information from manufacturers and suppliers. Any existing registers should be regularly updated for this purpose to see that they provide a complete and accurate picture. In the case of lifting drums, for example, the risk factors would include the size and weight of the drums, the height to which the drums are lifted, movement by the forklift and the methods of loading the drums. The worst-case scenario would be a drum falling from the pallet, forks or tines, or rack onto someone, resulting in death or permanent disability. The severity could increase if there was a toxic spill affecting one or two workers, but would be even more disastrous if it affected the entire workplace.

After consultation, the risk assessment might look like this (Figure 7.3).

Figure 7.3 *Assessment of risk*

PROCESS	HAZARDS	POTENTIAL INJURY	SEVERITY	PROBABILITY	RISK
Lifting drums with forklift	Items falling	Death, permanent disability	4	3	H
	Mast hitting fittings, dislodging items	Death, permanent disability	4	3	H
	Collision with bystander	Death, permanent disability	4	3	H
	Overturning	Permanent disability	3	2	M
Slicing food	Contact with blade	Lacerations	3	2	M
	Contact with electricity	Shock	3	2	M
		Burns	3	2	M
Forming panels with power press	Caught in machinery	Death, permanent disability	4	1	L

A risk evaluation would decide whether any of these risks were tolerable or not and what the priorities were.

STEP 3: CONTROLLING RISK

The next step is to use the hierarchy of controls to assess whether any existing controls can be improved on in order to further minimise the risk. As always, hazard elimination is the preferred option. An investigation into the options must take place and the information, data and advice on risk control options identified and sourced. Again, consultation with the operators, stakeholders and key personnel should occur throughout the development of controls.

Here, we highlight some of the common types of controls associated with plant.

Access and egress

Controls associated with plant often require consideration of access and egress; for example, when maintaining equipment under normal and emergency conditions. This could include:
- emergency lighting
- safety doors
- alarm systems.

Special attention needs to be paid to dangerous parts where there is the potential for contact or entrapment.

Guards

Plant is associated with the use of guards. Guarding controls typically include:
- permanently fixed physical barriers where no access of any part of a person is required (for example, fencing)
- interlocking physical barriers where access to dangerous areas is required during operation; these are barriers or guards, similar to fixed ones, but that have a movable (usually hinged) part connected to machine controls, so that if the movable part is in the open/lifted position, the dangerous moving part at the work point cannot operate; this can be arranged so that the act of closing the guard activates the working part (to speed up work) – for example, the front panel of a photocopier
- physical barriers securely fixed by means of fasteners or devices
- presence-sensing safeguarding systems are designed to automatically stop the machine stroke if the sensing field is interrupted; proper use of presence-sensing devices provides protection not only for operators but also for others in the area; these devices are commonly referred to as light curtains.

There are other sorts of guards as well. All of these have pluses and minuses.

Operational controls

Operational controls are used to control hazards associated with plant. They must be:
- suitability identified, with their nature and function clearly indicated
- readily and conveniently located

- guarded to prevent unintentional activation
- capable of locking in the OFF position to enable disconnection of all motive power and forces
- of a failsafe type.

Operational controls can include emergency stops and warning devices. They need to be prominent and clearly and durably marked; that is:

- coloured red (push buttons, bars or handles)
- unable to be affected by electrical or electronic circuit malfunction.

Signage is an important type of control, but needs to be used with other controls.

Figure 7.4 *Danger: out of service sign*

The following case study demonstrates some basic WHS lessons, particularly in regard to plant.

CASE STUDY

CUTTER AUTOMATES PUMPKIN CHOPPING AND REDUCES INJURIES

PROBLEM

Campbell's Soups process thousands of pumpkins each week for one of the company's most popular canned products: pumpkin soup. Until the implementation of the solution, several full-time staff were required to chop and seed the large, thick-skinned Mountain Blue pumpkins.

Chopping pumpkins required two people per team: one to lift and place the pumpkins on the chopping table; the other to slice the pumpkins into halves or quarters using large vegetable cleavers. The vegetable was held with one hand, and the cleaver raised with the other and brought down firmly on the pumpkin.

This continuous action resulted in injuries to the shoulders, hands, wrists and fingers of kitchen staff, and created a repetitive strain hazard. Between 1985 and 1993, 246 claims were made; 23 of these were long-term claims. This figure was considered above average for the industry.

SOLUTION

Management and employees decided it was time to automate the chopping process. Apart from the high injury rate, production was slow and unable to meet production demands. A survey of chopping equipment on the market was conducted but nothing suited the specific needs of the Campbell's process. An internal solution was sought.

Twenty employees, including production staff, fitters, engineers and forklift drivers, became involved in the design and construction of a pumpkin-cutting machine and the redesign of the work environment.

A pumpkin-cutting machine consisting of a conveyor belt and hydraulic ram with a six-bladed cutter and seed-corer was developed. Pumpkins are placed at regular intervals on the conveyor belt, which carries pumpkins to the cutting head, and the quartered and halved pieces are swept into a large crate underneath.

The structure is fully guarded by a steel enclosure, which minimises the risk of hands being caught under the chopper. Bending into the crate and lifting the pumpkins onto the processing belt has also been eliminated. A mechanical tilting stand has been devised and drum-loads of pumpkins are lifted onto the stand by a forklift. A hydraulically operated lever slowly tips the pumpkins onto the conveyor belt. This leaves the operator with just the one task: regularly spacing the pumpkins before they reach the cutting head.

BENEFIT

The initiative has had wide-reaching and positive effects at Campbell's because attention has been directed at a manual handling problem as well as the entire work system. There have been no injuries reported since the system was introduced, a major manual handling risk has been eliminated and productivity has increased. The level of employee satisfaction is high because all aspects of pumpkin handling and processing have been addressed. Employee consultation and involvement contributed to a successful outcome.

An added bonus is that Campbell's can recycle the seeds to local farmers and scrap pieces to pig farmers because the pumpkins are cored before cutting.

While the initial cost of the cutting machine and guarding was over $6000, management estimated the machine paid for itself in just three months. The machine is so effective it is being adapted for Campbell's Soups cabbage-processing operation.

Questions

1   What were the critical conditions making this solution a success?
2   What are the residual risks if any?

Registration, licensing, certification, permit to work

As with with cars, most plant must be registered, and operators of particularly dangerous plant must be certified by a recognised certifying authority. The regulations provide details.

Registration is a process whereby a certifying authority requires an organisation or industry to register plant, machinery and equipment and tasks requiring operator licensing and/or certification.

Operator licensing and/or certification refers to any form of regulation that restricts entry to an occupation or a profession to those who meet competency-related requirements stipulated by a regulatory authority. (This includes any physical or implied licence, registration, certification, approval or permit that is required by a person in order to gain employment/self-employment.)

Plant registration can be required for plant design as well as the plant item itself. Plant requiring design registration includes a wide range of plant from boilers to lifts to prefabricated scaffolding to amusement machines to tower cranes to vehicle hoists, and so on.

Individual plant items that require registration are:

- lifts
- boilers (identified in AS 3920 as hazard levels A–C)
- certain pressure vessels (also identified in AS 3920 as hazard levels A–C – some exceptions apply)
- tower cranes
- mobile cranes (working load > 10 tonnes)
- building maintenance units
- truck-mounted concrete-placing units with booms
- amusement structures (except Class 1 structures).

Permit to work procedures, licensing or certification are defined as a written authority document that may include:

- approval to undertake work and activities, including tests, measurements and monitoring, such as hot work permits for welding and cutting in hazardous environments, and confined space entry
- authorisation by a responsible or designated person directly in control of the work
- certification of appropriate precautions and controls to be followed
- checklists, conditions and actions, such as the frequency and duration of the work and atmospheric tests
- compliance with recognised industry-standard recording practices as required to assist in ensuring a safe working environment.

Plant that requires operators to be licensed normally includes

- pressure equipment (boilers, steam engines, turbines)
- scaffolding
- rigging
- forklifts
- cranes
- hoists.

Check with your regulator.

Information and training

All plant information must be documented and provided to management and key personnel such as operators, supervisors and maintenance personnel.

Irrespective of whether a plant item requires an operator to be licensed, training is essential for all plant stakeholders, including operators, maintenance personnel, supervisors and so on – that is, anyone who comes into contact with the plant.

Naturally, training needs will vary according to the role of the person in relation to the plant. Accordingly, a training needs analysis should be conducted prior to plant purchase to determine who should be trained in what. If the plant is already in place, a training needs analysis is still required.

Training should be undertaken prior to commencement of new plant operation as well as new or changed operating procedures for the plant.

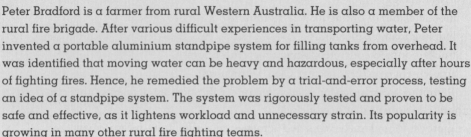

WHS IN PRACTICE

PW & CJ BRADFORD (WA)

Peter Bradford is a farmer from rural Western Australia. He is also a member of the rural fire brigade. After various difficult experiences in transporting water, Peter invented a portable aluminium standpipe system for filling tanks from overhead. It was identified that moving water can be heavy and hazardous, especially after hours of fighting fires. Hence, he remedied the problem by a trial-and-error process, testing an idea of a standpipe system. The system was rigorously tested and proven to be safe and effective, as it lightens workload and unnecessary strain. Its popularity is growing in many other rural fire fighting teams.

Source: Safe Work Australia, 2006, Category 3: Best workplace and safety practices in small business, http://www.safeworkaustralia.gov.au/AboutSafeWorkAustralia/NationalActivities/AnnualSafeWorkAustraliaAwards/2006Winners/Pages/PWAndCJBradford.aspx.

Danger tags

Locking switches that require keys to open the lock could be used in conjunction with a danger tag system that promotes greater safety consciousness among the workforce for all situations in which danger to people could arise from:

- the operation of machinery, plant or equipment
- the flow of steam, electricity, gases or liquids
- the use of faulty or unsafe plant and equipment.

Danger tags could include multiple locking systems and would require written authorisation by a competent person for them to be opened. Such systems would be implemented and monitored in liaison with relevant key personnel.

Other procedures could include controls such as those dealing with:

- purchasing and maintenance
- proposed changes to plant, associated raw material and operating materials, such as lubricants
- proposed changes to work processes, systems and contracts.

Some major categories of plant requiring specific controls are:

- plant under pressure: boilers, pressure vessels, gas cylinders
- plant with moving parts

- powered mobile plant: tractors, earthmoving equipment
- plant with hot or cold parts
- electrical plant and plant exposed to electrical hazards
- plant designed to lift or move: escalators, cranes, elevators, forklifts, hoists
- industrial robots and the like
- lasers
- scaffolds
- lifts
- amusement rides.

Many of these items of plant are dealt with by Australian standards.

Maintenance

Often, accidents occur while maintaining, inspecting, altering, repairing or cleaning plant. To prevent this, the regulations require employers:

- to provide necessary facilities and safe systems of work
- to follow the recommended procedures
- to maintain and test the safety and warning devices
- if plant is damaged, to gather advice from a competent person
- to see that only competent people are involved in repairing, inspecting and testing of plant
- to see that repairs respect the design limits of the plant.

Should an accident occur, the plant must be stopped and access to plant during maintenance controlled, using measures such as:

- lockout or isolation devices
- danger tags
- permit to work systems.

Employers should also document and keep appropriate records of all tests, repairs, maintenance and so on undertaken.

If the plant cannot be stopped, operational controls that permit controlled movement of the plant must be fitted and safe systems of work used. At this stage, you should have a hazard register with the controls identified, as per Figure 7.5.

After selecting the most suitable controls, it is necessary to ensure that everyone knows what those controls are by documenting the safe working procedures and providing everyone with the required training, information, instruction and supervision. The implementation must then be monitored and evaluated.

Figure 7.5 *Sample hazard register*

PROCESS	HAZARDS	POTENTIAL INJURY	SEVERITY	PROBABILITY	RISK	CONTROL	RESP. PERSON	IMP. DATE	CHECK DATE
Lifting drums with forklift	Items falling	Death, permanent disability	4	3	H	Separate racking from pedestrian paths; forklift-only lanes	FH	1.12.12	8.12.12
	Mast hitting fittings, dislodging items	Death, permanent disability	4	3	H	Move fittings out of reach	FH	1.12.12	8.12.12
	Collision with bystander	Death, permanent disability	4	3	H	Restrict pedestrian access	FH	1.12.12	8.12.12
	Overturning	Permanent disability	3	2	M	Display load weights prominently	FH	1.12.12	8.12.12
Slicing food	Contact with blade	Lacerations	3	2	M	Use steel mesh-cutting glove and safe working practices	CQ	8.12.12	15.12.12
	Contact with electricity	Electrocution	3	2	M	Use Residual Current Device; test regularly	CQ	8.12.12	15.12.12
		Burns	3	2	M	Use Residual Current Device; test regularly	CQ	8.12.12	15.12.12
Forming panels with power press	Caught in machinery	Death, permanent disability	4	1	L	Regular testing of system to ensure press does not work while door is open	PA	8.12.12	15.12.12

STEP 4: MONITORING AND EVALUATING CONTROLS

Without the controls being monitored and evaluated for their effectiveness, the whole process falls down. Guards have to be checked and maintained. Certification of operators needs to be up to date. You should also consider whether any hazards have been introduced by the control measures themselves; for example, a greater sense of safety contributes to higher risk-taking as a result. The results of monitoring may show deficiencies in the hazard identification and risk management process that need to be fixed. Often workplace and equipment changes will have occurred.

The nature and level of monitoring depends on the nature and level of risk. In any case, regular reporting needs to be carried out in an agreed form. Safe working procedures will need to be updated.

The key questions will be these:

- Are the control measures eliminating or reducing the risk?
- Are they introducing new hazards?
- Is the process of monitoring and evaluating the controls working effectively? For example, have there been any incidents during the process?

Reviewing controls

Controls need to be reviewed in light of any changes to the workplace and plant hazards. The question becomes: Does the risk assessment show a need for further risk control to reduce the risk to as low as reasonably practicable (ALARP)?

Records of this assessment would include:

- compliance with legislative requirements
- risk assessments
- noise and vibration analysis
- maintenance and modification records.

Any recommended improvements would need to be discussed and agreed on with all of those involved. It may be necessary to liaise with the plant manufacturers during this process.

Modifications

All modifications to plant, including the imposition of controls designed to make the plant safer, require a formal risk assessment to ensure that:

- they perform the task required
- they reduce the risk and make the plant and its operation safer
- there are no unforeseen consequences
  This involves ensuring that:
- the designer and manufacturer are consulted so that WHS issues are accounted for
- if design registration is necessary (for example, for cranes), the requirement for new plant design registration due to the modification is met

- the person carrying out the modification is competent to do the task
- the competent person follows the manufacturer's procedures
- the task is carried out according to all/any Australian standards.

Plant is isolated from any power sources prior to any modification. Before returning the modified/altered plant to service, the modifier of the plant should:

- introduce control measures to prevent or remove any risks created by the modification
- inspect and test according to the modified design specifications and relevant standards.

Plant is only one area where specific types of control have been developed. In the next chapter we look at ways of controlling risk using ergonomic principles.

Summary

- 'Plant' is the general term used for machinery, equipment, tools and appliances.
- The duties of employers with respect to plant are detailed and include consultation; hazard identification; risk assessment; training; information, instruction and supervision; control of risk; (contracting of) design, installation and commissioning; use, repair, alteration, dismantling, storage and disposal.
- Hazards should be identified before and during the introduction of plant into the workplace, before and during any alteration or change to the system of work associated with the plant, and when new or additional health and safety information becomes available.
- When identifying hazards associated with plant, systems of work associated with plant should be considered as posing potential hazards as much as the physical machinery or equipment itself.
- Plant requiring specific controls is referred to in the regulations and includes items such as plant under pressure (boilers, pressure vessels, gas cylinders), plant with moving parts, powered mobile plant (tractors, earth-moving equipment), plant with hot or cold parts, and others.
- Controls associated specifically with plant hazards include access and egress, guards, operational controls, registration, licensing and certification, lockout and tag-out, and danger tags.
- Controls need to be documented and everyone provided with the required training, information, instruction and supervision.
- Monitoring, evaluating and reviewing the entire management of risk associated with plant is intensive but critical to its success.

In your workplace

Streakers hair and beauty salon has just been sold to a new owner. The owner plans to appoint one of the current staff as manager but he also wants to make sure that Streakers is a safe place to work. He is not a hairdresser himself and is uncertain about the safety of all the different types of equipment, so he decides to undertake a comprehensive plant risk assessment.

1 Identify the plant hazards likely to be found at Streakers.

Hint: look up the Queensland Government's *Guide to the Health & Beauty Industry*.

2   Assess the risks in relation to three of the plant hazards.
    Hint: use the 'Risk management form – hairdressing' in the guide to help assess the risks.
3   Decide on appropriate control measures to reduce the risk of each of the three plant hazards.
    Hint: use the hierarchy of control when selecting your controls.
4   When you have decided on the controls, reassess the risk using the Hazpak tool and decide whether the new risk rating is acceptable.
    Hint: check whether the risk ratings conform to the ALARP principle. Is it cost-effective to introduce these controls? Is the risk too great not to implement them?
5   Carry out a training needs analysis (TNA) in respect of the plant hazards identified above.
    Hint: use the tool on how to conduct a TNA located at http://www.safework.sa.gov.au/contentPages/docs/swiY1A8T2TrainingNeedsAnalysis.pdf.
6   Develop a plant purchasing policy for future plant purchases.
    Hint: Refer to the pre- and post-purchasing tips on page 136.

Questions

1   What is the plant purchasing policy in your workplace? If you don't have one, what are the key items for consideration?
2   What are the risk management steps particular to plant?
3   What are the pros and cons of using the four main types of guards:
    a   permanently fixed physical barriers?
    b   interlocking physical barriers?
    c   physical barriers securely fixed?
    d   presence-sensing safeguarding systems?
4   Some plant, such as boilers, pressure vessels and lifts, require registration with the relevant WHS regulatory authority. Examine the regulations and identify any items of plant in your workplace that require registration. Have they been registered? What form did the registration take?
5   Using the case study of Cambell's Soup pumpkin cutter, complete a hypothetical hazard register.

Activities

1   Identify three items of plant at your workplace and complete a hazard register for each identifying your sources of information. Refer to the regulations dealing with plant. You may have to use Australian standards in some cases. It is preferable to do this activity with others.
2   Interview or invite an inspector to your class who has experience with plant. Ask them about some of the most common issues associated with plant inspections and for clues to working safely with plant in your industry.

Search me!

▶ | Search me! 🖱

Explore **Search me! management** for relevant articles on plant and machinery risk. Search me! is an online library of world-class journals, ebooks and newspapers, including *The Australian* and the *New York Times*, and is updated daily. Log in to Search me! through www.cengage.com/sso using the access card in the front of this book.

KEYWORDS

Try searching for the following terms:

▶ plant guards   ▶ failsafe guards

▶ physical barriers ▶ presence-sensing devices

▶ danger tags   ▶ permit to work

Search tip: **Search me! management** contains information from both local and international sources. To get the greatest number of search results, try using both Australian and American spellings in your searches, e.g. 'globalisation' and 'globalization'; 'organisation' and 'organization'.

Additional resources

- The websites of Commonwealth, state and territory WHS authorities provide good detailed guidance material on implementing plant regulations and plant registration. As one example only try http://www.deir.qld.gov.au/workplace/subjects/foundry/hazards/plant/index.htm.
- For machine guarding, go to the OSHA site, http://www.osha.gov/SLTC/machineguarding/index.html, and look at 'hazard recognition' and 'possible solutions'. There is plenty here.
- Safe Work Australia, National Standard for Plant [NOHSC:1010 (1994)] is essential reading; it can be downloaded from the ASCC website at http://www.safeworkaustralia.gov.au/About SafeWorkAustralia/WhatWeDo/Publications/Pages/NS1994Plant.aspx.
- CCH Australia's *Plant Safety: Managing Plant Hazard* (ISBN 1 86264 938 3) is a useful (loose-leaf) resource; it is available at www.cch.com.au.
- There are a number of videos available on YouTube that deal with plant safety; type in 'machine guards' and 'machine guards OSHA'.

Endnotes

1   The National Standard for Plant [National Occupational Health and Safety Commission, 1010:1994] is a bit old but is nevertheless very useful until other codes or standards are produced.

2   Go to WorkSafe Victoria Prosecutions at www.worksafe.vic.gov.au and search for 'Prosecutions'.

3   While we have used the hazard register as one way of recording and reporting hazards, other means can include

- policies and procedures, particularly WHS purchasing and contracting procedures
- standard operating procedures

- job and task statements
- documents describing how tasks, projects, inspections, jobs and processes are to be undertaken
- job safety analysis worksheets
- risk assessments
- plant and equipment registers
- maintenance and service logs, sheets, cards, diaries, etc.
- quality system documentation.

CONTROLLING RISK: ERGONOMICS

Learning Objectives

By the end of this chapter, the reader will have a general understanding of how to:

- apply ergonomic principles to control risk
- assess the degree of match between people and their activities, equipment, environment and systems
- design ergonomic interventions to enhance the match between people and their activities, equipment, environment and systems
- implement ergonomic interventions to enhance the match between people and their activities, equipment, environment and systems
- evaluate ergonomic interventions.

INTRODUCTION

Ergonomics[1] – sometimes called 'human factors'– is the science dealing with interaction between humans and their activities, equipment, environment and systems. Using this knowledge, ergonomics attempts to optimise human wellbeing and overall system performance.[2] Ergonomics evolved as a discipline during the Second World War to address problems arising out of the operation of complex military equipment; for example, cockpit design. Nowadays, even though ergonomics is popularly associated with office furniture and workstation design, its application is much wider.

Physical ergonomics deals with human anatomical, anthropometric, physiological and biomechanical characteristics, as they relate to physical activity. (Relevant topics include working postures, materials handling, repetitive movements, work-related **musculoskeletal disorders**, workplace layout, safety and health.)

Cognitive ergonomics deals with mental processes, such as perception, memory, reasoning and motor response, as they affect interactions among humans and other elements of a system. (Relevant topics include mental workload, decision making, skilled performance, human–computer interaction, human reliability, work stress and training, as these may relate to human-system design.)

Organisational ergonomics looks to optimise the entire social–technical system of work, including the organisational structure, policies and processes.[3]

In this chapter, we show how ergonomic principles are applied to the most common cause of workplace injuries; that is, undertaking manual tasks (often referred to as manual handling). In particular, we examine the approach that physical ergonomics brings, as demonstrated in the code of practice entitled *Hazardous Manual Tasks*.

Manual tasks involve more than just lifting or carrying something. The term 'manual tasks' is used to describe a much broader range of activities involving the use of force to lift, lower, push and/or pull, carry, move, hold or restrain any object, animal or person. It also covers activities that require repetitive movements, sustained postures and/or exposure to vibration at the same time.

As with other hazards, a risk management approach to manual tasks should be adopted to identify, assess, eliminate or mitigate the risks arising from performing manual tasks at work.

DID YOU KNOW?

In 2007–2008, 41 per cent of all serious claims arose from the performance of manual tasks. Of these claims 18 per cent arose from muscular stress arising from lifting/carrying/putting down objects and 15 per cent from handling objects.

Source: Safe Work Australia, 2010, *Compendium of Workers' Compensation Statistics Australia 2007–2008*

ERGONOMICS

We have said that potential hazards are identified after having first identified the context for investigation – usually, a workplace or function – and then listing the main activities or processes found there. At this point, ergonomics looks at the degree of match between the people and those activities or processes, including the equipment, the environment and the systems of work involved. This may be the actual situation or the proposed situation. Where there is not a fit that meets the worker's physical and psychological needs, there is usually a potential hazard.[4]

In the case of manual tasks, some of the key risk factors are movement, posture and forces. Below, we discuss movement and posture in manual handling to demonstrate physical ergonomic principles.

MOVEMENT AND POSTURE

At work, the activities, together with the equipment, environment and systems of work, make demands on posture and movement. Muscles, ligaments and joints align to adopt a posture, produce a movement and apply force. While the muscles, with the assistance of the ligaments, provide the necessary force, the joints enable relative movement of various parts of the body. Poor posture and movement put stress on the muscles, ligaments and joints, resulting in musculoskeletal complaints to the neck, back, shoulders, wrist and other parts of the body. Some movements not only produce body stressing, but also require an expenditure of energy by the muscles, heart and lungs.

To assess the demands for certain postures or movements, ergonomics draws on research principally in **biomechanics**, **physiology** and **anthropometry**.

Biomechanics

Biomechanics applies the physical laws of mechanics to the body to estimate the stress exerted on muscles and joints when a person adopts certain postures or carries out certain movements. From biomechanics, we gather principles such as the following.

* Keep joints in a neutral position; do not stretch the muscles and ligaments spanning the joints.
* Keep work close to the body.
* Avoid bending forward from the waist.
* Avoid twisting the trunk.

These principles can be – and often are – violated regularly by workplace demands, thereby increasing the danger of injury. Using scientific studies of movements and postures, biomechanics can be used to design and implement less stressful options. Biomechanics can specify the range of limb positions that optimise muscle effort without causing physical damage.

Physiology

Exercise physiology estimates the energy demands on the heart and lungs from muscular effort during movements. As we are all aware, there is a limit to the amount of energy that the heart and lungs can normally supply to the muscles when performing movements or adopting postures before experiencing general fatigue. Any task requiring expenditure up to that level is not considered heavy and does not require breaks or alternative light tasks. Knowing what that level is for particular tasks helps in the design of work; thus, for example, what are the limits on the rate of work and what is the right equipment in order to optimise output that will not cause any damage to the body? It can also help to identify the frequency and length of any rest breaks that might be required. Finally, physiology can also be used to estimate the fitness of workers and to develop personal health programs.

Anthropometry

Anthropometry concerns the size and proportion of the human body. Anthropometric tables have been constructed to assist industrial designers, among others, by identifying the standard dimensions – including weight – of short, average and tall people in various postures, either standing or sitting. However, the tables reflect certain populations.[7] This issue is important, especially with new migrants from Asia entering the workforce, many of whom are smaller than Europeans. For example, the positioning of control panels must take into account smaller people. Other groups of workers may also include tall people, big people, those with disabilities, the old, young and pregnant women, so issues such as door heights, for example, should be considered. It is important, then, when identifying potential hazards that consideration be given to the range of physical human variability.

Figure 8.1 *Estimated anthropometric data for Australian men (1990)*

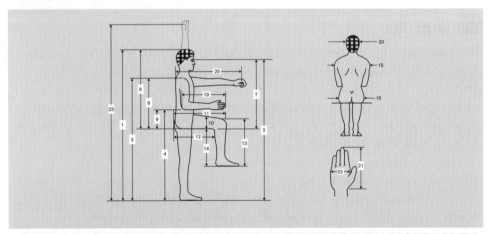

DIMENSION	PERCENTILES (mm)						
	1ST	2.5TH	5TH	50TH	95TH	97.5TH	99TH
1 Stature	1559	1587	1610	1733	1849	1871	1897
2 Eye height	1442	1471	1496	1621	1736	1758	1785
3 Shoulder height	1260	1285	1307	1422	1531	551	1575
4 Elbow height	945	965	983	1073	1160	176	1195
5 Knuckle height	641	661	677	754	819	832	848
6 Sitting height	812	828	842	907	966	977	991
7 Eye height, sitting	685	705	721	789	843	855	871

DIMENSION	PERCENTILES (mm)						
	1ST	2.5TH	5TH	50TH	95TH	97.5TH	99TH
8 Shoulder height, sitting	515	528	539	595	648	658	669
9 Elbow height, sitting	173	184	193	242	293	303	315
10 Thigh thickness	112	119	125	155	183	188	193
11 Buttock→knee	514	527	538	594	645	655	666
12 Buttock→popliteal	412	425	436	493	546	556	568
13 Knee height	456	470	482	541	594	604	617
14 Popliteal height	367	378	387	438	487	496	506
15 Shoulder breadth	385	397	407	460	508	517	528
16 Hip breadth, sitting	280	293	304	357	404	414	425
17 Chest depth	157	166	174	202	228	234	243
18 Abdominal depth	158	179	196	271	318	329	345
19 Elbow→fingertip	420	429	437	474	508	514	522
20 Head breadth	139	141	144	155	165	167	169
21 Hand length	166	170	173	189	206	209	213
22 Hand breadth	72	74	76	85	96	99	102
23 Vertical grip reach, standing	1854	1886	1914	2053	2188	2213	2244
24 Vertical grip reach, sitting	1090	1114	1135	1240	1338	1357	1380
25 Forward grip reach	667	684	699	772	832	843	856

Source: M.G. Stevenson, *Notes on the Principles of Ergonomics*, 2003.

Figure 8.2 *Estimated anthropometric data for Australian women (1990)*

DIMENSION	PERCENTILES (mm)						
	1ST	2.5TH	5TH	50TH	95TH	97.5TH	99TH
1. Stature	1454	1478	1499	1607	1712	1731	1754
2. Eye height	1338	1364	1387	1499	1601	1620	1643
3. Shoulder height	1168	1189	1209	1308	1406	1425	1446
4. Elbow height	878	896	911	989	1065	1080	1097
5. Knuckle height	598	619	637	721	782	793	808
6. Sitting height	756	772	786	850	907	918	931
7. Eye height, sitting	638	657	673	740	791	801	814
8. Shoulder ht., sitting	477	490	501	557	610	621	633
9. Elbow ht, sitting	166	177	186	233	283	294	305

DIMENSION	PERCENTILES (mm)						
	1ST	2.5TH	5TH	50TH	95TH	97.5TH	99TH
10. Thigh thickness	94	105	114	152	180	186	194
11. Buttock→knee	486	500	512	569	619	629	640
12. Buttock→popliteal	388	403	415	474	527	537	548
13. Knee height	422	434	445	496	542	551	561
14. Popliteal height	332	343	351	397	444	453	463
15. Shoulder breadth	338	347	355	395	435	442	451
16. Hip breadth, sitting	277	290	302	368	431	443	457
17. Chest depth	167	176	183	214	249	258	269
18. Abdominal depth	163	179	192	252	303	313	324
19. Elbow→fingertip	375	384	392	429	461	467	474
20. Head breadth	131	134	136	146	157	159	162
21. Hand length	152	155	158	174	190	193	196
22. Hand breadth	65	66	67	74	86	90	95
23. Vertical grip reach, standing	1719	1750	1776	1901	2036	2069	2111
24. Vertical grip reach, sitting	788	842	892	1127	1245	1257	1271
25. Forward grip reach	621	635	647	703	759	771	787

Source: M.G. Stevenson, *Notes on the Principles of Ergonomics*, 2003.

DID YOU KNOW?

The tallest man on earth according to the *Guinness Book of World Records* was Robert Pershing Wadlow of the USA, who was recorded a few weeks before his death in 1940 as being 2.72m (8'11") tall. He was only 18 years old.

Source: http://www.guinnessworldrecords.com.

Posture, especially prolonged posture in the same position, can also result in injuries. This applies to sitting, standing, and hand and arm postures; for example, bent wrists and unsupported, raised arms.

Combine poor posture with the application of force and repetition and you increase the chance of injury referred to as **occupational overuse syndrome (OOS)**. Here, the need for a sympathetic design of workstations and equipment is clear.

DID YOU KNOW?

Also known as repetitive strain injury (RSI), OOS is a collective term for a range of conditions characterised by discomfort or persistent pain in muscles, tendons and other soft tissues with or without physical manifestations. It is usually associated with tasks that involve repetitive or forceful movement or both, and/or maintenance of constrained or awkward postures.

In assembling this type of experience and information in the form of principles – essentially a list of evidence-based do's and don'ts – ergonomics is able to help identify potential hazards and either design out risk altogether or minimise it.

Turning to the hazards of manual handling and using ergonomic principles, how do we identify the hazards, eliminate them or, failing that, control them and finally monitor and review the effectiveness of the controls?

IDENTIFYING HAZARDS

Identification of hazards should preferably be done:
- before and during the introduction of new work processes, equipment, layout, environment and systems of work
- before and during any alteration or change to the above
- whenever new or additional health and safety information becomes available.

First, prepare a plan and consult with others, stating what you hope to achieve and the criteria or standards you are using (for example, a code of practice), which area(s) you are assessing, who you expect to involve and what resources you will need. The hazard register format used in Chapter 6 is a useful tool for setting out your plan, and is represented below.

site → processes → hazards → potential injury → severity → probability → risk → control → implement → monitor and evaluate or review

SOURCES OF INFORMATION

People

In developing the plan, draw on people who have a stake in the outcome, especially line managers, employees and their representatives. You may need direct help from professional ergonomists, as well as from those involved in safety engineering, occupational health and injury management. These people will be a prime source of information.

Records of incidents or injuries

Important evidence will include records of incidents involving manual handling found in an incident or injury register. The records should provide information on:
- the area of the workplace where the incident occurred
- the occupation, job or task of the injured person
- the part of the body injured; for example, back, neck or shoulder
- the nature of the injury; for example, strain, sprain, laceration or fracture
- the type of accident; for example, overexertion and physical stress from lifting objects, or slips and falls while handling objects
- the time of day the injury occurred, including the elapsed time of the shift worked by the injured worker.

If you are able to establish an incidence rate, you may be able to compare locations, occupations or tasks, which may assist in the analysis of the issues and the identification of systemic problems.

Internal sources

Other internal sources would be:
- manufacturers' manuals and specifications
- purchasing, contract and tendering procedures
- enforcement notices and actions
- minutes of meetings
- reports
- audits, questionnaires and surveys
- job and task statements
- documents describing how tasks, projects, inspections, jobs and processes are undertaken.

External sources

Other information sources would include:
- state and territory WHS authorities and Safe Work Australia
- relevant state or territory WHS codes of practice and guidelines
- related international and Australian standards
- national plant and certification standards, and associated guidance material
- professional associations, such as Human Factors and Ergonomics Society of Australia, Safety Institute of Australia, Institute of Engineers Australia, Design Institute of Australia and Building Design Professionals
- employer groups, unions and industry bodies
- WHS professionals, including those involved in ergonomics, safety engineering, occupational hygiene, occupational health, injury management, toxicology and epidemiology.

Direct observation

The final important source of information – in the case of a review – will be informed direct observation of the workplace and the tasks being performed. Workplace inspections, audits and walkthrough surveys, and the use of checklists, can assist in the risk identification process. The national manual handling code of practice[5] has checklists that can be used in any workplace inspection. In addition, a number of jurisdictions have developed industry-specific guidelines for manual handling.

ASSESSING RISK

Risk assessment is critical when incidents have occurred and when processes are introduced or modified. All risk factors should be taken into account when developing controls. The main risk factors involved in performing manual tasks are:

- repetitive or sustained awkward posture
- repetitive or sustained movement
- repetitive or sustained application of force
- application of high force
- exposure to sustained vibration
- handling loads that are unstable, unbalanced or difficult to grasp.

We look here at these and other risk factors, beginning with posture and movement.[6]

Figure 8.3 *Risk factors*

RISK FACTOR	DO'S	DON'TS
Repetitive or sustained posture	• Adopt several different, but equally healthy and safe, working postures. • Permit an upright and forward-facing posture and good visibility; perform the majority of tasks at about waist height and within easy reach.	• Remain in one posture for lengthy periods; any bending or twisting of the spine. • Avoid having to bend or reach.
Repetitive or sustained movement	• Should be performed smoothly, with control, in a balanced, comfortable posture. • Strive to have a variety of different healthy and safe activities.	• Avoid undue discomfort or pain; sudden, jerky movements; avoid overextension, repetitive bending, twisting and overreaching. • Avoid frequent, repetitive long-term manual handling of all types and for all muscle groups (for example, hands).
Forces, including high force	Consider the weight of an object in relation to: • frequency and duration • position of load relative to the body • distance moved – distances should be as short as possible; the longer the distance the lighter the load • characteristics of the load. Note that the posture and working conditions should support the application of force to push, pull or restrain an object, even where there is little or no movement.	• Lift loads in excess of 4.5 kg when seated; when standing, the risk of back injury increases significantly with objects above the range of 16–20 kg. • Avoid loads above the employee's shoulder height, below mid-thigh height; requiring extended reach, having to manoeuvre loads accurately into position.
Vibration	• Use remote control processes to isolate workers from source of vibration where possible. • Select equipment with lower vibration levels and/or use vibration-damping equipment. • Ensure equipment is maintained. • Reduce time exposed.	• Avoid exposure to high levels of vibration especially over long periods of time. • Neglect to consider the increased risk arising from the compounding effects of vibration and other risk factors such as force, posture, movement or thermal conditions.

RISK FACTOR	DO'S	DON'TS
Handling loads that are unstable, unbalanced or difficult to grasp	Attend to load and equipment dimensions, stability, rigidity, predictability, surface texture and temperature, grips and handles. Gloves or similar personal protective equipment should be assessed.	Underestimate the risks of handling animate objects; for example: • hospital patients require extreme care, often while attached to fragile medical equipment • disturbed patients or animals may require restraint.
Work organisation	Consider factors such as staff levels, availability of equipment, work schedules, shiftwork, work pace, task variety, rest breaks and recovery time, and work procedures. These may interact with other risk factors.	Deal with manual handling separately from the entire system of work.
Work environment	Climate, lighting, space and floors and other surfaces underfoot should be considered when assessing manual handling risk.	Neglect housekeeping and footwear as they affect the risk in manual handling.
Skills and experience	Employees should have the knowledge and ability required to perform the task.	
Age	Pay attention to the assessment of risk and control measures for young workers, who are still developing. Older workers may be subject to a decline in ability; for example, in eyesight, hearing.	Discriminate against young or old workers by failing to adapt the job to the person.
Clothing	Clothing (particularly, uniforms, footwear and PPE) should be carefully assessed for the risks they present for manual handling.	Wear uniforms or other forms of clothing that constrain movement or posture or otherwise put the body at risk.
Special needs	Assist employees with special needs, such as those returning from extended leave or with short-term or long-term disabilities.	

Note that the risk factors – work organisation, skills and experience, age, special needs – relate to or overlap with organisational ergonomics.

The data collected will then need to be analysed to provide an understanding of the potential risk. You must know the hazards, the potential injuries, the likelihood of them occurring and their severity to establish priorities for action. (See Chapter 6 for a discussion of estimating the level of risk based on the likelihood and severity of any injury.)

Having completed the risk assessment, the next step is to eliminate or control that risk by developing a preferred solution. In this context, ergonomists talk of optimising the match between people and their work.

CONTROLLING RISK

To optimise the match between people and their work, the preferred options are as follows.

1 Eliminate the risk by:
   • modifying the workplace design and layout
   • changing the nature of the load handled
   • changing the items used

- altering the working environment
- modifying the work systems, organisation and practices.

2 Minimise the risk by:
- using mechanical aids or other assistive devices (engineering controls)
- altering the workplace
- changing the item used
- modifying systems of work.

3 Training

4 Other administrative controls (for example, job rotation and breaks).

WHS IN PRACTICE

TOYOTA MATERIAL HANDLING AUSTRALIA

Toyota Material Handling Australia (TMHA) provides retail and rental sales, fleet management and customer support services across industries. In response to a workplace injury, TMHA management and technicians worked together to find a solution to manual handling risks associated with moving forklift tyres for repair.

The solution considered work restrictions and was purpose-built on site. From rudimentary beginnings, the device – based around a TMHA hand pallet jack – allows the user to safely and securely lift the tyre to the required height and easily rotate it to align the rim and wheel studs. It removes the manual handling task, with no need to lift, physically support or rotate the tyre.

Source: WorkCover NSW, Safe Work Awards 2010: Category 2: Best Solution to an identified OHS issue, http://www.safeworkawards.com.au/Awards-highlights/2010-Awards/Category-2-Awards.aspx.

The following case study is an example of an ergonomic solution. It does not necessarily represent the best solution, but indicates how ergonomic principles can be applied. It is an example of introducing mechanical handling equipment to reduce risk with a focus on engineering controls. It is worth noting that work organisation has changed as well.

MANUAL TASK: LOADING TUBS ONTO A PALLET

PROBLEM

Solvent-based adhesives (such as contact cement for use by carpenters) are poured into 20-litre metal tubs and stacked on pallets for despatch to customers. The finished product weight of each is approximately 20 kg. The manual handling of the tubs was identified as a source of musculoskeletal disorders (MSDs), affecting the back, shoulder and upper limbs.

RISK FACTORS

Risk factors included:
- repetitive movement through bending the back forwards and twisting; reaching forward; lifting and lowering
- force combined with awkward posture

- each tub only able to be lifted by one person
- certain employees rostered to the task, therefore higher exposure
- ageing workforce
- workers of varying strengths and capabilities.

SOLUTIONS

Short-term: A rotating self-height-adjusting palletiser was hired for use.

Medium-term: A palletiser was purchased and stands were built for the pallets so that the working height was raised and back bending and forward reaching was minimised.

Long-term: A conveyor belt was constructed to reduce carrying distance.

BENEFITS

Benefits included:
- eliminates manual lifting and stacking of heavy products
- easily installed
- flexible
- cost-effective solution.

Questions
1 Were any additional hazards introduced?
2 What other controls are involved?

CONTROLS AND DISPLAYS

As mentioned earlier, ergonomics initially dealt with some of the problems associated with complex military operations and still concerns itself with controls and displays, making them easier and safer to use. The following story from the inquiry report into the rail accident at Waterfall in NSW illustrates where a control – in this case, the deadman system used by the train driver – was inadequate and failed, despite being identified as faulty many years before the fateful accident. This case study also illustrates where ergonomics can contribute to dealing with the hazards associated with plant.

WATERFALL, AGAIN

CASE STUDY

Being able to satisfy myself that there was no defect in the track, no malfunction in G7 and no reckless or deliberate conduct by the train driver which caused the accident, the inference from the known state of his coronary arteries and other cardiac risk factors led me to the view that Mr Zeides suffered a sudden incapacitating heart attack at the controls of G7. It was not possible to determine whether Mr Zeides was dead or dying at the time of impact, but I was satisfied that he was so incapacitated that he had no control of G7 from the time shortly after it left Waterfall railway station.

That conclusion led me to examine why, in those circumstances, there was a failure of the system in Tangara trains which is supposed to prevent an accident of this kind from occurring if the train driver has a sudden heart attack. The deadman system depended upon the train driver keeping pressure either on the master controller, which was spring loaded and held in the right hand, or alternatively setting the master controller in the desired position then keeping appropriate pressure on the foot pedal to prevent an emergency brake application.

The foot pedal was designed so that a certain pressure was needed to put it in the set position, but if too much or too little pressure was applied, causing it to either be fully depressed or fully released, an electrical relay system triggered an emergency brake application.

Figure 8.4 illustrates the mechanism by which the deadman foot pedal operated.

Figure 8.4 *Internal mechanism of deadman foot pedal*

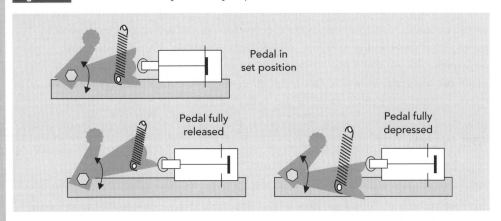

Dr Andrew McIntosh, Senior Lecturer in Biomechanics and Ergonomics, School of Safety Science, University of New South Wales, was retained by the Special Commission of Inquiry to conduct tests on the deadman foot pedal. Following exhaustive testing and careful analysis of the results of those tests, Dr McIntosh's conclusions were as follows:

The tests and analyses undertaken on the Tangara deadman system indicate with a very high degree of confidence that an incapacitated driver of body mass greater than 110 kilograms, such as the deceased driver Mr Zeides, could maintain sufficient force due to "dead weight" on the deadman's pedal to hold it in a "set" position. This could be achieved with both feet, one foot, with different foot placement on the pedal, wedging of the feet under the heater, and different seat positions.

Mr Zeides weighed 118 kilograms at autopsy. When the results of Dr McIntosh's empirical testing were considered with the other facts known about the accident, I was satisfied Mr Zeides was using the deadman foot pedal when he had a heart attack. The very system designed to protect the safety of passengers in those circumstances failed to operate.

Although the direct cause of the accident could be established, it was necessary to establish how a train with that inherent safety defect could be permitted to be built and utilised for public passenger transport and remain in service with that serious latent safety defect for many years. It became apparent that the then SRA had information for approximately 15 years that the deadman foot pedal in Tangara trains had the inherent deficiency that train drivers over a certain weight could set the pedal inadvertently if they became incapacitated for whatever reason. Dr McIntosh established that train motion would have no effect on this.

The interim report carefully analysed the knowledge of the SRA at various stages during that 15 year period, to attempt to establish why such a dangerous state of affairs had been permitted to prevail for such a long period. The simple answer was that there were serious deficiencies in the way in which safety was managed by that organisation over that period of time.

Source: NSW Ministry of Transport, 2003, *Final Report of the Special Commission of Inquiry into the Waterfall Rail Accident* (McInerney Inquiry), Executive Summary: pp. iii, iv. © State of New South Wales through ITSR.

Questions

1 How might this accident have been avoided, given the findings?
2 Would health surveys have helped, as Mr Zeides was quite big?

Developing a solution will require collectively thinking through and testing options, possibly with prototypes. The results need to be evaluated, discussed and documented before recommending the preferred option, of which there may be only one, other than continuing with the current situation. Evaluation, discussion and documentation are not only important for a legalistic or compliance point of view, but also for reviewing the implementation. Having documented the development of a solution enables you to refer to your notes and, if necessary, reassess your objectives. Often, unintended consequences – good and bad – may result. As mentioned, the new control could have an effect on other members of the organisation, such as cleaners and maintenance staff, who may need to be made aware of and consulted about any changes to their routines.

WHS IN PRACTICE

UNIVERSITY OF QUEENSLAND LIBRARY

Library staff at University of Queensland identified a significant manual handling issue when book trolleys were pushed into the book lift for transport between floors.

As books were stacked on trolleys and pushed into the lift, the wheels of the trolleys would fall down the gap between the floor and the lift. When this happened the operator had to exert force on the loaded trolleys to manoeuvre them into the lift. Back injuries were a common consequence of this manual handling task.

Several solutions were examined, including installing larger trolley wheels and limiting the number of books on trolley shelves.

Library employee Martin Rhodes developed a prototype Ergo-bridge, which has successfully overcome the problem. His idea has been modified and adopted by Schindler Lifts.

Figure 8.5 *University of Queensland library Ergo-bridge*

Martin's Ergo-bridge has improved the task of wheeling heavy library trolleys into the book lift. No injuries related to the book lift have occurred since the Ergo-bridge was installed.

Source: Queensland Work Safe Awards 2009, Category 2: Best Solution to an identified workplace health and safety issue, Highly Commended- University of Queensland Library- St Lucia, www.deir.qld.gov.au, © The State of Queensland (Department of Justice and Attorney-General) 2009.

IMPLEMENTING CONTROLS

Final check

Before implementing any ergonomic intervention or control, careful assessment needs to be made of the requirements set out in the legislation, codes of practice and standards. For example, not only must the general requirements for a hazard identification and risk management be met – consultation, documentation and record-keeping, for example – but also a search should be made for the latest and best information on the hazards being addressed. Assessment can involve not only Australian and international standards and guidance material but also databases. Fortunately, in most cases, this search is not too difficult an exercise; some expert advice from a professional ergonomist should help.

To repeat, key personnel, stakeholders and users need to be consulted when developing, selecting and implementing ergonomic interventions. Where possible, the impact on other functional areas and management systems, if any, need to be anticipated. Often where such controls are to be implemented, training will be required and training areas will need to be identified in any recommendations.

It is important that someone be given ownership of the intervention or control, if only to monitor and report on its implementation against the standards used.

Implementation strategy

An implementation strategy or plan should be developed once the solution has been agreed upon, a final check has been carried out and someone has been given ownership. The strategy should consider:

- confirmation of the purpose and the standards or criteria to be used
- communication with all of those affected
- possible steering committee oversight
- a phasing-in or trial period
- running the control or intervention while other parts of the organisation continue with the same processes or equipment
- testing methods and data collection
- training and recruitment requirements
- above-the-line costs and cash flow considerations, as well as below-the-line costs, such as downtime and project administration
- manual, IT and procedural documentation
- schedules and deadlines
- monitoring arrangements.

The health and safety manager's role in implementation and, indeed, the entire project needs careful assessment to ensure that the responsibilities of line management are supported. However much it may be the idea or initiative of the health and safety unit manager, ownership and responsibility should be laid out clearly beforehand in order to bring about the success of an ergonomic intervention as well as ensuring compliance with it.

Records

Records associated with implementation should be maintained in a central location and be available to the employees' health and safety representative(s). The records should include information on:

- the manual-handling injury-prevention program
- risk assessment reports
- design modifications to, and specifications for, plant and work processes
- risk control measures implemented
- training and education activities.

Evaluation and review

The evaluation at the end of a specified period should look at the outcomes:

- Did the intervention achieve its goals – fully or partially?
- Were there any unintended consequences of significance?
- What were the actual costs – direct and indirect – and how did they differ from the budget estimate?
- Is it possible to say there was a net benefit against the criteria used; for example, safety, compliance, improved efficiency? All up, did you go backwards or forwards?

The evaluation will be helped by gathering the views of those involved, the data collected and, possibly, an independent qualified assessor.

After an evaluation has been made, the review should see if the control *as is* will be continued with, modified and improved, or abandoned and something entirely different and new tried. If the intervention was not fully or even partially successful, the process needs to be reviewed to see whether improvements could have been made. The recommendations should be a matter for prior consultation before finalisation. As far as possible, the final report should not contain any surprises.

Summary

- Ergonomics deals with the interaction between humans and their activities, equipment, environment and systems. It attempts to optimise human wellbeing and overall system performance.
- Ergonomics can be broken down into three major areas: physical, cognitive and organisational.
- Physical ergonomists are often called on to deal with manual handling. They use the sciences of biomechanics, physiology and anthropometry.
- Ergonomic principles are demonstrated in the code of practice *Hazardous Manual Tasks*.
- The code sets out three main steps: hazard identification, risk assessment and risk control. Useful checklists are supplied.
- It is preferable that ergonomic principles are applied at the earliest stages; for example, at the design and purchase stages.

- It is important to plan in consultation with the users, be informed by an understanding of the law and use the best ergonomic information and data available. Qualified ergonomists can assist.
- Having identified the hazards and assessed their risk(s), preferred options should be developed in line with the hierarchy of controls. An agreed-upon implementation strategy should then be documented and used.
- Evaluation of the outcomes forms the basis for an effective review. Again, expert advice can be used to confirm – or reject – any recommendations.

In your workplace

Bottlebrush House is the unit of Casuarina Nursing Home that provides care for residents with dementia. The majority of the residents are elderly and require frequent clothing changes, especially in relation to toileting. A risk assessment of dressing/undressing residents identified the following manual-task-related risks to nurses, enrolled nurses and others responsible for dressing/undressing residents:

- frequent occurrence for all nurses/enrolled nurses during each shift
- awkward postures involving sustained side bending and twisting, combined with weight-bearing while dressing (especially when putting residents' pants on)
- bruising and/or tearing of residents' skin
- aggression and agitation of some patients resulting in potential injury to both staff and residents.

1 How would you reduce the identified risks?

   Hint: what could be redesigned to make the task easier and safer? The code for hazardous manual tasks is a useful starting point for general risk reduction. There is also a wealth of information on the Internet in relation to manual handling in nursing homes in Australia.

2 How would you go about implementing the changes?

   Hint: Who would you need to consult with? What checks would you need to undertake to ensure the controls were appropriate? Refer to this chapter for tips on implementation.

3 What benefits are likely to accrue?

   Hint: consider benefits in relation to both staff and residents.

Questions

1 Ergonomics is sometimes summarised as fitting the task to the person. What precisely is meant by this expression? Use an example from your own work.
2 What are the three major areas of ergonomics? Describe when you might use an ergonomist from each of those areas.
3 Workplace furniture and equipment are used by many people of different sizes and shapes. How would you deal with the problems associated with
   a conveyors, beds and benches (height)?
   b tool handles (diameter, length)?
   c machine guards (openings)?
   d library shelves (height, depth)?
   e lift buttons (height)?
   f door handles (height, diameter or width, clearances for hands)?

Activities

1 How might you use an anthropometric table in designing a workstation? As an example, consider a workstation you are familiar with. Provide photos or videos showing the issue.

2 In the examples of solutions given in this chapter, provide an alternative and possibly better solution to the problems using ergonomic principles. You may wish to do this as a group.

3 Using your own workplace as an example, select a process or set of processes for an ergonomic assessment, develop a plan in consultation with your manager and those affected, implement your plan and report on the outcomes. To ensure the success of the project, be careful to define exactly what the boundaries are and assess the risk carefully. If in any doubt, use professional assistance.

Search me!

Explore **Search me! management** for relevant articles on ergonomics. Search me! is an online library of world-class journals, ebooks and newspapers, including *The Australian* and the *New York Times*, and is updated daily. Log in to Search me! through www.cengage.com/sso using the access card in the front of this book.

KEYWORDS

Try searching for the following terms:

▶ human factors
▶ manual handling
▶ physical ergonomics
▶ occupational overuse syndrome
▶ cognitive ergonomics
▶ biomechanics
▶ organisational ergonomics

Search tip: **Search me! management** contains information from both local and international sources. To get the greatest number of search results, try using both Australian and American spellings in your searches, e.g. 'globalisation' and 'globalization'; 'organisation' and 'organization'.

Additional resources

- Safe Work Australia (SWA) hosts material from the former ASCC and NOHSC and is continuously building on the information available. Its website is http://www.safework australia.gov.au.
- The website of Human Factors and Ergonomics Society of Australia (HFESA) provides information on ergonomics and a list of certified members with contacts. Details can be found at http://www.ergonomics.org.au.
- International Ergonomics Association (IEA) is the most notable of the international and national ergonomics bodies that the HFESA website has links with. IEA can be found at http://www.iea.cc.
- Kroemer, K. & Grandjean, E., 1997, *Fitting the Task to the Human*, 5th edn, Taylor & Francis: London. Swiss Etienne Grandjean is the grandfather of ergonomics; see the updated version of his classic text.
- Oxenburgh, M., Marlow, P. & Oxenburgh, A., 2004, *Increasing Productivity and Profit Through Health and Safety: The Financial Returns From a Safe Working Environment*, 2nd edn, CRC Press: Boca Raton. This book on ergonomics illustrates how a return on investment can be demonstrated. The principles can be applied to other WHS interventions as well.
- Pheasant, S., 1986, *Bodyspace: Anthropometry, Ergonomics, and Design*, Taylor & Francis: London. This text is widely used by WHS professionals.
- See Stevenson, M., 2003, *Notes on the Principles of Ergonomics*, Mike Stevenson Ergonomics: Sydney, for an excellent introduction to ergonomics and its health and safety aspects. The book has the additional benefit of referring to Australian material.

Manual tasks

Although ergonomics addresses other WHS problems, manual tasks remain a very big issue. The following titles are dated but remain useful reading on this issue. They can found at SWA's website: http://www.safeworkaustralia.gov.au.

* *Guidance Note for the Prevention of Occupational Overuse Syndrome in Keyboard Employment* [NOHSC: 3005 (1996)], 2nd edn, Australian Government Publishing Service: Canberra.
* *Guidance Note for the Prevention of Occupational Overuse Syndrome in the Manufacturing Industry* [NOHSC:3015 (1996)], 2nd edn, Australian Government Publishing Service: Canberra.
* The *National Code of Practice for the Prevention of Musculoskeletal Disorders from Performing Manual Tasks (2007)* provides practical advice on meeting the requirements of the National Standard for Manual Tasks 2007. The *National Code of Practice for the Prevention of Occupational Overuse Syndrome* [NOHSC:2013 (1994)] should be consulted on OOS problems.
* Many of these codes have been adopted in part or whole by the various WHS authorities. Check your own authority's website.

Endnotes

1 The root of the term 'ergonomics' is the Greek *nomos*, meaning 'rule', and *ergo*, meaning work.

2 These definitions are taken from the International Ergonomics Association website at http://www.iea.cc.

3 These definitions are taken from the website of the Human Factors and Ergonomics Society of Australia at http://www.ergonomics.org.au.

4 There may be no health and safety issue in the case of a mismatch, but simply an inefficiency.

5 The *National Code of Practice for the Prevention of Musculoskeletal Disorders from Performing Manual Tasks* (2007).

6 We have summarised the key points from the *National Code of Practice for the Prevention of Musculoskeletal Disorders from Performing Manual Tasks* (2007). More details can be found in the national code of practice together with checklists.

7 Note that the anthropometric tables in this text were developed in 1990, accordingly dimensions for both men and women will have changed significantly due to increases in size of people generally, particularly in width dimensions, and a changing ethnic mix.

CONTROLLING RISK: OCCUPATIONAL HYGIENE

Learning Objectives

By the end of this chapter, the reader will have a general understanding of how to:

- identify health hazards that may result from features of the workplace or working environment
- apply occupational hygiene principles to assess and control risk of worker exposure to potentially harmful agents and factors
- design risk control strategies and advise on their implementation
- monitor and evaluate control strategies to minimise workplace exposures.

INTRODUCTION

Australia has the dubious honour of having the highest mesothelioma and melanoma rates in the world. Mesothelioma is a cancer of the lining of the lung or peritoneum and is almost exclusively caused by exposure to asbestiform mineral fibres. Australia's legacy arises from the mining of crocidolite (blue asbestos) at Wittenoom in Western Australia in the years after the Second World War, and the extensive use of asbestos cement sheeting in construction. Current exposure arises through building demolition and DIY renovation of houses.[1]

Melanoma is an aggressive form of skin cancer that is caused by exposure to sunlight. Outdoor workers, particularly those in construction, open-cut mining and electricity and telecommunications lineworkers, are particularly susceptible to overexposure to sunlight, or more specifically, the ultraviolet radiation in sunlight.[2]

To adequately control these and similar exposures, it is necessary to be able to identify, measure and control them. Occupational hygiene is the WHS discipline that deals with such hazards and is generally defined as the art and science dedicated to the '*anticipation*, *recognition*, *evaluation*, *communication* and *control* of environmental stressors in or arising from the workplace that may result in injury, illness, impairment, or affect the wellbeing of workers and members of the community. These stressors are normally divided into the categories biological, chemical, physical, ergonomic and psychosocial'.[3]

In this chapter, we look at how occupational hygiene is used to identify hazards and control risk, with particular reference to hazardous chemicals and noise. In Chapter 10, we look at methods of measuring a range of workplace hazards.

TYPES OF HAZARDS

The following table in Figure 9.1 summarises the major types of hazards in the workplace.[4]

Figure 9.1 *Major types of hazards dealt with in occupational hygiene*

TYPE OF HAZARD	WHAT IT DOES	EXAMPLES
CHEMICAL HAZARDS	CHEMICALS ENTER THE BODY, PRINCIPALLY, BY INHALATION, ABSORPTION THROUGH THE SKIN OR INGESTION	
Corrosives	Severe damage to skin, eyes and digestive system after contact with corrosive chemical.	Concentrated acids and alkalis, phosphorus
Irritants	Contact with skin irritants may cause reactions such as eczema or dermatitis. Eye irritants cause stinging and watering of eyes. Severe respiratory irritants might cause shortness of breath, inflammatory responses and oedema.	Skin: acids, alkalis, solvents, oils Respiratory: aldehydes, alkaline dusts, ammonia, nitrogen dioxide, phosgene, chlorine, bromine, ozone
Allergens	Chemical allergens or sensitisers can cause allergic skin or respiratory reactions.	Skin: colophony (rosin), formaldehyde, metals such as chromium or nickel, some organic dyes, epoxy hardeners, turpentine Respiratory: isocyanates, fibre-reactive dyes, formaldehyde, many tropical wood dusts, nickel

TYPE OF HAZARD	WHAT IT DOES	EXAMPLES
Asphyxiants	Asphyxiants interfere with the oxygenation of the tissues. Simple asphyxiants replace oxygen in air. Chemical asphyxiants react in the body to prevent oxygen function in the tissues.	Simple asphyxiants: methane, ethane, hydrogen, helium Chemical asphyxiants: carbon monoxide, nitrobenzene, hydrogen cyanide, hydrogen sulphide
Carcinogens	A cancer is a malignant growth or tumour caused by abnormal and uncontrolled cell division. Known human carcinogens are chemicals that have been demonstrated to cause cancer in humans. Probable human carcinogens are those chemicals demonstrated to have caused cancer in animals but the evidence is not definite for humans.	Known: benzene (leukaemia); vinyl chloride (liver angiosarcoma); 2-naphthylamine, benzidine (bladder cancer); asbestos (lung cancer, mesothelioma); hardwood dust (nasal or nasal sinus adenocarcinoma) Probable: formaldehyde, carbon tetrachloride, dichromates, beryllium
Reproductive toxicants	Reproductive toxicants interfere with an individual's reproductive or sexual functioning.	Manganese, carbon disulphide, monomethyl and ethyl ethers of ethylene glycol, mercury
Developmental toxicants	Developmental toxicants are agents that may cause an adverse effect in offspring of exposed people, effects such as spontaneous miscarriages, birth defects or developmental delays.	Organic mercury compounds, radiation, carbon monoxide, lead, thalidomide
Systemic poisons	Systemic poisons are agents that cause injury to particular organs or body systems.	Brain: solvents, lead, mercury, manganese Peripheral nervous system: n-hexane, lead, arsenic, carbon disulphide Blood-forming system: benzene, ethylene glycol ethers Kidneys: cadmium, lead, mercury, chlorinated hydrocarbons Lungs: silica, asbestos, black coal dust
BIOLOGICAL HAZARDS	**BIOLOGICAL HAZARDS MAY BE GROUPED INTO INFECTIOUS, NON-INFECTIOUS AND ALLERGENIC AGENTS**	
Infectious hazards	Workers at risk of exposure to bacteria, viruses, moulds, fungi or prions include employees at hospitals, laboratory workers, farmers, sewage and sludge treatment workers, slaughterhouse workers, veterinarians, zoo keepers and cooks.	Examples include hepatitis B and C, tuberculosis, anthrax, brucellosis, tetanus, chlamydia psittaci, salmonella, SARS, legionnaires' disease.
Non-infectious hazards	Workers at risk include cotton mill workers, hemp and flax workers, grain-silo workers.	Examples include byssinosis, grain fever
Allergens	Allergens might be found in many industrial environments, such as those involving fermentation processes, drug production, bakeries, paper production, wood processing (sawmills, production, manufacturing), as well as in biotechnology and spice production. Exposure to allergens may induce symptoms such as allergic rhinitis, conjunctivitis or asthma.	Occupational asthma: wool, furs, wheat grain, flour, red cedar, garlic powder Allergic alveolitis: farmer's disease, bagassosis, bird fancier's disease, humidifier fever, sequoiosis

TYPE OF HAZARD	WHAT IT DOES	EXAMPLES
PHYSICAL HAZARDS		
Noise	Exposure to high levels of noise (above 85 dB(A)) over a significant period of time or impulsive noise (above 140 dB(C)) may cause temporary and chronic hearing loss, as well as tinnitus.	Foundries, woodworking, textile mills, metalworking, tarmacs
Vibration	Manual work using powered tools is associated with symptoms of peripheral circulatory disturbance known as vibration-induced white finger (VWF). Vibrating tools may also result in reduced grip strength, low-back pain and degenerative back disorders.	Mining loaders, forklift trucks, pneumatic tools, chainsaws
Ionising radiation	Ionising radiation includes X-rays, gamma rays and radioactive particles including alpha and beta particles. Exposure to ionising radiation can cause DNA damage and cancer, including leukaemia.	Nuclear reactors, medical and dental X-ray tubes, particle accelerators, radioisotopes used as density or other gauges
Non-ionising radiation	Non-ionising radiation is electromagnetic radiation such as ultraviolet radiation, visible radiation, infrared, lasers, microwaves, radio frequency. Direct exposure to non-ionising radiation can cause tissue damage from heating of the tissues. In addition, ultraviolet light can cause skin cancers; infrared radiation might cause cataracts; high-powered lasers may cause eye and skin damage.	Ultraviolet radiation: outdoor work; arc welding and cutting; UV curing of inks, glues and paints; disinfection Infrared radiation: furnaces, glassblowing Lasers: communications, surgery, construction
Heat and cold	High environmental temperature, high humidity, strenuous exercise and impaired heat dissipation may cause heat stress disorders. Cold temperatures can cause hypothermia and frostbite.	Working indoors: furnaces, freezers Working outdoors: extreme climatic conditions
PSYCHOSOCIAL HAZARDS[5]		
Stress	Workplace stress is the harmful physical and emotional response that results from a poor match between job demands and the capabilities, resources or needs of the worker. Stress is capable of producing physiological, emotional, cognitive and behavioural effects, which can lead to poor health or injury.	Various working environments
Bullying	Bullying is an act of repeated aggressive behaviour with the intention of hurting another person. Workplace bullying is often associated with new, younger, female or immigrant workers being intimidated by established workers. It can result in health effects similar to stress (see above).	Various working environments, including construction, manufacturing and defence forces
Violence	Violent attacks can come from internal and external sources.	Various working environments, including cash-handling, law enforcement, custodial, hospital and welfare services

In the remainder of this chapter, we look at how the principles of occupational hygiene apply specifically to workplace hazards. This chapter looks at two specific examples of workplace hazards – noise and chemicals – and how occupational hygiene is used to assess and control them. Occupational hygiene methodologies can be used on most of the hazards noted in Figure 9.1. Finally, aspects of an overall health program in a workplace are examined in the context of a case study.

IDENTIFYING OCCUPATIONAL HYGIENE HAZARDS AND RISKS

Information on hazards is available from a number of sources. In the first instance, the legislation in your local jurisdiction should be consulted. This will include the Work Health and Safety Act and regulations for hazards in general. In relation to hazardous chemicals, the Dangerous Goods Act and relevant regulations under that Act cover their transportation, and the Work Health and Safety Regulations[6] provide direction in relation to storage and use on site. The Work Health and Safety Regulations also contain specific obligations in relation to hazardous chemicals, noise and other specific hazards. In addition, legislation other than these regulations may apply to specific hazardous chemicals, such as radioactive substances, in each jurisdiction.

The regulator in each jurisdiction normally also provides a range of guidance information covering specific hazards and industries. These may include codes of practice, guidance notes and other documentation. Safe Work Australia also provides model national standards, as well as research and statistical information – for example, covering workers' compensation claims – that would be helpful in identifying hazards within an industry or occupation. Safe Work Australia has published information on exposure to various hazardous chemicals, including asbestos, in a range of industries in Australia.[7]

Occupational hygiene applies the basic risk management model (see Chapter 6) in the workplace. That is:

- establish the context or situation that applies in the workplace
- identify what hazards, such as those discussed in Figure 9.1, are present
- assess the risks associated with those hazards; for many chemical and physical hazards, part of the risk assessment will involve measurement (see Chapter 10), either in the atmosphere or through biological or medical surveillance
- when the risk is deemed to be unacceptable (for example, when the measured level is greater than the exposure standard), undertake appropriate control action to eliminate the risk or, when that is not reasonably practicable, to reduce the risk as low as reasonably practicable
- routinely assess the control measures to ensure that they achieve regulatory compliance in relation to the hazard as a minimum, and that the controls remain effective.

NOISE HAZARDS AND HEARING CONSERVATION

Noise can be defined as unwanted sound and is present in nearly all industry sectors. It can result in noise-induced hearing loss (NIHL) in noisy environments such as the mining industry or mechanised workplaces, annoyance caused by stray loud conversations in open-plan offices or acoustic shock in call centres.

Between July 2002 and June 2007 there were approximately 16 500 successful workers' compensation claims for NIHL in Australia.[8] Apart from the cost to the workers' compensation system, this also represents a significant burden on the victims and their families.

Noise physics

To better understand the requirements of legislation, and to understand how to control noise, it is necessary to briefly describe some aspects of noise physics.

Sound is perceived as pressure fluctuations (for example in air) that the human ear can detect. The sound of a voice, or any industrial noise, is generally a mixture of different frequencies, which are measured in hertz (Hz). For example, the range of frequencies of the notes on a piano is 27.5 Hz to 4186 Hz. A healthy young adult can hear frequencies in the approximate range of 20 Hz to 20 000 Hz. As a person ages, they generally lose the ability to hear the higher frequencies (a hearing loss called presbycusis, which is different from NIHL).

The human ear does not perceive each frequency with equal sensitivity, and is most sensitive to what are termed the middle frequencies – around 2000 to 5000 Hz. It is less sensitive to the very low frequencies, and very high frequencies. It should be noted that consonants in human speech are perceived at these middle frequencies.

Apart from frequency, the other main quantity used to describe a sound is the size of the pressure fluctuations. Normally we measure such sound pressure levels (SPL) in terms of decibels (dB), which are based on a logarithmic scale that is calculated relative to the weakest sound that the human ear can hear (zero decibels). The threshold of pain for sound is around 140 decibels.

With the concept of frequency and SPL, we can now describe the way that noise is measured. Since not all frequencies are sensed in the same way in the ear, most sound-level meters (noise meters) deconstruct the sound as it is picked up by the microphone into individual frequencies and then modify (weight) each frequency as it would be perceived by the ear. Meters then reconstruct this new weighted sound into a measure called 'decibels – A weighted', or dB(A). The noise exposure standard is given in dB(A). Most sound-level meters also have a second inbuilt weighting scale, the 'C' weighting, which is used for measuring peak levels.

In a normal workplace, the noise level is never constant, but fluctuates continuously from very quiet to sometimes very loud. Sound-level meters (cumulating type) and noise dosimeters (discussed further in Chapter 10) average those fluctuations so that an eight-hour equivalent SPL can be obtained. This allows those multiple fluctuations to be assessed for their risk of causing NIHL by comparison against the exposure standard.

An occupational hygienist may be required to assess the noise risks within a workplace using relevant instrumentation. However, a rule of thumb is that if you have to raise your voice to talk to a worker at about one metre away, or have ringing in your ears at the end of the day, you are probably in a situation that puts you at risk of developing NIHL.

DID YOU KNOW?

You can calculate noise dose from plant sound pressure levels. The Health and Safety Executive in the UK provides an online noise dose calculator that allows conversion of sound pressure levels – say of individual machines or operations – into an eight-hour equivalent exposure. You need the times of exposure to the nearest 15 minutes to each of the sound pressure levels for the calculation. See http://www.hse.gov.uk/noise/dailycalc.xls.

Health effects

Noise is detected via a network of sensors within the cochlear in the inner ear. Any sustained exposure to noise levels over around 80 dB will result in a temporary numbing of those sensors and temporary threshold shift. If the ear is rested in quiet surroundings, the sensors will recover. However, repeated noise assaults on the ear will, over time, result in the temporary threshold shift (TTS) becoming a permanent threshold shift, or NIHL. NIHL can be identified by an audiologist by the characteristic hearing loss at the middle frequencies. This results in a reduced ability to differentiate consonants within speech, hence reducing communication capabilities. Over time, it will generally result in a reduction in the quality of life for the sufferer.

Exposure to high noise levels (over 85 dB(A)) over a long period of time causes NIHL. The higher the noise level and the longer the time of exposure, the more extensive will be the NIHL. There generally is no physiological warning that hearing is deteriorating as it is very gradual, but early NIHL can be picked up during audiometric testing. Typical noise levels (in dB) can be:

- library   40
- business office   60
- heavy truck   90
- pneumatic hammer   105
- jet take-off   125.

DID YOU KNOW?

Does your workplace noise cause a temporary threshold shift?

Repeated TTSs can lead to permanent threshold shifts or NIHL. If you drive to work, you can do a simple test to assess whether you develop TTS at the end of a shift. Here is how to do it.

1. When you arrive at the factory's car park in the morning, turn off the engine but leave the radio/stereo on with the key in 'accessories' position.
2. Turn the volume down so that you can just hear the radio/stereo, then fully turn off the ignition, remove the key and go to work.

3. At the end of the shift, get back into the car and put the key back to 'accessories' (don't start the engine) – which should turn on the radio/stereo, without you touching the volume knob.
4. If you cannot now hear the radio/stereo that you could hear that morning, you are suffering a TTS from the noise experienced during the shift.

Other effects of noise can be annoyance and acoustic shock. It should be noted that these do not generally cause NIHL, but can have other physiological or psychological effects. Annoyance can arise in environments such as open-plan offices, where employees can be distracted from their jobs by conversations at nearby desks. Research shows that the most annoying aspect of office noise is speech by other workers (46 per cent), followed by the noise of office machines (25 per cent).[9] Such annoyance, if unresolved over a period, can result in employee stress.

Acoustic shock is a recent phenomenon that is particularly relevant in the call-centre industry. It is defined as:

> any temporary or permanent disturbance of the functioning of the ear, or the nervous system, which can be caused to the user of a telephone earphone by a sudden sharp rise in the acoustic pressure produced by it.[10]

It generally results from a high frequency shriek or other loud sound in the earpiece that might be of human origin (someone blowing a whistle into the phone mouthpiece) or the result of an electrical/electronic malfunction. The sounds are generally over a very short duration, as the operator quickly removes the headset. They can result in pain in the ear, nausea, tinnitus and other symptoms. These symptoms generally disappear over time, but the operator may remain wary and traumatised.

Legislative requirements

All jurisdictions in Australia have common noise exposure standards incorporated in their Work Health and Safety Regulations. The maximum allowable daily noise exposure level is 85 dB(A), as an eight-hour equivalent A-weighted sound pressure level (also shown as $L_{Aeq,8h}$). In addition, 140 dB(C) is set as a C-weighted peak sound pressure exposure standard, which could be thought of as an instantaneous maximum noise standard.

Organisations need to assess the risk of hazardous noise exposure of employees. Where such exposure is in excess of the exposure standard, the employer must implement appropriate control measures. In the first instance, exposure to noise by employees should be eliminated, so far as reasonably practicable. If that is not possible, the exposure must be reduced so far as reasonably practicable by substituting quieter plant or processes, or using engineering controls. If that does not reduce the exposure to below the exposure standard, then appropriate administrative controls or hearing protectors need to be employed. Where hearing protectors are required as part of a hearing conservation program, the employer needs to provide audiometric testing within three months of a person starting, and then every two years thereafter. The requirements of a hearing conservation program are discussed below.

Controlling noise

Noise always results from some vibrating source, follows a transmission pathway, and then is perceived by the receiver. By understanding this process, we can understand the essentials of noise control. Basically, we can reduce the noise at source, interrupt its pathway or isolate the receiver.[11]

Reduce noise at source

Reducing the noise at the source is the preferred approach, consistent with the hierarchy of control. There are some generic ways of reducing noise at source, including

- replacing the plant or operation by quieter machines or equipment
- maintaining plant properly – badly worn bearings and gears, poor lubrication, loose parts, slapping belts, unbalanced rotating parts and steam or air leaks all create noise that can be reduced by planned maintenance
- relocating noisy plant or equipment that need not be inside the factory walls; for example, pumps, fans or compressors could be located outside or in separate noise-proof rooms
- modifying processes so that impact or other process noises are reduced (for example, minimising the fall height of a product onto hard surfaces); using rubber mats on work benches or vibration dampers on machinery is effective in reducing noise.

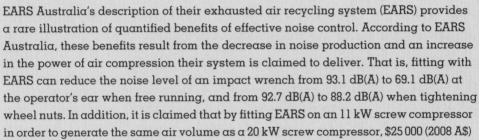

WHS IN PRACTICE

NOISE REDUCTION AT SOURCE

EARS Australia's description of their exhausted air recycling system (EARS) provides a rare illustration of quantified benefits of effective noise control. According to EARS Australia, these benefits result from the decrease in noise production and an increase in the power of air compression their system is claimed to deliver. That is, fitting with EARS can reduce the noise level of an impact wrench from 93.1 dB(A) to 69.1 dB(A) at the operator's ear when free running, and from 92.7 dB(A) to 88.2 dB(A) when tightening wheel nuts. In addition, it is claimed that by fitting EARS on an 11 kW screw compressor in order to generate the same air volume as a 20 kW screw compressor, $25 000 (2008 A$) can be saved over 10 years from savings on energy costs ($21 000) and capital costs ($4000).[12]

You can get ideas for controlling your noise problems through the HSE Sound Solutions database[13] or the (US) Noise Reduction Ideas Bank.[14]

Source: Safe Work Australia, 2010, *Occupational Noise-induced Hearing Loss in Australia*, © Commonwealth of Australia: Canberra, p. 32, http://safeworkaustralia.gov.au/AboutSafeWorkAustralia/WhatWeDo/Publications/Documents/539/Occupational_Noiseinduced_Hearing_Loss_Australia_2010.pdf

Engineering treatment of the noise transmission path

The next preferred approach is to interrupt the noise pathway by engineering means. Methods include isolating the noisy plant in an enclosure, acoustically treating the area to reduce noise or protecting the employee within a sound-reducing room. Examples of sound-reducing techniques include

- erection of noise barriers between the noise source and the exposed employee to reduce noise transmission; lead, steel, brick and concrete – all heavy and dense materials – make good transmission barriers
- use of absorbing material such as fibreglass or polyurethane foam on surfaces facing the noise source (for example, ceiling, walls) to reduce reflection and increase noise absorption
- use of acoustic silencers on air-intake and exhaust systems.

To be completely effective, enclosures need to seal all air pathways. Reducing noise at source or by treating the pathway calls for specialists such acoustic engineers. It is always easier to stop noise at the design or purchase stage. It does *not* require specialised knowledge to insist that specifications for all machinery require noise levels to be supplied and for this information, and its interpretation, to be provided to the relevant HS committee, prior to purchase or installation, as required by the Work Health and Safety Act.

Protecting the employee

Lower on the hierarchy of control are administrative control measures and provision of hearing protectors. Administrative controls include

- organising schedules so that noisy work is done when as few employees as possible are present
- rotating jobs so that employees are rotated through tasks to reduce the period of exposure for individuals.

Areas where persons may be exposed to noise levels in excess of the exposure standard must be identified as hearing-protection areas, and the boundaries clearly defined through the installation of mandatory signage consistent with AS/NZS 1319:1994 *Safety signs for the occupational environment*, as shown in Figure 9.2.

Where engineering and administrative controls do not reduce the noise exposure below the exposure standard, employees must be supplied with and wear effective hearing-protection devices. These could be earmuffs or earplugs of various types. However, the reason why hearing protectors are a less desirable control measure is that incorrect wearing or removal of the protectors for even a short time can significantly reduce their effectiveness and result in the exposure standard being exceeded by the employee. Information on selection and use of hearing protectors can be obtained in AS/NZS 1269.3:2005 *Occupational noise management – hearing protector program*.[15]

Before hearing protectors are issued, the need for their use, and where and how they are to be used, must be fully explained to those having to wear them. Supervision on correct wearing should be undertaken to ensure that hearing conservation is maintained. Absence of such supervision can seriously erode the program's effectiveness.[16]

When an employer has to provide hearing-protection devices to control noise exposure in an area to below the exposure standards, it is good practice and consistent with AS/NZS 1269.3:2005 for the employer to provide audiometric testing for employees within three months of commencing work in that area, and every two years thereafter. This is normally undertaken by an audiologist or an occupational health nurse under the direction of an audiologist. The employer must ensure that records of all noise and hearing testing are kept and reviewed periodically to ensure that the hearing conservation program is effective in control the risk of NIHL.

Figure 9.2 *Mandatory hearing-protection symbol (from AS/NZS 1319)*

MANUFACTURING OPERATION

CASE STUDY

PLANT DESCRIPTION

The Acme Artisan Company is a small Melbourne organisation making custom parts such as specialty metal handles, hinges, and so on, for an exclusive period furniture manufacturer. The parts are handmade by a team of five craftsmen that have been working in the organisation in excess of 10 years. The manufacturing process involves stamping metal parts using a press, grinding, drilling, finishing and polishing. The company adopts a batch process to the manufacturing so that on a daily basis they generally make one variety of parts. The noisy processes (stamping, drilling, grinding) happen to be carried out in the morning, with the afternoon spent in finishing the products and packing them in such a way that they are protected in transit.

There have been some articles in the industry newsletter about hearing loss, and the employer, after reading the articles, did notice that some of the craftsmen were a little hard of hearing and that, particularly in the morning production run, it was difficult to talk face to face to the people on the shopfloor without raising his voice.

RISK ASSESSMENT

An occupational hygienist was contracted to undertake a noise level and noise dose survey of the various processes and operators in the shop and provided the following data.

A – Sound pressure levels using a calibrated noise meter taken in the vicinity of the craftsmen showed the following average results.

Operation	SPL dB(A)	Duration (hours)
Stamping	90	1
Drilling	86	1
Grinding	92	2
Finishing and polishing	81	2
Packaging	70	2

B – Noise dose: all craftsmen carry out similar tasks. Calibrated dosimeter readings on two of them showed that they were exposed to an equivalent eight-hour exposure level of 88 dB(A) over the shift. This is double the exposure standard, so is unacceptable. Appropriate control action is required.

RISK CONTROL

The employer contracted an acoustic engineer to review the operation and advise on appropriate control action. The engineer looked at those operations having a noise level in excess of 85 dB(A) only, and recommended the following.

- If impact-resistant perspex was used in place of the open-mesh guards on the stamping machine so as to enclose the relevant noisy parts of the machine, the noise levels would be reduced to 86 dB(A).
- Sharpening the drill bits more frequently and modifying the drill mount with the use of rubber inserts to isolate the product being drilled would reduce the drill noise to 84 dB(A).
- The grinding was carried out on a steel bench. A solid rubber mat placed on the table would isolate the grinding action and the noise levels would reduce to 88 dB(A).

If these modifications were implemented, the new sound pressure levels would be as follows.

Operation	SPL dB(A)	Duration (hours)
Stamping	86	1
Drilling	84	1
Grinding	88	2
Finishing and polishing	81	2
Packaging	70	2

The equivalent eight-hour exposure level of the operators would then be reduced to 84 dB(A). This is now below the exposure standard, so hearing protectors are not required. However, the employer also purchased light earmuffs after consultation with the operators, so that they could wear them when the stamping and grinding operations were carried out if they wished. In addition, in recognition of past exposure, the employer paid for a baseline audiometry test for the operators to establish current hearing levels.

Questions

1 How do you know if you are in a potentially hazardous noise environment, without the use of measuring instrumentation?
2 In terms of controlling hazardous noise, describe the three areas where noise can be controlled over its pathway.
3 Describe the preferred ways of controlling hazardous noise exposure consistent with the hierarchy of control.

HAZARDOUS CHEMICALS

Persons conducting a business or undertaking have the following duties in regard to hazardous chemicals:[17]

- to assess and control risks arising from the use of hazardous chemicals
- to provide employees with information, instruction and training
- to consult with employees and their representatives
- where necessary, to carry out atmospheric monitoring and health or medical surveillance.

To begin the job of assessing and controlling the risks, an assessment team representing management, employees and, if necessary, specialists would need to be brought together. The team should

- know the relevant law and guidance material governing hazardous chemicals
- be able to read and understand information found on labels or in safety data sheets (SDSs; also known as material safety data sheets, or MSDSs)
- have access to specialist advice from HS professionals (occupational hygienists, and so on) or other advisors (ventilation engineers, equipment manufacturers) as needed.

Identifying the hazardous chemicals

Risk phrases on the SDS and pictograms on the chemical containers will help to identify **hazardous chemicals**[18](see Figure 9.3). Hazardous chemicals may be solids, liquids, gases, vapours, dusts, mists or fumes. Detailed information should be obtained about processes to identify the chemicals used, including:

- raw materials
- materials handled or added in the process, such as additives and catalysts
- final products and reaction by-products.

The assessment team should establish a hazardous chemical register to record their assessments. The register should record the amount of the chemical and where it is located.

Figure 9.3 *Pictograms from the UN Globally Harmonized System of Classifying and Labelling Chemicals*

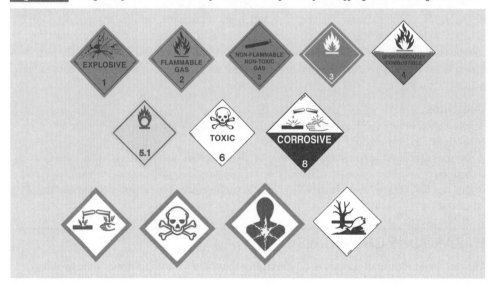

Safety data sheets

Safety data sheets provide information about the identity of a chemical, its hazards and how to use it safely. It contains information about first aid, fire-fighting, spills, handling and storage, exposure control, personal protective equipment, toxicity and ecological impacts. An accurate SDS must be obtained from the manufacturers or importers of hazardous chemicals and kept up to date (less than five years old) and must be made available to employees. A sample SDS is found as an appendix to this book.

DID YOU KNOW?

HAZARDOUS SUBSTANCES INFORMATION SYSTEM (HSIS)

Safe Work Australia maintains an Internet database, the Hazardous Substances Information System (HSIS). You will need the chemical name or CAS number, which is a unique numerical identifier for chemical compounds, polymers, biological sequences and alloys.

To interrogate the HSIS, enter the CAS number or the correctly spelled chemical name. The database will provide information on the hazardous chemicals classification and exposure standard information (see 'Additional resources' at the end of the chapter).

Evaluate any exposure

The next step is to determine if there are any exposures to the chemicals. To determine if there are potential exposures, a walk-through survey of the workplace should be undertaken, examining each of the processes and looking for evidence of chemical use and escape. Consult those involved in normal operations and non-production situations such as maintenance, cleaning and emergencies about when they inhale or come into skin contact with the chemicals. Injury and incident reports should also be reviewed.

Chemical processes might occur in a closed system without anyone being exposed except during maintenance work or process failure, while other processes may take place in open systems, which may or may not have local exhaust ventilation. Each of these will have different potential for exposure, with the closed system usually having the least exposure and the open system with no local exhaust ventilation having the potential for most exposure.

Atmospheric monitoring is required when there is an exposure standard for the hazardous chemical and if you are not sure whether the exposure standard may be exceeded, or if you cannot determine the risk to health with confidence by simply reviewing the information about the chemical and examining the nature of the work.

If the chemical is not released or emitted into the work area, then the exposure is not significant. Where there is potential for exposure, the exposure needs to be assessed and compared to the exposure standard within the HSIS. Exposure standards are generally based on the concentration of the chemical in air that should not adversely affect the health of the average worker for eight hours a day, five days a week, over a working lifetime. However, it should be noted that

> Exposure standards do not represent 'no effect' levels at which every worker can be guaranteed adequate protection, nor do they constitute a 'fine line' between satisfactory and unsatisfactory working conditions. Given the range of individual susceptibility, it is inevitable that a small proportion of workers who are exposed to concentrations at or below the exposure standard will suffer mild or transitory discomfort ... [or] illness.[19]

Accordingly, occupational hygiene best practice is to try to have a local action level for the control of hazardous chemicals at one half of the allowable exposure standard. This allows for the occasional excursion above the action level without breaching the legislated exposure standard, and provides a better situation for those workers more sensitive to the hazardous chemical.

Identify control actions

If the exposure is likely to exceed the exposure standard, then appropriate controls should be implemented, taking into account the hierarchy of controls. The legislation requires that where reasonably practicable, exposure to hazardous chemicals should be eliminated. Where this is not reasonably practicable, the risk has to be mitigated. Examples of the application of the hierarchy of control for chemicals follow:

* *elimination*; for example, elimination of asbestos cement-sheet walls
* *substitution*; for example, using a water-based paint instead of a solvent-based paint
* *isolation*; for example, separation of employees from the chemical by using closed systems
* *engineering controls*; for example, use of local exhaust ventilation (engineering controls are changes to the process or equipment that reduce or eliminate exposures to an agent)
* *administrative controls*; for example, restricting access, rotating workers through jobs with exposures, work practices that reduce exposure
* *personal protective clothing and equipment*; for example, respirators, chemical goggles, protective gloves and face shields.

A combination of the control methods described above may be required to ensure adequate control of the overall process. All controls must be maintained and monitored to ensure their effectiveness. For any control to be effective, workers must be able to fully perform their tasks with the control in place. If the control measures interfere with the tasks, workers may be reluctant to use them, which could result in increased exposures.

Scheduled hazardous chemicals (referred to in the Work Health and Safety Regulations, Schedule 14) may also require specific health surveillance. Examples include benzene, lead and asbestos. Such surveillance can include biological monitoring, such as determining the quantity of lead in blood, or medical tests, such as lung function related to asbestos or silica exposure.

Establish emergency procedures and first aid facilities when necessary. This is particularly important in the case of leaks, spills or other uncontrolled releases. Requirements may include showers and eyewash facilities as well as evacuation and clean-up procedures.

Documentation and training

Assessments and controls must be documented within safe work procedures. Information, instruction, training and supervision are required for anyone likely to be exposed to hazardous chemicals. In particular, training should allow employees to be able to demonstrate an understanding of:

* the labelling of hazardous chemicals
* the use of SDSs

- hazards to which they are likely to be exposed
- safe work practices
- risk controls
- effective use of personal protective equipment
- emergency and first aid procedures
- incident reporting.

Risk assessments should be recorded with all the details of the process and potential exposures, as described above. Minimum recording requirements are set out in the regulations.

Most importantly, everyone affected should be able to access the risk assessments and monitoring data for the chemicals and processes to which they are exposed. If any changes to work processes or controls are required, workers should be consulted about their implementation. A summarised report should detail how the workplace will be monitored and the monitoring results should be distributed to those affected; for example, as graphs on the noticeboard. Workers should have access to the contact details of someone who can explain the assessments, interventions or monitoring results. Health and safety representatives and HS committees should have access to aggregated health or medical surveillance data.

Assessments should be regularly reviewed, particularly when changes to the processes have occurred or incidents have occurred, monitoring or health surveillance indicate potential problems, or when better information or new controls become available.

Hazardous chemical health and safety program

Health and safety programs may be defined as programs instigated within an organisation to maintain the workers' state of wellbeing and freedom from occupationally related disease or injury. Best-practice organisations will take this beyond merely controlling workplace hazards to promoting healthy lifestyles in and beyond the workplace. This aspect will not be further developed here; however, readers wanting to learn more about employee wellness programs can read further at the Free Management Library.[20]

The discussion on the development, implementation and assessment of a health and safety program will be undertaken within the context of an extended case study of a lead-risk operation.

CASE STUDY

HANDLING DRY LEAD COMPONENTS IN A PVC MANUFACTURING PLANT

A small PVC parts manufacturing plant uses lead-based UV stabilisers in some PVC formulations.

An operator handles the stabilisers during batch mixing. The stabiliser is weighed out by scooping the powder from 25 kg bags into a plastic drum on a set of scales. Once all the raw ingredients are weighed, they are tipped into a dry blender. After mixing, the batch is transferred into hoppers which feed the extruders. Approximately 8–10 batches are prepared per eight-hour shift.

The operator has access to a disposable half-face piece respirator but he prefers not to wear it, especially on hot days, as he finds that the combination of dust and sweat around the rim of the respirator irritates his face.

The operator wears his own street clothes at work and does not change out of the clothes or wash when eating or leaving work. The weighing and blending areas are swept clean at the end of each shift.

ASSESSING THE RISK

- Form of lead: the stabiliser is a white dusty powder. It contains 8% lead by weight.
- Routes of exposure: the MSDS [the SDS] states that the main route of exposure to the stabiliser is through inhalation of the airborne dust, and that good housekeeping and personal hygiene need to be maintained to control the risk of inhalation and ingestion exposure.
- Level of exposure: Safe Work Australia's [HSIS] atmospheric exposure standard for inorganic lead is 0.15 mg/m^3. Biological monitoring of the operator showed that his blood lead level was 2.2 μmol/L indicating that there is a significant risk of lead exposure in the process [This is some 50 per cent over the allowable blood lead level for a male worker]. The biological monitoring results identify the process as a lead-risk job.
- Tasks undertaken: the operator's hands and forearms are covered with powder when he scoops the stabiliser out of the bags and airborne dust is being generated by the weighing and blender loading tasks. Dry sweeping of the process area generates airborne dust.

IS THERE A RISK?

The process is a lead-risk job and there is a significant risk to the operator from lead inhalation and ingestion. Because there is a risk, control measures need to be put in place.

Source: WorkSafe Victoria, 2000, *Code of Practice for Lead*, No. 26, p. 13; access http://www.worksafe.vic.gov.au for more information and future updates.

Legislative requirements

The employer's responsibilities for lead-risk jobs are set out within the Work Health and Safety Act and Regulations in terms of consultation, provision of information, instruction and training, risk assessments, risk controls, and atmospheric and biological monitoring to ensure the exposure standard is not exceeded, and the program reviewed to ensure its effectiveness. These aspects will now be discussed.

Consultation

Chapter 3 identifies the requirements for HS consultation in the workplace. In this case study, the employees and/or health and safety representative should be provided with relevant information on the process, including the *Code of Practice for Lead*, SDSs for any products used, incident reports, historic atmospheric monitoring data and averaged biological surveillance data for the operation.

Information, instruction and training

As part of background briefing, the employer may call upon a medical practitioner, who carries out blood testing of the employees and discusses potential health issues associated with lead exposure. These issues can include

- how lead enters the body
- toxicity related to specific body organs, and the male and female reproductive systems
- specific toxicity (teratogenicity) of lead for the foetus and special precautions that have to be applied to women of reproductive capacity
- susceptibility of infants to the effect of lead if carried into the home on clothing.

Job applicants must be provided with this information at the application stage, including the legislative requirement for periodic blood testing.

This information would be part of an operator training program and included for initial training and then follow-up instruction for anyone working in and supervising lead-risk jobs. Such training provides employees with the skills and knowledge they need to perform their job safely. Essential parts of this training take into account the special needs of employees – including work experience, gender, language and literacy – and would include

- safe work procedures including access to relevant SDSs
- the requirement and use of control measures in the operation
- medical examinations and biological monitoring.

Procedures and training should be adjusted whenever there is a change in the process, or additional information – for example, on the effectiveness of the risk controls – becomes available.

Training on HS issues should be carried out by a person who is competent to provide that training. This might mean that the trainer has a Certificate IV in Assessment and Training, or equivalent, and is also knowledgeable about the subject matter[21] – in this case, lead-risk processes. The effectiveness of the training and information process can be tested in the short term by testing the knowledge of the participants immediately after the training and then, say, the following week. However, it is also important to review the whole risk control program, of which training is a part, to review whether blood lead values are elevated or are retained within biological exposure standards.

Risk assessment

Risk assessments must be carried on all lead-risk jobs. This process should include people who understand the process, including the health and safety representative, but may also require specialist skills, including those of an occupational hygienist who routinely assesses exposure to lead dust or fume. All aspects of the process should be considered, including cleaning, maintenance and similar situations.

Biological monitoring is the most effective way of measuring the amount of lead that is actually absorbed by an employee. Blood lead might be extracted by an occupational health nurse, analysed in an appropriate NATA[22]-registered laboratory, and then reviewed and reported on by a medical practitioner.

In terms of risk assessment, women of reproductive capacity, as well as pregnant or breastfeeding women, have a special susceptibility to the effects of lead and have to be treated differently from women not in those categories and differently to men. The legislated allowable blood lead levels and the frequency of biological testing differ for the two groups. Other individuals that might be more susceptible to the effects of lead include those with anaemia or kidney disease, who should be detected at the pre-employment medical examination.

Risk controls

Controls need to be consistent within the hierarchy of control, with emphasis on substitution, isolation or engineering controls of lead dust or fume. Local exhaust ventilation is normally used in processes such as those described in the case study. Cleaning should be carried out with vacuum or wet methods and never by dry sweeping. Administrative controls in the form of safe work procedures will be mandatory, and the use of personal protective equipment, such as special clothing, gloves or respirators, may be required, depending on the process.

Personal hygiene, including removal of overalls and other protective equipment, and thorough washing prior to eating or leaving the plant are essential. Smoking within the work area should be prohibited because of the risk of lead dust contaminating the cigarettes and hence entering the body through cigarette smoke.

CONTROL MEASURES

After having assessed the lead exposure risk, a number of control strategies were considered by the employer. Elimination and substitution of the stabilisers with less toxic substances were rejected as control measures because they would alter the properties of the PVC and make it unsuitable for use.

Engineering controls were looked at, and it was decided that the most efficient method of controlling the airborne lead dust in the operator's breathing zone was to install local extraction ventilation around the scales and at the mixer loading point. This was done with the use of a system with a flexible arm so that the same extractor could be used for weighing and loading by simply swinging the flexible duct arm into the right position. The extraction system allows for a connecting flexible hose, which can be used to vacuum the floor area around the scales and mixer. This eliminates the sweeping task.

In order to reduce the contamination of the operator's clothing and body, the employer provided the operator with personal protective equipment in the form of overalls with long sleeves and elbow-length rubber gloves. Two sets of lockers were provided in the change room and the operator was instructed that he must use one locker for his street clothing and the other for his overalls.

An administrative policy was introduced that required the operator to remove his overalls and wash before eating or leaving the plant at the end of the shift. The overalls and other personal equipment were laundered by specialist laundries, and at the employer's cost.

HS PROGRAM EFFECTIVENESS

The training, testing, controls and procedures will have to be reviewed as an integrated system to assess their effectiveness in controlling the risk of lead diseases. There are a number of local information sources that might be used by the HS committee and/or management to routinely assess the program's effectiveness. These include the following.

- Observation through routine inspections: Are employees following the safe work procedures? Is the ventilation system working well, or is dust on surfaces evidence of inadequacy of the ventilation? Is airborne dust visible in the shafts of light in the factory? Do employees follow good personal hygiene? Is work clothing segregated from street clothing?
- Airborne monitoring: Does routine air monitoring show that the exposure to airborne lead dust is always below the legislated exposure standard of 0.15 mg/m^3?
- Biological surveillance: Does the blood lead data show that blood lead is below legislated requirements for each of the target groups, including women of reproductive capacity?

If any of the above indicators identify that the controls are not working as intended, then the deficiencies need to be investigated and remedied. For example, filters on ventilation systems may become clogged and this reduces the effectiveness of the ventilation system. However, in this case, the important issue is not that the filters were clogged, but why did the maintenance program not have the filter cleaning on the routine plan? Such root-cause analyses will allow ongoing compliance in these high-risk jobs.

Questions
1 What are the likely health effects from exposure to lead dust?
2 Why are there different biological exposure standards for women compared to men?
3 What are preferred ways to control a toxic dust, consistent with the hierarchy of control?

Source: WorkSafe Victoria, 2000, *Code of Practice for Lead*, No. 26, p. 13.

Summary
- Occupational hygiene deals with chemical, physical, biological and psychosocial hazards. Occupational hygienists or other suitably qualified professionals may be required if there is any doubt about appropriate risk assessment and control.
- Employers must consult with employees and their representatives on workplace risks and provide employees with information, instruction, training and supervision on workplace hazards.
- Employers, in consultation with employees, must assess and control the risks in the workplace. Where necessary, they may have to carry out relevant exposure monitoring and health or medical surveillance.
- Risk control measures have to be consistent with the hierarchy of control.
- Employees have to be appropriately trained in hazards and relevant risk control.
- Records of risk assessments, exposure monitoring, control measures, health or medical surveillance, and training must be kept and regularly reviewed to ensure that the health and safety program is achieving its objectives of protecting employees from workplace hazards.

In your workplace
At the International Engineering Co., the period between mid-December and mid-January is the time of the annual shutdown, when production ceases and planned maintenance is undertaken. This generally involves some or all of the following activities.
- Stripping down the machines to examine parts for wear and subsequent replacement. This may involve exposure to various oils and greases used to lubricate the machines, and the use of kerosene to clean accumulated muck. Water-based products are not used since they cause rusting of the machinery.
- Disassembly of the machines can involve the use of impact wrenches (similar to those used by garages to fit tyres) to unbolt/refit parts, which can be noisy. This occurs most of the time during the planned maintenance.
- Some of the parts being disassembled or assembled have sharp edges and can weigh up to 50 kilograms.

You are the safety officer and need to develop a safe work procedure for the planned maintenance job described above.
1 Identify the hazards likely to be involved in the job.
   Hint: for chemical hazards, locate an appropriate SDS on the Internet and identify the relevant hazards associated with the chemicals used. For noise, identify the appropriate noise levels from examples in this chapter. For manual handling, refer to Chapter 8 for appropriate hazard identification.

2   Assess the risks in relation to these identified hazards.
    Hint: review the Work Health and Safety Regulations to assess legislated requirements. Do
    you need additional hygiene monitoring to help you assess the risk?

3   Identify appropriate control measures that could be used to minimise the risks to the
    maintenance team.
    Hint: take into account the hierarchy of control but remember 'reasonably practicable'. Use
    the SDS as well as information in this chapter as a starting point.

4   How would your answer change if the maintenance team had to work for 14 by 12-hour shifts
    immediately before Christmas Eve, and then again 14 by 12-hour shifts after New Year's Day?
    Hint: refer to Chapter 11.

Questions

1   What are the principal types of hazards dealt with by occupational hygiene? Give examples of
    each of these types.
2   What are the employer's specific duties in relation to hazardous chemicals? Check the
    regulations before you respond.
3   When do you need to do environmental monitoring or health surveillance?
4   What are the exposure standards for noise?
5   What are the possible adverse health effects from noise exposure?
6   Why does planned maintenance generally keep noise levels lower?
7   Identify the hierarchy of control as it applies to noise control.
8   Describe the essential elements of a hearing conservation program.

Activities

1   In your workplace, identify any hazardous chemicals. Does your workplace have a hazardous
    chemicals register? If not, look up on the Internet safety data sheets that give you further
    information on these chemicals. Raise this issue with your supervisor or health and safety
    representative.
2   Read the SDS in the appendix to this book and answer the following questions.
    a   What is the product and where might it be used?
    b   What are the hazards associated with its use and how might the body be affected?
    c   What are the exposure standards?
    d   What are the recommended types of control?
    e   If you spill this product, what material or equipment do you need to have available?

Search me!

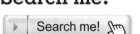

Explore **Search me! management** for relevant articles on
occupational hygiene. Search me! is an online library of world-class
journals, ebooks and newspapers, including *The Australian* and the *New York Times*, and is
updated daily. Log in to Search me! through www.cengage.com/sso using the access card in the
front of this book.

KEYWORDS

Try searching for the following terms:
▶ globally harmonised system
▶ noise control
▶ carcinogen
▶ chemical hazards (or search for a specific chemical; for example, epoxy, petrol, etc.)

Search tip: **Search me! management** contains information from both local and international sources. To get the greatest number of search results, try using both Australian and American spellings in your searches, e.g. 'globalisation' and 'globalization'; 'organisation' and 'organization'.

Additional resources

The websites of the state, commonwealth and territory WHS regulators contain information not only on legislation specific to the jurisdiction, but also guidance material that covers occupational hygiene issues.

While this chapter focuses on hazardous chemicals and noise, some links dealing with biological, physical and psychosocial hazards, as well as links to other authorities and research bodies follow.

- Safe Work Australia (www.safeworkaustralia.gov.au) contains a range of national standards relating to hazards. Specific documents relevant to this chapter include
  – Hazardous Substances Information System (HSIS), found at http://hsis.ascc.gov.au, is an Internet database that provides hazard classification information on over 3500 chemicals.
    Note: At the time of writing, the *Model Work Health and Safety Regulations* noted that, from 2012, exposure standards would be published by Safe Work Australia in the *Atmospheric Contaminant Workplace Exposure Standards*, which would replace the *Adopted National Exposure Standards for Atmospheric Contaminants in the Occupational Environment* [NOSHC:1003 (1995)]. It is expected that the HSIS will reflect this change.
  – National Online Statistics Information (NOSI) is a database providing information on workers' compensation claims by industry and occupation.
  – National standards on asbestos, lead, carcinogenic substances, storage and handling of dangerous goods, major hazards facilities, safety data sheets, etc.
- Australian Radiation Protection and Nuclear Safety Agency (http://www.arpansa.gov.au) contains all relevant information about legislation and codes for ionising and non-ionising radiation issues.
- Australian Institute of Occupational Hygienists (http://www.aioh.org.au) provides information on selection of occupational hygiene consultants by expertise and geographic location.
- Association of Australian Acoustical Consultants (http://www.aaac.org.au/au/aaac) is a not-for-profit peak body representing professionals who are involved in delivering acoustic solutions to a wide range of clients and the community.
- Safety Institute of Australia (http://www.sia.org.au) provides information on selection of HS professionals and HS trainers.
- Health and Safety Executive in the UK (http://www.hse.gov.uk) provides much useful information suitable for use by health and safety representatives on identifying and controlling all types of workplace hazards, including psychosocial hazards. This information includes a range of calculators, training materials and survey materials.
- International Labour Office (ILO), an agency of the United Nations, provides the Encyclopaedia of Occupational Health and Safety at http://www.ilocis.org/en/default.html. This site also provides references to all aspects of health and safety with an emphasis on training and policy documents.
- The International Agency for Research on Cancer (IARC), an agency of the United Nations, provides a series of books on carcinogens and chemicals suspected of causing cancer at http://monographs.iarc.fr/ENG/Monographs/PDFs/index.php.
- Grantham, D., 2001, *Occupational Health and Hygiene: Guidebook for the WHSO*, 3rd edn, D.L. Grantham: Brisbane. This excellent book gives a basic understanding of the principles of workplace health and occupational hygiene, as well as practical guidance on implementation

of occupational hygiene solutions. (WHSO refers to the workplace health and safety officers appointed under the *Workplace Health and Safety Act 1989–90* (Qld).) It does not cover psychosocial hazards.

• Tillman, C., 2007, *Principles of Occupational Health and Hygiene,* Allen & Unwin: Crows Nest, NSW, is a modern Australian text on occupational hygiene and goes into more detail than can be covered here.

Endnotes

1   Safe Work Australia, 2010, *Mesothelioma in Australia: Incidence 1982 to 2006, Mortality 1997 to 2007,* Commonwealth of Australia: Canberra.

2   Cancer Council Australia: http://www.cancer.org.au/aboutcancer/cancertypes/melanoma.htm.

3   Australian Institute of Occupational Hygienists definition.

4   The table is based on the International Labour Office's *Encyclopaedia of Occupational Health and Safety,* 4th edn.

5   Psychosocial hazards are discussed more fully in Chapter 11.

6   Chemical regulations in each jurisdiction are based on the National Standard for the Control of Workplace Hazardous Chemicals, 2009, published by Safe Work Australia. They are part of the broader Work Health & Safety Regulations in each jurisdiction.

7   Safe Work Australia, 2010, *Asbestos Exposure and Compliance Study of Construction and Maintenance Workers.*

8   Safe Work Australia, 2010, *Occupational Noise-Induced Hearing Loss in Australia.*

9   Kroemer, K. & Grandjean, E., 1997, *Fitting the Task to the Human,* 5th edn, Taylor & Francis: London.

10 Standards Australia (2006), ACIF G616 *Industry Guideline – Acoustic Safety for Telephone Equipment,* Australian Communications Industry Forum: Milsons Point, NSW.

11 Control measures are adapted from WorkSafe Victoria, 1992, *Code of Practice for Noise.*

12 See http://www.auears.citymax.com/f/EARS_Brochure.pdf for more information.

13 See HSE Sound Solutions Case Studies at http://www.hse.gov.uk/noise/casestudies/soundsolutions/.

14 See the Washington State Department of Labor & Industries Noise Reduction Ideas Bank at http://www.lni.wa.gov/safety/topics/reducehazards/noisebank/.

15 The AS/NZS 1269 series is an excellent reference source of information for health and safety representatives on most aspects of noise control and hearing conservation, including:
    • Overview and general requirements
    • Measurement and assessment of noise emission and exposure
    • Noise control management
    • Hearing protector program
    • Auditory assessment

16 Health and Safety Executive, 2009, *Real World Use and Performance of Hearing Protection,* Research Report RR720, at http://www.hse.gov.uk/research/rrpdf/rr720.pdf.

17 A useful guidance note on identifying and controlling hazardous chemicals in the workplace is available from WorkSafe Victoria: *A Step by Step Guide for Managing Chemicals in the Workplace,* 2001.

18 From January 2012, Australia is adopting the Globally Harmonized System of Classifying and Labelling Chemicals, sponsored by the United Nations. See http://www.unece.org/trans/danger/publi/ghs/ghs_welcome_e.html.

19 WorkSafe Victoria, 2000, *Code of Practice for Hazardous Substances,* p. 38.

20 Go to http://managementhelp.org/emp_well/emp_well.htm.

21 The Safety Institute of Australia (http://sia.org.au) provides information on HS professionals who can provide relevant WHS training.

22 National Association of Testing Authorities; see also Chapter 10.

USING EQUIPMENT TO MONITOR WORKPLACES

Learning Objectives

By the end of this chapter, the reader will have a general understanding of:

- the general process of monitoring agents or conditions in the workplace
- the selection of measuring devices
- the preparation required to collect workplace information and data
- use of devices to collect workplace information and data
- the documentation and evaluation of results.

INTRODUCTION

The Work Health and Safety Act requires that persons in charge of a business or undertaking have a duty of care in relation to their undertaking. This includes providing a safe workplace, and safety when working with plant and hazardous chemicals. Occasionally, to ensure that a workplace is safe, it will need to be monitored for agents or conditions such as chemicals, noise, vibration, light, radiation, fibres, dust, fumes, heat, humidity, radiation or biological agents.

Undertaking such assessments is often beyond the internal expertise and capabilities of individual small and medium enterprises, and occupational hygienists or other professionals may be called in to provide advice on monitoring and interpreting the results within the context of what is 'safe' or 'unsafe'. Monitoring devices may be needed to identify the agents or conditions, measure the exposure and determine the effectiveness of controls. Exposure standards and other regulatory or advisory requirements are used to assist in developing an appropriate monitoring plan, interpreting the exposure data and evaluating the results.

A health and safety adviser or manager must have a general understanding of the process of monitoring in order to know when to engage an occupational hygienist and how to use such professional services effectively.[1]

Directories of Australian HS consultants can be found as follows.

Occupational hygienists	http://www.aioh.org.au/providers.aspx.
Ergonomists	http://www.ergonomics.org.au/membersearch/
General OHS professionals	http://www.sia.org.au/membersearch/

This chapter provides an overview of the monitoring process and some of the key issues involved. An initial point – it is important to consult with the workplace stakeholders about your intended monitoring strategy and sampling plan, and ensure that results are shared with all those concerned.

MONITORING

Monitoring[2] is the process of measuring the concentration of agents or conditions that workers are exposed to in their work. In this chapter, we are talking of workplace environmental monitoring, rather than biological monitoring or other forms of monitoring. Biological monitoring involves measuring the amount of material or its metabolised product in a sample of blood, urine or expired breath, or occasionally in hair, nails or breast milk. Health monitoring or health surveillance involves examining exposed people for health effects that result from exposure. Workplace environmental monitoring involves measuring the amount of the material in workplace air, on surfaces or in workplace water.

For risk assessment purposes, you need a reliable estimate of exposure as well as an exposure standard to compare it against. Generally, if the workplace amount is significantly lower than the exposure standard, such exposure is compliant with legislation and no additional controls may be needed. However, there are numerous issues related to exposure estimates and exposure standards that make such a comparison challenging. Best practice requires continual review of the workplace risks and improvements where reasonably practicable.

Workplace exposure can vary greatly in different locations, at different times, with differing processes and different environmental conditions. As such, if one sample[3] or area is different from the others, how do you interpret it? Is that one sample representative of all the different locations, times and conditions?

Using atmospheric contaminants as an example, the exposure standard[4] is the concentration of a substance in workplace air that, according to current knowledge, should not cause adverse health effects nor cause undue discomfort to nearly all workers over their working lifetime. Exposure standards should not be seen as fine lines between what is safe and unsafe. Exposure standards change over time; for example, as new information is developed. When new data indicated that respirable silica could cause silicosis after prolonged exposure at lower levels than previously understood, the national exposure standard was reduced from 0.2 mg/m^3 to 0.1 mg/m^3 in 2004.[5]

An exposure standard for airborne contaminants can be of three forms: *time-weighted average (TWA)*, *peak limitation (PEAK)* or *short-term exposure limit (STEL)*. In addition, some chemicals have a skin notation that indicates that the material may also be absorbed through the skin.

- Time-weighted average (TWA) means the average airborne concentration of a substance for a normal eight-hour working day, five days per week. Nearly all monitoring programs estimate the time-weighted average exposure as this is used to identify and prevent chronic health effects.

- Peak limitation (PEAK) means a maximum or peak airborne concentration that should not be exceeded. It is determined over the shortest analytically practicable period of time that does not exceed 15 minutes. PEAK limits are usually set for substances that can have immediate health effects at high doses such as chlorine.

- Short-term exposure limit (STEL) means a 15-minute TWA exposure that should not be exceeded at any time during a working day, even if the eight-hour TWA average is within the TWA exposure standard. Exposures at the STEL should not be longer than 15 minutes and should not be repeated more than four times per day. There should be at least 60 minutes between successive exposures at the STEL. STELs are usually set for substances that have acute toxic effects at high doses, such as styrene, which is used in the manufacture of fibreglass.

Airborne contaminants are measured and reported in units of:

- *ppm*: parts of vapour or gas per million parts of contaminated air by volume
- *mg/m^3*: milligrams of substance per cubic metre of air at 25°C and one atmosphere pressure
- *f/mL*: fibres per millilitre of air as determined by the membrane filter method.[6]

Specific exposure standards for atmospheric contaminants are available from Safe Work Australia's Hazardous Substances Information System (HSIS). Using the HSIS database, we find the following exposure standards for amosite (brown asbestos) and styrene.

Figure 10.1 *Exposure standards for amosite and styrene*

STANDARD NAME	SYNONYMS	CAS NO.	TWA (PPM)	TWA (MG/M³)	STEL (PPM)	STEL (MG/M³)	CARCINOGEN CATEGORY
Amosite		12172-73-5	0.1 f/mL (P)	–	–	–	1
Styrene	Phenyl-ethylene Vinyl benzene	100-42-5	50	213	100	426	–

The CAS registry number is a unique number assigned by the Chemical Abstracts Service to a specific chemical. A Category 1 carcinogen is a known human carcinogen, Category 2 carcinogens are probable human carcinogens and Category 3 carcinogens are substances suspected of having a carcinogenic potential. '(P)' in the amosite TWA indicates that prohibition is recommended (note that the importation and use in Australia of all asbestos products have been prohibited since 2007).

OVERVIEW OF THE MONITORING PROCESS

Figure 10.2 summarises the main steps in the process of monitoring and evaluating exposures in the workplace. The individual steps are explained below.

Figure 10.2 *The main steps in monitoring*

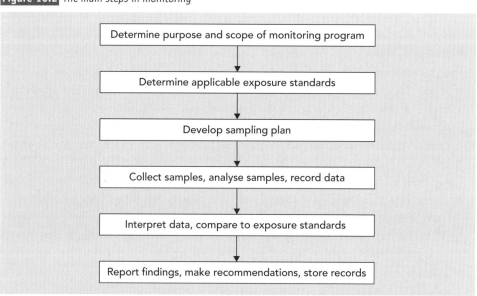

Step 1: Determine purpose and scope of monitoring program

The need for a monitoring program may be triggered by a risk assessment that indicates that a substance is being used but there is no information about how much of the substance is actually in the workplace. There may be complaints about noise, or irritating smells or heat. Or there may be regulation that requires regular monitoring, such as for Legionella in cooling towers. Before embarking on a monitoring program, you should understand the purpose of the monitoring and what you are trying to achieve. Usually, the purpose of a monitoring program is either:

- *exploratory*, in that monitoring is trying to determine what and/or how much of the agent or condition is present in the workplace. This information will be used in risk assessment to determine whether appropriate controls are in place.
- *compliance*, in that a known agent or condition is in the workplace and the monitoring program is checking to ensure that the exposure is below the exposure standard, implying that the controls are working properly.

Before monitoring, you should understand the scope of the project. You need to know things about the workplace, the work processes and the workers before you start. In particular, you should know:

- the tasks and activities being undertaken: precisely what tasks you are monitoring, where they occur, during what times
- the attributes of the agent or condition you are looking for; for example, whether it is a single chemical, a mixture of chemicals, a known raw material or product, or something generated by the process
- the way in which the agent or condition is being generated: which pieces of equipment or process use or generate the agent?
- the rate of generation: is it continual, intermittent, associated with certain tasks?
- physical features of equipment: does it leak, interfere with or experience interference from other equipment?
- the number of people in the area and the timeframe of occupying the area: number of people exposed, how long each day, over what shifts
- existing controls: what controls are in place already? are they being used consistently?

For ease of communication, you should record this information and share it with the workplace stakeholders. Once you have an understanding of the workplace and the potential for exposure, you should determine what standards apply to the situation.

Step 2: Determine applicable exposure standards

As indicated above, an exposure standard is required to determine if the exposure found in the workplace is acceptable. On the whole, workplace exposures below the exposure standard are acceptable. In addition to the exposure standards for chemicals we have already discussed, there are exposure standards for noise and ionising radiation. Although not defined in regulations, recommended standards for light illuminance, vibration, heat and cold can be found in Australian standards or advisory documents issued by regulators. Regulations must be complied with. Employers should also seek to comply with exposure standards recommended in codes of practice, Australian standards, regulators' guidelines and similar sources to meet their general duty of care. WHS regulators and professionals can assist you in finding and interpreting this information.

Some agents will not have an Australian exposure standard but there may be one from overseas. Where no exposure standard exists in Australia, useful sources include the American Conference of Governmental Industrial Hygienists (ACGIH[7]), the British

Health and Safety Executive[8], the (US) National Institute for Occupational Safety and Health[9] or Occupational Safety and Health Administration.[10]

In some cases, monitoring and comparison to the exposure standard may not be required because the agent or condition can be controlled easily. In these cases, the risk can be reduced because the agent or condition can be safely eliminated or substituted, or because controls can be applied immediately and directly. However, if applying controls, some monitoring may be required to ensure the ongoing effectiveness of the controls.

Step 3: Develop a sampling plan

Based on the purpose and scope of your monitoring, once you have defined the agent or condition you want to assess and you have defined the area and tasks to be assessed, the next step is to develop the sampling plan that describes who, what, when, how and how many samples are to be taken. In your sampling plan, you should address:

- whether you are collecting personal or area samples – personal samples measure the amount of contaminant in the breathing zone of the worker.[11] Area samples measure the amount that is in the work area; personal samples are a better indication of the actual dose received by the worker.
- how many samples you expect to take – the aim is to get representative samples of the various exposures in the workplace. This will depend on the variety of tasks in the workplace. If workers do exactly the same task, in the same way, in the same environmental conditions, then relatively few samples need to be taken as they will each be representative of each other. However, if the workers do different tasks for different lengths of time, in different conditions, you will need more samples to cover all conditions.
- types of sampling equipment and techniques to be used – this will depend upon the type of agent, condition or chemical that you are monitoring for. Figure 10.3 describes some of the issues that need to be addressed and the types of monitoring equipment that can be used.
- analytical methods to be used – some equipment is direct reading; the results will not have to be taken to a laboratory for analysis. Some monitoring will require the sample to be analysed in a lab. In each case, there must be a reliable and validated analytical method for producing results.

DID YOU KNOW?

CONTRACTING A SUITABLY QUALIFIED PERSON

If you decide to contract an occupational hygienist or other professional to assist in assessing risk in a workplace, how do you know whether they are competent to do the job properly? WorkSafe Victoria[12] suggests a number of factors to be taken into account. These include the person's knowledge and technical expertise, industry experience, communication skills, reputation and professional association. It is generally safer to employ a person who is a member in good standing of a professional association that requires the attainment of and continuing development of relevant knowledge, skills and experience for membership.

Figure 10.3 *Monitoring issues and equipment for different agents and conditions*

AGENT/ CONDITION	KEY ISSUES TO BE ADDRESSED BEFORE MONITORING	TYPES OF MONITORING EQUIPMENT[13]
CHEMICAL AGENTS		

Vapours and gases	• Single or mixed exposure
	• Likely concentration range
	• Appropriate and validated analytical method
	• Active or passive sampling
	  – flow rate
	  – collection device/medium
	• Potential for skin contact/absorption
		• Direct reading indicator tubes

		Drager CO indicator tube and Accuro pump
		• Direct reading instruments such as continuous CO monitors
		QRAEII multigas detector
		• Active sampling whereby pumps pull air into the collection device
		SKC 210-1002 PocketPump, with charcoal tube sampling head
		• Passive sampling where sampling badges are in contact with environmental air
		3M organic vapour passive sampler

AGENT/ CONDITION	KEY ISSUES TO BE ADDRESSED BEFORE MONITORING	TYPES OF MONITORING EQUIPMENT[13]
Mists and aerosols	• Appropriate collection method • Appropriate and validated analytical method	• Direct reading indicator tubes • Active sampling with liquid impingers SKC Airchek 2000 pump with liquid impinger
Fibres	• Likely contaminants and their concentration range	• Active sampling whereby pump pulls air through a collection filter SKC Airchek 224-PCXR4 pump with IOM dust sampling head
Dust and particulates	• Likely particle size • Appropriate and validated analytical method	• Active sampling whereby pump pulls air through, where appropriate, a size separator and a collection filter SKC cyclone with 25 mm sampling head • Direct reading instruments TSI Dusttrak 8520 aerosol monitor with cyclone separator • Direct indicating wipes (limited number of analytes)

AGENT/ CONDITION	KEY ISSUES TO BE ADDRESSED BEFORE MONITORING	TYPES OF MONITORING EQUIPMENT[13]
BIOLOGICAL AGENTS		
Infectious agents	• Is there a known agent? • How is the agent to be cultured (grown) in the lab? • May need biological monitoring of blood or urine to determine if exposure has occurred or health effects are present	For Legionella in cooling towers, take water samples and culture them in a lab
Non-infectious agents	• Issues similar to dust and particulates	
Allergens	• These are usually proteins. Proteins vary in size, which determines the collection process. Is there a reliable collection process for these materials? • Is there a validated analytical method and standard?	
PHYSICAL CONDITIONS		
Noise	• Background noise levels • Personal exposure or area maps • Continuous, intermittent or peak noise • Additive sources • Calibration and maintenance • dB(A), dB(C)	• Sound level meters Bruel & Kjaer 2250 light precision sound level meter with Type 4230 calibrator • Noise dosimeters Quest NoisePro DLX dosimeter with CA-12B calibrator

AGENT/ CONDITION	KEY ISSUES TO BE ADDRESSED BEFORE MONITORING	TYPES OF MONITORING EQUIPMENT[13]
Light	• Time of day • Season of year • Interfering objects	• Direct reading illuminance (light) Extech 407026 light meter
Vibration	• Continuous or intermittent exposure • Periodic or random vibration • Additive sources	• Vibration meter/accelerometer Bruel & Kjaer type 4332 accelerometer with integrator for connection to B&K Type 2209 SLM
Temperature and humidity	• Is there a need to measure both temperature and humidity? Use wet bulb globe temperature (WBGT) index for heat stress. • What actions do you take once you calculate the WBGT index?	• Psychrometer to measure wet bulb and dry bulb temperature JRM sling psychrometer • WBGT is a composite temperature used to estimate the effect of temperature, humidity and solar radiation on humans. QUESTemp 36 thermal environment monitor

AGENT/ CONDITION	KEY ISSUES TO BE ADDRESSED BEFORE MONITORING	TYPES OF MONITORING EQUIPMENT[13]
Radiation	• Type of radiation: e.g. ionising, non-ionising • Background levels • Peak or continuous exposure	• Ionising: direct reading Geiger counter Ludlum Measurements Model 3A survey meter with probe • Non-ionising: ELF, RF, EMR, EMF measurement devices Extech 480826 Triple Axis EMF tester with probe

Note: Figure 10.3 shows examples of monitoring equipment used in a teaching environment. There is a wide range of equipment available on the market for most monitoring applications, and users should seek advice on equipment that meets their needs, particularly in relation to application, accuracy and price.

Step 4: Collect and analyse samples, record data

Based on the sampling plan, collect the samples and have them analysed. As summarised in Figure 10.3, air contaminants are collected on an appropriate sampling media, either by actively pulling an air sample through the medium or by passively allowing the air to diffuse to the medium (personal monitoring tabs). Gases, vapours, particulates and bio-aerosols are all collected by active sampling methods; gases and vapours can also be collected by passive diffusion sampling.

For many particulates, once the sample is collected, the mass of the contaminant is measured on a microbalance and the concentration calculated by dividing the mass by the volume of sampled air. Gases, vapours and some particulates – for example, crystalline respirable silica – are collected on an appropriate medium that then has to be analysed in a laboratory. Concentrations of gases and vapours are expressed as parts per million (ppm) or mg/m^3; for particulates, concentration is expressed as mg/m^3.

A number of techniques can measure directly in the workplace and remove the need for subsequent laboratory analysis, such as

• direct reading indicator stain tubes (gases and vapours)
• direct reading passive absorption badges and tubes (gases and vapours)
• direct reading infrared, laser or piezo crystal monitors (aerosols and dust).

All physical agents can be measured directly in the field using appropriate instrumentation. Much modern instrumentation is able to data-log – for example, over the whole shift – for subsequent computer analysis of exposure.

Prior to carrying out the sampling, the operability of the equipment will need to be checked. Batteries must be tested; the availability of appropriate attachments, leads and filters should be assessed; the functionality of the equipment should be tested; and measuring devices must be calibrated and appropriate scales selected. Direct reading equipment needs to be routinely calibrated at a NATA[14]-accredited laboratory. When equipment needs testing in analytical laboratories, NATA accreditation of that laboratory for that analysis has to be confirmed. When a consultant is used to take measurements, ensure that any equipment used is NATA-certified and subsequent analysis is undertaken in a NATA-certified laboratory. Some equipment, such as sampling pumps and noise measuring equipment, should be calibrated with a field calibrator before and after each use. The calibrator should in turn be routinely tested in a NATA-accredited laboratory. Regardless of the monitoring method used, you must understand the limitations and accuracy of the method and equipment. For example, noise meters will vary in price from less than $100 to over $10 000. Clearly there will be differences in capability and accuracy between these extremes.

Ensure that the results from the monitoring are recorded, with clear information about the date, location and activity being monitored; whether it is an area or personal sample; the name of the person wearing the monitoring equipment; the type of sample and its duration; and the results. Obviously, you will need to consult with the workers in the area so that they understand what you are trying to achieve and what their role is. Ensure that all concerned workers and managers have access to any findings from the monitoring.

Step 5: Interpret data, compare to exposure standards

If the workplace complies with the duty of care, all samples will be well below the exposure standard and you will feel confident that the exposures are controlled. However, should you find that some samples appear to be above the exposure limit, you may need professional advice to interpret the data.

While it is not within the scope of this book to introduce all of the methodological issues associated with assessing and analysing monitoring data, there is one very common and important topic that needs explanation.

After taking a number of spot measurements over a fixed period of time to gather a TWA, graphs representing the concentration of contaminants often show a large amount of variance in concentration levels. Figure 10.4 is an example.

Obviously, the variable factors found in the workplace produce estimates that are not distributed about an average.[15] You might, for example, have taken 30 sample measurements with the results showing:

1, 2, 2, 9, 5, 1, 2, 5, 3, 4, 3, 7, 2, 8, 3, 6, 7, 11, 3, 1, 6, 12, 4, 2, 3, 4, 2, 5, 15, 4

Figure 10.4 *Variance in contaminant concentration levels*

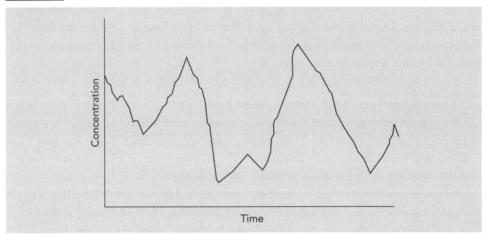

If you were to plot the number of times a worker was exposed to each various concentration, the frequency versus concentration graph would look like the following.

Figure 10.5 *Frequency versus concentration*

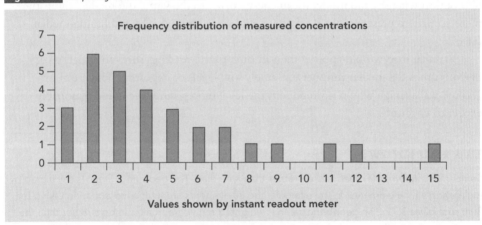

The curve would resemble the following.

Figure 10.6 *Frequency versus concentration curve*

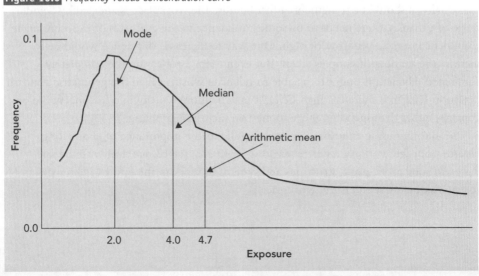

The *mode* or most common value is 2.0. The arithmetic *mean* or average is equal to the sum of all your readings divided by 30 (4.73). The *median* is 4.0. This is calculated by ordering the figures and finding the value that sits at the middle. If there are even numbers then the two middle figures are added and divided by two. For example, in the series presented above, the order would be:

1, 1, 1, 2, 2, 2, 2, 2, 2, 3, 3, 3, 3, 3, 4, 4, 4, 4, 5, 5, 5, 6, 6, 7, 7, 8, 9, 11, 12, 15

Which figure represents the true exposure level?

We can disregard the mode, for that only reveals a common figure and is misleading. However, if we look at the mean or average, it is affected by a few very high readings, thereby making it unrepresentative. The median, then, appears as the exposure level the worker would reasonably expect in the area sampled.

A comparison with real estate may help. You are looking for a $400 000 home to buy and want to know in which districts you are most likely to find a home at that price. Do you choose the districts where the median price is $400 000 or the districts where the mean or average price is $400 000, remembering that a few mansions will jack the average price up or many very cheap dwellings will bring the average price down? It should be clear that, in general, when you have skewed distributions and not a normal distribution whereby the mode, mean and median are the same, the median offers the more accurate representation. Real estate guides recognise this by publishing median prices.

A similar story would apply if the vast bulk of the readings showed a high level of exposure and a smaller number extremely low levels of exposure. The mean or arithmetical average would misrepresent the level of exposure one could reasonably expect to encounter.

DID YOU KNOW?

Sometimes a *geometric mean* is used rather than a median. The geometric mean is calculated by multiplying all the elements. In the example, the 30 elements are multiplied and then taking the 30th root gives 3.71. The geometric mean is weighted for all the small numbers rather than the few higher ones and is considered a more accurate representation of the exposure level. Geometric means are useful summaries for highly skewed data.

Finally, it should be remembered that because the workplace is affected by a wide range of variables, there needs to be some confidence in the estimates of exposure made. Confidence may be very low or high. One way to increase confidence would be to increase the number of samples taken. But even then, error cannot be completely eliminated. Hygienists ought to be able to calculate what is called the geometric standard deviation (GSD). If there is a high GSD, it may be more worthwhile to concentrate on controls, rather than spending more money on increased sampling.

Monitoring using exposure standards highlights the importance of eliminating hazards from the workplace wherever possible. In chapter 12, we deal with the safe design of substances, plant, structures and systems of work in the effort to eliminate and reduce risk before it enters the workplace.

WHS IN PRACTICE

THE DUSTY AND NOISY GOLDMINE

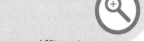

The health and safety representative in the surface crusher and mill area of Victoria Gold NL has had complaints about noise and dust from workers in the area.

Gold is contained as flecks in underground quartz seams. This ore is mined and carried to the surface on skips that deposit the ore in large hoppers. From there, it is fed to a jaw crusher that reduces the ore to chunks smaller than 2 cm. From the crusher it is fed as an aqueous slurry into a series of rod and ball mills to reduce the ore to powder size for subsequent treatment and recovery of the gold.

The health and safety representative observed the following:

- The crusher and mill areas are generally an open structure. Apart from the jaw crusher area, the rest is roofed but there are no walls around the works.
- Extensive amounts of dust are escaping around the jaw crusher. Water is sprayed onto the ore to suppress the dust, but this is generally ineffective. The operator mainly stays in the control room, but frequently comes out to release blockages in the crusher. The control room is air-conditioned but the desk and other interior surfaces are generally dusty. The control room, including desk surfaces, is cleaned every night. There are obvious slurry spillages around the rod and ball mills. Some of these have dried out and operators walking through raise visible dust with their feet.
- It is difficult to carry on a conversation in the vicinity of the crusher and ball mills without shouting.
- The whole surface works are a mandatory hardhat, eye protection and hearing protection area, and this is generally enforced and complied with.
- There are no specific SDSs on site.

The representative has to determine whether the crusher and mill area comply with the exposure standards for noise and respirable silica, as defined in the Work Health and Safety Regulations. He goes about this in the following way.

1 He identifies what are the exposure standards for noise (the Work Health and Safety Regulations Part 4.1 note an exposure standard of 85 dB(A) $L_{Aeq,8h}$) and respirable silica (the HSIS shows the exposure standard as 0.1 mg/m^3).

2 Using a simple sound-level meter he identifies that the noise level is over 90 dB(A) at times around the crushers. This confirms the observation that it is difficult to converse in the area and indicates it is likely that the noise exposure standard has been breached.

3 He is not able to measure respirable silica directly but has access to a prior occupational hygiene report in which a spot check using a Dusttrak monitor measured respirable dust at levels up to 5 mg/m^3 on the crusher platform. While the report gave no indication of the composition of the dust measured, the following facts suggest strongly that the exposure standard was breached:

   - the Dusttrak dust levels were so much above the respirable silica standard
   - an Internet search showed that the composition of quartz rock varies up to 90 per cent pure crystalline silica
   - no remedial work had been completed since the Dusttrak report had been received.

4 Based on that information, the representative issues the employer with a provisional improvement notice (PIN) requesting that an occupational hygienist be contracted to assess noise dose and respirable silica average concentrations to which operators in the area would be exposed.

5 Further control actions will depend on the results provided by the occupational hygienist.

Step 6: Report findings, make recommendations, store records

The report should address the regulatory requirements and address the project objectives in a clear, logical manner, taking into account the nature of the audience. The results and records must be retained and stored in a format that enables them to be readily retrieved in accordance with regulatory requirements or standards.

THE CAR-BODY REPAIR SHOP

CASE STUDY

The Port Melbourne site of a Japanese car company that imports cars has a panel-beating shop that repairs cars that have been damaged in transit from Japan. There are three people working in the shop: two panel-beaters and a spray painter. Car damage, although small on individual vehicles, keeps the shop busy because of the numbers of vehicles involved.

Cars usually require sanding of damaged paintwork, hammering of dents to rough proportions, filling minor imperfections with body 'goo' and then smoothing out of the cured 'goo' with an electric sander, and hand-finishing with fine sandpaper. The car is then spray painted to bring the body up to showroom condition. The paintwork is baked under strong spotlights that raise the temperature of the bodywork to around 150°C.

Risk assessment 1 – your walk-through survey identifies the following issues:

- The spray-paint contains toluene diisocyanate (TDI). The painter uses an airline full-face respirator during the actual spraying within the downdraught spray booth, but you notice that immediately the painter stops spraying, he takes off the respirator to examine the quality of paintwork, and is exposed to a fine mist of spray still in the air. The painter mixes the paints himself to match the car colour.

- The body 'goo' is an epoxy two-part mix with epichlorhydrin and bisphenol A as the active ingredients, and the filler being mainly calcium carbonate and fibreglass. Much dust is generated during the sanding operation.

- The main solvent used for thinning both the paint and goo is toluene, and this is also used to clean implements such as the spray gun. Petrol is used for cleaning gross spillages, and general removal of grease, and the like.

- Apart from the air-supplied respirator used by the painter and general coveralls worn by the staff, no PPE is used.

- There are no specific written procedures, and no information on the chemicals other than that on the containers.

Based on your walk-through survey, you contract an occupational hygienist to measure exposures of TDI, dust, solvents and noise.

Risk assessment 2

1 The occupational hygiene report evaluated the total dust content (respirable and inhalable) throughout the workplace generated by the sanding of body putty. On the day of the survey, two operators were

doing intermittent work on two vehicles. One operator wore an IOM open-face filter and the other a SKC cyclone sampler. Total sampling time was eight hours for each operator.

The results were:

IOM total dust sampler	15 mg/m^3
SKC cyclone for respirable dust	6.5 mg/m^3

Discussion: HSIS does not have specific standards for total and respirable dust 'not otherwise classified'. National Exposure Standards in NOHSC:3008 (1995) recommend 10 mg/m^3 as a maximum for total dust. ACGIH have recommended a maximum of 3 mg/m^3 for respirable dust not otherwise classified. The dust was tested and showed no free epichlorhydrin and bisphenol A in the sample. Based on this, the operators were exposed to dust levels above the recommended standards and control measures should be initiated.

2 The report evaluated the levels of TDI that the employees are exposed to through the spray-paint. The painter worked on one car in the paint booth during the morning, and again in the afternoon. Total spraying time was one hour each time. A sampler including low-flow pump with a special TDI-specific sampling tube was worn by the spray-painter for the whole day. Results of TDI sampling were 0.27 ppm.

Discussion: HSIS provides an exposure standard for all isocyanates (including TDI) of 0.02 mg/m^3 as a time-weighted average. HSIS also notes that TDI is a sensitiser. The operator was protected for part of the time by the respirator. However, best practice is to limit short-term exposures to not more than three times the exposure standard. The exposure experienced by the spray-painter was 13.5 times the exposure standard. On this measure, control actions need to be initiated.

3 The report evaluated the exposure to organic solvents (toluene and petrol) in the workplace. Because of the intermittent nature of the exposure, Drager hydrocarbon indicator tubes were used for spot sampling alongside the operator and the results (converted to mg/m^3) were as follows:

Mixing paint (toluene)	100 mg/m^3
Cleaning implements (petrol)	250 mg/m^3

Discussion: HSIS provides exposure standards for toluene at 191 mg/m^3 as a TWA and it carries a 'skin' rating, indicating that it can be absorbed through the skin. The exposure standard for petrol is 900 mg/m^3 as a TWA. Given that the samples were the peak exposures during the workday, it is assessed that the operators would not exceed the TWA exposure standard. However, both these compounds, if contacting skin over a period of months or years, can cause dermatitis, and splashes to the eye can be injurious, so impervious gloves and aprons, as well as eye protection, should be worn while mixing paint and cleaning implements. Petrol is highly flammable and a fire hazard, so that it is recommended that a less volatile cleaning agent, such as kerosene, be adopted.

4 The report evaluated noise exposure generated by the sanding of vehicles, hammering of dents, the air compressor and other ambient noise. A calibrated noise-dose meter was worn by each operator over an eight-hour day. Results for the three operators averaged in the range 79–82 dB(A).

Discussion: Noise doses over the shift were below the 85 dB(A) exposure standard set out in the Work Health and Safety Regulations.

SUMMARY

The company is in breach of its duty of care in terms of dust and TDI exposure, and control actions should be implemented. It is also recommended that appropriate PPE be worn while mixing paint and cleaning implements. Kerosene should be substituted for petrol as a cleaning agent.

RISK CONTROL

1 To control the dust arising from sanding, a new sander with built-in vacuum extraction was introduced. This visibly reduced the dust from the sanding process.
2 To control TDI exposure, a new air-supplied mask was purchased that allowed the operator to lift the visor to inspect his work, while maintaining a clean breathable air supply throughout.
3 Kerosene was introduced as a main cleaning agent and petrol was phased out.
4 PVC gloves and aprons, and a face shield, were purchased for each operator and new procedures were developed to make using this PPE compulsory while cleaning.
5 SDSs for all chemicals were obtained and discussed with the operators.
6 A training program to acquaint the operators with the new equipment and procedures was provided. During a subsequent visit by a WorkSafe inspector, the work practices were deemed acceptable.

Questions

1 How would the manager of the repair shop go about selecting a competent occupational hygienist to measure exposures?
2 What consultation should the manager have undertaken to determine the appropriate control measures to be implemented?
3 How would the management and staff of the repair shop ensure that the new procedures are appropriate and effective, and will continue to be implemented?

Summary

- Monitoring is the process of conducting a measurement or series of measurements of the concentration of agents or conditions workers are exposed to in their work.
- For risk assessment purposes, a reliable estimate of exposure as well as a standard to compare it against is needed.
- Monitoring requires careful consideration of the factors affecting sampling, as measurements may vary widely.
- An exposure standard means an airborne concentration of a particular substance in the worker's breathing zone, exposure to which, according to current knowledge, should not cause adverse health effects nor cause undue discomfort to nearly all workers.
- An exposure standard can be of three forms: time-weighted average (TWA), peak limitation or short-term exposure limit (STEL).
- In addition to information on SDSs, the Hazardous Substances Information System provides national exposure standards for many atmospheric contaminants.
- The median or geometrical mean provides the best measure of workplace exposure, particularly when there are skewed results.

In your workplace

With professional guidance, the right equipment and cooperation from your workplace, carry out an environmental monitoring project to assess the risks associated with:

a noise (you will need a sound-level meter if you only want to measure the machine noise levels and/or a noise dosimeter to measure the actual exposure of individuals)
b lighting (you will need a luxmeter)
c temperature (you will need a sling psychrometer or other thermometry).

Do this activity individually or as part of a team. Prepare a report on your activities, findings and recommendations. Discuss with others the issues you encountered and how you resolved them.

Hints: Exposure standards for noise will be found in the Work Health and Safety Regulations; recommended illuminance (lighting levels) are found in AS/NZS 1680.1:2006 *Interior and workplace lighting: general principles and recommendations*; recommendations for thermal comfort in office environments can be found in WorkSafe Victoria's 2006 *Officewise*. If thermal stress is an issue refer to HSE at http://www.hse.gov.uk/temperature/information/heatstress/.

Environmental monitoring equipment can be hired. Look up 'gas detectors' (or similar tags) in a phone directory to find a local supplier in your state.

Questions

1   What is environmental monitoring and why is it carried out?
2   What are the basic steps in environmental monitoring?
3   Describe what TWA, STEL and peak limitation standards are and their specific purposes.
4   What are the advantages and disadvantages of using exposure standards to promote health and safety?
5   What is the difference between 'mode', 'mean' and 'median'?

Activities

Using the HSIS database, determine the exposure standards of a chemical found in your workplace or home.

Search me!

Explore **Search me! management** for relevant articles on occupational hygiene instrumentation and monitoring. Search me! is an online library of world-class journals, ebooks and newspapers, including *The Australian* and the *New York Times*, and is updated daily. Log in to Search me! through www.cengage.com/sso using the access card in the front of this book.

KEYWORDS
Try searching for the following terms:
▶ dust monitoring
▶ vapour monitoring
▶ noise measurement

Search tip: **Search me! management** contains information from both local and international sources. To get the greatest number of search results, try using both Australian and American spellings in your searches, e.g. 'globalisation' and 'globalization'; 'organisation' and 'organization'.

Additional resources

• As our knowledge develops about chemical, biological and physical hazards, regulations and standards come under review. To keep up with changes, refer to the website of your WHS regulator.
• Safe Work Australia (www.safeworkaustralia.gov.au) contains a range of national standards relating to hazards. Specific documents relevant to this chapter include:
  • Hazardous Substances Information System (HSIS), found at http://hsis.ascc.gov.au, is an Internet database that provides hazard classification information on over 3500 chemicals. At the time of writing, the Model Work Health and Safety Regulations state that, from

2012, exposure standards will be published by Safe Work Australia in the Atmospheric Contaminant Workplace Exposure Standards, replacing the Adopted National Exposure Standards for Atmospheric Contaminants in the Occupational Environment [NOSHC:1003 (1995)]. It is expected that the HSIS will reflect this change.

- National standards on asbestos, lead, carcinogenic substances, storage and handling of dangerous goods, major hazards facilities, safety data sheets, etc.
- Australian Radiation Protection and Nuclear Safety Agency at http://www.arpansa.gov.au contains all relevant information about exposure standards and codes for ionising and non-ionising radiation issues.
- ACGIH Threshold Limit Values: see www.acgih.org/home.htm for purchase of TLV/BEI booklets and related documentation.
- Australian Institute of Occupational Hygienists at http://www.aioh.org.au provides information on selection of occupational hygiene consultants by expertise and geographic location.
- National Chemical Information Gateway provides links to a range of sources on chemicals at http://apps5a.ris.environment.gov.au/pubgate/cig_public/!CIGPPUBLIC.pStart.
- Standards Australia provides for the purchase of Australian and ISO standards at http://www.saiglobal.com/.
- Health and Safety Executive (UK) at http://www.hse.gov.uk provides much useful information for assessing all types of workplace hazards. The Health and Safety Executive List of Workplace Exposure Limits (WELs) is downloadable as a PDF file from http://www.hse.gov.uk/coshh/table1.pdf.
- US exposure standards (called permissible exposure levels – PELs) can be found on the Occupational Safety and Health Administration (OSHA) website at http://www.osha.gov/. Useful information is also available from the US OHS research body, the National Institute for Occupational Safety and Health (NIOSH) at http://www.cdc.gov/niosh/.
- HSE, 2006, *Monitoring Strategies for Toxic Substances*: a free pdf of this text is downloadable at http://www.hse.gov.uk/pubns/priced/hsg173.pdf.
- Grantham, D., 2001, *Occupational Health and Hygiene Guidebook for the WHSO*, 2nd edn, Brisbane. This is an excellent practical guide to occupational hygiene in the Australian setting. It covers monitoring techniques and devices.
- National Code of Practice for the Control of Work-related Exposure to Hepatitis and HIV (blood-borne) Viruses [NOHSC:2010 (2003), 2nd edn] provides guidance on meeting requirements under existing Commonwealth, state and territory workplace health and safety legislation as it relates to HIV/AIDS and hepatitis B in the workplace.
- AIOH, 2001, *Simplified Monitoring Strategies: A Guidebook on How to Apply NOHSC's Exposure Standards for Atmospheric Contaminants in the Occupational Environment to Australian Hazardous Substance Legislation*, Australian Institute of Occupational Hygienists: Melbourne.
- Tillman, C., 2007, *Principles of Occupational Health and Hygiene*, Allen & Unwin: Crows Nest, NSW, is a modern Australian text on occupational hygiene and offers more detail than can be covered here.

Endnotes

1   Information on what to expect from a competent consultant who offers monitoring services can be found at http://www.hse.gov.uk/pubns/guidance/g409.pdf.

2   We use the terms 'monitoring' and 'sampling' to indicate a program of sampling; sampling refers to single measurements, while monitoring is the entire procedure required to estimate exposure.

3 As with note 2 above, sampling is the single measurement in a monitoring program.

4 The exposure standard is broadly taken as the quantum of the exposure defined in relevant regulations as allowable or 'safe'. Examples include allowable noise levels and airborne concentrations of harmful chemicals, as set out in the HSIS (see http://hsis.ascc.gov.au/). HSIS is the Hazardous Substances Information System, an Internet database that provides hazard classification information on over 3500 substances classified as hazardous according to the approved criteria. See description in Chapter 9.

5 Source: NOHSC, from *Commonwealth of Australia Chemical Gazette*, 2004 12.

6 NOHSC:3003 (2005) *Guidance note on the membrane filter method for estimating airborne asbestos fibres*, 2nd edn.

7 See http://www.acgih.org.

8 See http://www.hse.gov.uk/.

9 See http://www.cdc.gov/niosh/.

10 See http://www.osha.gov/.

11 The breathing zone is defined as a hemisphere of 300 mm radius extending in front of a person's face, measured from the midpoint of an imaginary straight line joining the ears. Source: WorkSafe Victoria, 2000, *Code of Practice on Hazardous Substances*.

12 WorkSafe Victoria, 2008, *Employing or Engaging Suitably Qualified Persons to Provide Health and Safety Advice*, Edition No. 1, October, http://www.worksafe.vic.gov.au/wps/wcm/connect/14f103804071fb6db254fee1fb554c40/WorkSafe+Position.pdf?MOD=AJPERES.

13 Photographs in this chapter are of instruments owned by RMIT's OHS Teaching and Research Unit and photographed by Gail Spring and Leo Ruschena, 2010.

14 National Association of Testing Authorities.

15 This example is adapted from David Grantham's *Occupational Health and Hygiene Guidebook for the WHSO*, pp. 36–37.

MANAGING PSYCHOSOCIAL HAZARDS

Learning Objectives

By the end of this chapter, the reader will have a general understanding of how to:

- explain the nature of the psychosocial hazards – stress, violence and bullying
- discuss the causes of psychosocial hazards
- discuss strategies to eliminate and control psychosocial hazards
- monitor and review strategies to eliminate and control psychosocial hazards.

INTRODUCTION

'Psychosocial hazards' refers principally to work-related stress arising from work pressure, workplace violence, bullying, sexual and other harassment, and exposure to traumatic events. Only in recent years, as the number and costs of compensation claims have increased, have such incidents been fully recognised as workplace health and safety issues. Stress-related claims for compensation still remain relatively small in number, but they are increasingly costly.

These compensation costs are just a fraction of the real cost of workplace stress because workers tend to take sick leave rather than lodge claims. Stress-related absenteeism is a major hidden cost to industry. Other hidden costs include decreased productivity and higher turnover. In addition, claims arising from violent and aggressive behaviour are also of concern because of health and safety legal implications, possible **common law** actions and the impact on business operations.

As employers have a duty of care to provide workplaces that are safe and do not cause psychological injury, health and safety managers – and managers and supervisors in general – need to know how to identify and deal with psychosocial hazards.

In the first part of this chapter, we look at the principles used to identify the hazard of workplace stress and assess and control the associated risk, after which we examine workplace violence and bullying.

WHAT IS STRESS?

In general, stress is the psychological and physical reactions experienced when someone is faced with demands – low-level or high-level. When you first find yourself in a stressful situation, your body responds by increasing your energy, thereby preparing you for greater levels of action. This increase in energy comes from an increased heart rate, raised blood pressure, muscle tension and general physical and mental alertness.

Often, confusion exists between arousal and stress. Highly active sport can be arousing and lead to physiological reactions but it is, mostly, enjoyable. Business deals can be challenging and demanding, but they can also be rewarding and enjoyable. It is when our reactions are experienced negatively, when we can't get pleasure from the demands or deal with them satisfactorily that we usually talk of stress as opposed to arousal – or what some call 'positive stress'. For this reason, stress is often referred to as 'psychological injury'.

Note that for compensation purposes, it is the stress-related medical conditions such as anxiety, panic and depression that are compensable.

We define 'workplace stress' as the negative response to workplace demands that go beyond our ability to enjoy or cope with them.

WHAT CAUSES STRESS?

Workplace demands come from outside the organisation – for example, from the public, clients, customers and other organisations – and from inside, for example, from supervisors, managers, co-workers and other departments.

Individuals and groups will respond differently to the same type of workplace demands, depending on factors such as

* individual perceptions, personality, skill levels, knowledge and health
* the level of control or decision making allowed to deal with the demand
* the social and technical support received from the workplace and our family and friends, as well as from professionals, such as counsellors or doctors.

Such factors are said to *mediate* or affect our response to the same type of demands. In certain cases, factors such as the lack of control and support, can be causes of stress or stressors in their own right.[1] It is the combination of workplace demand and mediating factor that determines whether the workplace demand is a stressor.

Figure 11.1 *Workplace demands and mediating factors*

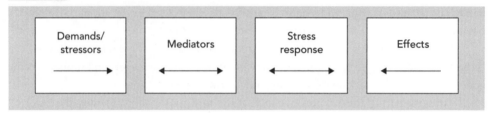

The negative effects or consequences of stress can include, but are not limited to, those identified in Figure 11.2.

Figure 11.2 *Some negative effects of stress and their consequences*

PHYSIOLOGICAL	EMOTIONAL	BEHAVIOURAL
• rise in blood pressure	• tension	• addictions to food, drugs, alcohol
• insomnia	• anxiety	• smoking
• rise in heart rate	• depression	• poor work performance
• gastric reflux	• irritability	• absenteeism
• headaches	• mood swings (emotional lability)	• antisocial behaviours
• fatigue	• volatile temper	• irregular eating pattern
• cardiovascular disease	• tearfulness	• acting out; e.g. breaking things
• hair loss	• apathy	• nail biting
• menstrual irregularity	• negativity/pessimism	• social withdrawal
• increased susceptibility to illness	• despair	• accident proneness
• loss of concentration	• hopelessness	• absenteeism
• muscular tension	• dependency	• quitting job

The longer-term effects can be quite severe and life-changing. Moreover, they can go on to lessen our ability to respond to demands, in turn making things even worse.

WHO IS AFFECTED BY STRESS?

Based on workers' compensation claims data, occupations commonly associated with stress claims include schoolteachers, police officers, emergency service workers (firefighters and ambulance officers), corrective services personnel, and health and community service workers. Workers in these occupations can face major stress situations, often involving threats of physical danger or major accidents, because of the nature of their workplace demands. (Later in this chapter, we discuss workplace violence.) While such occupations represent the high end of stress claims, there does not appear to be an occupation that is completely free from stress.

DID YOU KNOW?

- That serious claims for mental stress in 2006–07 were much more prevalent in the medical and dental services (15 per cent) and community care services (13 per cent) than the industry average of 8 per cent.
- That 20 per cent of mental disorder claims in rail transport in 2006–07 resulted from exposure to a traumatic event, whereas 39 per cent of claims were due to vehicle accidents and 22 per cent to other mental stress factors (for example, work pressure, bullying, harassment, etc.).[2]

MANAGING WORKPLACE STRESS

IDENTIFYING STRESS

Workplace stress is often identified by symptoms such as:
- changes in a person's mood or behaviour, such as deteriorating relationships, irritability, indecisiveness, absenteeism, reduced performance or increased mistakes
- evidence of substance abuse, including 'over the counter' (legal) drugs, alcohol, tobacco and illicit substances
- health complaints, such as frequent headaches, lack of sleep or nausea
- complaints of stress
- workers' compensation claims for psychological injury.
    Other means of workplace stress identification include:
- HR records of turnover, absences, annual leave (for example, identifying sections in which excessive amounts of annual leave are being accrued)
- HS incident reports (accidents can sometimes result from cognitive lapses due to workplace stressors)
- workplace climate surveys
- job satisfaction surveys.
    Workplace stressors – the causes of psychological injury – can take many forms. Examples include excessive workload, being treated unfairly, abusive remarks or emails, rumours of job shedding, personal conflicts, workplace change, poor work conditions and facilities, poor communication, lack of recognition of good performance, insensitive supervisors, racial or sexual harassment, lack of adequate training, career frustration, ambiguity about job and role, to name a few. (We discuss issues such as job demand and control below, and workplace violence and bullying later.)

Identifying the demands placed on our ability to enjoy or cope with them – the stressors – may require specialist expertise; for example, an organisational psychologist or counsellor. Carefully constructed stress surveys might be used. But, more often than not, it simply requires managers or supervisors to discuss matters with workers in a sympathetic environment, provided, of course, that they have the skills and policy direction needed. More of this shortly.

A preventive approach would not wait for symptoms or complaints to occur, but instead would involve regular discussions with staff on matters such as appropriate workload, training, support and future changes to avert any stress occurring in the first place.

In workplaces today, what often presents as the medical condition 'stress' sometimes may be more about the communication of dissatisfaction with work than about illness. As most organisations do not provide avenues for the effective management of employee problems, individual employees seek assistance from the most accessible and legitimate source – their doctor. Consequently, human resource management problems become crystallised as medical problems and are, potentially, compensable.

> Stress is often a symptom of poor employment relations and can seriously affect productivity. Organisations who talk regularly with their employees and have sound systems and procedures in place for dealing with issues like absence and discipline are much more likely to avoid work-related stress and to be able to deal with potentially stressful situations when they arise.
>
> Source: Advisory, Conciliation and Arbitration Service, cited in HSE, 2008, *Working Together To Reduce Stress At Work: A Guide for Employees*, p. 1.

ASSESSING THE RISK

Assessing the risk of stress first requires gathering information on the demands and the workplace mediating factors that moderate or contribute to that stress. Assuming that workplace stress already exists, questions to be asked include the following.

- Who is affected?
- How are they affected; that is, what are the risk factors – demands and mediating factors – and how do they operate to produce stress?
- When does the stress occur? Is it continuous or concentrated at certain times?
- What controls exist? Are there procedures to deal with stress? Are they used?
- What are the effects on health, morale, operations?
  In trying to assess risk, it is useful to have a model.

The demand–control model

While all workplace demands and mediating factors can contribute in various ways to stress, four factors and the relationships between them, appear to be core. These are:

- psychological demand
- job control
- organisational support
- job uncertainty.

Stressful work would be characterised by high psychological demand, low job control, low organisational support and high job uncertainty. However, it is the first two factors of psychological demand and job control that appear to be more significant than the others.[3] The following model, developed by Robert Karasek, illustrates how the two factors of psychological demand and control (decision-making latitude) interact.

Figure 11.3 *Interaction of psychological demands and control*

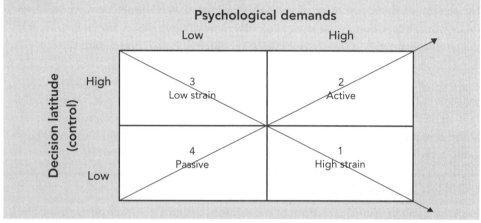

Source: Karasek, 1998.

In quadrant 1, where there is high demand and low control, you have high strain or stressful jobs. Here, you are likely to find stress-related symptoms of exhaustion and cardiovascular disease. In quadrant 3, where there is low demand but high control, you have low-strain jobs. Here, you would expect lower than average levels of stress reactions. In quadrant 2, you have active jobs in which there is high demand and high control. Here, there is more opportunity to be motivated, learn and grow as the demands are converted into problem solving and direct activity. The demands are coped with positively, not negatively; however, similar to any other situation, if the demand is excessive, irrespective of a positive attitude, a physical toll may be incurred. In quadrant 4, you have low demand and low control or passive jobs. Jobs with high control and low demand tend not to challenge employees or tap their creative capacities. Such jobs would include blue-collar production work, especially machine-paced work that involves boring and repetitive tasks. The model has been tested to show that:

- the social organisation of work, not just physical hazards, leads to illness and injury
- stress-related consequences are related to the social organisation of work activity and not just its demands
- work's social activity affects stress-related risks, not just person-based characteristics
- the possibility of positive stress and negative stress can be explained in terms of combinations of demands and control.

Since first being developed, the model has been changed by some researchers to include the factor of workplace social support. Where there is low social support, for example, those with high-strain jobs (quadrant 1) are more likely to experience stress. There is also evidence that job uncertainty can combine with one or more of these factors to increase the likelihood of stress.

It is important to remember that stress may be due to factors other than job demand and job control. Stressors involve a wide range of issues, which we referred to earlier in this chapter. The solutions are just as widely varied. Just as one example, sexual harassment is a significant cause of stress and therefore a WHS issue. However, like some other workplace stressors such as violence and racial discrimination, sexual harassment can also be dealt with using strategies based on different laws – in this case, the federal *Sex Discrimination Act 1984* (Cwlth).

After an appreciation of the size and nature of the problem has been gathered, a judgement has to be made about whether it is important or not and if it is significant, how significant. It could be a temporary phase that is already under control and no action is required, or it could be something that has been festering and shows no signs of going away – in which case, we need to look at controlling it.

CONTROLLING STRESS

Depending on the particular nature of the stressors, a number of controls are available. The preferred option is the removal of the stressors entirely: better communication, team building, disciplining offenders, improved supervisory training, capping overtime, and so on. However, in many cases, this may not be as straightforward or practical as we would like; for example, when meeting budgets and deadlines, facing inevitable organisational change, and dealing with customers or other organisations. In which case, controls are needed that minimise stress. These controls need to be developed with the input of workers themselves and possibly professional assistance.

Recognising the problem

Managers can begin by providing leadership:
- acknowledging that stress may be a problem or potential problem in their organisation
- designing and implementing formal systems with documented policies and procedures to prevent and, should it occur, manage dissatisfaction (for example, establishing grievance procedures, instituting performance management programs, implementing performance planning and development programs, establishing employee assistance programs, and so on)
- encouraging openness in the communication of dissatisfaction
- managing, rather than ignoring, conflict situations
- involving those affected in the process of finding solutions
- giving effective and timely feedback on workplace problems.

Problem solving

Leadership can also be shown through addressing particular problems by:

- providing programs for at-risk employees, such as cash handlers, accident and emergency workers, police and related services, and so on
- attending to workload, job design and organisational training
- providing professional and confidential support services; for example, employee assistance programs
- facilitating liaison between line managers, human resources staff and training staff
- providing clear performance expectations for supervisors.

Anticipating issues

Recognition and problem solving ought to be part of normal organisational management; however, in times of significant change, such as downsizing, major corporate restructuring, technological change and the like, it is particularly important to have strategies established early in the planning phase. An individual strategy can give stress a status it does not deserve, so it is not necessary or desirable for organisations to have a separate stress strategy. Rather, the management of stress-related problems ought to be a normal part of effective management strategy.

Importantly, managers need to consider intervening before using any medical options or investing entirely in (expensive) 'stress management' courses that focus on the individual coping with stressors rather than removing them or mitigating them at source. 'Change the mind, not the world' is at best short-term and limited when dealing with workplace stress. It is no substitute for a safe and healthy workplace.[4]

Management strategy

Having a strategy for dealing with these problems is not admitting defeat, nor is it shielding employees from the normal challenges of the workplace. When properly developed, management strategies can continue to provide interesting and challenging work while assisting employees to cope with those demands that they find difficult.

It is important then that the achievement of the core goals of the organisation makes reference to the wellbeing of the workforce; that is, of those centrally involved in the delivery of these goals. Naturally, this must go beyond rhetoric and be reflected in corporate practice.

A good way to make this clear is to set agreed management standards and measure performance against them. The Health and Safety Executive in the UK has drawn up a number of useful management standards to address key areas of workplace stress, which are summarised below.

THE MANAGEMENT STANDARDS

Demands

Includes issues such as workload, work patterns and the work environment. The standard is that:
- employees indicate that they are able to cope with the demands of their jobs
- systems are in place locally to respond to any individual concerns.

Control

How much say the person has in the way they do their work. The standard is that:
- employees indicate that they are able to have a say about the way they do their work
- systems are in place locally to respond to any individual concerns.

Support

Includes the encouragement, sponsorship and resources provided by the organisation, line management and colleagues. The standard is that:
- employees indicate that they receive adequate information and support from their colleagues and superiors
- systems are in place locally to respond to any individual concerns.

Relationships

Includes promoting positive working to avoid conflict and dealing with unacceptable behaviour. The standard is that:
- employees indicate that they are not subjected to unacceptable behaviours; for example, bullying at work
- systems are in place locally to respond to any individual concerns.

Role

Whether people understand their role in the organisation and whether the organisation ensures that the person does not have conflicting roles. The standard is that:
- employees indicate that they understand their role and responsibilities
- systems are in place locally to respond to any individual concerns.

Change

How organisational change (large or small) is managed and communicated in the organisation. The standard is that:
- employees indicate that the organisation engages them frequently when undergoing an organisational change
- systems are in place locally to respond to any individual concerns.

Source: Health and Safety Executive, What are the Management Standards, http://www.hse.gov.uk/stress/standards/.

Sunnybrook College is a community college, with its main campus in a large regional centre. Overall, it is estimated that 20 per cent of the teaching staff belong to the National Tertiary Education Union (NTEU). The college was inspected by WorkCover and was told its policies and practices dealing with stress were woeful, with reports of harassment and high levels of sick leave. It was required to carry out a stress audit, as no overall stress management strategy was in place.

Management used a recognised consultancy firm, who prepared the terms of reference and objectives for the HS committee. The HSE Management Standards approach was used as a general framework to develop the audit. Based on results, the consultancy group used focus groups to identify hotspots and drafted action plans for the committee's approval. The plans included training in their implementation by managers and supervisors as well as a short-term and a longer-term method of reviewing against agreed targets.

The outcome saw a steady decline in sickness leave and an improvement in employee survey ratings. In terms of other impacts, staff felt that the college was more aware of stress and the main work-related stressors encountered by staff. More open communication was also cited as a spin-off.

Questions

1 Which aspect of the exercise appeared to be most successful?
2 Which lessons do you think could be used in your organisation?

WORKPLACE VIOLENCE AND BULLYING

Stress may be caused by violence and bullying or lead to violence and bullying. In the following section, we look at a topic that has only emerged as a headline WHS issue in recent times.

WHAT IS WORKPLACE VIOLENCE?

Workplace violence can be defined generally as incidents in which workers are abused, harassed, threatened or assaulted in the course of their work. It can also cover incidents that occur when a person is commuting to and from work, as well as malicious damage to property.

The three basic categories, based on the source of workplace violence, are shown in Figure 11.4.

Figure 11.4 *The three basic categories of workplace violence*

TYPE	SOURCE	VULNERABLE INDUSTRIES, OCCUPATIONS	MAIN RISK FACTORS
External	Perpetrated against workers by people from outside the organisation	Banks, post offices, taxis, retail traders, liquor outlets, service stations, pharmacies	Cash, drugs, property that can be easily resold
Client-initiated	Inflicted on workers by customers or clients of the organisation	Police, guards, fire services, teachers, welfare workers, health care workers, tax officers	Face-to-face contact, as well as telephone and email contact
Internal	Involving workers inside the organisation; for example, a supervisor and employee, or a worker and apprentice – bullying, initiation rites, bastardisation	Military forces, police, high schools, prisons and many other organisations	Various

OVERT AND COVERT VIOLENCE

Workplace violence is an emerging WHS issue. It has been traditionally thought of as assault and injury by external aggressors, arising, for example, out of bank, pharmacy or petrol station hold-ups. However, many violent incidents also occur in government agencies that deal directly with the public, or in hospitals, schools and other institutions. In such cases, the perpetrators may not only be interested in money or drugs, but also are often expressing poorly met or unmet needs or other dissatisfaction. Customer service personnel in the public and private sectors, for example, may be subjected to violence from angry clients or customers. Nurses and other nursing home staff are often subjected to violence from confused elderly residents. Despite often resulting in injury to the carer, this form of violence is frequently not reported.

Much workplace violence, however, occurs within an organisation and is often covert. It may occur between workers or between a supervisor or manager and worker. Bullying and harassment are two forms of such covert workplace violence and can include humiliation, sabotage, spreading gossip, delaying tactics and practical jokes, as well as verbal abuse, nasty text messages and physical attacks.

Bullying

The concept of bullying occurs frequently in research and literature emanating from Europe and the United Kingdom and is usually equated to repeated incidents of harassment. In Australia, schoolyard bullying (for example, student to student, student to teacher) has received a wealth of media attention in recent times and the various states and territories have invested considerable (human and financial) resources in developing and implementing prevention programs to combat it. Bullying in other workplaces has recently been recognised as a major cost in the form of absenteeism, staff turnover and reduced productivity.

DID YOU KNOW?

A 2010 report by the Productivity Commission, *Performance Benchmarking of Australian Business Regulation: Occupational Health and Safety*, showed that bullying and harassment cost $15 billion a year, and this did not include the hidden costs, such as hiring and training employees to replace those who left as a result of workplace stress. Workplace stress claims tended to be more costly than claims for less serious physical injuries and resulted in more time taken off work. It also found that 2.5 million workers experienced some aspect of bullying during their working lives.

Source: based on Nicola Berkovic, 2010, Workplace bullies cost $15bn each year, *The Australian*, 28 January, http://www.theaustralian.com.au/news/nation/workplace-bullies-cost-15bn-each-year/story-e6frg6nf-1225824136075.

Extent and cost

Because workplace violence is covered by the criminal justice system as well as WHS authorities, the extent and pattern of it in Australia are not clear. There are difficulties with differing reporting systems as well as serious underreporting. Internationally, it has been estimated that, at most, only one in five incidents are reported.[5] Only work–related homicides are reliably reported.

Where WHS authorities have begun to report workplace violence, the figures show a significant number of claims and costs. In 2000–01, for example, the first year in which data on workplace bullying was compiled by WorkCover Victoria, 1099 claims for compensation for workplace bullying and violence were reported, at an estimated cost of $26 million.[6]

Like workplace stress, the costs of workplace violence have an impact on the individual, the organisation and the community. Individuals may be physically injured (even killed) or suffer from a series of mental health disorders (including post-traumatic stress disorder, adjustment reactions, depression and/or anxiety), the symptoms of which cover physical, behavioural, cognitive and emotional reactions. Compensable costs, although easy to document, are only the tip of the iceberg. The costs to the individual's (and their family's) quality of life are extensive but difficult to measure. The potential economic and human resource costs to an organisation can be far-reaching and encompass:

- increased turnover
- increased absenteeism
- reduced productivity
- negative public relations affecting client attitudes and usage
- negative investor relations
- fines and, potentially, jail (under WHS legislation)
- lawsuits under anti-discrimination legislation
- breach of (employment) contract lawsuits
- criminal lawsuits
- civil lawsuits.

MANAGING WORKPLACE VIOLENCE

There are three approaches used in managing workplace violence:

- reducing exposure to violence – *prevention*
- encouraging appropriate behaviour when violence appears imminent – *protection*
- dealing with the post-event impact – *treatment*.

All three approaches need to be established and operational. That said, in the remainder of this chapter, we concentrate on prevention, using the risk management methodology of hazard identification, risk assessment and control. In the following section, we will assume the organisation is embarking on an initial review of its exposure to violence.

We use the logic of the hazard register; that is, identify the context (the workplace and standards to be used), organise a team and suitable resources, prepare a plan, list the processes, identify the violence hazards, assess and evaluate them, prepare controls and implement them, monitor and evaluate their effectiveness and regularly review the process in order to improve the outcomes.

Step 1: Identifying the context

The area to be assessed needs to be defined. It may be the organisation itself or certain high-risk areas within the organisation. In some cases – for example, storefronts – the similarity in functions and locations may only require a representative assessment. The standards to be used also need to be set out. What standards of security and level of risk are we prepared to accept? These may be detailed in an already existing policy. The overall goal should be clear – a workplace free of violence.

Step 2: Organising a team

A small team representing the affected workforce, including health and safety representatives, needs to be organised and a plan prepared by management for consultation and agreement. Specialist assistance, such as appropriate consultants or local police, may need to be called on. Information on the potential for violence should be gathered from internal resources (for example, injury reports, compensation claims), as should information on workplace violence gathered from external sources such as WHS agencies. Many of these agencies have detailed fact sheets dealing with violence in different industries and occupations; for example, pharmacies, bottle-shops, service stations, hospitals and hospices. Industry associations often have guidance material as well. When possible, checklists should be prepared to ensure comprehensiveness and uniformity.

Step 3: Identifying the hazards

List the main processes in the workplace, being careful to include maintenance, repair and cleaning. Then, using the documented information and discussion with managers and employees, identify the potential for abuse, threats and assault from the three sources: external, client-related and internal. Figure 11.5 is based on a hazard identification framework from the Western Australian code of practice *Violence, Aggression and Bullying at Work*. It covers hazard identification as well as some risk assessment issues.

Figure 11.5 *Hazard identification form*

Hazard identification notes
Name of organisation: The Blue Hills Nursing Home
Information collected by: Mary Jones, Supervisor
Date: 2 April 2011

TASK AND LOCATION	HAZARDS	PEOPLE AFFECTED	HOW OFTEN	COMMENTS
Showering residents in the bathroom	Residents may become agitated and abusive; staff may become impatient with uncooperative residents	Nurses and other staff, and/or residents can suffer verbal and physical abuse	Daily, especially in the morning	Not enough time for showering; each resident can increase the pressure in this situation
Introducing new staff	Residents may not like to be undressed in front of staff who are unfamiliar to them	New nurses and other staff	Daily, especially in the morning	
Visitors meeting residents in lounge rooms	Aggressive and antisocial behaviour from some residents	Visitors may be frightened	During visiting hours	
Keeping personal belongings secure in bedrooms	Residents may accuse each other of removing personal belongings	Residents and staff who may become involved in arguments	At any time	

TASK AND LOCATION	HAZARDS	PEOPLE AFFECTED	HOW OFTEN	COMMENTS
Planning daily schedules in all areas	Some residents who are attached to certain staff members may be upset by a change	Staff who are seen to be responsible for the change	From time to time	Procedure to advise long-term residents of changes before they occur should help
Dispensing medication	Residents may not want to take medication; their behaviour may change when medication is changed	Visitors, other residents, staff, especially if it is unusual for the person to be aggressive	Daily	

This form covers all employees, residents and visitors who may be affected by work in the nursing home.

Source: Reproduced courtesy of WorkSafe, Department of Commerce, Western Australia (www.worksafe.wa.gov.au).

Step 4: Assessing the risk

The next job is to assess what the risk is for each hazard. Two groups of factors identified by researchers as the primary causes of workplace violence are:
- structural aspects of the workplace, such as cash handling, dealing with the public and work schedules
- psychosocial factors, such as co-worker and supervisory support and team culture.

Being careful to consider both types of causes, questions such as the following should be asked:
- What are the risk factors?
- How many are exposed?
- When are they exposed?
- What controls are in place?
- How effective are the controls?
- How likely are violent incidents?
- What are the potential injuries?

Answering these questions requires research and consultation. As mentioned, industry sources, as well as WHS authorities and specialists, can provide invaluable assistance. Checklists are available that will help with direct questions for particular industries and occupations. Onsite inspections are required, particularly for external and client-initiated violence.

After getting a picture of what the likelihood and impact of the hazards may be, the risk needs to be evaluated. Do the risks exceed the accepted standards? If they do and something must be done, what are the priority hazards? If they don't, then the situation only needs monitoring and future review.

Who is at risk?

The simple answer to the question 'Who is at risk?' is anybody. However, there are factors that can increase the risk for particular individuals. Individuals most at risk include:
- people (and women in particular) from cultural backgrounds that do not encourage speaking up and/or making complaints

- workers with little or no English
- employees working alone and/or in isolated areas
- young workers
- workers in precarious employment (for example, those in insecure employment including casual employees, seasonal workers, etc.).

Other factors relating to the workgroup size, workers' roles and responsibilities, the workplace culture and so can also increase the risk for some individuals.

COMPANY, WORKERS FINED $335K FOR WAITRESS'S BULLYING

A magistrate has fined a Melbourne cafe company $220,000 over a workplace bullying case that resulted in a waitress committing suicide.

Brodie Panlock, a 19-year-old waitress, took her own life in 2006 after enduring persistent bullying by her colleagues at Cafe Vamp in Hawthorn.

Company director Marc Da Cruz and three of his employees, Nicholas Smallwood, 26, now of Queensland, Rhys MacAlpine, 28, of Kooyong, and Gabriel Toomey, 23, of Abbotsford all pleaded guilty to charges under the occupational health and safety act.

The court was told Smallwood and MacAlpine mentally and physically bullied Ms Panlock during work hours and even taunted her about a previous suicide attempt.

The magistrate described their bullying as 'persistent and vicious' and said cafe owner Da Cruz condoned it.

Smallwood was fined $45,000. MacAlpine was fined $30,000 and Toomey must pay $10,000. Da Cruz was fined $30,000.

Prosecutor Gary Livermore told a pre-sentence hearing last week that witnesses had seen Smallwood and MacAlpine pour fish oil into Ms Panlock's kitbag and then pour it over her hair and clothes, reducing her to tears.

He also said they engaged in indirect bullying, such as calling her fat and ugly.

Step 5: Controlling the risk

As with other workplace hazards, the hierarchy of controls should be used, as shown in the example of a video store in Figure 11.6.

Figure 11.6 *Controlling cash-handling risk*

1 Eliminate the hazard entirely	No cash on premises
2 Substitute less hazardous procedures	Use drop safe or limited cash float
3 Put in engineering controls	Widen counters, install screens
4 Use administrative controls	Alarms, staff rotation through vulnerable zones, install CCTV
5 Provide training	Train staff in dealing with hold-ups

In the case of external or client-initiated violence, many techniques are available, including careful design and location of facilities, that will reduce the opportunity for and raise the perceived cost to perpetrators. Some of these techniques go under the heading of 'target hardening' – which means making it more difficult to commit acts of violence. These technical fixes can be very effective as, for example, the use of central locking, which has significantly reduced the number of car thefts.

Nevertheless, it must be said that the perception of difficulty may incline perpetrators to 'raise the ante' and use even more violent methods in order to achieve their goal. More subtle strategies include:

- increased visibility in contact areas, used together with closed-circuit television
- appropriate furniture and fittings; that is, those that are not potential weapons
- use of music, television, lighting, colours
- two doors to interview rooms.

Using the hazards identified at the video store (Figure 11.6) as a starting point, a vast range of organisational strategies could be applied. These should include strategies related to

- employees
- customers
- the physical environment
- emergency situations
- policy and procedures
- restraints
- training and information
- the response phase (incident management)
- the recovery phase (post-incident management), including information dissemination, team and management support, and debriefing and counselling.

Some of the best advice comes from industry experience. Figure 11.7 is a good example of strategies that are used in a workplace that is surprisingly prone to violence.

Figure 11.7 *Examples of organisational strategies to prevent and/or minimise aggression in aged care*

Workers	
	• Undertake communication/aggression problem solving
	• Improve personalised care through employee care teams and small groups of residents
	• Avoid rotating employees
	• Roster to avoid fatigue/stress
	• Employee training in defusing incidents, communication, negotiation, anger management
	• Avoid giving extra attention to at-risk residents, thus reinforcing inappropriate behaviour
	• Approach at-risk residents from the front
	• Work in teams or pairs
	• Adopt a team approach to necessary care procedures at the same time
	• Allow employees to choose their working partners
	• Consider aggression reduction when rostering
	• Match employee competency with assigned tasks
	• Look for signs of stress or burnout in employees

Residents	• Assign new residents to experienced employees • Explain all procedures to residents and ask permission • Find out residents' likes and dislikes and account for same • Plan and structure activities to meet individual needs • Consult with residents' doctors regarding medication and health in respect of potential aggression • Be alert to pain or constipation • Account for 'sundowning' syndrome • Don't hurry or rush residents • Involve residents' families • Focus on maintaining residents' mobility • Positively reinforce non-aggressive behaviour (use a praise and reward system) • Consult with families to provide easy-dressing clothing and footwear
Physical environment	• Minimise noise • Ensure furniture and fittings are not breakable or potential weapons • Ensure building is fitted with safety glass • Ensure clear signage and identification cues • Reduce sliding doors • Use plain colour schemes with calming colours • Ensure there are routines, but also ensure the routines are not regimented • Provide safe, secure outdoor recreation area with interesting features, such as birdbath, statue • Ensure residents, employees and specialists are consulted before redecorating or making building alterations

Policy and procedures

While safe design and engineering controls are important, suitable administrative controls are necessary to implement them. Above all, there needs to be a clear policy of zero tolerance towards any violence, together with procedures based on regular risk assessments and reviews. The policy and procedures should be made clear to everyone involved, as should the sanctions if the policy and procedures are violated. If incidents are likely, staff need to be trained in how to spot and deal with them. Any incidents or breaches must be reported. All new staff must be informed of the policy and procedures as well as of the consequences for any breaches. A clear, sharp statement of policy that is communicated to everyone by the head of the organisation is the most effective form of control, particularly when dealing with internal and client-initiated violence.

With internal- or client-initiated violence in particular, designing out the potential risk in some situations may not be simple or even possible. This does not mean that there is an absence of experience in reducing or minimising the potential for violence in these cases. On the contrary, there is a great deal of research and experience. It is a matter of gathering it from those directly involved and those with wider knowledge and expertise, then implementing the most suitable controls. Nowadays, most WHS authorities have codes of practice or guidance material addressing workplace violence in its main forms.

The management of an incident that results in workplace violence should be part of an emergency management and response system set up to deal with emergencies of all kinds.

Response phase

Even with the best controls, it may not be possible to eliminate or reduce all risk. Procedures and employees trained to use them are needed to deal with the possibility of incidents.

The response to an act of violence is a real test of the system. The aim is to have an effective immediate response that controls and defuses the situation, and reduces the risk of long-term psychological harm for employees. Everyone should know who has the authority to take charge of the situation. That person should be trained to coordinate the response, including taking care of employees who may be injured or in shock or are otherwise affected by the incident.

To minimise the effects of trauma, employee assistance should be available as part of the immediate response and the recovery phase. The main focus is to provide immediate professional counselling and support.

General arrangements – such as providing a safe place to retreat to, controlling media access, providing communication with families and arranging transport home – are also important to relieve the immediate pressure.

Recovery phase

The recovery phase deals with the reorganisation and reconstruction required to return the workplace to normal operations. At this point, the workplace should have been made safe, first aid and medical assistance arranged and immediate support provided. The workplace may be in disarray if there has been property damage as a result of the incident, but the situation has to be brought under control.

As it is important health-wise that employees return to normal duties as quickly as possible after the disruptive incident, plans previously agreed to should be implemented as quickly and efficiently as possible. The following actions should be included:
- Provide clear information regarding the situation to all employees.
- Provide ongoing professional counselling and support services for employees and their families.
- Allow employees time to recover, but encourage early return to work.
- Provide advice on legal matters and workers' compensation arrangements.
- Investigate the incident and review management procedures.

We have completed the hazard identification, risk assessment and control stages of dealing with psychosocial hazards. The final stages are monitoring and reviewing.

Step 6: Monitoring and reviewing

The process of managing psychosocial hazards should be monitored to make sure the action taken to eliminate hazards and reduce risk is effective. Hazard identification, risk assessment and risk control are all parts of a continuous process that should be regularly reviewed to ensure that the action taken is still effective and that new hazards have not been introduced.

The key to this part of the process is a reporting system that encourages employees to note incidents that may have a bearing on the effectiveness of the system. Whether verbally or written, the reports of incidents should be discussed to see if others have noticed similar issues. All of these procedures reflect on the quality of the risk assessment and the decision to implement certain controls. Feedback on the system may be reported to the team as a whole, as with client-initiated violence and externally initiated violence. With internal violence, more suitable ways of conveying information that would better protect any victims may need to be decided on. In any case, a thorough system of regular reporting of incidents and ongoing communication is critical. It is at this point that the controls and any training in anti-violence procedures can be evaluated for their effectiveness. If the system clearly remains risky, a review may need to be brought forward.

When a system for monitoring and review is set up, it may be easier to make the management of psychosocial hazards part of the whole safety management system in which all hazards are monitored and reviewed on a regular basis.

With any WHS program or activity a review against the objectives, on a regular basis and in the case of specific incidents, is necessary. Particular attention should be paid to the validity of the risk assessments that underpin controls and training. It may be useful, depending on the incident's potential severity or as a result of changes to the organisation, that an independent review be conducted. HS committee or HS representative input is necessary at this stage, as the consultation can ensure the quality of any review and build confidence among staff. Benchmarking, or simply sharing experiences with other organisations, can lead to big improvements in quality. Lessons can also be learnt from dissimilar organisations.

Summary

- Stress claims are the costliest compensable workplace injury or disease. The hidden costs, such as absenteeism, increased turnover, reduced productivity, make occupational stress one of the most serious workplace hazards in financial and economic terms alone.
- Stress is defined as the psychological and physical reaction experienced when one is faced with demands that cannot be met. When you find yourself in a stressful situation, your body responds by increasing your energy, thereby preparing you for greater levels of action.
- Stress normally refers to situations in which the demand is experienced negatively, not positively as with sports. There is some individual variation in response to similar demands. This variation depends on individual, social and other factors that mediate your experience; for example, the support you may or may not receive from your manager or supervisor. The effects of stress can be significant and affect your psychology, physiology and behaviour.
- While many factors have been cited as stressors, research strongly indicates that it is the organisation and management of work that plays a critical role in determining the level of stress in the workplace; in particular, the nature and relation of job demand, job control, organisational support and job uncertainty.
- Managing stress requires understanding of the particular causes, which, in turn, requires successful communication among employees, supervisors and managers. A good understanding of the work culture is needed before effective strategies can be developed.

- Unless such strategies are developed, stress may become a medical problem, which involves costly compensation premiums.
- Workplace violence is a significant cause of occupational stress and physical injury, affecting not only those facing threats, harassment, abuse and attacks from the public, but also those facing equally stressful relations with other employees, managers and supervisors. Here, too, the insured and uninsured hidden costs are intolerable.
- Successful strategies require treatment of workplace violence using a risk management approach together with a zero-tolerance policy.
- There is a growing awareness of workplace violence in all its forms, which includes a body of well-documented resources to use in its identification and management.
- Not only are prevention strategies required, but so also are strategies to deal with incidents – during and after.
- Monitoring, evaluating and reviewing systems depend heavily on an effective reporting system in which people are encouraged to raise issues that may appear to be minor.

In your workplace

Heroic High School is located in a large town in south-western Queensland. It has 1000 students. The feeder area of the school has mixed demographics, ranging from a small proportion of middle-income earners to a large proportion of people on basic wages. A significant proportion of the feeder population are unemployed due to the closure of the town's major employer, the local abattoir. This has impacted on the general economic wealth of the town, especially the retail industry.

Heroic High School has had the same principal for five years, but there is a high turnover of staff generally. A number of new staff were appointed at the beginning of the year, including two maths teachers, who are also required to teach science. The maths department head teacher went on maternity leave at the end of first term and there is an acting head filling in.

The principal is concerned because the maths department has had a number of workers' compensation claims for psychological injury citing work-related factors in the past six months.

You are the deputy principal. The principal has asked you to find out what the problem is and fix it.

1 Identify the work-related factors potentially causing stress.
   Hint: for this activity, use the WorkSafe Victoria Stresswise Toolkit Worksheet available for download at http://www.worksafe.vic.gov.au/wps/wcm/connect/wsinternet/worksafe/home/forms+and+publications/tools/stresswise+toolkit+worksheet.
2 Determine the stress-related risks and evaluate them.
   Hint: use the information on risk assessment in Chapter 6 to evaluate the risks and determine the risk rating.
3 Suggest suitable control measures for each of the risks, based on the priority of the assessed risk ratings.
   Hint: consider the hierarchy of control discussed in previous chapters and use the higher levels where possible, also taking into account the ALARP principles (refer to Chapter 6).

Questions

1 Define 'stress' or 'psychological injury'.
   a How does it occur?
   b What are its effects on people?
2 What are the employer's legal obligations in relation to workplace stress? Which sections of your WHS Act apply?

3 How does stress differ as a hazard from other physical hazards such as, say, a toxic chemical? Consider how you identify, assess and control workplace stress.

4 What is workplace violence and what are the major categories?

5 In most jobs, stress is inevitable. Discuss this statement.

6 Are there psychosocial hazards (stress, violence, bullying) in your workplace? If so, what are management's methods of dealing with them? Are they successful? How would you improve upon these methods?

Activities

1 With the cooperation of your employer, conduct a (confidential) stress survey in your workplace. For assistance, search for 'stress surveys workplace' on the Internet to find forms that you can use or adapt. See, for example, http://www.vieu.org.au/bullying_survey.pdf. Prepare an analysis of the results for a report back to your employer.

2 With regard to activity 1 above, examine what is on offer from a (small) number of professionals who offer workplace consultancies dealing with stress. Compare the products and prices. Ask for references. Prepare a report on the preferred option.

Search me!

 Explore **Search me! management** for relevant articles on workplace stress Search me! is an online library of world-class journals, ebooks and newspapers, including *The Australian* and the *New York Times*, and is updated daily. Log in to Search me! through www.cengage.com/sso using the access card in the front of this book.

KEYWORDS

Try searching for the following terms:

▶ **stressors**   ▶ **workplace violence**
▶ **demand and control**   ▶ **bullying**
▶ **job support**   ▶ **harassment**
▶ **job uncertainty**

Search tip: Search me! management contains information from both local and international sources. To get the greatest number of search results, try using both Australian and American spellings in your searches, e.g. 'globalisation' and 'globalization'; 'organisation' and 'organization'.

Additional resources

• The websites of most regulators offer guidance on dealing with workplace stress, violence, bullying and aggression.

• The International Labour Office's *Encyclopaedia of Occupational Health and Safety* contains excellent articles on psychosocial hazards, as well as on all other WHS matters. It can be found at http://www.ilocis.org/en/contilo.html. You will find Karasek's article 'Demand/ Control model: a social, emotional, and physiological approach to stress risk and active behaviour development' there.

• See various international sites such as:
  – Canada: http://www.ccohs.ca/keytopics/
  – USA: www.cdc.gov/niosh/topics/stress/
  – UK: www.hse.gov.uk/stress/.

• Because stress is emerging as a growing health and safety issue, more writers have focused on it and so the available literature is immense and expanding. A lot is of the '7 steps …' type of books with, of course, accompanying DVDs and audiotapes – all of which is very general and of mixed value. Some of the most practical material is industry- or occupation-centred and based carefully on research. The best source of such information are the websites referred to above.

- Mayhew, C. & Chappell, D., 2003, The occupational violence experiences of 400 Australian health workers, *Journal of Occupational Health and Safety – Australia and New Zealand*, 19(6).
- Mayhew, C. & Chappell, D., 1995, Managing the stress phenomenon at work, in P. Cotton (ed.) *Psychological Health in the Workplace: Understanding and Managing Occupational Stress*, Australian Psychological Society: Melbourne. This text contains a lively debate on the proper approach to workplace stress and how it should be identified.
- Turnbull, J. & Paterson, B. (eds) 1999, *Aggression and Violence: Approaches to Effective Management*, Macmillan: London.
- Wirth, K., 2003, Bullying and violence in the workplace: the legal perspective, *Australian Master OHS and Environment Guide 2003*, CCH: Sydney. See also articles by Helen Borger, Katherine Wirth, Paul McCarthy et al., Claire Mayhew, Jan de Jonge and Maureen Dollard in this book.

Endnotes

1   Other mediating factors could include pay and conditions, career development, physical environment, relationships at work (conflict), home–work balance and domestic or personal problems.

2   See Safe Work Australia's *Compendium of Workers' Compensation Statistics Australia 2007–08*, at http://www.safeworkaustralia .gov.au/AboutSafeWorkAustralia/WhatWeDo/ Publications/Documents/177/Compendium OfWorkersCompensationStatistics_2007_2008_ PDF.pdf.

3   Karasek, R., 1998, 'Demand/Control model: a social, emotional, and physiological approach to stress risk and active behaviour development', in ILO, *Encyclopaedia of Health and Safety*, 4th edition.

4   Readers may wish to look at the QUT 'wellness program' at http://www.wellness.qut.edu.au/ resources/.

5   Turnbull, J. & Paterson, B. (eds), 1999, *Aggression and Violence: Approaches to Effective Management*, Macmillan: London.

6   Wirth, K., 2003, Bullying and violence in the workplace: the legal perspective, *Australian Master OHS and Environment Guide 2003*, CCH: Sydney.

CONTROLLING RISK: SAFE DESIGN

Learning Objectives

At the end of this chapter, the reader should be able to apply safe design principles to control risk and:

- advise on the HS requirements of the design process
- develop a systematic hazard identification and HS risk evaluation system for safe design
- advise on principles of HS risk control
- advise on consultation processes between people involved in the lifecycle of the designed product
- advise on contractual arrangements and procurement systems to minimise 'purchased' WHS risk
- recognise the application of safe design to precarious employment.

INTRODUCTION

It is clear that if you can make things safe *before* they are used, potential risk can be eliminated or minimised better than trying to deal with hazards *after* they have arrived in the workplace. 'Designing out' risk – whether with machinery, substances, buildings or systems of work – is prevention at its best. It is also cost-effective to fix problems at the design stage, rather than later, especially after an accident.

This chapter provides information on eliminating hazards through safe design. We describe the principles of safe design and their application. We also discuss the specific implications for hazard identification and risk management, consultation and procurement or purchasing.[1]

WHAT IS SAFE DESIGN?

Safe design is about *upstream* decisions that impact positively on safety *downstream*. Safe design eliminates hazards and controls risks to health and safety 'at the source'. This covers items such as:

- work premises, construction projects and structural materials
- plant (machinery, equipment, appliances and tools)
- substances
- work methods and systems of work.

Safe design tends to focus on products, 'hardware' – plant, substances and structures. This chapter reflects that focus but also points out the need to look at the safe design of the work involving plant, substances and structures.

A safe design approach begins in the conceptual and planning phases, defining options about design, methods of manufacture or construction or use to enhance safety. Safety should be part of the 'fitness for purpose' objectives.

Risk will exist as designed products are modified or the environments in which they are used change. This means any person who controls decisions taken during the lifecycle of a designed product should consider the potential risk implications.

WHO IS INVOLVED IN SAFE DESIGN?

Safe design is relevant to:

- design professionals (for example, architects, engineers, building surveyors)
- other groups with significant influence over design decisions (for example, developers, owners, employers, financiers, insurers, project managers, purchasers, customers and supervisors)
- suppliers (including manufacturers, importers, plant-hire), constructors, installers and trades/maintenance personnel
- government regulators and inspectorates
- workers.

Consultation is critical at all stages of the process for safe design, particularly with users. Consultation and feedback are generally much easier for employers, as they have established channels for communicating with employees. Designers, manufacturers and suppliers, on the other hand, need to establish effective ongoing consultation mechanisms to identify existing and potential hazards (see below).

Designers and manufacturers should also consult with suppliers, importers, installers and users of similar designed products while doing their technical and market research.

CASE STUDY

A publishing company has a busy warehouse in Sydney. Large book orders are dispatched throughout the day and overseas shipments are delivered regularly. The company has decided to implement a system of forward-only vehicle movements to remove the hazard to pedestrians in the warehouse.

At the design stage a system of forward-only movements can be considered for certain types of loads. The example shown illustrates a forward-only interface. Roller-doors at the exit end of the building are normally closed. These make the thermal conditions more comfortable. Further the normally closed doors must be opened to exit. The opening of the door is an indication to any personnel outside and in the vicinity that a truck is about to exit. The door opening can also be linked to an alarm and warning light. (Culvenor 2004)

Figure 12.1 *Forward-only system for the movement of trucks*

Photograph and caption © John Culvenor. Used with permission.

The control over the decision about such a safely designed system would be held by the facility owner, the architect and the engineer working together and anticipating the risks of vehicles backing up.

Questions

1 What risks remain after the design for the forward-only system has been put in place?
2 How would you control these risks?

WHY SAFE DESIGN?

The opportunities to create safer workplaces and plant are most cost-effective in the earliest phases of the lifecycle of designed products. In contrast, by the time the designed product is ready for import, supply or commissioning (in the case of a building) there are likely to be fewer options to make the product safer. In addition to the human cost of injury, illness and disease, poor design can result in a range of economic costs, such as low productivity, higher maintenance, higher employment and workers' compensation expenses, and reduced asset life.

DID YOU KNOW?

Research commissioned by the National Occupational Health and Safety Commission indicated that:

- Seventy-seven (37 per cent) of 210 identified workplace fatalities definitely or probably had design-related issues contributing to them; in another 29 (14 per cent), the circumstances were suggestive that design issues were involved.
- Design contributed to at least 30 per cent of work-related serious and fatal injuries.
- Design-related issues were most prominent in the 'machinery and fixed plant' group and 'mobile plant and transport' group.
- Similar design problems are involved in many fatal incidents.
- Design-related issues were definitely or probably involved in at least half of the incidents in the mining, transport, agriculture, construction, trade and manufacturing industries.
- Solutions already exist for most of the identified design problems.

The main finding from the study is that design continues to be a significant contributor to work-related serious injury in Australia. This is the case with a wide variety of machinery, plant and equipment, although the extent of involvement varies between them. Limitations of the data sources mean that the design contribution identified in this analysis is likely to be underestimated.

Source: NOHSC (2004), *The Role of Design Issues in Work-related Injuries in Australia 1997–2002*, Commonwealth of Australia: Canberra, pp. 1–2.

DUTY-OF-CARE RESPONSIBILITIES

The WHS Act imposes a duty of care on designers, manufacturers, importers, suppliers, installers and erectors (among others). These parties have a role in ensuring health and safety in relation to particular designed products, such as plant, buildings, structures and substances.

Section 22 of the Act refers to 'Duties of persons conducting businesses or undertakings that design plant, substances or structures'. In general, 'the designer must ensure, so far as is reasonably practicable, that the plant, substance or structure is designed to be without risks to the health and safety of persons [at a workplace]'. (s. 22(2))

Specifically, the designer must carry out any calculations, analysis, testing or examination that may be necessary and provide adequate information to users and with regard to any hazardous properties of substances. The designer must also identify the conditions for safe use. (s. 22(3, 4, 5))

THE FIVE PRINCIPLES OF SAFE DESIGN

As we see below, the safe design approach is a systematic approach that can help parties to meet their legal obligations. The health and safety manager should know what the general principles of safe design are in order to assist the organisation with contracting or purchasing and with any designing, manufacturing and supplying of goods and services.

PRINCIPLE 1: PERSONS WITH CONTROL

Persons who make decisions affecting the design of products, facilities or processes are able to promote health and safety at the source. These include designers, manufacturers, suppliers, leasing or hire agents, purchasers, installers, users, importers, erectors and maintainers. It is important to recognise that if someone alters the design of, say, a machine in a workplace, they become 'designers' and are subject to the law as such.

WHS IN PRACTICE

Fall hazards from the upper deck of car-carriers are a hazard that has been around for many years. Fitting railings to the trailer can significantly reduce the risk of falling.

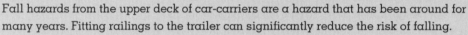
Figure 12.2 *Accessing a vehicle on a car-carrier with the railing fitted*

Photograph and caption © John Culvenor. Used with permission

The person with the control over the decision for this change would be the plant designer and manufacturer. Those that benefit from this solution are the truck drivers transporting cars, and possibly workers performing maintenance on the trailers. Information on the maintenance of the railing systems would need to be transferred from the manufacturer on purchase.

Source: Australian Safety and Compensation Council, 2006, *Guidance on the Principles of Safe Design for Work,* © **Commonwealth of Australia 2006.**

PRINCIPLE 2: PRODUCT LIFECYCLE

Safe design applies to every stage in the lifecycle from conception through to disposal. It involves eliminating hazards or minimising risks as early in the lifecycle as possible.

Designed products are conceived, exist and 'die' within a lifecycle. The lifecycle of a designed product must be considered. This means eliminating the hazards at the design stage or controlling the risk as the designed product is:

- constructed or manufactured
- supplied or installed

- commissioned, used and/or operated
- maintained, repaired, cleaned and/or modified
- decommissioned, demolished and/or dismantled
- disposed of or recycled.

Develop concept phase

Concept development provides the functional specifications and may include a number of options or approaches. Safety requirements for all phases of the lifecycle should be identified and included in the functional specification. Consultation with workers and users is required, as well as research, such as review of risk assessments for such or similar designed products. All issues identified through research and consultation should be collated and registered to be used in phases of the lifecycle; in particular, the *design phase*.

Figure 12.3 *The lifecycle of a designed product*

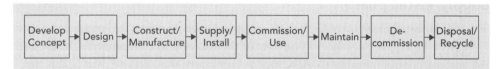

Employers/purchasers should have contractual arrangements and procurement systems that operate to minimise the purchased designed product's HS risk. Such arrangements should ensure that:

- purchasing and contractual arrangements (for example, specifications, supplier prequalification and tender documentation) include a requirement to eliminate HS hazards, minimise HS risks and provide residual HS risk information
- the design brief or draft specifications include an agreement to carry out a safe design approach; the agreement should also include production of a lifecycle HS risk evaluation and a residual risk register.

Design phase

The design phase involves development of design options, evaluation plans and trials, in consultation with downstream users. It should include as part of the design plan:

- assessment of the risk in each of the phases beyond the design phase
- development of a trial and evaluation plan
- development of risk control options
- appropriate instructions for safe construction/manufacture, supply/installation, commissioning/use, maintenance, decommissioning and disposal/recycling.

It is desirable to design to suit the capacity of the widest possible range of people in the workforce, taking into account physical dimensions and diversity. Designed products should also be evaluated for all reasonably foreseeable uses and harm that may affect users. Effective trials and evaluation of the designed product and any risk control options, in consultation with the users, is critical to the design phase. The trial and evaluation of design should extend into all phases of the lifecycle.

Construction or manufacture phase

The construction/manufacture phase involves manufacturers/constructors following design plans. Design plans should detail processes for safe construction/manufacture, as well as safety requirements/features to be included in the designed products.

Monitoring and evaluation of the risk controls communicated with the design plan should be factored into manufacturer/constructor's risk assessments and WHS management systems to ensure safe production processes. Trials should confirm the effectiveness of risk controls in the designed products before they are provided for supply or commissioning/use.

Supply/install phase

The supply/install phase involves the safe receipt, storage, handling and transfer to a user. It requires the supplier/installer to be aware of the risks and to communicate the residual risk and risk control measures to users, such as employers, workers and their health and safety representatives.

Suppliers should also conduct risk assessments for the safe receipt, storage and handling of designed products. Consultation between designers, manufacturers/constructors, suppliers and users can be a great help in identifying and effectively eliminating or controlling risks.

Suppliers should encourage discussion of the associated health and safety issues with workers using the products, and pass relevant risk information back to designers and manufacturers/constructors.

Commission/use phase

The commission/use phase requires:
- confirmation of trial results and ongoing evaluation activities
- effective passage of information
- appropriate training, instruction and supervision.

Persons in control of workplaces need to assess the risk of implementation and use of products with the knowledge of the residual risk passed from designers, manufacturers and suppliers. Any additional design issues identified at this stage should be fed back to the designer through the manufacturer, supplier and/or importer.

Maintain, decommission and dispose/recycle phases

Each of these phases also requires risk assessment, using the information passed through the lifecycle from the designer about the residual risk and risk control measures. Additional design issues identified in these phases should also be fed back to the designer.

It is important that any modification to designed products in the maintenance phase initiates reapplication of the processes detailed in the concept and design phases. This ensures that new hazards are not introduced and that safety features already designed in are not affected, and other opportunities for improved elimination/control of risks are identified.

PRINCIPLE 3: SYSTEMATIC RISK MANAGEMENT

This principle involves the application of hazard identification, risk assessment and risk control processes to achieve safe design.

The primary duty of a designer, manufacturer/constructor or supplier of designed products is to eliminate any hazards that may create a risk of harm from use or exposure to the designed product throughout its lifecycle. If it is not practicable to eliminate the hazard, then the designer, manufacturer/contractor or supplier should control the risk. Taking a systematic risk management approach will allow the parties to manage these duties.

To achieve their duties, designers, manufacturers/constructors and suppliers are required to:

- identify design-related hazards
- conduct risk assessments
- eliminate hazards and control risks
- monitor and review the risk control measures
- maintain records of risk assessments
- consult with users on manual-handling risk
- provide information on the intended use of designed products as they transition through the lifecycle phases.

Applying hazard identification and risk management during lifecycle phases

Some of the specific objectives of risk analysis are:

- *concept development and design phases*
    - to identify major risk factors
    - to provide input and assess the adequacy of the overall design
    - to identify and evaluate possible safety measures for the design
    - to provide input into the assessment of potentially hazardous facilities, activities or systems
    - to provide information on procedures for normal and emergency conditions
    - to evaluate risk with respect to regulatory and other requirements
    - to evaluate alternative design concepts
- *construction/manufacture, supply/install, commission/use, and maintenance phases*
    - to monitor and evaluate experience in order to compare actual performance with relevant requirements
    - to provide input into the optimisation of normal operating, maintenance/ inspection and emergency procedures

- to update information on major contributors to risk and influencing factors
- to provide information on the significance of the risk for operational decision making
- to evaluate the effects of changes in organisational structure, operational practices and procedures, and system components
- to focus training efforts

- *decommissioning and disposal phases*
  - to evaluate the risk related to system disposal activities and to ensure that relevant requirements can be met
  - to provide input into disposal procedures.

Hazard identification and risk management process

Identifying hazards requires the following procedures to be carried out.

- *Research* – information from injury and incident data kept by users or other suppliers, manufacturers and/or designers of similar designed products, to records of research and trials previously conducted by any of these parties, will assist the identification of hazards.
- *Consultation* – consultation should occur with all parties involved in the lifecycle of designed products about hazards.
- *Guidance material* – checklists for hazard identification may be found in or formed by reviewing related standards, codes of practice, guidance notes or technical standards.

Identifying hazards

There are two broad sources of hazards relevant to designed products.

- *Hazards relating to the designed products themselves* – designed products are likely to have a range of hazards that need to be identified. For example, a patient trolley in a health care facility will pose hazards relating to its mobility, its moving parts and its load-carrying capacity, while a building or structure will have hazards relating to access and egress.
- *Hazards relating to how the product will be used and the environment where it will be used* – the patient trolley, for example, may pose hazards stemming from the kind of loads that it is used to move, the gradient and type of surface (for example, unstable or slippery flooring) on which it is used. A designer should consider hazards posed by the environment in which the item will be used.

  Risk management requires designers to evaluate the context of the risk of the product – where, how and when it is being used – and ensure appropriate risk management systems and tools are in place.

  Risk management systems include:

- assigned roles and responsibilities
- guidance on acceptable levels of risk (ALARA)
- trade/specialist and risk management training
- consultation requirements and mechanisms (How are the parties affected by the risk involved in the identification, assessment, control and/or ongoing monitoring of the risk? How will someone know about the risk(s) after the current phase?)

- risk monitoring, review and continuous improvement processes (What trial or evaluation is to be conducted and how are risk controls to be checked for their effectiveness?)
- risk assessment tools to be used.

Risk assessment tools should be selected as appropriate; for example, Hazard Operability Studies (HAZOP), event tree analysis, fault tree analysis, and others. Other tools are detailed in Australian and New Zealand Standard 3931 *Risk analysis of technological systems – application guide.*

Risk assessment is used to see if any subsequent phase of the lifecycle of the designed product has the potential to result in harm. Designers, manufacturers, constructors and suppliers need to analyse and evaluate the risk. Analysis utilises research to determine:

- if there are any existing controls
- the likelihood of a harmful event occurring
- the consequence of the harmful event
- the resulting estimated level of risk.

Evaluation allows for comparison of the estimated risk levels against the guidance provided on acceptable levels of risk. It also prioritises the risks.

Risk control is the next step. When an assessment results in unacceptable levels of risk, a designer should consider whether the risk can be designed out by redesigning aspects of the product. However, if design risk is assessed as extreme or very high, the design approach may need to be reconsidered. A fundamentally different design approach may be required to remove those risks.

If the risk cannot be eliminated, the designer should attempt to minimise the risk by using the hierarchy of controls. Designers need to make sure that any control put in place does not create another risk or introduce a new hazard for users. If, after attempts to eliminate or control risk, the residual risk remains too high, the designer should provide information on the remaining or residual risk and advise on measures required to control this in the workplace. The measures should reflect the hierarchy of controls discussed elsewhere in this book.

Monitoring and reviewing the residual risk and effectiveness of risk control measures is the next phase. Designers should confirm the effectiveness of risk controls through designed products and work trials. This may include controlled prototype studies across the identified range of tasks or uses. Designers should then ensure the ongoing evaluation and correction/amendment of the risk controls as the product and systems of work transit through the lifecycle phases. Manufacturers and suppliers should monitor and review the risk controls communicated by the designer, as well as those identified and implemented internally. New information and more effective risk controls should be communicated to users as well as back to the designer. They should also monitor new information that informs improved risk controls and ensure this is communicated to all parties.

Assessment records must be maintained. A designer should keep a record of the risks identified during the design process and the steps taken to eliminate or minimise those risks. The designer should keep the record for as long as the designed products remain in use in a workplace. Additionally, when new information becomes available, and the design is modified to take into account this information, a record should be kept of this. Designers may find that the most effective way of communicating risk to manufacturers, suppliers and users is to make the risk assessment available to them. This would not necessarily preclude the need for manufacturers, suppliers and users to conduct their own risk assessment, as the people and work environment may vary significantly from one workplace to another.

PRINCIPLE 4: SAFE DESIGN KNOWLEDGE AND CAPABILITY

Safe design knowledge or capability should be either demonstrated or acquired by persons with control over design. Skills and knowledge required by designers include:

* knowledge of WHS regulations
* knowledge of WHS in procurement
* hazard identification and analysis
* risk evaluation and risk control
* the ability to source, identify and analyse data on human behaviour
* the ability to integrate knowledge from a range of sources and disciplines into a new solution
* consultation, negotiation and influencing skills
* planning methods.

PRINCIPLE 5: INFORMATION TRANSFER

Effective communication and documentation of design and risk control information between all persons involved in the phases of the lifecycle is essential for the safe design approach.

People who will work with the product should be aware of the risks involved, the control measures and any specific training requirements. Key information required to control risks should be recorded and transferred from the design phase to all users in later phases of the lifecycle. Users should be informed about any residual risks and the mechanisms to control them. Everyone should provide feedback to upstream parties regarding newly identified risks.

In summary, applying the five principles of safe design helps the organisation – as producer or consumer – to fulfil its health and safety obligations and reduce costs. One way of understanding the impact of safe design is to look at it from the point of view of someone in the purchasing department needing information.

CONTRACTING OR PURCHASING

When purchasing equipment or entering into contract arrangements, the PCBU will want to ensure that hazards are not being introduced. If it is a design brief, the contract will need to specify that a safe design approach has been applied and include evidence to that effect. When residual risk does exist, the measures to deal with it should be provided.

In many cases, the PCBU will be dealing with the purchase or hire of plant – new machinery, tools, appliances, equipment. When purchasing or leasing items of a type requiring plant design notification, the PCBU will need to obtain and retain written proof of the design notification. Government WHS authorities should be able to assist in determining the requirements for design notification.

This chapter has looked at safe design while concentrating principally on plant and equipment used in the workplace. Clearly, workplaces themselves as well as the associated systems of work must be designed in a manner that minimises risk. We conclude with a discussion of the hazards of precarious or non-standard employment as a matter for safe work or employment design.

SAFE WORK DESIGN

PRECARIOUS EMPLOYMENT

Precarious employment refers to non-standard employment contracts such as part-time work, casual or temporary work, outsourcing or subcontracting, and home-based work.[2] It is also often marked by limited benefits and legal entitlements, poor working conditions, job insecurity, low wages and, as might be expected, increased risk to health and safety. Precarious employment has been growing in recent years and poses distinct problems for the health and safety manager.

In 2005, professors Michael Quinlan and Philip Bohle (UNSW) reviewed 106 studies published between 1966–2005 that measured the HS effects of job insecurity and workplace change using a variety of indices including injury, disease, hazard exposure, stress, compliance with WHS laws and management systems. The results were compelling. Of 61 studies of job insecurity/downsizing, 53, or 87 per cent, found adverse health and safety effects. Among 23 studies of outsourcing/subcontracting and home-based work, all 23, or 100 per cent, found an adverse effect on health and safety; and of 22 studies of casual work/labour-hire, 15, or 68 per cent, found worse health and safety compared to that of permanent workers.[3]

The 'existing laws and guidance material on worker involvement largely presume a permanent work arrangement between employer and employees and, as such, take little or no account of the presence of subcontractors, leased or temporary workers,' Quinlan said.

Management response

The fact remains that the increased risk associated with precarious employment does not alter the PCBU's duty of care. It simply makes it more difficult to fulfil that duty. HS managers need to identify the risks posed by precarious employment in consultation with the workers affected and, just as dealing with other hazards, use the hierarchy of controls to design them out or reduce their impact. That means taking all reasonably practicable steps to ensure that practices such as contracting and subcontracting, and using labour-hire, part-time workers and telecommuters do not pose an unacceptable risk. Specific risk management strategies need to be developed for each of these non-standard practices and monitored for their effectiveness. Anything less could result in a breach of the law or company policy and, most importantly, death, injury and disease.

For the HS manager, it means reminding management at all levels of *their* legal and corporate responsibilities and assisting them with suitable risk management programs to deal with work design. Fortunately, there is increasing experience of dealing with the risks of precarious employment. Guidelines and models have been developed that can be applied, say, to the use of (sub)contractors that senior and line managers as well as supervisors need to be aware of. There may also be situations in which a practice such as subcontracting presents unacceptable risk, and alternative forms of employment, possibly standard employment, need to be used.

When showing why such precautions and possible changes are needed, it will be difficult for many companies, as such arrangements are often introduced to save money. The fact that the law may be broken, and the consequences for the organisation and particular individuals will need to be spelt out clearly.

DID YOU KNOW?

INSECURE JOBS TRIGGER MORE HEALTH PROBLEMS

Precarious employment is associated with poor mental and physical health, World Health Organization (WHO) researchers say.

A new landmark report looked at the social determinants of health, particularly concerning temporary contacts or part-time work with low wages and no benefits, i.e. precarious employment.

Study author Dr Carles Muntaner said that when compared with those with full-time work with benefits, workers who report employment insecurity experience 'significant adverse' effects on their physical and mental health.

The study also found that stress at work is associated with a 50 per cent excess risk of coronary heart disease, and there is consistent evidence that jobs with high demands, low control and effort-reward imbalance are risk factors for mental and physical health problems (major depression, anxiety disorders and substance use disorders).

Dr Muntaner noted that Australia and a number of other wealthy countries such as New Zealand, the United Kingdom and the United States all face similar challenges. 'Access to healthcare is not the only determinate of a healthy community', he said. 'All aspects of our lifestyle, including how we work, are intrinsically linked to our wellbeing and our quality and length of life'.

The report calls for three overarching recommendations to achieve health equality, including improving employment and working conditions. The WHO study is the culmination of three year's work by a group of policy makers, academics, former heads of state and former ministers of health who have been investigating the differences between and within countries that result from the social environment where people are born, live, grow, work and age.

Source: Copyright © 2007 Australian Business Pty Limited (ABN 077 016 874) and contributors. WorkplaceOHS, www.workplaceohs.com.au, 23 September 2008.

So far in this book, we have dealt with the development and implementation of a systematic approach to health and safety, or what is used here – a workplace health and safety management system. This system should be checked regularly to see that the elements are in place and working. It is the task of WHS auditing to which we turn in the next chapter.

Summary

- 'Safe design' is about designing out hazards before they are introduced into the workplace (or where products are used by the public).
- Safe design is prevention at its best. It is also less costly to deal with hazards in this way than having to deal with them later.
- Organisations have a duty of care to their employees and the public, both in common law and under WHS legislation.
- The health and safety manager should know what the general principles of safe design are in order to assist the organisation with contracting or purchasing, and with the designing, manufacturing and supplying of goods and services.
- The five principles of safe design are:
  - Principle 1: Persons with control – persons who make decisions affecting the design of products, facilities or processes are able to promote health and safety at the source.
  - Principle 2: Product lifecycle – safe design applies to every stage in the lifecycle from conception through to disposal. It involves eliminating hazards or minimising risks as early in the lifecycle as possible.
  - Principle 3: Systematic risk management – the application of hazard identification, risk assessment and risk control processes to achieve safe design.
  - Principle 4: Safe design knowledge and capability should be either demonstrated or acquired by persons with control over design.
  - Principle 5: Information transfer – effective communication and documentation of design and risk control information between all persons involved in the phases of the lifecycle is essential for the safe design approach.

In your workplace

When there is a failure or defect in a product or another factor such as loss of power, then the product should remain in a safe condition, as the following story reminds us.

WORKER CRUSHED IN A RUBBER TYRE ASSEMBLY MACHINE

During the fall of 2000, a 46-year-old worker at a tyre assembly plant was caught and crushed in a tyre assembly machine. The machine was making prototype agricultural tyre, which differ significantly in assembly procedure from other tyres manufactured at this facility. The large computer-controlled machine normally operates in automatic mode while workers build tyres on a routine basis during their work shift. On the day of the incident, the machine malfunctioned while working on a prototype tyre, and a maintenance crew was called in. The operator cut out the partial tyre and removed it from the machine. When they finished the repair, the machine was reset to zero, in manual mode, to a 'start' position, in order to build another tyre. However, the machine's computer control system jumped to an 'operational mode' and caught the victim off guard from his backside, crushing him in the left pelvic region. Co-workers immediately assisted the man, and he remained alert and conscious during transport to the hospital and during his evaluation prior to surgery. Following surgery he was placed in intensive care where he deteriorated and died 33 days later from multiple system failures and sepsis.

Initial investigation of the tyre assembly machine determined that computerised command and control information from the previous tyre production run was still stored in the machine's computer system, even though it had been manually reset to zero. Consequently, the tyre machine's unanticipated operation resulted from this 'residual' computerised command and control information. The tyre company immediately shut down the machine and later addressed the software problem. Company officials also shut down a similar machine being used at a different tyre plant in another state. Multiple safeguards were incorporated into the operation of the machines to eliminate the possibility of recurrence.

Source: Centers for Disease Control and Prevention.

Assume your company was responsible for the design, manufacture, supply and installation of the rubber tyre assembly.

1   What was the nature of the breakdown in design?
2   How could the accident have been avoided, given the principles of safe design?

Questions

1   What is 'safe design' and its benefits?
2   What are the phases of a 'product' that safe design must take into consideration?
3   Which factors or considerations can tend to compromise safe design?
4   What are the five principles of safe design? Briefly explain what each means.

Activities

1   Examine the practical safe design examples in *Guidance on the Principles of Safe Design for Work* (go to http://www.safeworkaustralia.gov.au and search under 'Publications'). Think of an example from your workplace or home of a product or aspect of building construction that exhibits some risk. Referring to the principles of safe design, describe how this risk might have been introduced and how it might be eliminated.
2   The South Australian publication *Safe: Information for the Safe Design of Commercial Kitchens* (at http://www.safework.sa.gov.au/contentPages/docs/ hospSafeDesignComKitchen.pdf) offers a good methodology for designing a safe workplace. Using one or more of the sections dealing with aspects of a safe workplace, apply it to your workplace to see if any improvements can be made.

Search me!

▶ | Search me! 🖑

Explore **Search me! management** for relevant articles on safe design. Search me! is an online library of world-class journals, ebooks and newspapers, including *The Australian* and the *New York Times*, and is updated daily. Log in to Search me! through www.cengage.com/sso using the access card in the front of this book.

KEYWORDS

Try searching for the following terms:
▶ safe design principles
▶ safe product design
▶ precarious employment

Search tip: **Search me! management** contains information from both local and international sources. To get the greatest number of search results, try using both Australian and American spellings in your searches, e.g. 'globalisation' and 'globalization'; 'organisation' and 'organization'.

Additional resources

- Culvenor 2004, Principles of Safe Design, unpublished report to the National Occupational Health and Safety Commission.
- In May 2006, ASCC, the body that preceded Safe Work Australia, drafted *Guidance on the Principles of Safe Design for Work*. It argues the case for safe design and sets out the principles, while providing examples as well.
- Australian and New Zealand Standard 3931 (1998) *Risk analysis of technological systems – application guide* offers a good overview of the issues and the risk assessment tools that are available.
- A useful text is Christensen, W.C. & Manuele, F.A. (eds) 1999, *Safety Through Design*, National Safety Council, USA.
- Antonelli, P. & Yelavich, S., 2005, *Safe: Design Takes on Risk*, The Museum of Modern Art: New York.
- Much safe design literature applies to plant and construction for which technical standards apply. WHS authorities are a useful source of information. Standards Australia has many standards dealing specifically with safe design.
- An excellent guide to the safe designing of a workplace is the South Australian publication *Safe: Information for the Safe Design of Commercial Kitchens*, available at http://www.safework.sa.gov.au/contentPages/docs/hospSafeDesignComKitchen.pdf. The principles apply to a wide variety of workplaces.
- There have been many tragic design faults. The Ford Pinto is perhaps a classic, with its fuel tank exposed to rear-end collisions (see http://en.wikipedia.org/wiki/Ford_Pinto). Closer to home we have the F-111 deseal/reseal problem for fuel-tank maintenance workers (see http://www.airforce.gov.au/projects/f111/index.aspx).
- The SWA publication *Safe Design for Engineering Students* 2006, Commonwealth of Australia, at http://www.safeworkaustralia.gov.au/SafetyInYourWorkplace/SafeDesign/Pages/EngineeringStudents.aspx, advises engineering students on safe design principles. There are some good case studies as well.

Endnotes

1 This chapter draws on the document *Guidance on the Principles of Safe Design for Work*, issued by the Australian Safety and Compensation Council in May 2006. The authors wish to acknowledge the contribution of Dr John Culvenor to the 2004 report to NOHSC that was adapted for the 2006 ASCC publication used here, in particular the examples found in Figures 12.1 and 12.2.

2 For an analysis of precarious employment in Australia, see Watson I., Buchanan J., Campbell I. & Briggs J., 2003, *Fragmented Futures – New Challenges in Working Life*, Federation Press: Sydney. Also see Rafferty, M. & Yu, S., 2010, *Shifting Risk – Work and Working Life in Australia*, produced for the ACTU by the Workplace Research Centre, University of Sydney.

3 Quoted from 'WorkChoices: How it will affect workers' health and safety', paper presented by Professor Michael Quinlan to the ACTU Choose Unions for a Cleaner, Safer, Healthier Workplace Seminar, Melbourne, 11 May 2006.

AUDITING AND EVALUATING WHS ACTIVITY

Learning Objectives

At the end of this chapter, the reader should have general information on how to:

- plan a WHS audit
- develop a WHS audit plan
- use a WHS audit tool
- gather relevant information, data and HS records
- undertake HS audit activities
- report on the outcomes of the WHS audit
- evaluate HS activity against industry-specific standards
- benchmark HS activity.

INTRODUCTION[1]

Organisations need to be audited, checked regularly, to see whether their WHS management system meets required legal and corporate standards and where it may be improved.[2] Together with performance measurement discussed in Chapter 4, auditing is a way of evaluating your system and bettering it. Benchmarking, which we discuss briefly here, is another method of reviewing your system to see if it can be improved.

To begin with, an independent professional auditor – or team of auditors – can be hired to carry out an external audit.[3] Alternatively, people from within the firm trained in auditing standards may do it as an internal audit. The health and safety manager can audit the organisation. However, this may be seen as involving a conflict of interest and not providing enough independence. Generally, it is preferable to use fresh eyes.

After gathering information (usually by onsite inspections), interviewing and examining records and data, the auditors report their findings to management, provide a score and highlight areas for improvement. By evaluating the workplace health and safety management system (WHSMS) and identifying areas for improvement, audits assist the organisation to continually improve its performance.[4]

WHS auditing is a skill that requires proper training and considerable experience. This chapter provides only general information on planning an audit; documenting the plan; using an audit tool; gathering information, data and records; performing the audit; and, finally, reporting the audit. It will enable the health and safety manager to understand the audit process when engaging qualified auditors. For the purposes of presentation, however, here we presume that you are conducting the audit.

The chapter concludes by outlining how an organisation can evaluate itself against industry-specific standards and how to learn from others through benchmarking.

DID YOU KNOW?

AUDITING, INSPECTING, MONITORING, MEASURING, EVALUATING AND REVIEWING

WHS auditing, inspecting, monitoring, measuring, evaluating and reviewing should not be confused.

- *Auditing* is checking to see if the required WHS *system activities* – training, notification of incidents, managing risk, etc. – exist and that they meet the standards.
- *Inspecting* is looking for hazards and checking the controls.
- *Monitoring* is observing and recording over a period of time anything of relevance to health and safety.
- *Measuring* is gauging if goals are being met.
- *Evaluating* is judging whether you did well or not.
- *Reviewing* is trying to find ways to improve.

WHAT IS A WHS AUDIT?

A **WHS audit** is simply a check of the HS system to see whether or not it meets standards. Is the organisation doing everything it is supposed to be doing as required by law and the firm's standards? This may be done to get a 'snapshot in time' as, for example, part of a due diligence check simply to check if the firm complies or, further, as part of a program of continuous improvement. Here, we will assume that WHS auditing, as part of the WHSMS, is designed to help the organisation continuously improve its HS performance.

Suitably trained internal or external auditors use a type of checklist, an audit tool, to assess whether all the required activities exist and meet the required standards. They gather information and data, inspect workplaces and conduct interviews. After interviews they prepare a report identifying those areas that comply with the standards and those that don't. For areas that don't comply, they make recommendations, actively highlighting any critical areas. Often they provide a score.

The audit process may be staged, with a preliminary audit conducted to prepare the organisation for a complete audit. After a preliminary audit, surveillance audits of special areas may be carried out.

The focus of a WHS audit is on the system used to promote health and safety. The main system elements are set out below.

Figure 13.1 *Continuous improvement in the WHSMS cycle*

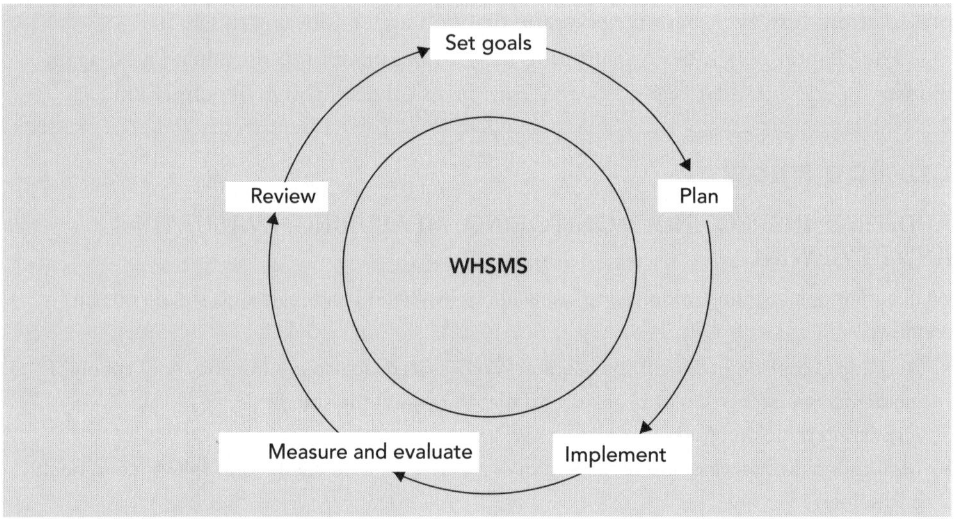

PLANNING AN AUDIT

Audits generally form part of an audit program. Depending on the nature and size of the organisation, audits are programmed over a set period – one, two, three years. In large organisations, the program should be a *rolling* program so that over the period the *whole* organisation gets audited against *all* the HS system requirements.

A documented risk analysis is used for planning most audit programs. Where are the critical areas? They could be facilities, functions, business divisions, operational units or projects. Is it purchasing? The facility at Port Lincoln? The warehouse? The new bridge construction? These form your priorities and are audited more often than other areas during the period of the audit program. The program then needs to be reviewed annually as circumstances change.

If your organisation has an audit team to deal with other business matters, such as financial, IT, quality, environment or performance audits, contact them to see how they go about business. They should be happy to share their experience and provide advice.

The audit program, together with the documentation supporting it, needs to be consulted on and, finally, endorsed by the HS committee, if you have one. It may also be endorsed by a relevant board committee. Endorsement gives the auditors authority to open doors.

Individual audit plans then flow out of the program. Plans deal with the specific areas or sites using some or all of the HS system requirements in each case. To prepare each plan, a number of questions should be asked.

Figure 13.2 *Example audit questions and responses*

1 Scope What exactly are you auditing? • which HS system requirements are you checking – all or some? • which parts of the organisation are you checking to see if the requirements are being met – all or some? Specify boundaries: space, time, function.	The safety procedures for hiring of contractors and labour-hire by human resource and purchasing departments in Tasmania and Victoria over the current financial year.
2 Objectives Why are you auditing it? • specific outcomes	To determine whether the procedures used conform to the company's policy, duty of care and specific obligations to contractors and labour-hire, and, if not, what action needs to take place.
3 Standards What are you using to measure • HS legislation, Australian or international standards, standards developed by WHS authorities, industry standards, standards developed internally by the organisation or by commercial organisations?	Company policy and procedures; Victorian and Tasmanian WHS Acts and relevant regulations and codes of practice; WorkSafe VIC SafetyMAP standards relating to supervision, use of contractors, permit to work and access controls.
4 Requirements What do you need to complete the audit? • management system documentation, including policies and procedures, position descriptions and duty statements • operational documentation including completed forms, schedules, checklists, logbooks, minutes of meetings, action plans, maintenance reports and health surveillance records, training materials and records • information and data that includes changes since last audit such as new equipment, processes, products, substances or projects	• Documented or online company policy and procedures, relevant WHS Acts, regulations and codes of practice • Copies of organisational charts of the departments, documented procedures, statistics detailing number and nature of contractors and labour-hire used during current financial year, sample contracts • Contact details of HR directors and finance directors • Contact details of line managers using contractors and labour-hire • Contact details of contractors and labour-hire staff • Audit tool • Time to meet management, staff and contractors, labour-hire

4 Requirements (Continued)

• claims, legal reports, complaints, hazard logs and incident and injury reports, enforcement notices and actions • reports and management reviews • previous management system reports and industry risk profiles • equipment • trained professionals • time for interviews, inspections, analysis, reporting back • access to management, persons in control of the workplace, supervisors, employees and other parties across a range of levels and roles including health and safety representatives, HS committee members, design personnel and, where appropriate, contractors, customers/clients	
5 Strategy What do you need to do to achieve the audit objectives? • hold meetings • carry out inspections • examine documentation • conduct surveys • interview • analyse • provide findings • corroborate	Two three-day site visits at the Victorian and Tasmanian regional offices to • hold meetings with regional director, finance and human resource managers • examine the contracts and procedures for tendering • meet local supervisors at four representative sites where contractors and labour-hire are used • interview a small sample of contractors and labour-hire • analyse and prepare report.

In planning an audit, the auditor should be prepared for reasons or excuses for delays, inability to provide the required information and lack of time or access. It means having fall-back plans that will enable the auditor to collect the required objective evidence, at least as much as possible. Any adjustments to the plan or limitations set on the evidence-gathering should be noted in the final report. If, however, the auditor meets insurmountable obstacles, they need to report on why the audit was not carried out and arrange for another time. For this reason, it is very important to have the authority of senior management and the WHS committee for the audit program.

DEVELOP A WHS AUDIT PLAN

The audit plan is developed, documented and submitted as a draft for comment to the area or site management and details:
• the scope of audit
• the standards to be used
• the personnel involved and the audit team manager or lead auditor
• access and facilities: keys, passes, room, phones and computer
• timelines

- meetings to be scheduled, people to be interviewed; normally, an introductory and final meeting are held with management with end-of-day briefings held throughout the course of the audit
- locations to be inspected
- any information and data required to be on hand
- any sampling methodology, including statistical measures
- any HS requirements for the auditors; for example, PPE, induction training.

As it is a rare manager who enjoys being audited, particular attention should be paid to

- identifying the benefits to management (what concerns them?)
- minimising the impact on the operations of the area being audited
- providing plenty of advance warning
- assuring management of respect for confidentiality
- reaffirming that a draft report will be sent for comment to local management before submission to senior management.

After receiving feedback and modifying the agreed draft, the next step is to use (or develop/adapt) an audit tool. It should be forwarded to the local manager beforehand as a courtesy.

The WHS audit tool

An audit tool is a type of checklist that you use to record whether elements of the WHS management system conform to the required standards. Having a prepared audit tool is a systematic way of checking the WHSMS and provides consistency when different teams use it at different times; that is, of course, when everyone is trained to use it in the same fashion.

If you don't already have one, it is generally preferable to examine the tools currently available before beginning this task on your own. Many audit tools are available, such as the International Safety Rating System and the National Safety Council of Australia's five-star rating system. Victoria has produced the (free) SafetyMAP. Your industry association may be able to help you determine which is most suited to your industry.

Once you examine the ones available, you will probably find that there is one suitable to your organisation's needs and your particular WHSMS. Then, if required, you can simply add any specific issues you wish to consider for your particular organisational risks or structure.

The audit tool is usually constructed with headings taken from the WHS system, such as policy, commitment, resourcing and so forth. Under each of those headings, the specific requirements or criteria of the system are spelt out.

Figure 13.3 is a sample page adapted from a corporate audit tool. '6.3 Contractor safety' is the WHSMS element being audited. 6.3.1, 6.3.2 and 6.3.3 are the audit criteria. The criteria specify the standard to be met and must be accurate.

A scoring system is provided, with 0 indicating nothing in place, 1 and 2 indicating partial compliance, and 3 indicating full compliance. Sometimes a simple 'Yes' or 'No' may be used.

The aids suggest ways of collecting evidence and the notes section is for observations or references enabling the auditor to make findings. Other evidence, such as spreadsheets, copies of procedures, photos and interview notes, should go together with the rest of the audit tool as the basis for the audit report.

Figure 13.3 *A sample page adapted from a corporate audit tool*

6.3 Contractor safety

6.3.1	HS performance is a criterion in the location's contractor selection process	0	1	2	3	N/A
6.3.2	Contractors/subcontractors have an HS program consistent with company standards and local regulations	0	1	2	3	N/A
6.3.3	Location informs all contractors of specific rules, hazards and risks, and vice versa	0	1	2	3	N/A

Auditor's aids

- Review contractor selection criteria
- Check site's review process of contractor safety
- Check any available documentation to ensure adequate exchange of information. What process is used?

Auditor's notes

_____

_____

_____

_____

With such an audit tool – and agreement and training in its use – you have the opportunity to assess the organisation consistently across units and across time. Done well, you are able to use the tool to measure progress and compare performance reliably, accurately and comprehensively.

Now you have an audit tool and plan, you are ready to gather the required information.

GATHER INFORMATION, DATA AND HS RECORDS

Any remaining issues concerning the audit plan should be negotiated before the audit actually begins. An initial meeting with local management should take place to confirm the plan and become familiar with the worksite at the outset.

It is important in auditing that a wide range of different sources is used to gather an objective picture. Policies, procedures or work instructions may be merely words or pieces of paper that people are not aware of or do not understand or use. You only find this out by talking to different people or examining records, checking manuals, sampling and observing.

Alternative methods may need to be identified and used when evidence is unavailable, using methods to address the gap such as:

- interviewing
- alternative sampling methodologies

- discussion groups
- surveys
- observation
- alternative information and data
- modified audit checklists.

When you identify non-conformances or discrepancies, or the required activity is not there or up to standard, it is important that the reasons and evidence be noted carefully. For this reason, the audit report should be viewed as a piece of engineering in which the findings are carefully built on solid facts and not hearsay or assumptions. Wherever possible, look for additional evidence to corroborate facts and conclusions. The strength of the finding should reflect the strength of the supporting evidence. Records of evidence and findings should be progressively documented in an appropriate format and retained. Similarly, the information-gathering should be sensitive to the needs for security, confidentiality, impartiality and equity. The collection of all information and data should be done ethically.

It is useful at the end of each day to debrief the local management, present any concerns and observations, ask for comments and clarifications, and update them on the progress of the audit to assure them the schedule is being met. Any hazards identified during the audit should be reported promptly to the appropriate people, including any health and safety representative. Finally, an exit meeting with key personnel and stakeholders should be arranged at which summary audit findings and recommendations are presented.

COMMON AUDITING PROBLEMS

Common problems with internal audits fall into two major areas:

1 Inadequacies of the program
- Some programs fail to understand audits are not about 'hazard spotting' but seek to understand why and how the hazard has been managed ineffectively.
- While programs may appear to be reviewing systems, gaps remain. For example, the purchasing system may assess all new equipment, yet associated systems such as maintenance or workflow impacts are ignored or the system does not extend to parts or materials.
- Key risk components are neglected. For example, a manufacturing company may focus on site risks but ignore the risks associated with salespersons driving long distances or travelling overseas

2 Inadequate auditor skills or knowledge
- Poor understanding of the risks to the organisation and industry. For example, an auditor must understand community care organisations have physical, behavioural and psychosocial hazards and the system needs to manage each one of these.
- Auditors may rely solely on documentation and neglect observation and verbal evidence.
- Poor audit planning can result in systems only being addressed narrowly or superficially.
- Auditors sometimes don't understand fully the legislation and associated codes/Standards and how these should be applied.

Source: Jenny Barron, Director, Practical Work Solutions.

Discussion questions

1 How does the health and safety manager ensure that the audit covers the necessary ground?
2 How does the organisation commission a suitable firm that has:

- the correct level of audit experience
- comprehensive experience in statutory compliance, including both self-insurance regulatory requirements and any other relevant statutory issues
- a strong knowledge base and resources, including relevant industry knowledge where applicable
- proper accreditation for the audit operations required?

REPORT ON THE WHS AUDIT

A draft report is prepared for comment as soon as possible after the audit. Typically, a WHS audit report contains the following headings:

- executive summary
- introduction
- system strengths
- findings against standards or criteria
- audit process
- scope
- audit procedures
- scoring.

As audit reports are sensitive, objective evidence – information, data, observations, measurements, tests – they should be presented with clear and concise findings. The benefits of adopting the audit report recommendations should be set out in the report. Where you can expect challenges, build your case carefully.

The audited site then has the chance to comment on the draft report. Once both the site and the audit team have reviewed the comments, the lead auditor prepares a final version of the report and sends it to the site and senior management for final comment and response.

CATEGORISATION AND SCORING OF AUDIT FINDINGS

Each finding is usually categorised in terms such as 'critical', 'major' or 'minor'. A numerical score is tallied and the site is assigned a 'level'; for example, on a scale of 1–10. The score and level achieved are normally provided in the executive summary of the draft audit report and at the end of the final report.

In some situations – for example, internal audits – the audit team may have the power to see that the recommendations are acted on. In this case, the site manager would send the audit leader an answer to the report with an action plan to close the findings. The site management would then report to the lead auditor the status of the action plan: closed findings, works in progress, problems and so on. If necessary, a visit to the site might take place to assess the problems encountered. After a set period, a follow-up audit can be organised to reassess the HS situation of the site.

It is important to recognise that a WHS audit deals with the HS system. It is not intended as a HS consultancy. The role of the auditor is to assess the system, see where it meets the standards and where it doesn't. Their training as professional auditors is to point out any gaps and hence highlight what needs to be improved. Auditors may recommend ways to address gaps but it is not their primary role. It is up to (site) management to find the best ways and means of addressing the identified gaps.

It is important to emphasise that compliance with the audit criteria doesn't assure compliance with the law, particularly when you are using limited criteria or when the audit scope is restricted. Nor does an audit rule out action by a regulatory authority. Finally, a successful audit does not mean you are necessarily meeting your WHS goals. However, if you do comply, you are more likely to be 'legally compliant' and on your way to meeting those goals. In this way, it may help in any defence *if* the audit has been professionally conducted and management has acted in good faith on the findings.

EVALUATING COMPLIANCE AGAINST INDUSTRY STANDARDS

We have talked in general terms of what is an audit. However, it is useful to include in the audit an evaluation of the organisation's WHS system against industry-specific standards. In some respects, this is the most valuable form of evaluation because of its specific relevance. The issue is finding those industry standards and incorporating them into an audit so as to evaluate your organisation's practice against them. In some cases, your industry association or WHS authority can assist. The following example, *Guide to Best Practice for Safer Construction*, developed by the construction industry, is a useful model for other industries.[5]

The guide suggests a framework for improving safety performance on construction projects. It addresses all stages of the construction process: planning, design, construction and post-construction. While being a guide to implementation, it can also be used to evaluate safety performance. It identifies specific tasks, describes them in detail, and lists the key benefits, desirable outcomes, performance measures and task leaders. Examples are also provided. The 'WHS in practice' box below quotes one task from this guide (Stage 2: Design, Principle 1 – Demonstrate safety leadership).

WHS IN PRACTICE

Task 2.4 Establish assessment criteria for prospective constructors

Action	The client should specify assessment criteria for the evaluation of tenders – including project safety management and performance.
Description	Tenders can be assessed using a number of criteria, such as price, quality, construction period, amenity and aesthetics. The weightings given to these attributes will vary from project to project, and often price is the only consideration – with quality and time requirements built into specifications.
	Safety management is also a valid attribute in assessing tenders. Weightings given to these criteria will be influenced by

	the nature and size of the project and its proximity to public areas. Tenders can also be assessed quantitatively (price, time), qualitatively (quality) or subjectively (aesthetics, amenity) – or any combination of these.
	It is the responsibility of the client to determine the appropriate assessment criteria and the weightings to be applied in order to evaluate tenders. Some suggestions for assessing safety competence include
	• the submission of a draft construction safety plan as a precursor to Task 3.1
	• a written response to the project safety charter with suggestions for improvements or modifications
	• presentations on safety management by tenderers
	• project data sheets outlining safety performance on previous projects
	• curricula vitae of proposed personnel responsible for managing safety on the project.
	A percentage weighting could be applied to these responses to be taken into account along with other selection criteria.
Key benefits	An appropriate weighting can be given to safety according to the scope, nature and risk profile of a project.
Desirable outcomes	Tenderers have a full understanding of the importance given to safety management for a project, and will strive to submit the most attractive proposal in a competitive environment.
Performance measures	A specified weighting for safety in the contract documents.

Establishing criteria for the selection of a 'safe' constructor at the Morwell River Diversion

Constructors were chosen on account of their ability to demonstrate that they could maintain safety as a key priority. In the tender phase, potential constructors needed to develop a detailed safety management plan and identify appropriate safety systems upfront. The client established a project team who undertook independent assessments of these plans and the constructors were then selected on the basis of their plans. The translation of the project management plans to the actual site was the critical aspect analysed.

The client also required the names of the key personnel who would be involved in the project and, as part of due diligence, undertook interviews with those people in order to identify whether safety was a priority and the way in which safety was to be managed 'because at the end of the day, companies can lay out their magnificent documentation, but if you don't get the key people, that is where you fall down'.

Source: Cooperative Research Centre for Construction Innovation, 2007, *Guide to Best Practice for Safer Construction: Tasks*, p. 19, http://www.construction-innovation.info/images/The_Guide_Tasks_lo_rez.pdf.

Not all industries will have such best-practice frameworks that can be used to evaluate performance. However, HS networks, consultants or events such as conferences can be the source of useful information for this purpose.

Evaluating performance is only one step on the path to improving performance. While it is possible to use in-house experience and external expertise such as consultants to further improve, some organisations use the process of benchmarking themselves against others. In this way, they may hope to speed up the learning process.

BENCHMARKING BETWEEN ORGANISATIONS

Benchmarking allows you to assess the activities and service performance of your enterprise against those who have attained best practice. The most useful form of HS benchmarking is qualitative, involving processes and procedures. By contrast, numerical or quantitative benchmarking – for example, comparing outcome figures or rates (LTIFRs) – may show areas for improvement but not how to get there. That requires people to analyse the way they carry out work, setting out the steps, tools, time, standards and so on. For example, the activity of handling compensation cases can be quite intensive and costly, making it a good candidate for benchmarking with those who have a reputation for excellence. To analyse the activity accurately requires training in techniques such as process flow-charting and cause-and-effect analysis (fishbone charts) and various problem-solving tools.

The scope of HS benchmarking may be big – the entire WHS management system – or small, as in the case of compensation. Newcomers are advised to start with a small project to develop an understanding of the issues and build confidence. Management is more likely to endorse a gradual approach as the process requires time and resources. It will also want to see a return and that means careful identification of those projects that will have a recognisable impact. Eventually, it could be applied to HS in mainstream areas such as maintenance, training, purchasing, work system design, engineering design and production planning. In any case, a benchmarking project, like any project, needs to be carefully scoped with terms of reference and be properly managed. The process is set out in Figure 13.4.

Many organisations confuse 'benchmarking' with simply 'comparing yourself with another organisation'. While this may be helpful, benchmarking means actively seeking out the *best* and learning from them.

A key stage, then, is the selection of a benchmarking partner, usually found through networks or identified by external parties such as consultants, industry associations or insurers. For an organisation to become a benchmarking partner, they must be willing to share their experience at some cost to their time and resources. This often rules out direct industry competitors who fear 'spies'. The benefits for a benchmarking partner are seeing any effort to reduce workplace injuries as worthwhile and the opportunity to show off their leadership and brand. Benchmarking partners needn't come from the same industry and often the most interesting lessons can come from 'best practitioners' in different areas from the economy. It depends on the areas being benchmarked.

Figure 13.4 *The benchmarking process*

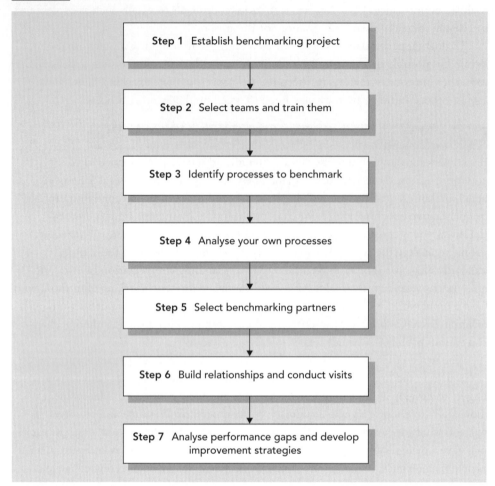

Source: NOHSC, 1999, *Benchmarking Occupational Health and Safety*, Australian Government Publishing Service: Canberra.

Other conditions for successful benchmarking by both partners include

- a commitment, particularly from senior management to WHS benchmarking (time, resources)
- a commitment to a preventive and systematic approach to WHS
- use of consultation.

TEAMS

Teams allow a range of expertise, experience and representation to be involved. Benchmarking teams should

- involve management and employee representatives with the required expertise in the areas being benchmarked
- be limited to six at the maximum
- receive training in the required skills and knowledge.

An important by-product of benchmarking is the training and experience acquired by those involved. While it can be tricky and resource-consuming, benchmarking can be very beneficial and not just for HS performance.

In this chapter, we have examined WHS auditing to demonstrate how the health and safety manager may evaluate the effectiveness of the WHSMS, or elements of it, in improving performance. The importance of industry-specific standards was highlighted as well as the benefits of benchmarking against best practice as methods of improving performance.

However, things may still go wrong. In the next chapter, we look at emergency procedures.

Summary

- A WHS audit is a check of the HS system to see whether the required legal and corporate activities exist and are being implemented properly. In this way, audits assist the organisation to continuously improve.
- The audit program should be planned to cover all parts of the HS system as it applies to the organisation in its entirety.
- Auditors must be trained and can come from within the firm or be contracted from outside.
- The key factors to be considered in planning an audit are the scope, the specific objectives, the standards or criteria to be used for each site, the requirements to complete the audit such as site information, meetings and so on, and a strategy to meet the objectives.
- The plan must be developed carefully to ensure cooperation from local management. It should have support from senior management and be endorsed by the HS committee.
- Audits use tools or checklists to evaluate compliance against each one of the criteria or requirements. These ensure thoroughness and consistency.
- Gathering information should be done carefully to ensure robust findings. It should also be done ethically.
- A draft report highlighting areas for improvement should be provided to the site manager for comment before a final report is developed and sent to local and senior management.
- Follow-up activity is often required, with action plans submitted to the lead auditor by local management.
- A valuable source of information about how to further improve is industry-specific standards used as benchmarks. Networks, industry associations and WHS authorities should be used to identify the main standards.
- Another valuable source is to compare activities and performance against those of organisations that have demonstrated best practice. As benchmarking with a different organisation requires time, training and resources, and can be tricky, it is best to begin with a small project to build confidence and trust.

In your workplace

A bank has set up a new call centre employing three shifts in the suburb of a major regional city. The employer is required to consult on HS matters with the employees in accordance with the regulations. You have to audit the centre and have to develop a plan.

1   How would you describe the scope and specific objectives of the audit?
2   How would you go about identifying the standards to be used?

3 What sort of information and other requirements are needed?

4 Outline your audit strategy.

Questions

1 What is a WHS audit? Describe its purpose and the processes in general terms.

2 How does an audit differ from a normal workplace inspection?

3 How does your organisation evaluate its HS performance? Comment on the quality of the evaluation and outline how you might improve it.

4 Your employer is required to have a drug and alcohol policy in place and operating. What would you, as an auditor, look for to see if it was conforming to this requirement? Develop your answer using the audit tool format in the example '6.3 Contractor safety' on p. 260. Consider alternative forms of information gathering in the 'auditor's aids' section.

Activities

With the cooperation of your employer, conduct an audit of the emergency procedures of a small office or facility. Preferably work with one or two others as an audit team. Prepare a report and recommendations.

Search me!

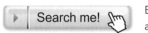

Explore **Search me! management** for relevant articles on health and safety auditing. Search me! is an online library of world-class journals, ebooks and newspapers, including *The Australian* and the *New York Times*, and is updated daily. Log in to Search me! through www.cengage.com/sso using the access card in the front of this book.

KEYWORDS

Try searching for the following terms:

▶ health and safety audit tools

▶ health and safety benchmarking

▶ health and safety industrial standards

Search tip: **Search me! management** contains information from both local and international sources. To get the greatest number of search results, try using both Australian and American spellings in your searches, e.g. 'globalisation' and 'globalization'; 'organisation' and 'organization'.

Additional resources

• There are two standards often referred to in WHS audits. The first is AS/NZS 4801:2001: *Occupational health and safety management systems – Specification with guidance for use.* This standard specifies requirements – auditable criteria – for a workplace health and safety management system. The other is AS/NZS 4804:2001: *Occupational health and safety management systems – General guidelines on principles, systems and supporting techniques.* This standard provides guidance on the development and implementation of workplace health and safety management systems and principles and their integration with other management systems.

• Victoria's SafetyMAP can be found at http://www.worksafe.vic.gov.au/wps/wcm/connect/wsinternet/worksafe/home/forms+and+publications/publications/import_safetymap_+measuring+health+_+safety+management.

- For a detailed presentation of management system auditing, see the International Standards Organization (ISO) quality or environmental management system auditing standards, ISO 10011 series and ISO 14010/1/2, available from Standards Australia.
- Audit tools contain standards for hazard identification, risk management and monitoring. However, they should be checked against current legal requirements and codes of practice before using them in any evaluation process.
- WHS performance measurement has been affected by developments in general business performance measurement as well as quality systems. D. Norton & R. Kaplan's 1996 *The Balanced Scorecard: Translating Strategy into Action* (Harvard Business School Press: Boston) is a classic.
- NOHSC's 1999 *Benchmarking Occupational Health and Safety* (Australian Government Publishing Service: Canberra) provides useful guidance for those wishing to undertake WHS benchmarking.

Endnotes

1   This chapter has benefited from comments by Jenny Barron of Practical Work Solutions.

2   Auditors like to distinguish compliance audits and performance audits. Generally, a compliance audit checks to see if the organisation is meeting standards of behaviour such as legal requirements or criteria set by the business. A performance audit checks to see if the organisation is meeting its goals effectively, efficiently and economically. In this chapter, WHS audits are considered compliance audits, not performance or 'value-for-money' audits.

3   Organisations may gain certification from accredited certification bodies such as Quality Assurance Services if, of course, the organisation passes the audit.

4   Audits of the WHSMS may assist the organisation to comply with the law but are not required under WHS law. Instead, they are good business practice.

5   This guide (2006) was commissioned by Engineers Australia, and the Cooperative Research Centre (CRC) for Construction Innovation provided the industry research leadership in coordinating and funding this key project (see www.construction-innovation.info/index.php?id=1053).

DEALING WITH EMERGENCIES

Learning Objectives

By the end of this chapter, the reader will have a general understanding of how to:

- develop and implement emergency management processes
- identify sources of risk
- analyse and evaluate sources of risk
- advise on requirements for emergency management
- monitor and report on the effectiveness of emergency management
- participate in the emergency control organisation
- advise and support key personnel in the post-response/ recovery phase to minimise consequences.

INTRODUCTION

Probably the most basic HS requirement organisations have to deal with is the risk of an emergency or crisis, such as fires.[1] This means it is necessary to develop a plan that identifies the risks, the emergency control organisation and the procedures, training, drills and review.

Dealing with emergency plans and procedures is usually the job of the health and safety manager. However, a number of organisations give the responsibility to someone else, such as the facilities manager.[2] Whoever is responsible, emergency procedures need to be produced and implemented.

We begin with the law and the requirement to prepare and implement an emergency plan. Then we use AS3745-2010 *Planning for emergencies in facilities* to look at how you would do this, focusing on fire and bomb threats.

THE LAW AND EMERGENCY PLANNING

Part 3.4 of the Regulations requires the person conducting a business or undertaking (PCBU) to prepare and implement an emergency plan that would cover:
- emergency procedures
- testing of the procedures
- provision of information, training and instruction to workers on the procedures. Those procedures must include:
- an effective response to an emergency
- evacuation procedures
- notification of emergency services at the earliest opportunity
- medical treatment and assistance
- effective communication between the person authorised by the PCBU to coordinate the emergency response and all persons at the workplace. (s. 3.4.1)

Given this obligation, what is the range of emergencies that require attention?

TYPES OF EMERGENCIES

Emergencies, or 'hazardous events' as they are sometimes called, can be grouped into those relating to:
- major hazard facilities
- hazardous substances spills
- dust explosions
- natural disasters
- pandemics
- civil disorder
- bomb threats
- fire.

MAJOR HAZARD FACILITIES

Some firms, such as oil refineries, fireworks factories, chemical plants and major fuel depots, may be classed as 'major hazard facilities' because they handle dangerous goods such as explosives, gases, flammable liquids and solids, oxidising substances, toxic and infectious substances, radioactive substances and corrosives. Not only are there regulations detailing control measures, but also, where certain levels of dangerous goods are present, there are specific regulations to deal with emergencies (see Chapter 8 of the regulations). The special issues related to such organisations are not covered here.

One of the biggest accidents affecting an Australian hazard facility was the 1998 gas explosion that occurred at the Esso natural gas plant at Longford in Victoria's Gippsland region. On 25 September 1998, an explosion took place at the plant, killing two workers and injuring eight. Gas supplies to the state of Victoria were severely affected for two weeks.

HAZARDOUS SUBSTANCES SPILLS

Hazardous substance spills are uncontrolled releases of hazardous materials. The spill may range from minor and easily cleaned up, moderate (for example, contained on site but requiring some emergency assistance) to major or catastrophic (for example, a spill not contained on site and entering the watertable and potentially risking many lives). Risk assessments on all hazardous substances in the workplace should be carried out and, if there is the risk that a spill may require emergency response, then plans specific to hazardous substances spill management must be developed in addition to the organisation's general emergency plan. Chapter 7 of the regulations deals with hazardous chemicals, controlling risk and emergency plans and equipment.

Spills, big and small, occur regularly and practically everywhere; for example, while transporting oil across the country or while working with chemicals in factories. They affect workers and the environment. On 21 August 2009, the Montara platform drill rig in the Timor Sea, off the northern coast of Western Australia, suffered a well-head accident, resulting in the uncontrolled discharge of oil and gas. The discharge of oil and gas was only stopped on 3 November that year. It is considered one of Australia's worst oil disasters. Fortunately, no one was injured.

DUST EXPLOSIONS

Dust explosions are the result of a combination of factors: firstly, the three elements required for a fire (known as the fire triangle) – *oxidiser* (oxygen in the air), *heat* (ignition source) and *fuel* (combustible dust) – and, secondly, *diffused fuel* (dispersion of sufficient quantity of dust particles) and, thirdly, *confinement of the dust cloud*. Combustible dust may be formed from most organic materials as well as some metals.

Dust explosions can occur in (but are not limited to) industries such as textiles, wood, food (feed, starch, flour), furniture, fossil fuels, pharmaceuticals. Explosions have happened in coalmines, grain elevators and flour mills. A dust explosion in the Mount Mulligan coalmine in Queensland killed 75 workers in 1921.

NATURAL DISASTERS

Numerous different natural disasters affect Australia, such as bushfires, floods, earthquakes and extreme weather events: cyclones, thunderstorms, severe blizzards and hailstorms.

DID YOU KNOW?

Severe earthquakes are common in Australia. The strongest recorded earthquake occurred in Tennant Creek, NT, when three quakes on 22 January 1988 measured 6.3–6.7 in magnitude, exceeding the February 2011 earthquake in Christchurch, New Zealand (6.3). It was felt in Perth and Adelaide but little damage was registered. The most devastating was in Newcastle in 1989 when an earthquake measuring 5.3 left 13 dead, 160 hospitalised and resulted in $4 billion damage.

PANDEMICS

Pandemics are sudden widespread outbreaks of disease that affect a region, a country or the world. Historically, in Australia there have been a number of major pandemics, including the Spanish influenza in 1918, which led to around 10 000 deaths and, more recently, swine flu (H1N1 virus) with over 37 000 notified cases (and 191 deaths) in 2009.

CIVIL DISORDER

Civil disorder includes riots, sabotage and demonstrations such as illegal sit-ins or marches that get out of control. A recent example in Australia was the rioting related to protests against the G-20 Summit in Melbourne in 2006, involving invasion of the Orica building and closure of all ANZ banks in the Melbourne CBD as a health and safety precaution. The *Emergency control organisation* standard (AS 3745-2010) includes a section on civil disorder and illegal occupancy.

BOMB THREATS

Bomb threats occur from time to time and planning for their management should be included in all emergency planning. Bomb threats may be received through the mail (as letters or articles), by phone or electronically; for example, via email. There may be no warning but a suspicious article might be sighted.

FIRE

As fires are a common form of emergency, the following section focuses on the planning and procedures to deal with them (but not their prevention).

DID YOU KNOW?

On 25 March 1911, fire erupted on the eighth floor of the Triangle Shirtwaist factory in New York and spread to the floors above. Locked doors and inadequate fire escapes led to the deaths of 146 workers, mostly immigrant female workers. The tragedy stunned the nation and spurred a broad range of reforms. Over the next few years, New York adopted new laws to protect the public from fires and ensure the health and safety of workers. The laws were the most advanced and comprehensive in the country and served as models for other state and local ordinances and for the federal labour legislation of the New Deal era, 20 years later. Centenary commemoration events were held throughout the country in 2011, linking the fire to similar dangerous conditions and accidents throughout the world, especially in developing nations.

Source: Landmarks Preservation Commission, Brown Building, http://www.nyc.gov/html/lpc/downloads/pdf/reports/brown.pdf.

MANAGING EMERGENCIES

In this chapter, we look at how the health and safety manager is to help manage emergencies. As the basis for this discussion, we have used AS 3745-2010 *Planning for emergencies in facilities*. It should be noted that AS 3745-2010 focuses on buildings and how to evacuate them, as they present the most likely location for the risk of fire and bomb threats. Keep this in mind when dealing with different types of worksites and emergency scenarios.

We begin, then, by focusing on fire emergencies, but the methodology could apply equally to a general emergency or crisis management. The case study below is used throughout this chapter to elaborate on this methodology.

CASE STUDY

A large state public-service department providing hospital and aged care facilities requires a program to cover the event of fires, emergencies and evacuations in properties it owns. Properties mainly include hospitals, boarding houses, community-based houses and nursing homes. The main issues are a diversity of properties located across the state, multilevel buildings (with lifts), sick and immobilised patients, visitors and volunteers, gas used in surgical operations and gas used for cooking.

Questions
1 What do you think are the immediate issues in dealing with patients?
2 Where might you go to find advice on emergency procedures?

STEP 1: ESTABLISH AN EMERGENCY PLANNING COMMITTEE

The first step is to establish an emergency planning committee (EPC) or team that will prepare a plan and appoint an emergency control organisation (ECO) to initiate an appropriate response to emergencies.

The EPC should represent management and employees, and include the chief and deputy wardens, as needed; it should also include people who have specialist knowledge or responsibility, such as a facilities manager or the landlord. It is also wise to aim for

Figure 14.1 *The management steps*

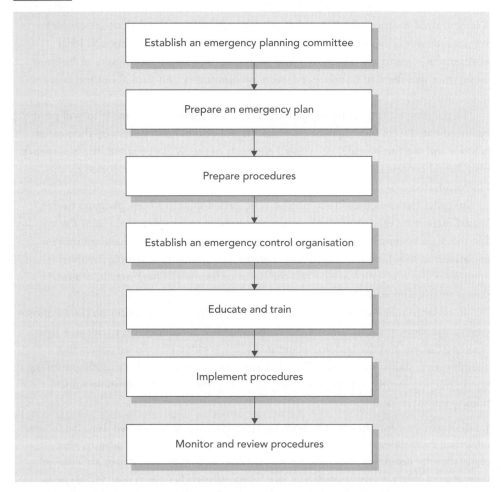

EPC membership that reflects the different sections/areas and activities of the workplace to ensure adequate coverage of the types of emergencies and local conditions. For example, in a hospital, the laboratory and nuclear-medicine department emergency scenarios would most likely differ significantly from those of the office or clinical areas. Often, facilities requiring a coordinated response to emergencies are shared by a number of organisations, so the issue of who is legally in control of the workplaces or how duties are to be shared must be settled before the committee becomes active.

The EPC should provide emergency authority to the ECO and indemnify the ECO and themselves against any civil liability arising out of the exercise of their duties.

The EPC should meet regularly – at least annually – in the first instance to:
- prepare and implement the plan
- establish the ECO, particularly the chief warden group, and arrange its training
- arrange evacuation exercises and drills
- review the effectiveness of exercises, procedures and training.

STEP 2: PREPARE AN EMERGENCY PLAN

You will need to know the law and regulations applying to the various sites, which will include not only any Commonwealth, state and territory laws, but also local government regulations. There may also be certain unwritten community or business sensitivities that need to be addressed, such as community concerns about the safety of the site itself.

Depending on the nature of the hazards and the risk involved, the plan will need to be coordinated with local agencies, such as the police emergency services, the nearest hospital and the fire brigade. As with all elements of the WHS program, the emergency plan should be developed in consultation with those involved and endorsed by the HS committee.

In order to develop each site plan, it is suggested that, as a basic planning tool, a hazard register be used that lists the main processes or activities carried out at the site. List the main activities from operational through to administrative, making sure you pay attention to where the activities are located, the numbers of people involved – employees and non-employees – and the hours of business. There may be seasonal factors to consider as well.

In order to make such a list in this way, you will need information on the location, general functions and structures of the site(s), which will require you to obtain a map detailing the site and the building plans, including possible evacuation routes and assembly areas, both onsite and offsite. Information needed may also include prevailing wind direction, nearby sensitive facilities, such as childcare centres, schools, nursing homes, transport routes.

CASE STUDY

The department provided a framework by which the facilities could prepare their own plans. The document categorised the facilities and set out specifications for planning according to each category. After consultation, the department established the main processes applying to each category and examined the emergency history to provide pointers for local facility managers to consider when drafting plans. Important to this process was assessing the degree to which local managers had control over security and the speed with which patients could be evacuated.

The next step would be to list the emergencies – the hazards – that could disrupt employees, contractors and visitors in their work activities. This means looking for the range of possible scenarios or circumstances under which a crisis may occur. Such emergency scenarios might include:

• fires and explosions
• medical emergencies
• bomb threats
• severe weather
• natural disasters
• spills

- loss of utilities
- security emergencies, such as armed robberies, disturbed people or other intruders
- terrorism and bio-terrorism (for example, anthrax)
- civil disturbance
- internal emergencies, such as loss of power or water supply.

Some emergencies will appear more likely than others; however, at this stage, it is important to regard them all as being the same level of risk.

Scenario development is, arguably, the most critical stage in the development of emergency plans and procedures; therefore, it is important that a reliable set of sources be called on to identify the emergencies and assess their risk.

We have mentioned the usefulness of holding a workshop with key people involved. The process of such a workshop could be helped along by some prior homework and looking at documentary sources such as:

- inspection and incident records
- enforcement notices and actions
- organisational records and files
- research literature
- international and national standards, codes of practice and guidelines
- material safety data sheets (MSDSs)
- meteorological report of local weather and climatic conditions.

It is essential that local conditions are accounted for, especially in determining emergency scenarios (for example, cyclones, floods and bushfires may be the most likely emergencies in some parts of Australia yet never occur in others).

It is also useful to enquire about the emergency hazards related to the industry. Information may be gathered from your industry association or employer group, your insurer and regulators.

Once you have identified the various potential emergencies, the results should be entered into a risk register (see example in Figure 14.2). The register should cover all the identified potential emergencies (fire, bomb threat, flood, civil unrest, and so on).

By now, you should have a reasonable grasp of what types of emergencies the site is most likely to face, when it is likely to encounter them, where and whom the emergency is most likely to affect. The next step is to analyse and evaluate the risk.

Analyse the risk

The risk may be analysed using a standard risk analysis tool; for example, the risk ratings for each of the identified emergencies can be entered into the organisation's emergencies risk register (as shown in Figure 14.3).

Figure 14.2 Sample emergency risk register (risk identification)

DATE:	MANAGER/SUPERVISOR:	VERSION NO.:
Codes	C = Consequences (severity of outcome)	RCS = risk control summaries
	L = Likelihood (of event occurring)	RA = risk assessment
	R = Risk rating (C × L)	SOP = safe/standard operating procedure
	Ca = Catastrophic	PPE = personal protective equipment
	E = Extreme	
	H = High	
	M = Moderate	
	Lo = Low	

EMERGENCY	INITIAL RISK RATING (WHEN NO CONTROLS IN PLACE)			CONTROL MEASURES (INCLUDE REFERENCES TO OTHER DOCUMENTS SUCH AS SOPS, PLANS, ETC. AS APPROPRIATE)	RESIDUAL RISK RATING (WITH CURRENT CONTROLS)			PLANNED CONTROL MEASURES	RESIDUAL RISK RATING (WITH PLANNED CONTROLS)		
	C	L	R		C	L	R		C	L	R
Fire from electrical fault											
Bomb threat											
Gas leak from natural or bottled gas supply, causing fire, explosion, asphyxiation or poisoning											
Flood (inundation into basement from heavy rain)											
Bushfire											
Civil unrest											
etc.											

Figure 14.3 *Sample emergency risk register (risk identification)*

DATE:	MANAGER/SUPERVISOR:		VERSION NO.:
Codes	C = Consequences (severity of outcome) L = Likelihood (of event occurring) R = Risk rating (C × L) Ca = Catastrophic E = Extreme H = High M = Moderate Lo = Low		RCS = risk control summaries RA = risk assessment SOP = safe/standard operating procedure PPE = personal protective equipment

EMERGENCY	INITIAL RISK RATING (WHEN NO CONTROLS IN PLACE)			CONTROL MEASURES (INCLUDE REFERENCES TO OTHER DOCUMENTS SUCH AS SOPS, PLANS, ETC., AS APPROPRIATE)	RESIDUAL RISK RATING (WITH CURRENT CONTROLS)			PLANNED CONTROL MEASURES	RESIDUAL RISK RATING (WITH PLANNED CONTROLS)		
	C	L	R		C	L	R		C	L	R
Fire from electrical fault	H	M	H	EWIS system Regular electrical checks of plant Electrical tagging Ban on personal electrical equipment policy implemented Fire equipment current and checked regularly Emergency plan Wardens trained Staff trained	H	Lo	M	No additional controls required Risk acceptable (ALARA principle) with current controls			
Bomb threat	H	Lo	M	Secure entry Staff identification before entry Mail room isolated from offices Emergency plan Wardens trained Staff trained	H	Lo	M				
Civil unrest	M	Lo	Lo	Secure entry to building Swipe card for entry to offices from foyer Emergency plan Wardens trained Staff trained	M	Lo	Lo				
etc.											

The department found that the major risks were fires and explosions, bomb threats, security and internal emergencies, such as power loss in remote communities.

The purpose of this stage is to determine whether the risks require any emergency planning and, if so, what are the priorities. Before that can be done, the risks need to be analysed to ascertain the ways in which people could be exposed to the hazards, how many, what would be the impact on them and how likely this would be.

In the case of fire, there is no option for most workplaces: fire regulations specify the requirements for various types of buildings and structures. For other types of risk, planning may be an option; for example, if there is no significant amount of cash or goods such as drugs or DVDs on the premises, specific emergency planning for armed robbery is not required. Your risk analysis and the external or internal standards you use will help you to gauge what level of risk is acceptable.

Document the plan

An emergency or crisis management plan now needs to be developed and documented for each site. The plan must:
- be approved at the highest levels of the organisation
- focus on management control
- identify responsibilities for decision making
- detail communication and support processes
- address any arrangements with any contractors or shared tenancy
- integrate the emergency response as well as the recovery plans
- incorporate dealings with external agencies and support
- address any planning for recovery before crisis occurs.

Documentation may include:
- policy
- emergency response structure (ECO)
- initial response instructions for various roles and areas
- responsibility and authority of individual roles
- warning systems
- training requirements
- resource inventory for response and recovery
- program review and monitoring processes.

STEP 3: PREPARE PROCEDURES

Procedures should address:

- evacuation routes
- people with disabilities
- lifts and escalators
- accounting for people, including contractors, volunteers and visitors
- assembly areas – which may differ for different emergency scenarios; for example, in severe weather or civil disturbance it would not be appropriate for the assembly point to be outdoors
- receptionist and/or switchboard operator
- floor or area marshalling
- restrictions on vehicular movement
- control and coordination – the location of the chief warden and communication procedures with ECO personnel and emergency services
- communication systems – warnings, alarms, telephones, PA systems
- first aid personnel
- emergency response equipment – extinguishers, reels, first aid kits, breathing apparatus
- life safety features – specialist fire-engineered or life safety features
- security guards and specialist staff
- third parties.

There is also a need for procedures to deal with recovery from an emergency (see below).

Document the procedures

The procedures need to be documented and formatted appropriately. They need to

- state their purpose and scope
- state the workplace(s) they apply to
- be based on the assessed risk
- address the specifics of the workplace
- identify roles and responsibilities
- provide flexibility for the ECO to allow for various circumstances
- take into account the hours when people are onsite
- be easy to understand and amend.

The procedures need to be publicised, accessible and used in training as well as, of course, in drills.

WHS IN PRACTICE

DO STAFF FIGHT FIRES OR SHOULD THEY LET THE FIRE BRIGADE DO IT?

Where staff are properly trained, have the right equipment and know when a fire is within their capacity to control – for example, a fire in an office wastepaper basket or small kitchen fire – then, yes, they may fight the fire.

If there are any unnecessary risks associated with attempts to control a fire, then, no, they may not. Occupants should withdraw, closing – but not locking – the doors behind them as they go.

STEP 4: ESTABLISH AN EMERGENCY CONTROL ORGANISATION

The ECO should consist of:

*   a chief warden
*   a deputy chief warden
*   a communication officer
*   floor or area wardens.

These positions must be filled by trained staff at all times. A register needs to be made to ensure that this occurs. Often, first aid officers are allocated emergency response roles as well. The Australian standard specifies the roles and responsibilities, selection criteria and training requirements for ECO personnel.

Everyone needs to know who their wardens are – this is usually made clear by colour-coded equipment, such as helmets – and how they can be contacted.

The roles and responsibilities of the ECO personnel must be set out, with the primary role of ensuring that life takes precedence over asset protection.

CASE STUDY

The government department was faced with having to establish a number of EPCs and ECOs centred on facilities with appropriate levels of wardens. They put together an organisational chart representing a simple hierarchy, showing how the hierarchy was linked to directors and, ultimately, the director-general of the department. Generic roles, responsibilities, competencies were outlined so that the managers at the facility level could establish local ECOs.

STEP 5: EDUCATE AND TRAIN

The EPC is responsible for ensuring the facilitation of training and education in emergency procedures. In addition, ECO personnel must be familiar with:

*   the layout of the area for which they are responsible
*   evacuation routes and safe places
*   alarms and communication procedures
*   the number, location and means of assistance for people with disabilities
*   the operation of fire detection and suppression systems

- any special procedures to deal with strategically significant items
- any dangerous goods
- the operation of portable fire extinguishers, fire-hose reels and fire blankets.

The EPC should also ensure that third parties are aware of the procedures, evacuation routes, safe places and fire-fighting equipment.

STEP 6: IMPLEMENT PROCEDURES

Implementation requires that the procedures form part of routine management programming. This means ensuring that everyone is aware of and trained in the procedures, with particular emphasis on the ECO itself. A training program based on the procedures needs to be scheduled, implemented and reviewed.

The importance of periodic evacuation exercises or drills cannot be overstated. External professional advice is valuable for picking up any shortcomings and how these omissions might be addressed. A checklist of all the requirements for a satisfactory exercise, including targets, should be developed and maintained. Before any full-scale evacuation, the EPC may test procedures by requiring the ECO to evaluate their effectiveness. Prior notice of all drills should be given, with the occupants being briefed beforehand. Importantly, the ECO should always debrief afterwards to assess effectiveness for review purposes.

A system for regular checks of emergency response equipment should also be instituted. Typically, this includes checking fire-fighting apparatus, but can extend to a wide variety of equipment such as emergency communication systems, alarms and the like.

The crisis management plan and procedures need to be regularly audited and reviewed, particularly as personnel and processes may have changed. Such an audit and review should be done at least annually and cover:

- the ongoing relevance of emergency and crisis plans – have the risks changed?
- the ability of the organisation to respond, given the current resources, training, knowledge and skills of the key personnel.

The ECO should meet as required or at intervals not greater than six months.

Reports on the status of crisis management, including emergency response processes, should be made to management on a regular basis.

It is the testing and monitoring of crisis management that lets down most organisations and is the area in which management is most exposed. As a health and safety manager, it is chilling but useful to imagine what it would mean to you if there were an emergency and someone died as a result.

We turn now to the post-response and recovery phase in the context of general crisis management.

POST-RESPONSE OR RECOVERY PHASE

The phase that is often overlooked is preparation for any recovery. Procedures need to be developed that focus on minimising the consequences to the people involved, to the environment and the organisation.

For people under stress as the result of an emergency, recovery can involve psychological counselling and trauma management. Professional resources can assist in developing appropriate procedures for managers to follow in the event of a hold-up, for example. Often, people appear to be coping until, say, a week later, when memories of the event affect staff quite profoundly. It is an area in which experience has helped to develop a number of rules to handle the psychological impact. Counsellors can often provide a session of training to frontline managers and workers who are especially exposed to this risk.

The ECO, for simple operational reasons, will need to understand how to cope after an emergency. The ECO has important communication responsibilities as well. Internal and external communication should be coordinated through someone responsible for seeing that messages are made clearly and accurately; if they are, people will listen and read with great interest and, as a result, be less confused about what they have to do next. It can be extremely stressful if, after a serious emergency, misinformation or rumours are spread. This cannot be prevented completely, but can be minimised by having a single source identified as reliable and trusted, and to whom all staff refer. Messages should be sent around as soon as the facts have been verified and updated in response to enquiries or as further details come to hand and have been clarified. In most cases, the person responsible will be the managing director or the communications officer on the ECO.

Appropriate reports should be sent internally to staff and externally to the appropriate agencies, which could include government health departments, the State Emergency Service, local government, environment authorities and union and employer associations.

After any emergency (or drill), a debriefing should take place with key personnel and, when appropriate, external agencies. The debriefing would focus on reviewing the emergency response and the effectiveness of the recovery procedures.

WHS IN PRACTICE

You want everybody to know what to do and quickly. The following simple evacuation procedures in the case of fire are provided by the NSW Fire Brigade.

Remain calm and don't panic.

ALERT

Alert the chief warden and other staff. Ensure that the emergency services have been notified (ring 000 and ask for fire, police or ambulance).

ASSEMBLY

Tell staff which assembly areas are to be used.

EVACUATE

Evacuate staff and visitors in the following order:

1 Out of immediate danger (for example, out of room)

2 Out of compartment (for example, through the fire doors or smoke doors) or to a lower level of the building

3 Total evacuation of the building.

CHECK

Check all rooms, especially change rooms and toilets, as well as behind doors, storage areas, etc.

RECORDS

Save as many records as possible, but only if it is safe to do so.

HEAD COUNT

Do a head count of all staff, contractors and visitors.

REPORT

Report to the chief warden and notify emergency services of any people unaccounted for.

Some organisations use the acronym REACT to help employees remember what they must do in the event of smelling smoke or seeing a fire:

Remove persons in immediate danger, if possible.

Ensure the door(s) is closed to confine the fire and smoke.

Activate the fire alarm system.

Call the fire department and/or notify switchboard to do so.

Try to extinguish the fire or concentrate on further evacuation.

Source: Fire & Rescue NSW, Evacuation, http://www.nswfb.nsw.gov.au/page.php?id=75.

DEALING WITH BOMB THREATS

Procedures for dealing with bomb threats form part of the EPC's responsibility. The Australian standard provides procedural guidelines and a phone threat checklist. Public safety organisations may be able to help with plans and advice may be gathered from your own industry association. The Australian Federal Police Bomb Data Centre has published a handbook providing guidelines for bomb threat planning as part of an ABDC Bomb Safety Awareness kit.

Bomb threats may come in the form of

- written threat – avoid unnecessary handling and place in a plastic envelope
- telephone threat – *do not hang up*; complete the phone threat checklist
- suspect object.

The threat needs to be evaluated as either specific – for example, providing details on the device, motive, location, time of detonation – or non-specific. Every threat needs to be treated seriously unless and until proven otherwise. The evaluation may result in:

- no further action
- a search without any evacuation
- evacuation and search
- evacuation without search.

Police should be notified; however, they may not conduct a search but instead provide advice.

SEARCH

Occupants should carry out the search for any suspect object. If one is found, it should not be touched, covered or moved. Outside areas, building entrances and exits, and public areas within the building, should be given priority for checking before looking inside and on the roof. Care should be taken not to use electrical equipment or any other equipment emitting electromagnetic radiation around the suspect object.

EVACUATION

Total evacuation needs to be evaluated against risks such as the location of the bomb outside the building, inability to carry out a search, panic, disruption to essential services and loss of business. Partial evacuation may be preferred in the case of specific threats. Evacuation procedures in the case of bomb threats, such as opening and not closing windows, may differ from those used for fire. In the case of (bomb threat) evacuation, people should remove personal belongings, such as briefcases and purses, to facilitate identification of suspect objects.

Procedures for how to deal with suspect mail bombs or other such articles can be obtained from the Australian Bomb Data Centre.

Lastly, it is important to remember that procedures related to bomb threats differ from fire emergency procedures. These differences may include but are not necessarily limited to those identified in Figure 14.4.

Finally, it is essential that people are aware of the basic procedures in the simplest form. A laminated, wallet-sized card outlining the procedures is one useful way of ensuring that everyone knows what to do. These should be distributed to everyone at their induction into the organisation as part of their WHS training; such a card could also be fixed to workstations.

In the case of fire, bomb threat or civil disorder, follow the facility emergency procedures and the instructions of your warden. Phone the ambulance service and the police on 000, the national phone number for emergencies.

Figure 14.4 *Procedures for dealing with bomb threats versus fires*

BOMB THREAT	FIRE
Open windows and doors (to diffuse the blast).	Close windows and doors (to contain the fire).
Take all personal belongings when evacuating (to reduce the quantity of items to be checked for a bomb).	Leave personal belongings behind (to speed up evacuation).

Summary

- Managing emergencies is a basic HS program, although it may be administered independently of the HS manager.
- It is a legal requirement to provide for emergencies. Managers should refer to the law and regulations, as well as to any standards that are based on the legislation.
- The steps to managing emergencies are:
  - establish an emergency planning committee (EPC) or team
  - prepare an emergency plan
  - prepare procedures
  - establish an emergency control organisation (ECO)
  - educate and train
  - implement procedures.
- The plan and procedures must be based on a risk assessment that involves scenarios.
- Monitoring and reviewing using evacuation exercises, as well analysis of any changes to the workplace, is critical to success.
- The post-response or recovery phase must not be overlooked when developing procedures.

In your workplace

You work in the claims department call centre of TIGOZ (Tightwad Insurance Group Australia), an insurance company specialising in domestic insurance in the Brisbane CBD. Your company leases floors 8 to 12 of the building. The call centre is located on floor 11. Following the 2011 Queensland floods, the call centre phones have been constantly ringing with people anxious to make claims for flood damage to their homes and contents. The claims manager has informed all call centre operators that unless a policy specifically states that it covers floods, policyholders' claims will be disallowed. You have had to tell at least half of the callers that they are not covered for flood damage. It has been very stressful as some have become tearful and others quite angry and abusive. You have just received an anonymous telephone threat: 'There's a bomb in your office that is going to detonate in two hours. It's your turn now. You lot deserve to find out what it feels like to lose everything, just like me and my family.'

1 What should you say to the caller?
  Hint: Look up the standard AS 3745-2010.
2 Who should you tell?
  Hint: refer to the section on the emergency control organisation in this chapter.
3 Develop an evacuation plan for the call centre specifically for dealing with bomb threats.
  Hint: the Rockingham local government area in Western Australia has a good set of guidelines (available for download from their website) based on AS 3745 for developing an evacuation plan.

Questions

1 What are the main types of emergencies addressed in crisis management plans?
2 Who is responsible for fighting fires in your workplace?
3 Without looking at any documentation, what is your understanding of the procedures in case of an emergency? Compare your understanding with the actual documentation.
4 Your organisation has received a non-specific bomb threat and you are the chief warden. What steps do you take? (Refer to the guidelines prepared by the Australian Federal Police's Australian Bomb Data Centre to answer this and the next question.)
5 A mysterious-looking parcel arrives in the mailroom of the company where you are the chief warden. What steps do you take?

Activities

1 Survey a section of your workplace to see if they know who their wardens are and what the emergency procedures are. Report back.
2 Find out if you have an emergency planning committee or emergency control organisation in your workplace (or institution). Find out who are the floor wardens and first aid officers. Does your workplace have a plan and schedule of evacuation procedures? After answering these questions, assess to what degree the organisation meets AS 3745.

Search me!

 Explore **Search me! management** for relevant articles on workplace emergencies. Search me! is an online library of world-class journals, ebooks and newspapers, including *The Australian* and the *New York Times*, and is updated daily. Log in to Search me! through www.cengage.com/sso using the access card in the front of this book.

KEYWORDS

Try searching for the following terms:
▶ emergency planning ▶ fire warden training
▶ evacuations ▶ emergency procedures

Search tip: **Search me! management** contains information from both local and international sources. To get the greatest number of search results, try using both Australian and American spellings in your searches, e.g. 'globalisation' and 'globalization'; 'organisation' and 'organization'.

Additional resources

• WHS regulators' websites provide guidance on developing emergency procedures.
• Since practically all workplaces have emergency procedures, it is useful to look at some examples – the National Archives (www.archivists.org/mayday/MayDayEmergencyProcedures.rtf) would be just one of many thousands.
• For information on dealing with bomb threats, kits are available from the Australian Federal Police: https://forms.afp.gov.au/online_forms/abdc_bomb_safety_kit.
• The Australian standard AS 3745-2010 *Planning for emergencies in facilities* are the basis for compliance.

Endnotes

1 We use the terms 'emergency' and 'crisis' interchangeably to describe hazardous situations requiring an immediate response by some or all parts of the organisation.

2 The responsibilities may be coordinated with programs that deal with unplanned events affecting the general business – 'business continuity' – such as utility failures, supply disruptions, product recalls, product tampering, severe weather, environmental spills, IT system crashes, and so on. Crisis management teams may deal with HS and business emergencies.

NOTIFYING, REPORTING AND INVESTIGATING INCIDENTS

Learning Objectives

At the end of this chapter, the reader should be able to:

- know how to respond to incidents
- describe basic first aid requirements
- notify and report incidents externally and internally
- distinguish incident categories
- carry out an investigation into a workplace incident
- prepare an accident report.

INTRODUCTION

When a workplace injury or illness occurs, the following four steps should be taken as soon as possible:

1 **Help the worker (or non-worker)**: provide first aid and any assistance in receiving medical or hospital care. If helping a worker, supply them information on making a compensation claim and assist with the submission. Monitor the claim closely and keep in touch with the worker regularly while they are away from the workplace. Depending on the severity, keep management informed throughout.

2 **Inform the regulator**: if it is a 'notifiable incident' – a fatality, serious injury or illness, or dangerous incident, as defined in the Act – tell the regulator. You may have to secure the site.

3 **Record and investigate the incident**: record details in a register of injuries. Find out why the controls didn't work and implement recommendations to prevent a reoccurrence.

4 **Notify the insurer**: notify your insurer of a fatality, injury or illness and provide details, normally within two days of learning of the incident. Advise the insurer if the worker will be claiming compensation.

In this chapter, we look at steps 1, 2 and 3. In the following chapter, we look at step 4 and the arrangements for compensating workers, managing their injuries and return to work.

INCIDENT PROCEDURES

As the most basic requirement, every workplace needs a simple set of procedures for dealing with incidents. Depending on the workplace, such procedures could combine with those covering emergencies – fires, floods, bomb threats (see Chapter 14).

A small wallet-sized card containing the basics and distributed to all workers is one step towards making sure procedures are followed. Besides forming part of the training for everyone, procedures should be provided to contractors and labour-hire. They should be checked regularly to reflect changes to the law, workplace and personnel and to see whether people are actually aware of them.

A full set of procedures should contain:

- definitions of incident categories – injury or illness with or without lost time, near-misses
- responsibilities of employees, managers, first aid officers, medical personnel, authorities, insurers
- rights of employees; for example, to compensation information
- required activities and timeframes to cover treatment of injuries; notifying, reporting, investigating and record keeping
- any maps
- contact details.

As mentioned, the documentation ought to be reviewed regularly, by the HS committee, where you have one. This chapter and the following contain material relevant to those procedures. The regulators as well as insurers, industry associations and HS advisers provide guidance material that can be used to prepare drafts.

CASE STUDY

A sewer worker entered an underground pumping station via a fixed ladder inside a 1-metre-diameter shaft. Because the work crew was unaware of the procedures to isolate the work area and ensure that the pump had been bypassed, the transfer line remained under pressure. When the worker removed bolts from an inspection plate covering a check valve, the force of the wastewater blew the inspection plate off. Sewage flooded the chamber, trapping and eventually killing her.

We will refer to this case study throughout the chapter.

Discussion questions

1 Before continuing, what is the immediate cause of the incident or unsafe act?
2 What are the possible root causes?

STEP 1: HELP THE WORKER OR NON-WORKER

Under Part 3.3 of the regulations, the law requires employers to provide first aid – equipment and people trained in first aid – sufficient to meet the needs of the workplace. Consideration must be made of the nature of the work being carried out:

- the hazards at the workplace
- the size and location of the workplace; for example, the proximity to local services (doctors, hospital, ambulance)
- the number and composition of the workers and other persons at the workplace. Facilities can include:
- first aid kits of different sorts, including travelling kits
- first aid rooms (or 'rest rooms', 'sick bays')
- occupational health centres with trained staff.

First aid kits should be checked regularly to see if the medicine, dressing or equipment is sufficient and appropriate.

A trained, certificated first aid officer should be onsite at all times, including during all shifts. It is recommended that there is more than one designated first aid officer in case of absences.

Above all, everyone needs to know where the first aid facilities are located, who their first aid officer is and relevant contact details. This information should be advertised on a noticeboard, the Intranet, near a lift or entrance, or wherever is appropriate. It is essential that the information is kept up to date. Apart from being useless, it is potentially life-threatening to still have the name and extension of a first aid officer who has left the company.

Regulators have published guidance material on first aid to assist employers, and readers are referred to them for further details. Many firms specialise in first aid, such as the Red Cross and St John Ambulance, and also offer advice.

In the case of serious injuries or illnesses, you will need to help the worker or non-worker get medical or hospital care, and possibly an ambulance. This may require someone from the workplace to go with them. The family will also have to be notified and contact details exchanged. Senior management should be kept informed, as well as the work team and health and safety representative.

Right to compensation

Workers have a right to know what their entitlements to compensation are. Information from the insurer should be given to the injured worker irrespective of whether you think they are entitled or not.

If the worker decides to go ahead with a claim, provide them with a receipt of the claim and forward the claim to the insurer with any further information required. Keep in touch with the worker regularly while they are away from the workplace and track the progress of the claim closely. (For more details on compensation, see Chapter 16.)

In the case study, the incident has resulted in a fatality and an ambulance needs to be called, management informed and a registry form raised. The deceased's family need to be contacted and, at an appropriate time, visited by the employer and told of compensation arrangements. The work crew will have experienced trauma and should be offered counselling. The effects of this incident on the crew and possibly others in the workforce will need to be monitored. A counsellor should be able to provide advice.

STEP 2: INFORM THE REGULATOR

The law requires 'notifiable incidents' – death, serious injury or illness, dangerous incident – to be notified to the regulator immediately after becoming aware of it by the fastest possible means. (ss. 35, 38 (1–2))

A *serious injury or illness* is one that requires:

- immediate treatment as an inpatient in a hospital
- immediate treatment for an amputation, serious head or eye injury, a serious burn, separation of the skin from the underlying tissue, spinal injury, loss of a bodily function or serious lacerations
- medical treatment within 48 hours of exposure to a substance
- any other injury or illness prescribed by the regulations but that does not include an illness or injury of a prescribed kind. (s. 36)

A *dangerous incident* is one that exposes a worker or any other person to a serious risk to a person's health or safety from an immediate or imminent exposure to:

- an uncontrolled escape, spillage or leakage of a substance
- an uncontrolled implosion, explosion or fire
- an uncontrolled escape of gas or steam
- an uncontrolled escape of a pressurised substance
- an electric shock
- the fall or release from a height of any plant, substance or thing

- the collapse, overturning, failure or malfunction of, or damage to, any plant that is required to be authorised for use under the regulations
- the collapse or partial collapse of a structure
- the collapse or failure of an excavation or of any shoring supporting an excavation
- the inrush of water, mud or gas in workings, in an underground excavation or tunnel
- the interruption of the main system of ventilation in an underground excavation or tunnel
- any other event prescribed by the regulations, but that does not include an incident of a prescribed kind. (s. 37)

The person with management or control of a workplace where a notifiable incident has occurred must ensure the site is not disturbed until an inspector arrives. (s. 39(1)) This is subject to the need to assist an injured person, remove a deceased person or make the site safe and minimise any risk of a further notifiable incident. The site may be disturbed if it is associated with a police investigation or when an inspector or the regulator has given permission. (s. 39(3))

The employer must keep a record of each notifiable incident for at least five years from the day that notice of the incident is given. (s. 38(7))

In the case study, the regulator would be notified. The regulator would ask that the site be secured until the inspector arrives. It is not normally a police matter but the regulator could advise. A record of notification must be kept, normally in the register of injuries.

STEP 3: RECORD AND INVESTIGATE THE INCIDENT

Register of injuries

As soon as possible, someone such as the HS manager or first aid officer, should record details in a register of injuries. The very useful standard AS 1885.1-1990 *Workplace injury and disease recording* contains a workplace injury and disease recording form for employers using standardised terms and coding. It also covers fatalities as well as near-misses in which no one is injured. Although it is used for workplace injuries, it may be used for commuting injuries as well.

The register is a collection point for data used to measure HS performance such as the lost-time injury frequency rate (LTIFR). It can also be used to identify hot spots, review preventive measures and return-to-work outcomes (days lost). This data can then be fed into reporting systems – monthly, annual. Because it is in a standardised form, comparisons can be drawn with other business units and against industry or occupational averages.

It is a well-known fact that comparing (negative) outcomes over time and against others – a bit like league tables – focuses management attention on health and safety and incorporates it into performance assessments. Used together with other HS information sources, such as inspections, investigations, audits, environmental monitoring and compensation data, the register plays a key role in understanding organisational HS effectiveness. The register also demonstrates compliance with the legal requirement to ensure 'that the health of workers and the conditions at the workplace are monitored for the purpose of preventing illness or injury of workers arising from the conduct of the business or undertaking'. (s. 19(3)(g))

A number of off-the-shelf software programs deal with the whole gamut of WHS requirements and cover injury data collection. However, spreadsheets are easy to use and may be adapted to your internal reporting requirements.

Incident investigation

Incidents, as we saw in Chapter 4, are usually categorised as:

- *Lost time injuries/diseases* – those occurrences that resulted in a fatality, permanent disability or time lost from work of one day/shift or more. These would include 'serious injuries and illnesses' defined in the Act as notifiable.
- *No lost time injuries/diseases* – those occurrences that were not lost time injuries but for which first aid and/or medical treatment was administered.
- *Near-misses* – any unplanned incidents that occurred at the workplace that, although not resulting in any injury or disease, had the potential to do so. These would include 'dangerous incidents' that are notifiable in the Act.

To prevent a reoccurrence, possibly more serious, incidents big and small should be promptly investigated. Incidents occur when hazard controls are ineffective or don't exist at all, exposing people to danger. Investigations try to find out why the controls were ineffective and then recommend the steps to be taken. In this book, the model of WHS shown in Figure 15.1 has been used.

Figure 15.1 *The WHS model*

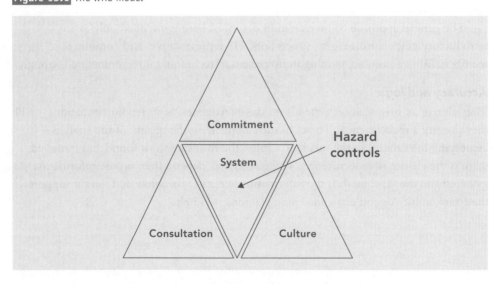

To be effective, all four elements must be present and working well. If an accident occurs, then one or more of these elements is either not present or not working properly. To begin with, however, investigations focus on the *controls* that make up the core of your WHS management system.

There may be situations whereby accidents occur largely out of your control; for example, natural disasters or third-party negligence – a driver passes through red lights and hits one of your company's vehicles. These limiting cases still require investigation into the controls you have set in place to see if they were, in fact, there or effective – emergency procedures in the case of natural disasters, and motor vehicle maintenance, airbags and safe driver training in the case of road accidents.

Investigation procedures

Organisations need procedures to ensure all investigations are carried out correctly. They need to cover

- when an investigation occurs – the occasion and the timing: *asap*!
- the roles and responsibilities – who should be involved (site manager, HS manager, HS representative, government inspector, specialist) and their authority
- the steps to be taken, including isolation of the accident site and equipment to be used
- the report format
- nature of recommendations – correction, prevention and follow-up
- the report lines – senior management, health and safety committee
- keeping of records and evidence
- confidentiality requirements.

Before introducing procedures, management should consult with workers on their content, as they need to have widespread understanding and acceptance. They also need to be easily available; for example, on the Intranet, together with any prescribed investigation forms. After some experience using them, they should be reviewed for their effectiveness.

The general approach to investigation described here is intended only as an introductory guide for managers, supervisors, HS representatives and committee members. Where possible, training in investigation techniques is recommended strongly.

Accuracy and logic

The value of an investigation depends on the effectiveness of its recommendations – will they prevent a reoccurrence? These, in turn, depend on the quality of the analysis – identifying the cause(s) of the incident. Unless the root cause(s) is found and removed, there is the chance of reoccurrence. The quality will depend then on the information gathered and the logic used: Is the information accurate, complete and does it support the conclusions? A good team and some planning will help.

Figure 15.2 *The investigation process*

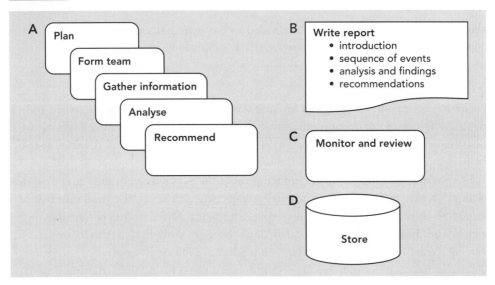

1 Plan your activities

While you should investigate as soon as possible after the incident has occurred, it is important to do a bit of quick planning. Before assembling a team, identify the scope and purpose of the investigation – your terms of reference – and plan your activities accordingly. This means identifying the incident clearly to limit the activities and information gathering required. You will need to be clear that you are not investigating to cast blame, but to prevent a reoccurrence of a similar type. People will recognise that there may be disciplinary outcomes, but that does not form part of your investigation or your recommendations.

Be clear about what 'reoccurrence of a similar type of incident' means. Does it mean all underground accidents or all pumping station accidents, for example? This will affect what you identify as root or underlying causes. The wider the brief, the number and size of the causes increase. In other words, be precise in your planning so that your investigation is manageable and the recommendations are credible.

2 Form the team

Investigations into major incidents, in particular, require a team, usually led by the health and safety manager and whoever is suitably trained. The local manager or supervisor needs to be part of the investigation team and an employee representative should be present both to assist and liaise with other employees. In-house or external professionals can also assist, depending on the nature of the incident. For the situation in the case study, you may wish to have your most senior engineer present. Discuss your plan with them. Have site meetings arranged.

A government-led inspection will need to be carried out in the case of a fatality or certain serious incidents. If in doubt, check with the authorities before proceeding on your own.

DID YOU KNOW?

Accident investigation forms can be downloaded for free from sites such as http://www.safetygroup.com.au/resources/accident_investigation_form.pdf.

3 Gather information

Gathering information begins with looking at the accident itself – what happened and what was the course of events immediately leading up to it? This is simply a factual description and not a causal explanation. The explanation takes place at the later stage of analysis, after you have collected all the relevant information.

Of course, you will already be thinking about the possible causes and those thoughts or hunches may influence your information-gathering. However, the good investigator should be objective and open-minded, collecting all the pertinent data before drawing conclusions. In the case study, the details could be more complicated than set out. Having a team will help you see what you might have missed by yourself.

Apart from a pen and notepad (with numbered pages for possible court purposes), you will usually need equipment such as a camera, a small tape recorder, tape measure, plastic bags or containers, gloves and protective equipment, depending on the type of accident. Other specialist equipment, such as noise and light meters, can be used provided they have been properly tested and calibrated. In the case study, equipment such as a respirator would be needed to deal with sewer gases.

The investigation should start *promptly* to observe conditions as they were and to locate witnesses. As mentioned, if there has been a death or notifiable incident, the site should be left undisturbed – as far as possible – subject to the permission of a government health and safety inspector.

Before collecting information, gather a quick overview, take steps to preserve evidence and identify witnesses. In the case study, this would include everyone in the work crew and general vicinity and those who came to the rescue. Check on their employment status and time and location in respect to the incident.

Physical evidence As physical evidence can change quickly, make an early record of

* where the injured workers were when the incident occurred
* the equipment, substances, devices and control measures used; in the case study, what was the lockout system? Were there danger tags?
* the position of any machinery guards and controls
* any damage
* the state of housekeeping and environmental conditions, such as noise, lighting, weather.

Take photos both of the general area and specific items using everyday items in the photo to indicate the comparative size and position – for example, coins, people. In the case study, a re-enactment photo or two would be useful. Prepare a sketch of the scene and note measurements.

For further analysis by experts, remove any broken equipment, debris and samples of material involved but only after checking first with the government inspector. Notes should identify where these items came from.

Eyewitness accounts Interview witnesses as soon as possible. A small handheld tape recorder is ideal for this purpose. Pointers include the following:

- Interview witnesses individually rather than in a group to gather individual perceptions of what happened.
- Try to put the witness at ease: be supportive, non–intimidating, non–judgemental.
- Assist with any language, literacy or educational problems; avoid technical jargon.
- Emphasise the reason for the investigation – to prevent a reoccurrence.
- After identifying the witness, time and location, allow the witness to talk about what happened. Do not interrupt, prompt or ask leading questions; use simple, positive, open questions instead.
- Take short notes during the interview when significant points are mentioned.
- If making a written record only, confirm with the witness that the record is correct. A general line of questioning would be as follows.
- What happened?
- When did it happen?
- Where were you at the time?
- What were you doing?
- Who was with you?
- What did you see or hear?
- What were the conditions at the time (weather, noise, fumes, light, etc.)?
- What were the injured workers doing?
- Why did it happen?
- How might similar incidents be prevented in the future?

Type up a written record as early as possible and have the witnesses confirm the details.

DID YOU KNOW?

LEADING AND OPEN-ENDED QUESTIONS

The difference between a leading question and an open-ended question is shown in the following: 'Was the lockout system not in use?' versus 'What precautions were taken at the time?'

Asking open-ended questions is not only less threatening, but also increases the chances of getting additional details and greater accuracy from that person's perspective. By gathering as much information as possible in the first instance, you avoid having to conduct stressful and annoying re-interviews. Closed questions requiring simple responses can be helpful for directing attention toward relevant facts after basic information has been gathered.

Workplace information Once you have a picture of the accident and how it occurred – the physical story – you will probably need further information on the specific workplace that cannot be gathered by pictures and witness accounts. For example, in the case study, other information that should be checked are technical data sheets dealing with the pumping plant, maintenance reports, past reports of incidents, work processes, safe work procedures and training records. Remember that you are trying to find out why the hazard controls were ineffective. Here, you may come across company pressure, tight schedules, awkward rules that are hard to follow, long working hours, inadequate rest, lack of ongoing training, or lack of safety awareness practices.

Organisational information The next level up is the organisation itself. You may need to collect information on company structure, plans, budgets, policies, procedures or practices to determine whether they exercised any influence on hazard controls. Poor communication or unclear responsibilities at the company level may have been factors. Purchasing and contract policies may have been flawed. The policies may have been correct but their implementation inadequate. Building, plant, equipment and fleet maintenance programs could have affected controls.

In the WHS model used in this text, we have said that factors such as management commitment, HS culture and consultation play important roles in affecting HS performance. Information on these factors may also be relevant.

Gathering such information at the organisational level lets you get the big picture and understand the importance of management factors affecting the control of hazards.

At some point, you will feel that you have sufficient information to begin your analysis. You will know what happened and the course of events leading up to the incident, as well as the relevant workplace and organisational factors affecting hazard control. If important information or data is not available, then it should be noted.

4 Analyse and draw conclusions (findings)

Once investigators know what happened and how it happened, the next step will be to consider why the incident happened, why the controls were ineffective. To do that a model is useful. Here we use a causal analysis tree model that first identifies the incident and then sets out the causes leading up to it.

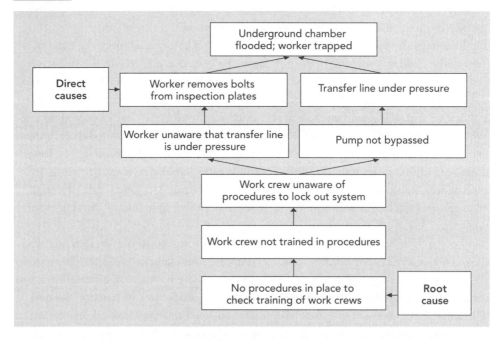

Figure 15.3 *Causal analysis tree model of an investigation*

The immediate or *direct causes* of the incident are 'worker removes bolts from inspection plate' and 'transfer line under pressure'. There could be more, such as poor lighting. These make up the *horizontal* dimension to the analysis.

The event – 'worker removes bolts from inspection plate' – is sometimes referred to as the 'unsafe act' or 'breakdown event', the point at which things go wrong. These events give an immediate technical explanation of why the underground chamber flooded and trapped the worker. But why did the worker remove the bolts from the plate when the transfer line was under pressure? She would not have done that unless she believed the transfer line was not under pressure or was unaware that it was. Why was the transfer line under pressure? Because the pump had not been bypassed. But why was the pump not bypassed? Because the work crew was not aware of the procedures, the same reason the worker was not aware that the transfer line was under pressure. Had they been aware of the procedures they would have locked out the pump beforehand, knowing that the transfer line could have been under pressure. Why were they not aware of the procedures? Because they had not been trained. Had they been trained in the procedures, there was every chance that this accident would not have occurred. But why were they sent out untrained? There were no procedures for ensuring that workers were trained before sending them to work. At this point, we have reached a root cause of the incident – lack of procedures to check that workers were trained to work safely in those conditions. This line of questioning makes up the *vertical* dimension of the analysis.

There may well be other root causes – factors whose removal would prevent a reoccurrence – that the investigation may determine must be dealt with. The point is that there were no procedures to check that everyone in the work crew had been trained to take the required safety precautions. Had there been such procedures, there was every likelihood that an untrained crew would not have been sent and the accident would not have occurred. Furthermore, putting in such procedures could be expected to prevent a reoccurrence. This, then, is a root cause.

What are the principles used in this intuitive method?

You begin by asking 'what caused the incident?' If, say, you identify A as one factor causing the incident, you will need to point to the evidence gathered in the first stage of your investigation to back the claim. (Imagine yourself being cross-examined in a court and asked to demonstrate your reasoning.) You then ask 'what caused A?' If the answer is B and C, you will again need to provide evidence for your answer. Then you ask, 'what caused B and C?', and so on. Keep asking the question 'what caused that?' until the line of questioning no longer identifies factors that could be demonstrated to have made a significant contribution – directly or indirectly – to the incident occurring. In other words, you have come to the end of the causal chain. As a *general* rule of thumb, investigators have found you need to ask 'why' at least five times before arriving at the root cause.

To check that you have covered all the possible causes, go to the WHS model and use the list of activities or practices that make up the four elements as a checklist, starting with the WHS management system. Did any one of these have any significant impact in making the controls ineffective? As we saw in the case study, lack of training was one. There may have been others – lack of consultation (over training), risk-taking culture, management commitment to deadlines at all costs, and so forth. However, be careful to clearly document your evidence as your search spreads. It is generally advisable to be as concise and focused as possible to make the most impact.

Having identified the causes, it is a matter of identifying those causes that, had they not been there, would have prevented the incident *and* its recurrence. These are your *root* or underlying causes. They are normally contrasted with the *direct*, immediate or technical causes of the accident (for example, 'faulty machine guard,' 'repeated lifting of heavy patients'). You may wish to type the causes further – major, minor or contributing. However you do it, set out your reasons for categorising the causes.

For work that is covered by relevant regulations or approved codes of practice, look to the specific requirements, as these should be part of your HS system. For example, if there is a manual handling injury, then the investigation should identify the factors that caused the injury, as described in *Hazardous Manual Tasks*. In the case study, the regulations dealing with plant or work in confined spaces may be applicable.

By now, you should have an account of what happened, how it occurred and why it occurred. Check once again that your conclusions are supported by the evidence through discussions with others in your investigation team.

DID YOU KNOW?

INDIVIDUAL AND ORGANISATIONAL ACCIDENTS

Many use their experience of individual accidents – slipping in the shower or cutting one's finger while carving – as a model for understanding organisational accidents. This usually means ending the analysis after identifying the unsafe act – taking the bolts off the inspection plate. The result is to blame human error or carelessness. The analysis does not go on to ask what other factors contributed to making the act unsafe if, indeed, human error or carelessness did play a role.

With individual accidents at home, we are normally in control of the factors resulting in the incident. Unless, for example, we have bought a faulty appliance or the gas plumbing had been done badly, we normally only have ourselves to blame. We could have put a proper mat in the shower or taken the time to sharpen the knife blade.

However, in an organisation, we don't exercise that same level of control. At best, an individual employee shares control over what occurs in the workplace with the supervisor, the managers, the purchasing department, suppliers, building owners, site controllers and others. Sometimes, we have no control apart from refusing to do the work at all. The model of the individual accident simply doesn't apply to the organisation. Moreover, the number of hazards and level of risk is usually much higher. Compare, for a moment, a refinery or rail-goods yard with your flat or house. In sum, we need to look at a wider range of factors to explain organisational accidents.

Some managers tend to ignore this and try to shift responsibility down the line to the careless worker or human error. They don't ask why the worker was careless or allowed to be careless, if indeed they were. Where were the supervision, instruction, procedures and training? If, in fact, the worker was careless or incompetent, why wasn't he or she replaced, especially if the risk was high? More importantly, why was the situation allowed to be so hazardous that human carelessness or error had the consequences it did? In other words, we should not ignore unsafe acts, but locate them within the larger context of the workplace and organisational factors to find the root cause or causes. To this end, the various jurisdictions have enshrined the 'system' approach to HS in legislation. Look for the system failures when trying to prevent incidents or when investigating them.

5 Make recommendations

First, see if there is any immediate *corrective* action that can be taken to reduce the risk and have it put in place urgently. For example, ban all further maintenance until supervisors have assured management that relevant training has been provided to everyone in the teams.

Generally, the root causes require more time to address in order to prevent a reoccurrence. Such *preventive* recommendations should:

- comply with corporate and legal standards
- be clear about what exactly needs to be done
- be practical – be effective and fit in with operations
- be cost-effective – represent the best value compared to any other options
- present a timeframe for implementation
- allocate responsibilities.

A review period should be set for *follow-up* on recommendations and the person responsible to report on the implementation. Before finalising them, relevant supervisors and health and safety representatives should have the opportunity to comment on and contribute to the recommendations.

6 Prepare report

Finally, prepare a written report as a record of the investigation for consideration by relevant management, health and safety representatives, and others who need to know.

This report should include the previously prepared draft of the sequence of events leading up to the occurrence and all relevant information sufficient to explain to third parties just what happened. Once more, check that you have the facts right and that the conclusions are supported by the evidence. As the report may be read by many, some of whom will draw their own conclusions, it must be written carefully and objectively so that 'the facts speak for themselves'. The report could be structured as follows:

- Introduction – a brief summary of the incident and the investigation
- Sequence of events – activities leading up to the incident
- Analysis and findings – immediate and root causes
- Recommendations – steps to prevent a reoccurrence, monitoring and review period.

The report and recommendations need to be referred to management in all but the most minor cases, however defined. Your procedures should identify how the report is to be signed off or otherwise dealt with. The recommendations may be rejected or amended. The HS committee should also be told of the outcomes as investigations form part of its agenda.

BREAKDOWN IN BEACONSFIELD OHS COMMUNICATION FAILED LARRY KNIGHT

Poor communication at the Beaconsfield Gold Mine (BGM) prior to Anzac Day 2005 undermined the site's Occupational Health and Safety (OHS) procedures, a report by Professor Michael Quinlan has found.

On Anzac Day 2005, a rock fall led to the death of Larry Knight and trapped Todd Russell and Brant Webb in the 925 west level of the mine.

Professor Quinlan from the Australian School of Business was appointed to assist independent investigator Greg Mellick by researching and writing a report on OHS at Beaconsfield prior to the incident that would inform the Coroner's Report into the death of Larry Knight.

He found that many workers and shift bosses didn't believe there was an effective mechanism for reporting safety issues to management, with some feeling that comments made by underground manager Pat Ball reflected an overall lack of concern for worker feedback that could have assisted in minimising the incident.

Dennis Newson, a Jumbo operator quoted in the report, said: 'Something was brought up in a toolbox meeting once ... and his comment was "We can do whatever we want here unless somebody dies" ... I just ... walked out, you shouldn't have management saying things like that.'

'[He] just said youse do the mining and we'll do the engineering,' Mr Newson said.

Shift supervisor Stephen Homan said in the report, '... this is the third place I've been a supervisor and this was the hardest to get communication or change on safety issues. It was the hardest of the three.'

However, Matthew Gill from BGM said while it may have seemed like Mr Ball did not listen at toolbox meetings, it was often the case that workers just didn't get what they wanted.

Professor Quinlan said that BGM management was not uninterested in safety and if workers' concerns had been treated more seriously, they may have changed their approach and helped prevent or minimise the incident.

'I don't really have the geotechnical expertise to say conclusively whether the event could have been prevented. But if the mine had undertaken a proper risk assessment and monitored their interventions following rock falls in October 2005 and taken due account of worker concerns, I think the likelihood of the events of April 25 could have been significantly reduced,' Professor Quinlan said.

'They were having a rock fall every four weeks, and one with an average of 50 tonnes every 10 weeks. Now that's a lot of rock falls and there were rock falls all around the area where Larry Knight was killed. That alone should have given them cause for concern, but they hadn't set themselves a series of warning indicators.'

However, Professor Quinlan said Beaconsfield was by no means the worst example of OHS practices in Australian mining.

'Inspectors mentioned other mines in Tasmania that were worse. Renison mine on the west coast had three fatalities in rock falls that year.'

He said he hoped his report would lead to changes for Beaconsfield, other mines, legislation and related authorities.

'A lot of money was spent on the Beaconsfield investigation. It would be a tragedy if the lessons learnt weren't used and we faced another incident like this. I criticised many organisations in my report, not just the mine. The unions should have taken a more active role in promoting workers' views on safety and aspects of the Tasmanian legislation on OHS were inappropriate. Hopefully not just mining but health and safety authorities and management will examine the report and take steps to make sure failures are addressed,' Professor Quinlan said.

'A lesson to be learned from Mr Knight's tragic death is the critical importance of proper risk management practices to worker safety, particularly in a mining environment,' Coroner Rod Chandler said in the Coroner's Report.

Professor Quinlan found that Larry Knight, Todd Russell and Brant Webb were well trained in the tasks they were undertaking and not at fault in any way.

'Larry Knight, Todd Russell and Brant Webb were undertaking their activities according to specified safe work procedures at the time of the incident and there is no evidence that their actions or inattention with regard to safety in any way contributed either to the rock fall or to their injuries.'

Professor Quinlan's report drew on documents provided by the mine and Workplace Standards Tasmania (WST), analysis of WST and coronial records relating to fatalities in Tasmanian mines in the last decade, recent government reports and inquiries into safety in mining, other relevant information and interviews with all relevant managers at BGM, 41 miners including Brant Webb and Todd Russell, officers of all unions with members at BGM and other relevant persons.

Source: Breakdown in Beaconsfield OHS communication failed Larry Knight, 22/6/2009. © Copyright University of New South Wales.

7 Monitor and review

As mentioned, a period of review should be set to see if the recommendations have been put in place and whether they have been effective. There may need to be a period of time set aside for supervisors and workers to implement and monitor the changes, before coming up with a decision on whether the recommended changes are having the desired effect. A judgement will have to be made and possibly further changes made. These should be noted in an attachment to the investigation report.

8 Keep a record

Valuable information on organisational hazards and the effectiveness of risk management can be obtained from records of work-related incidents, first aid treatment and incident investigations. The law requires records to be kept of work-related incidents resulting in injuries – including illnesses and diseases.

We said above that the Australian Standard 1885.1 *Workplace injury and disease recording standard* includes a form setting out how the information should be recorded. This includes details of the job that was being performed, the injury or disease, and what happened to cause the injury or disease. After the investigation report has been made, summary details of the action taken to prevent a reoccurrence should be entered. The law requires organisations to keep records of incidents and investigations.

The standard also explains how to analyse the records of injury to build a picture of the more serious or common problems and what is causing them, enabling you to identify priorities and trends and to monitor performance.

As discussed earlier, there are limitations on the use of such negative outcome indicators. You need other information to measure performance and set objectives, particularly if your data is small. Nevertheless, they remain important measures, for larger firms especially.

Injured workers often need to be compensated, rehabilitated and returned to work so that they can take up a productive life once more. In the next chapter, we look at these requirements and how they may be implemented effectively.

Summary

- When an incident occurs, the employer should first of all help the worker get first aid or medical assistance, then inform the regulator if the incident is notifiable, record the incident in a register of injuries, investigate the incident and inform the insurer.
- All workplaces must have procedures to deal with incidents. The procedures should be simple and known by everyone.
- A trained first aid officer is needed, together with suitable facilities as required by law.
- The three major categories of incidents are lost time, incidents without lost time and near-misses.
- Incidents occur when hazard controls are ineffective. Investigations are carried out to find out why the hazard controls were ineffective and how to prevent a reoccurrence.
- Investigation procedures are needed so that everyone knows how to conduct investigations correctly.
- The value of an investigation lies in the effectiveness of its recommendations. The quality of the investigation depends on the information gathered and the analysis done.
- Investigations look for the root causes of why controls were ineffective. Root causes are those whose removal would prevent a reoccurrence.
- The investigation must not only find out what happened but also the workplace and organisational factors affecting the hazard controls before an analysis can occur and recommendations can be developed. The activities making up commitment, consultation, culture and, above all the system, should be used as a checklist to complete the analysis.

- A useful model of analysing accidents and identifying root causes, direct causes and contributing factors is the causal analysis tree.
- It is important not to equate individual accidents with organisational accidents. Organisational accidents do not fall under the direct control of one person.
- Recommendations may include immediate corrective actions, longer-term preventive activities and follow-up activities.
- Drafts of the written report should be commented on by the investigation team before finalising.
- There are legal requirements for the length of time records of the investigation must be kept.

In your workplace

A construction worker was working on the second level of a building, erecting formwork for a column. Between 1.30 pm and 2.30 pm, he required a piece of timber for the column's formwork from a stack on the floor. The floor was fairly smooth finished concrete. The worker had walked to and from the stack of timber a number of times during the preceding days. On this particular day, after walking to the stack, he selected a piece of timber, which he then held in the crook of his left elbow. While he was walking back to the column, he slipped in a small pool of water. The worker claimed he was not aware of the existence of the water before he slipped on it, claiming that it was in an area of the floor that was 'pretty dark'. He put his right foot into the pool, which then slipped forward, overbalancing him and making him fall onto his right side. In trying to break his fall, he severely injured the base of his right thumb.

You are the onsite health and safety coordinator.

1 What immediate steps would you need to take?
2 Illustrate the steps you would take to investigate the incident.

Questions

1 Define a 'lost time injury', an 'injury without lost time' and a 'near-miss' or 'dangerous occurrence'.
2 What are the requirements for the notification, reporting and recording of incidents?
3 What incident procedures apply to your workplace or organisation? Are they easily accessible and clear? Who is your workplace first-aid officer?
4 What are your workplace investigation procedures?
5 What is the purpose of an investigation into an incident?
6 What are the main types of information needed in an investigation?

Activities

1 Using one of the following case studies for a role play, have someone play the investigator and interview a witness – a fellow worker in the case study – played by a second person. How effective was the questioning? How could it have been improved?
2 Using these case studies (adapted from compensation court cases), construct a causal analysis tree, identifying the direct causes, root causes and any contributing factors. Prepare some draft recommendations for immediate corrective activity, preventive activity and follow-up activity.

Fall through a roof

Darryl Arnold and seven others had been employed by a firm to remove and replace the roof of a warehouse on an industrial estate in Perth. Arnold had never worked on a roof before. While on the roof, Arnold stepped backwards onto a fragile roof light on an adjoining warehouse, which gave way. He fell approximately 6.75 metres, landing on the ground floor directly below, and died as a result of his injuries. No safe system of work had been prepared before work began and no safety precautions were in place at the time of the incident.

Injury in manufacturing plant

A contractor was hired to perform a series of jobs at a manufacturing plant. The foreman was responsible for ensuring safe work practices by his team. While helping an associate attach a pipe to one of the machines, the foreman stretched across the machine's conveyor belt, which interrupted an infrared beam and caused two probes to descend. The probes pinned the foreman to the conveyor belt, causing substantial bodily injury. Examination of the machine controls and displays indicated proper functioning. Evidence indicated the foreman was unfamiliar with the machine, was in a hurry to complete the task and did nothing to determine whether the machine was off.

Fall while unloading concrete

Kevin was injured at Devonport while working in the employment of a concrete supplier as a permanent casual driver of a concrete truck. While attempting to clean the chute on the back of his truck, Kevin lost his balance and fell about 1.5 metres backwards onto the ground, landing on his buttocks. At the time he was unloading concrete being delivered to a third-party building site. He regained his feet after a short while but suffered pain in his back and legs and felt a tingling sensation down his legs.

Fatality while working alone

Denise was employed as an overseer on a rural station. It was part of her duties to supervise the jackaroos, to plan the activities of the day and to allocate tasks to them. She had succeeded a very experienced employee, having herself been employed as a jackaroo for over two years. There were no qualifications required for the work performed by Denise, but a jackaroo could be groomed to take opportunities for higher positions, such as overseer or station manager. A jackaroo's training was acquired on the job. One day, Denise was supervising the work of two jackaroos. The task was to separate bulls from cows in a very large paddock, which was distant from the homestead. At the beginning of the day's work, Denise used a horse to locate groups of cattle in this large paddock, while the two jackaroos rode their horses in order to separate the bulls. This method resulted in the jackaroos coming into contact with Denise from time to time, but when they returned to the place where they had left a four-wheel-drive vehicle in order to have lunch, Denise was not present. It was not until some time after that the jackaroos became aware of Denise's horse standing by itself nearby. A search of that area led to the discovery of her body. She had suffered serious head injuries. No helmets were provided by the employer or used by the riders.

Search me!

▶ | Search me! 🖑

Explore **Search me! management** for relevant articles on notifying, reporting and investigating accidents. Search me! is an online library of world-class journals, ebooks and newspapers, including *The Australian* and the *New York Times*, and is updated daily. Log in to Search me! through www.cengage.com/sso using the access card in the front of this book.

KEYWORDS

Try searching for the following terms:

▶ first aid
▶ workplace health and safety incidents
▶ incident record keeping
▶ accident analysis
▶ workplace incident reporting

Search tip: **Search me! management** contains information from both local and international sources. To get the greatest number of search results, try using both Australian and American spellings in your searches, e.g. 'globalisation' and 'globalization'; 'organisation' and 'organization'.

Additional resources

- The websites of the regulators provide further advice on first aid, notification of incidents and accident investigation. Those websites can be found at http://www.safeworkaustralia.gov.au/AboutSafeWorkAustralia/WhoWeWorkWith/StateAndTerritoryAuthorities/Pages/StateAndTerritoryAuthorities.aspx.
- The Australian Standard 1885.1 *Workplace injury and disease recording standard* is a must.
- Chapter 10, Accident/incident investigation and reporting, in *Australian Master OHS Environment Guide* (2nd edn, 2007, CCH: Sydney), provides further useful advice on investigation and reporting.
- There are many models of accident analysis. Most of them have an engineering heritage and apply particularly to high-risk industries – airlines, nuclear, chemical – or major hazard facilities. James Reason, in his two major books, *Human Error* (Cambridge University Press: New York, 1990) and *Managing the Risks of Organizational Accidents* (Ashgate: London, 1997), has provided a lively discussion of the topic of industrial accidents from the perspective of a psychologist. Both are good introductions.
- Andrew Hopkins, Professor of Sociology at the Australian National University, has written on a number of major accidents. His books include *Lessons from Longford: The Esso Gas Plant Explosion* (1st edn, 2000, CCH: Sydney), *Lessons from Gretley: Mindful Leadership and the Law* (2007, CCH: Sydney), and *Failure to Learn: The BP Texas City Refinery Disaster* (2008, CCH: Sydney). These books are highly recommended for those interested in incident investigation.

16

COMPENSATING INJURED WORKERS AND MANAGING INJURIES

Learning Objectives

At the end of this chapter, the reader will have a general understanding of how to:

- describe the goals of workers' compensation and injury management
- outline the legal requirements of employers and workers under the law
- discuss the roles of health service providers, rehabilitation providers, insurers and treating doctors
- describe the main features of good injury management.

INTRODUCTION

In addition to the impact of injuries on workers and their families, the cost of workers' compensation and the days lost through injury are often performance indicators for the employer, managers and health and safety officer. For these reasons, a good appreciation of what compensation and injury management mean is critical to effective HS performance.

In this chapter we begin by looking at the law governing workers' compensation. We outline the steps involved in the compensation process and the responsibilities of employers, workers, insurers, rehabilitation providers, treating doctors and others. Then we see how best to manage injuries with the aim of a safe and speedy return to work.

LEGAL REQUIREMENTS

COMMON LAW AND COMPENSATION

Depending on the jurisdiction, compensation may be provided under common law or statute law.

Under common law, you must prove employer negligence; it must be shown that the employer breached a duty of care to the worker and that damage was suffered as a result. Workers may bring common law actions directly against employers for the employer's own actions or the actions of third parties, or directly against third parties. Negligence is demonstrated by proving that an employer breached a general duty of care or a statutory duty.

Breach of general duty of care

Employers have a general duty to provide workers with a 'safe system of work'. Among other things, this includes a duty to

- employ reasonably competent staff
- provide information, instruction and supervision on HS matters
- take reasonable care to ensure a safe place of work
- provide, inspect and maintain safe plant and equipment.

Where an employer fails to satisfy the duty of care and a worker suffers loss as a result, damages may be recovered by the worker as long as common law actions are not ruled out by legislation. Employers may be held liable for their own acts as well as those of workers or third parties; for example, contractors.

An action for breach of a statutory duty may be available under WHS regulation. Since WHS regulations are clearly established under the law, breach of statutory duty will often be easier to prove than a breach of a general duty of care.

Common law damages

Damages can be awarded for economic and non-economic loss. Economic loss is a measure of reduced earning capacity and injury expenses, such as treatment. This includes not only past earnings loss, but also future earnings loss. Non-economic loss relates to pain and suffering, reduced enjoyment of life, reduced expectation of life, impairment and disfigurement. Common law damages are normally paid as a lump sum and *can* exceed the maximum amounts available under the statutory schemes.

Common law actions on the other hand can be unfair, with workers with the same injury getting less than others or nothing at all. In addition, the lump sum payments may be insufficient or dissipated by medical or legal costs and repayments to Centrelink, leaving the injured worker and dependants with nothing.

STATUTE LAW AND COMPENSATION

Since the mid 1980s, 'no-fault' statutory schemes have been introduced in all jurisdictions. They are called 'no-fault' as it is not necessary to prove the employer was negligent for the worker to be paid compensation.

With the introduction of no-fault compensation schemes, access to common law and the ability to sue for negligence has either been abolished or restricted in most jurisdictions. All schemes that provide compensation through a statutory scheme and allow damages at common law prevent compensation by both, or so-called 'double dipping'.[1]

Compensation schemes under statute law

There are 11 major schemes set up under statute law. The principal Acts deal with both workers' compensation and rehabilitation or injury management. Only the main Acts are listed below. The administrator's website should be checked for any amendments. Some jurisdictions have legislation dealing with matters such as dust, asbestos, sporting injuries, terrorism and bushfire services. Others have industry-specific schemes, like that for miners in New South Wales.

Figure 16.1 *Compensation legislation reference table*

JURISDICTION	PRINCIPAL ACTS	ADMINISTRATOR
New South Wales	*Workplace Injury Management and Workers Compensation Act 1998* *Workers Compensation Act 1987*	WorkCover NSW
Victoria	*Accident Compensation Act 1985* *Accident Compensation (WorkCover Insurance) Act 1993*	WorkSafe Victoria
Queensland	*Workers' Compensation and Rehabilitation Act 2003*	WorkCover Queensland (insurer) Q-COMP (regulator)
South Australia	*Workers' Rehabilitation and Compensation Act 1986*	WorkCover Corporation of South Australia
Western Australia	*Workers' Compensation and Injury Management Act 1981*	WorkCover WA
Tasmania	*Workers' Rehabilitation and Compensation Act 1988*	WorkCover Tasmania
Northern Territory	*Workers' Rehabilitation and Compensation Act 2008*	NT WorkSafe
Australian Capital Territory	*Workers' Compensation Act 1951*	WorkSafe ACT

JURISDICTION	PRINCIPAL ACTS	ADMINISTRATOR
Commonwealth (Commonwealth employees and employees of authorities licensed to self-insure under the *Safety, Rehabilitation and Compensation Act 1988*)	*Safety, Rehabilitation and Compensation Act 1988*	Comcare
Commonwealth (seafarers)	*Seafarers' Rehabilitation and Compensation Act 1992*	Seacare
Commonwealth (defence force personnel)	*Military Rehabilitation and Compensation Act 2004*	Department of Veterans' Affairs

The Acts, together with the regulations, comprise the legislation and must be complied with. The administering authorities have also developed guidelines to explain how the Act may be implemented.

Lack of uniformity

Compensation law is complex and ever-changing, and varies across jurisdictions. While some schemes appear generous on one score, such as payment for lost earnings, they may look stingy in other respects, such as lump sum payments for permanent impairment. As mentioned, some provide access to common law, and others don't. The premium rates are variable as well, all of which means that comparing schemes can be tricky depending on how you weigh the elements.

For a national employer, multiple jurisdictions means additional administrative costs and difficulties measuring performance as requirements differ in each jurisdiction. Not only has this led to calls for greater uniformity, but it has also prompted larger eligible organisations to self-insure under the Comcare scheme, possibly threatening the financial viability of some state and territory schemes. For many workers, access to benefits and the size of benefits differs despite the fact that they may be doing the same job for the same employer but in a different jurisdiction. Workers working in more than one jurisdiction present additional cross-border problems.

In line with WHS law, there are efforts to harmonise workers' compensation arrangements across the Commonwealth, states and territories, and prepare national workers' compensation arrangements for employers with workers in more than one of those jurisdictions. A *National Workers' Compensation Action Plan 2010–2013* has been adopted to develop 'policy proposals which identify and assess sustainable opportunities for improved response to and management of work-related injuries, illnesses and deaths'.[2] So far, however, we have a mix of laws leading to confusion and inequity.

What follows then is necessarily a general introduction to the law and administration. For more detailed information, managers should contact the government authority, their own insurers or lawyers.

Objectives of statutory law

Generally, the objectives of statutory law are to:
* help secure the health, safety and welfare of workers by providing feedback through costs, incentives and data analysis

- provide adequate financial compensation in the event of workplace fatality, injury or illness
- provide appropriate early intervention, rehabilitation and return-to-work assistance
- ensure that employer contributions fully cover liabilities.

Who is covered?

If a person or business – private, public, not-for-profit or charity – employs or hires workers or apprentices on a regular, casual or contract basis, they are considered to be an 'employer' and must have a workers' compensation insurance policy. In broad terms, a 'worker' or 'employee' is someone who receives wages or commission, regardless of the number of hours worked, and whether or not they work on the employer's premises. The individual Acts and regulations provide further definition.

DID YOU KNOW?

'CONTRACT OF SERVICE' OR 'CONTRACT FOR SERVICE'

Under the law, compensation is normally only paid to employees ('workers'), not contractors the employer uses; for example, a glazier to replace a broken window. To draw the difference, an employee is usually defined in common law as one who works under a 'contract of service' while a contractor works under a 'contract for service'. There are criteria used by the compensation authorities to mark the difference. This difference is not only important for compensation law, but also is central to industrial relations. Furthermore, persons *may* be 'deemed' as workers for compensation purposes; for example, labour-hire and types of contractors. As all of this can be complicated and murky, managers should seek advice from their lawyers or compensation authority if they are in any doubt.

DID YOU KNOW?

Some employers use contractors rather than employees to perform work for them and avoid paying workers' compensation. If this is a deliberate attempt to avoid the cost, and such arrangements fall under the law, the employer could be prosecuted.

How are premiums calculated?

Generally, the basic premium or levy is calculated by multiplying the employer's total remuneration bill – not just payroll, but benefits as well – by the percentage premium rate set for the employer's industry. Determining which industry you are in can vary slightly across jurisdictions.

The premium is normally adjusted for the employer's claims history, with the exception being smaller enterprises. A good track record should see a lower premium; otherwise, there is no related incentive to improve health and safety or the return-to-work rate. In 2008–09, the Australian standardised average premium rate was 1.52 per cent of payroll.

In addition, some jurisdictions have played with other compensation-related incentives to improve outcomes, such as using experience rating schemes – for example, South Australia's bonus/penalty scheme – with mixed results. Your insurer or compensation authority should be able to provide information on any such initiatives.

What is a work-related injury?

An 'injury', 'disease' or 'disability' is defined in the Act. It includes psychological as well as physical injuries or diseases.

For an injury or disease to be work-related, it must 'arise out of or in the course of employment'. 'Arising out of' implies the immediate cause of the injury was a factor at work; for example, the drill press or paint fumes. Judging whether a certain injury or illness is work-related can be difficult when conditions have a long latency period (asbestosis) or are gradually acquired over a number of years of exposure (industrial deafness – technically called 'noise-induced hearing loss') and when there are a number of contributing factors.

'In the course of' implies during work. In some jurisdictions, compensation may cover injury travelling to and from work, so-called 'journey' or 'commuting claims'. It varies among jurisdictions and over time. Schemes may also cover scheduled recesses, such as lunch breaks, or employer-sponsored training or events like a sales conference.

Secondly, work must have contributed in a 'significant degree' or have been a 'substantial' cause of the onset, recurrence or aggravation of the injury. The phrase 'to a material degree' is also used. Be aware that the exact words used often vary from Act to Act and have been interpreted in the courts differently.

Finally, where the worker has had a pre-existing (non-compensable) condition affecting the injury, the effect of that prior condition may be taken into account.

When an employee has been injured as a result of 'serious and wilful misconduct' – for example, working under the influence of drugs or refusing to use provided protective equipment – compensation may not have to be paid. These are referred to as 'exclusionary provisions'.

As mentioned, injuries may be psychological as well as physical. In the case of stress-related injuries incurred from normal management activity – such as redeployment, retrenchment, demotion, discipline or dismissal – claims are usually rejected. However, this is not always the case, as, for example, the way in which the discipline was carried out may have been inappropriate rather than the fact of the discipline itself. The exclusionary provisions normally cover these details. Note that 'stress' is not a recognised medical condition, but stress-related injuries such as depression or anxiety are.

An employer or insurer may challenge a claim for compensation. Similarly, a decision by the insurer may be challenged. In either case, dispute procedures apply.

What is paid for?

Compensation is paid for
- lost earnings
- associated expenses, such as medical, hospital, pharmaceutical and any rehabilitation costs, as well as incidental travel expenses ('all reasonable costs')

- permanent impairment
- death.

Compensation usually covers damage to one's personal clothing, glasses or equipment, provided there has also been an injury. Other benefits may apply, such as legal assistance with a claim.

Calculation of the amount paid for lost earnings – 'income replacement' – varies from jurisdiction to jurisdiction. The amount is usually calculated on the basis of the worker's pre-injury earnings and indexed to keep pace with increases in average income. There are limits to entitlements depending on whether the injured worker is totally or partially incapacitated and the degree of incapacity. Income replacement payments are 'stepped down' by a percentage or to a set amount for workers who cannot earn an income because of a work-related injury. Step-downs in payments are supposed to act as an incentive for workers to return to work. They can be different across the jurisdictions and according to the level of income. Whether step-downs are fair or effective is a subject of debate, often without evidence or logic.

Financial and time limits to income replacement may be set. Restrictions on the accrual of normal leave may also apply. Under certain conditions, usually only after all return-to-work options have been exhausted, the injured worker may 'settle' for a 'redemption' and elect to receive a lump sum in lieu of further payments. Normally, compensation for lost earnings ceases with retirement age: currently 65 years (for men).

Payment for associated medical and rehabilitation expenses is often set at prescribed rates and, in some cases, may be capped. Compensation may also include attendant care, home help and provision of equipment; for example, wheelchairs and cost of modifying the injured worker's home or workplace in some circumstances.

When there is a permanent impairment – for example, the loss of a limb – payments in addition to income replacement may be provided in the form of a lump sum. Maximum limits apply. In the past, the amount for the particular disability was paid according to a scheduled list of all disabilities, or what was grimly called a 'table of maims'. Nowadays, most assessments are made in terms of the impact on one's life using medical guidelines.

In the event that a workplace injury results in death, all jurisdictions provide death benefits. A spouse or dependant of a worker who died in a work-related incident may be entitled to certain benefits to assist the family with funeral costs and ongoing living expenses.

The continuity of payments depends on the medical condition of the injured worker and the requirement that the worker returns to work as soon as deemed able to. As there is the potential for ignorance, non-cooperation and fraud, the employer must make every effort to closely monitor processes of compensation and return to work. In the end, providing early treatment and return to work is best for everyone. It helps a worker's recovery and morale while reducing claims and premiums costs.

DID YOU KNOW?

Compensation fraud exists but, as the scheme administrators themselves point out, it may be perpetrated by employers and insurers as well as workers. The popular focus on workers' fraud ('malingerers') – a theme dear to shock jocks and producers of current affairs programs – may be explained by the equally popular myths that workplace accidents are random events or the result of accident-prone or careless workers. Such myths help shift the costs of workplace injury onto the worker and absolve employers of living up to their duty of care.

Remember, too, that nearly half of all legitimate claims for compensation are never made! Safe Work Australia reports that the main reasons for not applying are:

- 'Male and female employees did not apply for compensation for nearly four-tenths of their injuries that involved some time lost from work because they considered the injury too minor to claim. For a further one-tenth of these injuries, male and female employees felt it was inconvenient or too much effort to apply.
- Male employees did not apply for compensation for over two in ten injuries because they did not know they were eligible for compensation.
- For female employees, nearly two in ten did not apply due to concerns about their current or future employment.'

Source: Safe Work Australia, 2009, *Work-Related Injuries in Australia, 2005–06: Factors Affecting Applications for Workers' Compensation*, © Commonwealth of Australia, p. 2. http://www.safeworkaustralia.gov.au/AboutSafeWork Australia/WhatWeDo/Publications/Documents/426/Work_Related_Injuries_2005_06_factors_affecting_application_ WC.pdf.

THE COMPENSATION AND INJURY MANAGEMENT PROCESS

In the preceding chapter, we identified the three key steps that must take place when an incident occurs and someone is injured or made ill: help the injured worker (and any non-worker), inform the regulator if it is a notifiable incident, finally, record the injury and investigate the incident. Here we look at the process of compensating and rehabilitating the worker and returning them to work.

As mentioned, there are provisions for the employer or insurer to challenge a claim and for the worker to challenge any denial of compensation. Dispute-settlement arrangements vary among jurisdictions and information is available from the insurers and compensation authorities.

The step-by-step procedures of workers' compensation can be complicated and are relative to the particular schemes. Information on the detailed administrative procedures can be obtained from your insurer or compensation authority. A summary flowchart gives you a generalised overview of the employer's role in the process.

INJURY MANAGEMENT

In the past, when a worker suffered a significant injury, their workplace and employer often provided very little assistance (or even contact) until the worker was fully recovered. Sometimes the only contact from the workplace was notice of termination.

Figure 16.2 *Key steps in the compensation and injury-management process*

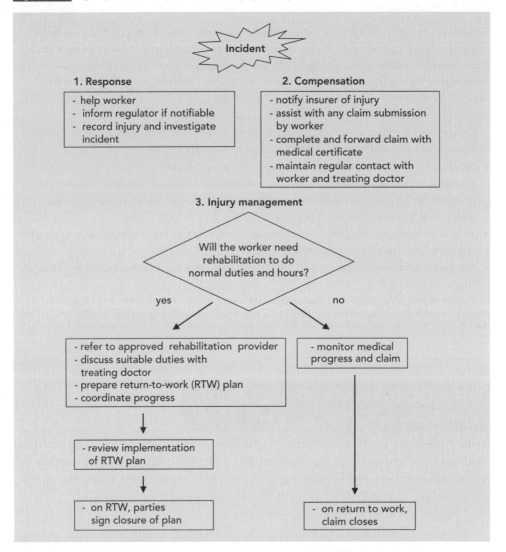

The following story is taken from WorkSafe Victoria's 2010 publication *What To Do If A Worker Is Injured: A Guide For Employers*. While it reflects the specific arrangements of Victoria's scheme, it also illustrates the processes involved in successful injury management.

Mike is a 42-year-old storeman and forklift driver who works for a packaging and distribution company.

During the hectic Christmas period, Mike feels a sharp pain in his back as he reaches down for a box on the conveyor belt. The pain is so intense it stops him from bending further and gets worse when he tries to sit down.

He reports the incident to his supervisor, who records the incident in the Register of Injuries book, sends him home early to rest and suggests he see a doctor the next day if he is not better. Mike's supervisor also informs Theo, the company's Return to Work Coordinator.

Mike sees his doctor, who diagnoses a low back strain and provides him with a Certificate of Capacity stating that he needs 10 days off work. She refers him to a physiotherapist for treatment and a program of exercises to improve his strength and flexibility.

During this time, Theo calls Mike to ask how he is feeling and offer support. He also sends Mike a Worker's Injury Claim Form and helps him complete it.

Theo starts to plan for Mike's return to work. He talks to his Agent, reviews the information contained in Mike's Certificate of Capacity, talks to Mike about what he thinks he may be able to do. Theo then lists possible duties Mike could do in the foreseeable future on WorkSafe's template Return to Work Arrangements and discusses this with Mike's foreman. He sends the proposed duties to Mike, the doctor and the physiotherapist. Theo also sends Mike a copy of the brochure Introducing WorkSafe: A Guide for Injured Workers to provide Mike with information about making a claim and entitlements.

Mike attends a number of physiotherapy sessions, takes pain medication and rests as much as he can. His pain improves a little, but he still has difficulty bending forward and can only sit for about 20 minutes at a time.

He attends a second appointment with his doctor and receives another certificate for two weeks off work and a recommendation to continue with the treatment, stay active and walk as much as he can.

Theo calls the doctor to discuss the suitable employment options and sends her a brief fax listing the tasks Mike normally does and other duties he could do while recovering. Theo also meets with the foreman to modify the roster and workload to accommodate Mike's return to work in a restricted capacity. He keeps Mike's colleagues informed of his recovery, the action the company has taken to support his early return to work and encourages staff to keep in touch with Mike.

Mike makes steady progress and can now sit for longer periods without pain. His doctor gives him a certificate stating he can return to work on reduced hours with restrictions on sitting and bending activities.

Theo updates the proposed suitable employment options based upon this new information and provides clear and accurate information regarding the return to work arrangements. He sends a copy of this to the doctor and drops off a copy to Mike on his way home. They agree on the best date for him to return to the workplace when Mike's supervisor will be available to support his return and check that everything is progressing as planned.

A few days later, Mike returns to work and over the next four weeks, with Mike and his doctor's agreement, his duties and hours are gradually increased.

On one occasion, Mike experiences an increase in pain after a new task is added to his workload. Theo modifies the return to work arrangements to cut back on the time spent at this task. He also makes sure Mike can leave early on certain days to attend physiotherapy appointments. Mike keeps Theo informed of his progress and together they agree on activities and rest breaks.

After eight weeks, Mike was able to return to his normal job and hours. Theo also made permanent changes to the way work was organised around the conveyor belt to reduce the likelihood of another injury.

While the extra effort of managing Mike's WorkSafe claim seemed inconvenient at times, Theo and his employer knew that getting Mike back to work as soon as possible was best for Mike and for staff morale – it was also good for the company's bottom line.

Source: WorkSafe Victoria, p. 38, 2010, *Appendix C: Example of an effective return to work, A guide for employers: What to do if a worker is injured*, pp. 37–8.
Access http://www.worksafe.vic.gov.au for more information and future updates.

Questions

1 Who do you think plays the critical role in facilitating Mike's return to work?
2 What are the motives of the employer in the process?

Workers feeling poorly treated or neglected by their employer after a significant injury were also more likely to sue for damages at common law – until recent times the primary driver of compensation cost escalation. Once an injury occurs, *duration of incapacity to work* is the primary driver of costs for both statutory and common law claims.

Nowadays, more active rehabilitation, or injury management, is required for ethical, legal and financial reasons, and it is this approach that we use here.

'Injury management' is a term that has grown more popular recently to describe 'rehabilitation', the restoring of a function. While **workplace rehabilitation** is rehabilitation specifically aimed at returning and keeping injured workers at work, 'injury management' refers to the entire range of activities dealing with injury or disease – medical intervention, treatment, retraining, return to work, claims management, management supervisory practices – as well as rehabilitation itself.

Importantly, injury management can be used whether or not the injury or illness was work-related. The fact that an employee was injured in a holiday accident, for example, does not prevent an employer from looking at ways that the worker can be returned to work as soon as possible. Providing suitable duties and hours during rehabilitation treatment makes good financial sense and sends a strong message to the workforce.

Figure 16.3 *Main players in the injury-management process*

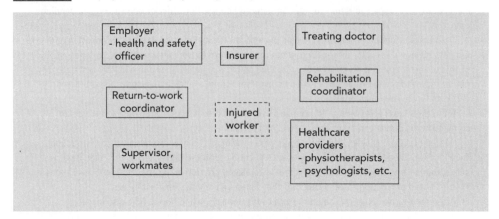

What are the employer's responsibilities?

In addition to providing the injured worker with first aid or transport for medical treatment, the employer needs to

- give the worker details of the insurer, an employer contact and a claim form
- notify the insurer of details of the injury, injured worker and treating doctor, and forward medical certificates, receipts and accounts for treatment
- provide any suitable duties while helping the worker to recover and return to work quickly, except when the worker has resigned voluntarily, employment is terminated for reasons other than the injury or when it is impracticable.

In general 'suitable duties' means those for which the worker is currently suited, given:

- the nature of their incapacity
- the nature of their pre-injury employment
- their age, education, skills and work experience
- their place of residence

- the return-to-work plan
- any occupational rehabilitation services involved.

The precise meaning of 'suitable duties' can vary across jurisdictions.

The employer should:

- appoint and train someone in the organisation to manage rehabilitation and return to work (a return-to-work coordinator)
- train everyone in their roles and responsibilities in the event of incidents and injuries.

It is recommended that the health and safety manager or the return-to-work coordinator know of recommended rehabilitation providers and other health providers so that early intervention is possible.

All of this should be set out clearly in an injury management program with policies and procedures detailing the employer's commitment, stakeholder responsibilities and steps in the return-to-work process. It should include staff training, performance indicators and mechanisms for review and improvement.

What are the worker's responsibilities?

The injured worker must:

- seek medical attention
- notify the employer as soon as possible if the incident has not been already notified
- record their name, the date and cause of the injury in the employer's injury register
- sign any prescribed medical certificates
- keep in touch with the employer
- cooperate with efforts to return to work.

The injured worker should be able to have their representative present in the development of any return-to-work plan.

A return-to-work plan should:

- be developed in consultation with the injured worker and the treating doctor
- set out the steps to achieve a return to work
- use appropriate expertise, such as approved rehabilitation and health care providers
- recognise the existing capacities of the injured worker so that suitable duties can be found
- if necessary, retrain or redeploy when it is not possible for the worker to return to pre-injury duties.

The preferred order is:

- same job and same employer
- similar job and same employer
- new job and same employer.

Failing that, the possibility of training and working for a new employer needs to be explored.

What are the insurer's responsibilities?

The insurer determines liability for workers' compensation and pays for insured costs as set out in the law.

They also must contact the worker, the employer and the treating doctor to ensure that the worker receives necessary assistance to recover and return to work.

Insurers *can* also assist the employer to develop an injury-management plan for the worker in consultation with the employer, the doctor and the worker, while keeping the employer informed of significant steps taken or proposed under the injury-management plan.

What is the role of the treating doctor?

Any injured worker off work for more than a specified period, usually seven days, must nominate a treating doctor. That doctor is responsible for:

- providing medical assistance
- completing certificates
- monitoring the worker's condition
- helping to coordinate treatment and any return-to-work management
- providing the employer and insurer with information relating to the injury and the worker's rehabilitation.

What is the role of health care providers?

Health care providers assist injured workers under the direction of the doctor, usually to provide necessary and reasonable treatment of the work-related injury. They include:

- chiropractors
- osteopaths
- physiotherapists
- psychologists
- exercise physiologists
- remedial massage therapists.
  Treatment may need to be approved by the insurer prior to its provision.

What is the role of the rehabilitation providers?

Accredited rehabilitation providers offer specialised services to help injured workers to return to work. They:

- assess the needs of the injured worker and the workplace requirements to develop a rehabilitation plan of action, listing the services needed to return the injured worker to work

- employ different health professionals, such as occupational therapists, physiotherapists, psychologists and rehabilitation counsellors
- are referred to by the employer, insurer or the treating doctor to help in complex cases
- are nominated by the employer in any return-to-work program.

What is the role of the health and safety manager?

When duties include injury management, the role of the health and safety manager is:
- to be aware of the responsibilities of everyone involved when someone is injured at work
- to assist where possible.

Training in the general requirements for compensation and injury management should be provided to everyone. In many jurisdictions, a return-to-work, rehabilitation or injury-management coordinator must be appointed and trained to assist in the administration of the injury-management program.

The big risk is that with ineffective injury management, the opportunity to return an injured worker is lost, costing both the worker and the employer. The longer the injured worker is away from work, the less chance there is of the worker returning to suitable employment and the bigger the premium becomes. Immediate, close and ongoing attention to a workplace injury is the key. Experience shows that it is psychological, organisational and work environment factors that block what would have been successful injury management. The earliest identification and removal of any of these factors is critical. From the employer's perspective, effective return to work not only reduces the chance of the worker suing for damages, but also reduces the chance of fraud. All of this means going beyond mere compliance and adopting 'active workplace injury management'.

ACTIVE WORKPLACE INJURY MANAGEMENT[3]

Active injury management means direct involvement by the employer in managing the return-to-work process from the time of injury and taking responsibility for outcomes. Success with workers, particularly those at risk of long-term incapacity, requires a positive approach:
- *Where possible, don't wait for the insurer.* An insurer can't act until a claim is lodged and accepted – statutory timeframes for applying for and determining compensation mean that this can take months. An employer can act as soon as an injury is reported. When the insurer ceases rehabilitation on termination of a statutory claim, an employer can continue to provide rehabilitation and assist the worker, reducing risks of future litigation.
- *Take the lead role.* Treating practitioners treat the damage to an injured worker's leg, arm, back and so on. They can rarely 'treat' the injury's functional impact at work or on workplace relationships, or the worker's problems in getting to and from

work. Treating practitioners may not have an accurate understanding of the demands of the worker's job, of suitable duties or of the environment in which the work is performed. With their knowledge, employers can play a positive role by acting early and seeing things through, by working cooperatively with the treating professionals and by ensuring clear communication with the insurer. This works with insurers, too. Tell them your needs and clarify each other's roles and responsibilities.

- *Where possible, avoid confrontation.* Resources should be used so that injured workers can earn a living rather than be used on adversarial medico-legal processes that crystallise incapacity and invalidity. An effective system identifies and addresses systemic barriers to early return to work (see below).

- *Allocate resources in proportion to risk.* To control risks, smart employers differentiate between different levels of risk and put together plans that work to minimise the likelihood of a high-cost outcome for themselves and their workers.

- *Recruit or contract qualified and experienced rehabilitation case managers and providers.* Smart employers ensure that high-risk cases are assigned to a rehabilitation case manager with the requisite level of expertise and access to necessary resources. 'Internalise' treatment resources where possible; that is, select a preferred medical provider and a preferred rehabilitation provider.

- *Take a long-term view.* Workplace injury costs take time to manifest, sometimes many years. Performance indicators and management information systems enable performance monitoring in the short term, predict long-term outcomes and support action by managers and workers in the workplace.

- *Identify and overcome barriers to implementation* such as the following:
  - Inertia: you need to convince decision makers that active injury management is necessary. The impetus for implementing best-practice rehabilitation systems often comes after a rude shock in the form of a workers' compensation premium notice. Demonstrate the return on investment in principle and in practice.
  - Financial and management systems: when these systems don't show the cause and effect of workplace injury it becomes hard to make an effective business case for workplace rehabilitation. If senior executives, accountants and business unit managers can't see the connection between active rehabilitation and achieving core targets, they won't support it. Work to change the system to reflect the business case in terms everyone understands.
  - Injury = failure: no organisation likes to focus on the fact that it may injure its workers. Some workplace cultures value safety so strongly that to put resources into rehabilitation is perceived as an admission of failure. This is counterproductive to effective management of accident consequences. Again, practical demonstration of the benefits needs marketing to the organisation.
  - Expertise: as a tiny number of cases can account for the majority of costs, employers need a system that ensures expertise is applied at the right time to

make a difference. Such cases need expert rehabilitation case management. Sourcing and internalising such expertise is a must for employers serious about their efforts.

- Long timeframes: in a world where performance is measured in ever-decreasing timeframes it is sometimes hard to get attention paid to issues that may have their greatest adverse impact in five years' time. Accounting systems need to recognise claims history and what this can mean for the employer in years to come.

- Does it really help workers?: an active workplace rehabilitation system will not work if it does not really help injured workers. If workers can't see the benefits, the system will not become part of the workplace culture. Market your successes and use injury management to deal with non–work–related injuries.

The following stories are based on success stories from the Queensland authority Q-Comp.[4]

Q-COMP – RETURN TO WORK ASSIST CASE STUDIES

A young cabinetmaker sustained a crush injury to his right thumb at work. After an amputation of his thumb, he found that he was unable to return to his previous position as the company had closed.

After initial discussions with Q-COMP's Return to work assist team, it was identified that his long-term goal was to be a trainer in his field of carpentry. He was referred to Skilling Solutions to look at career options and to the Australian Construction Training Services Pty Ltd for a trade assessment. At no cost to himself he subsequently completed Certificate IV in Training and Assessment, the mandatory qualification for being a trainer. Later that year he secured a subcontracting position as a shop-fitter to gain further experience which he plans to use in his future training role.

A 40 year old labourer was referred to Q-COMP by his insurer after sustaining a foot injury when a slope he was standing on gave way. His employment was terminated but he wished to stay in the construction area as he had experience and a number of machinery tickets in this area.

Return to work Assist referred him to Civic Solutions who were able to assist him with job preparation skills and assisted him to focus on his career direction. The injured worker had been contemplating a career change into horticulture and his discussions with Civic Solutions provided him with a variety of options. He was able to access a funded course in Horticulture and has now secured ongoing work in landscaping.

Following a re-occurrence of a back injury at work, a 35 year old warehouse supervisor/storeman was referred to Q-COMP.

The worker had been very proactive in delivering resumes to potential employers however had only been successful in securing short term work. After referral to the Return to work assist program he was linked with Civic Solutions and provided with job preparation assistance which refined his resume and selection criteria. He was also able to complete some additional computer training. All of this put him in a better position to apply for jobs and he is now happily working in retail four days a week in a job which doesn't require any heavy lifting.

A 29 year old gentleman sustained a lower back injury whilst digging a hole. He was referred to Q-COMP by Workcover as his injury made it impossible for him to return to his career of Plumbing.

With the help of Return to work Assist he was able to receive career direction from Skilling Solutions Queensland and he began looking at his options. He was assisted with job preparation through Civic

Solutions who helped him to further refine his career options. The worker identified that he wanted to start his own business and soon after he launched his own business repairing taps and doing minor plumbing work.

A young man was referred to Q-COMP following a back injury sustained whilst working as an Electrical trades assistant. On initial interview it was identified that the worker needed some assistance from Return to work assist in identifying a new career.

He was referred to Skilling Solutions Queensland to help him identify suitable career options which led to his enrolment in a job preparation course with Boystown. This course provided him with skills in resume writing, confidence building and further career counselling. At the completion of this course the worker decided he would like to complete his Year 12 certificate and has enrolled in a tertiary preparation course through Gold Coast Institute of TAFE.

Whilst completing his Year 12 certificate he was also upskilled through Boystown with courses in Responsible Service of Alcohol and Gaming which has allowed him to obtain a position working part time in a local tavern whilst completing his studies.

Source: Q-COMP, http://www.qcomp.com.au/services/return-to-work-assist/case-studies.aspx.

In 1995, the former National Occupational Health and Safety Commission drew up a list of 14 best-practice principles. These principles are recommended as part of your organisation's injury–management system.

PRINCIPLES OF REHABILITATION

Irrespective of the compensation and rehabilitation system or participant role, for example, injured employee, employer, etc., there are essential principles of rehabilitation, which can be promoted and maintained by all concerned. These principles are as follows.

(a) Maintenance at work, or early and appropriate return to work, is in the best interests of all employees who have suffered a work-related injury or disease and should be the prime goal.

(b) Commitment by all parties to the rehabilitation process is essential for successful outcomes.

(c) Recognition that the workplace is usually the most effective place for rehabilitation to occur.

(d) Rehabilitation should occur at the earliest possible time consistent with medical judgement.

(e) Rehabilitation intervention should ensure that
   - the dignity of employees is retained; and
   - employees participate actively in the process.

(f) Consultation between the employer and employee (and their representatives – where appropriate) should occur at all stages of the rehabilitation process.

(g) Employers and employees should be informed of their legislative entitlements and requirements under the relevant workers' compensation system.

(h) Information should be treated confidentially, with sensitivity and used only for the purpose for which it was supplied.

(i) All relevant rehabilitation expenses are to be met by the agent responsible under appropriate legislation.

(j) Return to work programs should aim to return the employee to work in either
   - same job/same employer
   - similar job/same employer
   - new job/same employer.

These are the first options to be considered when planning and implementing return to work programs. If these are inappropriate, or no position is available with the original employer, then the following apply

- same job/new employer
- similar job/new employer
- new job/new employer.

(k)   Work assigned through the rehabilitation process should be meaningful to the employee.

(l)   Graduated return to full time duties, permanent part time work or reduced hours relative to pre-injury hours should be considered when planning and implementing return to work activities.

(m) No injured employee should suffer financial disadvantage by participating in a return to work program.

(n)   Rehabilitation is most effective when linked to workplace-based occupational health and safety programs.

Source: National Occupational Health and Safety Commission, 1995, Guidance Note for the Best Practice Rehabilitation Management of Occupational Injuries and Disease, NOHSC:3021, Canberra. © Copyright Commonwealth of Australia, reproduced by permission. Currently, an adapted extract can be found in AS/NZS 4804 *Occupational health and safety management systems – General guidelines on principles, systems and supporting techniques*.

In the next chapter, we look at building an HS culture.

Summary

- No-fault workers' compensation schemes operate throughout Australia and require all employers to take out workers' compensation insurance policies.
- The principal aims of such schemes are to provide fair compensation and treatment for employees injured at work, while encouraging early return to work wherever medically possible and, at the same time, encouraging employers and employees to provide a safe and healthy workplace.
- While effective HS systems are the best way of reducing insurance costs, HS managers need to know the roles and responsibilities of everyone involved in the case of workplace injuries and diseases.
- Workers' compensation and injury-management law varies across all the jurisdictions, but there are a number of common principles and responsibilities applying to employers, employees, insurers, doctors, health care providers and rehabilitation providers.
- As the health of workers and the size of compensation premiums can be affected by ineffective injury management, managers and employees should be trained in their responsibilities.
- Above all, the key to success is immediate, close and ongoing attention by everyone involved.

In your workplace

A member of staff whose job location and management arrangements were changed, resulting in separation from family and reduced job satisfaction, was diagnosed with depression and mental breakdown. She was absent for six months on compensation with no action taken.

1   How would you as health and safety manager deal with this situation?
   Hint: Check the procedural guidelines issued by your compensation authority.

2   What steps would you take and with whom?
   Hint: Again, the steps should be supplied in the law and guidance material.

3   How would you prevent its reoccurrence?
    Hint: What sort of policy and procedures would you put in place?

Questions

1   Why do we have no-fault workers' compensation schemes?
2   In your jurisdiction
    a   how does the Act define a 'work-related injury'?
    b   what are the responsibilities of the employer?
    c   what are the responsibilities of the employee?
3   How does a contract of service differ from a contract for service?
4   How might the following people help in the return-to-work process?
    a   a rehabilitation provider
    b   a psychologist
    c   an occupational therapist.

Activities

1   Find out what your employer's workers' compensation arrangements are. Who does the employer insure with? What is the premium? Has it increased or decreased in recent years? Is there an excess, as with other forms of insurance? In general terms, what are the types of injures or diseases that have resulted in compensation?
2   Examine your workplace's injury-management policy. Compare it with those of others in your class. Does your workplace actively manage injuries in the manner described in this chapter? What is its approach to injury management and how could it be improved?
3   Visit a court where a compensation case is being held or read the transcript of a case. Summarise the case. Discuss the main issues of the case.
4   Interview a rehabilitation coordinator (or health care provider) or invite one to your class to discuss their experience and the lessons learned.

Search me!

 Explore **Search me! management** for relevant articles on workers' compensation and injury management. Search me! is an online library of world-class journals, ebooks and newspapers, including *The Australian* and the *New York Times*, and is updated daily. Log in to Search me! through www.cengage.com/sso using the access card in the front of this book.

KEYWORDS
Try searching for the following terms:
▶ workers' compensation   ▶ injury management
▶ return to work   ▶ rehabilitation

Search tip: **Search me! management** contains information from both local and international sources. To get the greatest number of search results, try using both Australian and American spellings in your searches, e.g. 'globalisation' and 'globalization'; 'organisation' and 'organization'.

Additional resources

• The websites of the government compensation authorities have copies of the legislation, together with information and guidance. A complete listing can be found at http://www.safeworkaustralia.gov.au/AboutSafeWorkAustralia/WhoWeWorkWith/StateAndTerritoryAuthorities/Pages/StateAndTerritoryAuthorities.aspx.

- A comprehensive comparison of the various compensation schemes, together with a short history of workers' compensation, entitled *Comparison of Workers' Compensation Arrangements in Australia and New Zealand*, can be found on the Safe Work Australia website. It is updated from time to time. It is a companion to the Workplace Relations Ministers' Council's Comparative Performance Monitoring reports entitled *Occupational Health and Safety and Workers' Compensation Schemes in Australia and New Zealand*, which provide detailed information on the operations of the schemes each year and examples of how aspects of scheme design are applied in practice. See http://www.safeworkaustralia.gov. au/WorkersCompensation/Pages/WorkersCompensation.aspx.
- For those wishing for detailed information on the law, CCH and the Law Book Company have produced books on this matter, and subscription services are available to keep one abreast of developments.
- The following references give further detail and discussion.
  - McDonald, W., 2007, Workers' compensation, in the *Australian Master OHS and Environment Guide 2007*, 2nd edn, CCH: Sydney.
  - Barnett, L., 2003, Rehabilitation, in the *Australian Master OHS and Environment Guide 2003*, CCH: Sydney.
  - Productivity Commission, 2004, *National Workers' Compensation and Occupational Health and Safety Frameworks*, Report No. 27, Canberra, March, is a useful overview and discussion of workers' compensation. Note that the conservative ideology used in the report has been criticised.
  - Purse, K., Meredith, K. & Guthrie, R., 2004, Neoliberalism, workers' compensation and the Productivity Commission, *Journal of Australian Political Economy*, No. 24, March.
  - Purse, K., 2005, The evolution of workers' compensation policy in Australia, *Health Sociology Review*, Vol. 14, No. 1, August, pp. 8–20. The author uses a political economy approach to workers' compensation.

Endnotes

1 Common law can have a significant impact on the statutory benefit structure. Schemes with little or no common law access – such as Comcare and in South Australia – tend to have benefits that cater for the ongoing needs of permanently impaired workers ('long-tail' schemes). Schemes with greater common law access – such as in Queensland and Tasmania – tend to have benefits directed towards workers with shorter-term illnesses or injuries. Such schemes look to the common law to meet the needs of the more seriously injured.

2 See the Safe Work Australia website for details: www.safeworkaustralia.gov.au.

3 This section has benefited from the paper by R.J. Hawkins, 2000, Active Rehabilitation Management: A Core Business Strategy delivered at Visions: The New Millennium, 8th Annual Safety Institute of Australia (Qld Division) and Division of Workplace Health and Safety Conference, Gold Coast.

4 For details, see http://www.qcomp.com.au/ services/return-to-work-assist/case-studies.aspx.

PROMOTING A HEALTH AND SAFETY CULTURE

Learning Objectives

At the end of this chapter, the reader should be able to:

- describe what a positive health and safety culture is
- select strategies to promote a health and safety culture
- describe the elements of a work–life balance program
- assess the current health and safety climate.

INTRODUCTION

The model of health and safety used in this book requires the core health and safety system to be supported by management commitment, effective consultation and a vibrant health and safety culture. It is the health and safety culture of an organisation that concerns us here.

A living health and safety culture is one in which people think and act as if human welfare is of prime importance. They are not only sensitive and informed about any risk and its effective management, but also to the opportunity to improve. Health and safety comes as second nature.

Where a positive HS culture is present, it is tangible. For example, when you enter workplaces in high-risk industries, people are dressed appropriately, warnings are issued, safety instructions and equipment provided, exits marked, and so on. You are made aware that there are risks and that your life, and that of everybody else, is of the highest importance. Furthermore, people encourage you to identify possible risks and will act on them immediately. All of this is done in a straightforward no-nonsense atmosphere. In many less risky and low-risk workplaces, the same level of everyday awareness and behaviour can often be experienced in an unselfconscious way.

Clearly, such a health and safety culture is desirable in all workplaces, if policies, consultation and systematic approaches are to combine to maximum effect. People have to think and act on the WHS policy, not merely comply with it minimally.

While HS culture-building is already happening as a result of other programs such as consultation, training, hazard identification and risk management, it needs to be treated as a program in its own right. This chapter identifies some key interventions in the workplace that develop not only a heightened sensitivity to safety but to health as well – as shown in Figure 17.1. In so doing, we go beyond the workplace to examine how a positive culture can be built by recognising the effect of non-work issues on workers' wellbeing.

Finally, we conclude by showing how HS culture-building can be measured using climate surveys.

Figure 17.1 *Health and safety culture*

SAFETY CULTURE	HEALTH CULTURE
• reporting culture • just culture • flexible culture • learning culture	• health and fitness programs • mental health awareness • trauma assistance • employee assistance programs • work–life balance programs
MEASURING A HEALTH AND SAFETY CULTURE	
• HS climate surveys	

BUILDING A SAFETY CULTURE[1]

Based on the analysis of a safety culture outlined in James Reason's book *Managing the Risks of Organizational Accidents*, an organisation with an active safety culture has:

- the capacity to drive the system towards the goal of maximising safety, regardless of the leadership's personality or current commercial concerns
- a clear respect for risk; that is, not being complacent or forgetting to be careful. Reason identifies four cultures that make up an informed safety culture:
- *a reporting culture* – one that is not afraid to report incidents and situations that threaten the health of workers
- *a just culture* – one that draws the line between acceptable and unacceptable behaviour and apportions personal responsibility and blame
- *a flexible culture* – one that adapts itself rapidly to organisational forms suitable for dealing with immediate hazards and then is capable of reverting back once the hazards have been controlled
- *a learning culture* – one that possesses 'the willingness and the competence to draw the right conclusions from its safety information system, and the will to implement major reforms when their need is indicated'.[2]

Obviously, the project for many organisations of building a dynamic health and safety culture is a long-term one, needing the understanding and cooperation of all employees, but beginning with senior management.

The very first step is to make the building of a health and safety culture a specific sub-program, along with others within the WHS program. The next step is identifying the particular thinking and behaviour required in the four cultures and devising ways to encourage it.

With the behaviours set as goals, Reason sets out the practices that would build those types of behaviours, or what he calls 'engineering' such cultures. Although his book concerns high-risk organisations, the lessons apply across all workplaces. We have amplified his suggestions with those drawn from our own experience.

ENGINEERING A REPORTING CULTURE

Getting people to report incidents or near-misses is up against the natural human instinct to avoid making a fuss, creating extra work or confessing one's own errors. Some methods for overcoming these inhibitors are as follows.

- Ensure that no one will be punished or discriminated against as a result of identifying risk however it is produced; rather, reward risk. This can be done through an explicit (policy) commitment to encourage reporting –'whistleblowing' – and managers or supervisors modelling such behaviour. Under-reporting then becomes unacceptable behaviour.

- It may be necessary to employ rules to protect the confidentiality of those reporting.
- Clearly separate any disciplinary function from the reporting function so that the two are perceived and trusted to be working separately.
- Provide for different methods of reporting, such as those requiring formal procedures and paperwork through to recorded and unrecorded discussions at team meetings or with specific staff members.
- Expand the range of possible incidents that can be reported to include anything that is thought to affect one's health when changes to the workplace could assist. Such 'incidents' could include work arrangements of any sort, such as carer commitments, workplace conflict, medical problems and domestic issues.
- Include performance appraisal questions for supervisors and managers such as 'Does your section/department encourage incident reporting? And if so, what have you done about the incidents?'

Such methods would ensure that reporting is made easier and health and safety has the central importance it should have. More important, however, would be the positive response to such reporting by the organisation. If the response is slow or ineffective, or if there is no feedback on the progress of the action, the reporting culture will be stifled. Publicising the learning achieved through reporting the changes that have been made is to be encouraged for precisely this reason.

ENGINEERING A JUST CULTURE

When a manager, supervisor or employee acts in a manner that puts them or others at risk, they should be told quite firmly. There should always be a clear line between acceptable and unacceptable behaviour. Whether they are to be held responsible is a separate matter and the possible subject of an investigation or disciplinary procedure. In any case, there is no room for a workplace that does not recognise unacceptable behaviour or personal responsibility. This is the meaning of a just culture.

Building a just culture can mean:
- communicating the WHS policy in the clearest way possible and having it reviewed and reaffirmed annually
- following carefully the procedures for 'law-making' in the workplace by consulting appropriately over policies and procedures
- publicising cases of how the organisation feels about unacceptable behaviour
- managers and supervisors modelling acceptable behaviour and openly identifying unacceptable behaviour
- adopting clear disciplinary procedures in regards to violations of WHS policy and procedures.

ENGINEERING A FLEXIBLE CULTURE

A flexible culture is one that adapts to contingencies and can revert to normal operating procedures as appropriate. Many of us work in some sort of hierarchy with other operational units surrounding our own. Ultimately, all of these report to a general manager supported by a management team. We will call these 'centralised bureaucracies' and contrast them with decentralised 'teams' or 'collegiate' organisations. More often than not, we work in both – forming a team with our workmates in an office, ward or shopfloor, while working in the larger hierarchical organisation.

When incidents threaten or happen, the people affected must respond quickly and in a fashion in which normal operating procedures do not apply. To some extent we can prepare ourselves with drilled procedures, as with emergency situations like fire, for example. But at other times, the hazardous situation may not be anticipated with prepared procedures, and instead we have to rely on our knowledge and skills. Formal authority is either remote or obstructs a rapid solution to the problem. You want experienced people on the spot, directing a response of which higher management may have limited understanding. You need a team in which everyone is heard but formal authority defers to experience, otherwise the situation can rapidly worsen. For this to work, and solutions to be implemented, there must be mutual respect for everyone's particular skills and experience. In a sense, another hierarchy emerges that may call on the lowest level of first-line supervisor or operator to fix the problem and control an incident because they have the needed skills. People in such situations must feel empowered to respond there and then with the support of those around them. After the situation has been dealt with, the organisation returns to normal operating procedures and the centralised regime takes effect.

In high-risk organisations, it is not uncommon to 'move' from working in one type of organisation to working in another. However, even in less risky and stressful workplaces, the ability to anticipate or respond to incidents rapidly is to be valued at any time.

Some of the ways that an organisation can help to build such flexibility are:

- Have different units within an organisation share the experience of dealing with situations requiring a rapid response: what specific lessons were learnt? Such telling of war stories should be encouraged to build confidence.
- Talk through near-misses or recent incidents to analyse what was done well and what didn't go so well.
- Take steps to ensure that everyone's experience is valued; the greater the diversity of experience, the greater the chance there is of building an effective response. This can mean carefully structuring team meetings so that everyone feels at ease and is encouraged to present their point of view – and not simply on health and safety matters either.

- When practical, looking to job sharing and rotation as a means to diversify experience; fresh eyes are often a great method of hazard identification.
- Again, encourage reporting of hazards to develop possible solutions from all perspectives. Study the process of how issues are raised and dealt with.

ENGINEERING A LEARNING CULTURE

> Learning disabilities are tragic in children, but they are fatal in organizations. Because of them, few corporations live even half as long as the person – most die before they reach the age of forty.[3]

Much has been written about learning cultures of organisations. In the case of WHS, it means more than simply having information systems that provide knowledge about hazards and incidents, and communicating that information throughout the organisation. It means *acting* on the information, much like a commercial firm anticipating and nimbly responding to changes in the market, or a government department acting on early policy signals from the minister.

A WHS learning culture can be developed by:

- gathering the latest information on relevant hazards, workplace health issues and changes to the law, and then providing it to the relevant areas of the business for discussion
- providing sufficient amounts of data from the firm's own experience to everyone, especially senior and line managers
- ensuring that training is carried out for all managers and employees, evaluating its impact on the workplace, reviewing the curricula and mode of delivery for improvement
- rewarding those who are alert to HS issues and the responses they make, especially managers and supervisors
- following up investigations, evaluating the corrective and preventive results and publicising the individual stories in the annual report.

Reason's four elements in building a positive culture are not the only elements needed. In the rest of this chapter, we look at other initiatives focusing on health.

DID YOU KNOW?

Australia's expert on safety culture is Andrew Hopkins of the Australian National University. He identifies culture with collective practices rather than individual values. Change the practices and you are able to change the values of those who work in an organisation and embed a culture of risk awareness. Andrew's books show how dysfunctional workplace cultures, such as narrow rule-based cultures and those involving organisational 'silos', led to a number of major accidents in Australia. (See the additional resources at the end of this chapter.)

The following is an example of a typical corporate safety culture program provided by Workplace OHS.

SAFETY CULTURE PROGRAM

The following advice from WorkCover NSW reinforces Reason's lessons on building a positive safety culture.

Beyond Compliance: A Positive Safety Culture

Beyond merely complying with the raft of harmonised work health and safety (WHS) laws that take effect in December 2011, businesses must also ensure they have a strong, safety-focused culture.

Speaking at Informa's National Workplace Safety Summit recently, the WorkCover NSW director of industry relationships group (OHS division), Jenny Thomas, spoke about the principles that underpin a positive workplace safety culture.

An organisation's safety culture, Thomas said, reflects its 'values, attitudes and behaviours' with regard to work health and safety.

Commitment from everyone

According to Thomas, a strong safety culture is underpinned by:

- an empowered workforce—workers not only know that they're entitled to work in a safe and healthy environment, but actually feel safe
- responsibilities—everyone acknowledges that the safety of others is important and accepts personal responsibility for ensuring the health and safety of both themselves and others in the workplace
- the behaviours and actions of supervisors and management demonstrate their genuine commitment to work health and safety. An organisation is 'genuinely' committed to safety, when it:
  - commits time and resources to workplace safety
  - consults with workers and listens to what they have to say
  - communicates messages, thoughts and reasons to everyone in a respectful way
  - ensures everyone has undertaken effective training and induction
  - develops and implements all necessary WHS and reporting systems and procedures
  - ensures return-to-work and injury management programs for injured workers are in place
- lower injury rates and lower workers compensation costs (as a result of the above).

Source: WorkplaceOHS, www.workplaceohs.com.au, 17 August 2010.

BUILDING A HEALTH CULTURE

HEALTH AND FITNESS PROGRAMS

Health and fitness programs are an important way of not only addressing the personal wellbeing of management and workers but also reinforcing a cultural awareness of the importance of workplace health and safety. These programs include those dealing with negative behaviour, such as smoking, and drug and alcohol abuse, but also those promoting health and fitness, such as gym memberships, corporate sporting teams, professional health assessments and seminars, healthier lifestyle programs (exercise and diet), yoga and Pilates classes, meditation and relaxation techniques, nutritional canteens and the like. Facilities such as quiet rooms, bike parking and exercise areas should also be considered.

There is a huge industry catering to the demand for health and fitness programs. After consulting and assessing the need for programs, careful scrutiny of providers is needed, as well as proper monitoring of their effectiveness.

Your compensation insurer should be advised of programs such as team sports and the use of in-house gym equipment as they may provide some additional risk. Insurers together with suppliers can provide information on how to manage that risk.

MENTAL HEALTH AWARENESS

While physical health and fitness is familiar, an area that is gaining more attention is mental health. For many, mental health problems have a stigma attached and managers and fellow workers may feel uncomfortable dealing with those suffering from them. Illnesses include clinical depression, substance-abuse disorders, anxiety, bipolar disorder and schizophrenia. While trying to manage their problem, sufferers of mental illness may not know how to raise it with others at work. There may be ignorance on both sides, leading to the danger of the workplace actually accelerating mental illness, preventing people from seeking early help or achieving a successful return to work.

In addition to the direct costs to the individual affected, depression, as one example, accounts for six million lost work days per year for Australian businesses.[4] By failing to provide early intervention for employees with mental illness, business loses more than $6.5 billion a year.

As one in five Australians experience a clinically diagnosed mental illness at some time in their lives, many workplaces employ people who are living with mental illness, making it an important issue for employers.[5]

DID YOU KNOW?

About 45 per cent of adult Australians will experience a mental illness, alcohol or substance abuse disorders at some stage in their lives.

Source: Australian Bureau of Statistics, 2008, *National Survey of National Survey of Mental Health and Wellbeing: Summary of Results, 2007.*

Anti-harassment and anti-discrimination policies, together with corporate programs to deal with workplace stress, form the basis for a psychologically healthy workplace, but additional work is needed to help workers with existing illnesses such as anxiety and depression.

It is beyond the scope of this chapter to canvas such a complicated problem except to say that, whether it is considered culture-building or risk management, mental wellbeing should be part of the corporate HS strategy.

With professional assistance, mental illness in the workplace can be handled with informed policies, procedures and training. Making yourself aware of the issues, raising them with others and treating people who experience mental health issues sensitively are first steps. Drawing on specialist resources is the next one (see additional resources below).

Trauma assistance

Occasionally, some employees experience traumatic events in their lives and the effects, both physical and emotional, can be long-lasting. Many experience feelings of anger, guilt, panic, emotional lability, depression and confusion. If the person does not deal with these feelings, they may suffer repercussions that affect personal and work relationships. Sleep, job performance, concentration and stress tolerance can also be affected.

Trauma counsellors can defuse any workplace trauma and counsel the people involved. Sometimes the after-effects are delayed and close liaison with sufferers and the employer can ensure that counselling is made available to people affected in this way (see additional resources below).

DID YOU KNOW?

The Australian Services Union and the Torquay-based Victorian Surf Coast Shire have made the first enterprise collective agreement that allows for an extra 20 days leave for victims of domestic violence. The Surf Coast agreement applies to around 260 council staff and is intended to help victims of family violence hold down a job. The agreement allows for up to 20 days a year of this leave and requires the employer not to breach the privacy of victims. It covers physical, sexual, emotional, financial, verbal or emotional abuse by a family member. The union intends to seek to include the family violence clause in all negotiations with employers.

Employee assistance programs

Employee assistance programs (EAPs) are another way of emphasising human wellbeing and building the health and safety culture. EAPs are short work-based programs designed to assist employees with work-related, health, family, financial or emotional concerns.

EAPs can help deal with issues such as high stress levels, conflict resolution, sexual harassment, violence, absenteeism, high staff turnover, declining productivity and work-related injuries and diseases.

EAPs are provided by professionally qualified counsellors and could include:

- confidential assessment
- short-term counselling or external referral if the person requires ongoing support
- organisational consultancy and training for organisational issues; for example, conflict resolution, change management.

It is estimated that, at any given time, a significant portion of the workplace has personal problems that diminish their productivity. EAPs have the ability to reduce sick leave, compensation claims, grievances, lost time, work-related accidents and associated administration time.

There are many EAP providers and a few are listed in additional resources below.

By now, you will have noticed that we have introduced non-work-related issues, going beyond the workplace to build a culture of human wellbeing. We continue this theme with an overview of the topic of work–life balance.

The term 'work–life balance' suggests that your real life is outside the workplace, when actually work is *part* of your life. This is why work must satisfy our human needs – the core theme of this book. Nevertheless, we use the term because of its widespread use.

BUILDING A WORK–LIFE BALANCE

Most of us – men or women – have home duties, although female workers still bear the brunt of this unpaid work. Home duties involve caring for family members young and old, whether they are fit or ill. We also have training and educational goals, as well as interests we want to maintain, such as hobbies, sports, community and the arts. Finally, we want leisure time with family and friends or simply to be by ourselves. All of these needs apply to the 'Generation X', 'Generation Y' and 'baby-boomers'.

Non-work activities and leisure require time and flexibility. If we can't strike a suitable balance, our work and our lives suffer. Stress levels increase. Other leave entitlements get swallowed up. Absenteeism rises. This is made all the more difficult as we are increasingly working longer hours. One-quarter of full-time workers put in 48 hours or more a week.[6] Health and safety managers have a role in helping to find that balance because of the potential consequences for workers' health if they don't.

It is also a larger economic issue as the workforce ages. To maintain our productivity and standard of living, the labour force as a portion of the total population cannot drop below a certain level – depending on other conditions such as levels of education and technology. One generally unwelcome option is to extend the years at work. For that option to be successful, working conditions must be attractive to attract and retain workers.

Finally, businesses don't want to lose skilled and valuable workers; they want to attract and retain them.

For a variety of reasons, then, organisations must first concern themselves with the total amount of hours worked by individuals; for example, capping the weekly total including overtime to 48 hours is an important beginning. Then employers should consider flexible arrangements such as:

- work-based childcare
- paid parental leave (see below)
- flexible timing of work
- job sharing rather than increasing individual working time
- working from home and telecommuting (though these have disadvantages).
  Other initiatives could include:
- developing support groups
- contracting counselling services
- assisting employees to find suitable childcare and elder-care facilities
- promoting study leave
- making sure holiday leave is used
- enabling people to have career breaks.

With assistance from consultants and professionals such as counsellors, health and safety managers could prepare the groundwork by conducting a survey of the organisation to determine what the issues are and who is affected. The Better Work–Life Balance Survey developed by the Queensland Government is one example.[7] From here, it is a matter of developing a suitable policy and suite of programs.

Paid Parental Leave scheme

Taking time away from work for a new baby is a common part of working life. The Paid Parental Leave scheme helps parents spend more time at home with a new baby, and helps employers keep skilled and valuable staff. It is one part of maintaining a balance between work and life.

In summary, the Paid Parental Leave scheme:

- is government funded
- is for eligible working parents of children born or adopted on or after 1 January 2011
- can be transferred to the other parent
- is paid at the national minimum wage (currently $570 a week before tax)
- is for up to 18 weeks
- can be taken any time within the first year after birth.

The scheme is administered by the federal Family Assistance Office, whose website contains a large amount of information for both employers and parents.[8]

Siobhan Renfrew is based in the University Centre for Staff Learning and Development, which is part of the Directorate of Human Resources, and is the Centre Administrator for external events. She has worked for the university for six years and has two young school-age children. For the past two years she has worked to the Directorate's standard flexi-time scheme. She says, 'Flexi-time does allow me the flexibility to drop off my children at school in the mornings and to have a flexi-day once a month. Flexi-time works well within a supportive team; someone is always in the office between 10 am and 4 pm and team members always take lunch breaks between 12 and 2 pm. Flexi-time has not had any adverse effect on my work'.

Fiona undertakes many activities outside work, one of which is being an adult instructor in the Army Reserve. This means that she attends a one-week annual camp, attends training courses and leads adventure-training groups. The university has allowed her time off to attend these functions within the guidelines of its special leave and other leave policy.

Fiona's flexible working pattern contributes to her Army Reserve activities, and allows her a day each month to catch up on home and family tasks. She says, 'I would quite like to work some sort of compressed hours pattern, taking two half days off rather than one whole day, and will perhaps propose this working arrangement to my line manager in the future after due consideration and planning'. Fiona has benefited from flexi-time and would like to see work–life balance policy information more widely disseminated. She feels it should be mentioned at interview, induction and introduction day. Fiona also successfully undertook an MBA in management, a work-based program, and was supported by her line manager through time off for study and writing reports.

Questions

1 What are the main drivers for Siobhan's use of flexi-time?
2 What factors lead to the success of her arrangements?

MEASURING A HEALTH AND SAFETY CULTURE

TARGET SETTING

We have covered some of the elements of a health and safety culture, dealing with internal as well as external factors. The next step is to measure where the culture stands at any given point. The best method of doing this is to find out what workers at all levels estimate as the health and safety climate.

Climate survey tools have been developed to assess what people think of the health and safety culture in their workplace. Progress is measured using such tools or surveys over periods of time, much like more general employee surveys or perception-mapping tools. A target could be, for example, a percentage improvement of the climate rating.

Climate survey tool

A good example of a climate survey tool is the Health and Safety Climate Survey Tool produced by the UK Health and Safety Executive, a licensed system.[9]

Climate surveys test issues by asking respondents to agree or disagree on a scale of, say, 1 to 5 to statements such as the following.
• I am clear about what my responsibilities are for health and safety.
• I fully understand the health and safety risks associated with the work for which I am responsible.

- I fully understand the health and safety procedures, instructions and rules associated with my job.
- Sometimes I am uncertain about what to do to ensure health and safety in the work for which I am responsible.
- The training I received covered all the health and safety risks associated with the work for which I am responsible.
- Training has given me a clear understanding of all those aspects of my job that are critical to safety.
- People here are consulted to establish their training needs.
  The main areas covered in the HSE climate survey tool are:
- training and competence
- job security and satisfaction
- pressure for production
- communications
- perceptions of personal involvement in health and safety
- accidents, incidents, near-misses
- perception of organisational or management commitment to health and safety (general and specific)
- merits of the health and safety procedures, instructions and rules
- rule breaking
- workforce view on state of safety culture.[10]

Climate survey tools can be bought off the shelf and adapted, or can be specifically constructed by consultants. They may be administered together with employee surveys. Provided they are completed with the required anonymity, they should be effective in letting you know how successful the health and safety culture is and where to make changes and improvements.

In the next and final chapter we look at emerging HS topics.

Summary

- A vibrant health and safety culture focuses on the primacy of human wellbeing.
- A health and safety culture supports a systematic approach to health and safety.
- There are four elements of a safety culture that focus on internal factors: a reporting culture, a just culture, a flexible culture and a learning culture.
- Building a culture sensitive to health could include health and fitness programs, mental health awareness, trauma assistance, employee assistance programs and work–life balance programs.
- The state of a health and safety culture can be measured using climate surveys.

In your workplace

Your firm, a medium-sized light engineering firm on the outskirts of a major regional centre, has experienced a similar number of incidents from year to year. Efforts to establish the reasons for the rate seem frustrated. Each time things are fixed up in one section, an incident will take place in another. From what the insurer tells you, your performance is well below standard for the type of business you carry out.

You have heard about the importance of a positive safety culture and think that this may be the element missing. But you are not too sure and the budget is tight. The insurer offers you some in-house assistance to develop a climate survey tool. Before you take up the offer, you want to make sure you understand what it means and whether it works.

Your marketing manager tells you about the free tool 'SurveyMonkey™' so you decide to try it and to call in the insurer if it doesn't work.

1   How would you develop a climate survey? (To start, go to www.surveymonkey.com or search for similar tools on the Internet. The New Zealand Department of Labour provides one at http://www.osh.dol.govt.nz/resources/tools/scs/scs-2.shtml.)
2   How would you 'road test' it? What steps would you take?
3   What sorts of graphics would you use to illustrate the findings?

Questions

1   Define what a health and safety culture is and state how it differs from the health and safety climate.
2   How does a health and safety culture support a systematic approach?
3   How would you describe your own organisation's health and safety culture using Reason's four elements?
    a   What does your organisation do well and what could be improved?
    b   What steps would you take to improve your organisation's HS culture?
4   What is the work–life balance in your organisation? What are its strengths and weaknesses? How would you improve it?
5   'A well-run WHS program has no need of an employee assistance program.' Discuss.
6   Do you think pay incentives for improved WHS performance would build a stronger health and safety culture? Provide reasons.

Activities

1   Select any one of Reason's four elements of a safety culture and demonstrate how it could be built within your workplace.
2   Find three providers of health and fitness programs that are suitable for your workplace and do an initial assessment against the criteria of quality (fit for purpose), service, price and timing (availability).
3   Develop a survey to assess the need for greater work–life balance in your workplace.

Search me!

▶ Search me! 👆

Explore **Search me! management** for relevant articles on health and safety culture. Search me! is an online library of world-class journals, ebooks and newspapers, including *The Australian* and the *New York Times*, and is updated daily. Log in to Search me! through www.cengage.com/sso using the access card in the front of this book.

KEYWORDS

Try searching for the following terms:

▶ workplace culture
▶ trauma counselling
▶ workplace health and fitness programs
▶ workplace health and safety climate
▶ workplace mental health
▶ work–life balance

Search tip: **Search me! management** contains information from both local and international sources. To get the greatest number of search results, try using both Australian and American spellings in your searches, e.g. 'globalisation' and 'globalization'; 'organisation' and 'organization'.

Additional resources

- Bohle, P., 2003, Work–life conflict, in *Master OHS and Environment Guide 2003*, CCH: Sydney.
- Hopkins, A., 2000, *Lessons from Longford: The Esso Gas Plant Explosion*, CCH: Sydney.
- Hopkins, A., 2005, *Safety, Culture and Risk: The Organisational Causes of Disasters*, CCH: Sydney.
- Hopkins, A., 2007, *Lessons from Gretley: Mindful Leadership and the Law*, CCH: Sydney.
- Hopkins, A., 2008, *Failure to Learn: The BP Texas City Refinery Disaster*, CCH: Sydney.
- Pocock, B., 2003, *The Work/Life Collision: What Work is Doing to Australians and What to Do About it*, Federation Press: Sydney.
- Reason, J., 1997, *Managing the Risks of Organizational Accidents*, Ashgate: Aldershot, UK. Reason provides a psychologist's perspective on the origins and prevention of industrial accidents.
- Schein, E., 1992, *Organisational Culture and Leadership*, 2nd edn, Jossey-Bass: San Francisco. This book makes a good attempt at defining the concept of culture, one of the most difficult things to define.
- Organisations providing help for those suffering from mental illness include beyondblue (www.beyondblue.org.au) and the Black Dog Institute (http://www.blackdoginstitute.org.au/). Organisations providing trauma assistance are Startts (www.startts.org.au) and the Trauma Centre Australia (www.traumacentre.com.au). Psychological counsellors are a good source of information and advice as well. The Australian Psychological Society (www.psychology.org.au) can help you find providers.
- The website of the Employee Assistance Professional Association of Australia (www.eapaa.org.au) can assist you in locating providers.
- The work–life balance issue will play an increasingly large role as the ageing of the population increases its hold on the workplace, and businesses press for precarious employment and extended working weeks. For a better understanding of the many issues involved see the Australian Work and Life Index (AWALI), a national survey of work–life outcomes among working Australians. The AWALI commenced in 2007 and has been repeated annually by the Centre for Work + Life at the University of South Australia in partnership with the SA and WA governments (www.unisa.edu.au/hawkeinstitute/cwl/projects/awali.asp).
- The National Safety Council of Australia has developed its own climate survey tool and administers it for organisations. See http://www.nsca.org.au/Programs__Products_Directory/OHS_Programs__Products/Safety_Climate_Survey.aspx.

Endnotes

1   This section draws on the work of James Reason in his book *Managing the Risks of Organizational Accidents* (1997, Ashgate: Aldershot, UK).

2   Reason, 1997, p. 196.

3   Senge, P.M., 1990, *The Fifth Discipline: The Art and Practice of the Learning Organization*, Century Business: London.

4   Hickie, I., Groom, G. & Davenport, T., 2004, *Investing in Australia's Future: The Personal,*

Social and Economic Benefits of Good Mental Health. Mental Health Council of Australia: Canberra.

5 Australian Institute of Health and Welfare, 2006, *Australia's Health 2006*, AIHW: Canberra, p. 97.

6 UniSA, 2010, Balancing work and life not getting any easier, media release, 3 August 2010, http://www.unisa.edu.au/news/2010/030810.asp.

7 See http://www.justice.qld.gov.au/fair-and-safe-work/industrial-relations/work-family-and-lifestyle/better-work-life-balance-survey2.

8 See http://www.familyassist.gov.au/payments/family-assistance-payments/paid-parental-leave-scheme/.

9 See www.hse.gov.uk.

10 The New Zealand Department of Labour has produced a (free) version of a climate safety tool. See http://www.osh.dol.govt.nz/resources/tools/scs/scs-2.shtml.

18

TOPICAL ISSUES

Learning Objectives

At the end of this chapter, the reader should be able to:

- appreciate the impact of the following contemporary issues on health and safety in the workplace and approaches to them:
  - climate change
  - nanotechnology
  - behaviour-based safety programs
  - corporate reporting.

INTRODUCTION

As we noted in Chapter 1, many external factors affect an organisation's health and safety performance: changes in law, politics, the environment, the community, research, the economy, technology, and so on. In this chapter, we look at some of the recent effects of those changes on HS performance in terms of the key issues of climate change, nanotechnology, behaviour-based safety strategies, and corporate reporting and accountability. We also look at some of the best ways of dealing with them.

CLIMATE CHANGE[1]

Climate change brings increased weather extremes resulting in fires, floods, violent storms and heatwaves, all of which can affect the workplace.

The WHS Act states that 'a person conducting a business or undertaking must ensure, so far as is reasonably practicable … the provision and maintenance of a work environment without risks to health and safety'. (s. 19(3)(a)) It is therefore a duty of PCBUs to address the weather extremes associated with climate change.

EMERGENCY PROCEDURES

Organisations have to factor the increased risk of fires, floods and storms into their emergency procedures. For example, if your workplace is near the bush or your workers work in areas prone to bushfires, procedures have to be put in place that incorporate warnings from public authorities such as the Bureau of Meteorology, put workers on alert and provide them with appropriate advice, such as how to evacuate their workplaces and where to go. Your organisation should already have these arrangements in place. However, they will need to be reviewed to see whether they are suited to any heightened risk. Drills and training may need to be changed or upgraded.

Similarly, if you are in a flood plain where the risk of sudden inundation is present, a review of your procedures is needed. Violent storms such as cyclones, wind gusts and hail also need to be recognised as hazards that may pose more risk than in the past. Such hazards will become more frequent and severe, so precautionary measures have to be heightened. Advice should be sought from public authorities such as state emergency and fire services, as well as building consultants.

AREAS OF INCREASED RISK

Heat: working indoors

Extremes of heat will be more common. In the case of working indoors, proper ventilation and air-cooling is needed just to make the workplace comfortable as much as avoiding heat stress.

Indoor air circulation and cooling is dealt with in AS 1668.2 *The use of ventilation and air conditioning in buildings* and readers are referred to it for technical details. The key aspects to focus on are the appropriate temperature range for the seasons, the rate at which air needs to be refreshed and the requirement for regular maintenance to prevent diseases such as legionnaires' disease.

Heat: working out of doors

Dealing with heat stress outdoors is, in part, addressed by codes such as Safe Work Australia's draft code of practice *Managing the Work Environment and Facilities* (December 2010) from which the following is extracted.

4.1 OUTDOOR WORK

Outdoor workers need to have access to shelter for eating meals and taking breaks, and to protect them in adverse weather conditions.

You should provide access to shelter such as sheds, caravans, tents, windbreaks or portable shade canopies. In some situations, vehicles or public facilities may provide appropriate short-term shelter.

You should also provide protection against solar ultraviolet (UV) exposure, for example by:

- reorganising outdoor work if possible so that workers carry out alternative tasks, or work in shade, when the sun is most intense; that is, between 10.00 am and 2.00 pm (11.00 am and 3.00 pm when there is daylight saving), and
- providing personal protective clothing (wide brim hat, long-sleeved collared shirt, long pants, sunglasses) and sunscreen.

Source: Safe Work Australia, 2010, *Managing the Work Environment and Facilities*, Draft code of practice, p. 21, http://www.safeworkaustralia.gov.au.

With extremes of hot weather, workers performing duties out of doors will need to know how to deal with heat stress – generally agreed to become an issue at about 26°C but possibly lower for certain individuals in certain conditions.

Workers must know

- what the consequences of heat stress are: stroke, dehydration, cramps, exhaustion, rashes, as well as increased risks of injury through fatigue and exhaustion
- what the safe limits are for working in hot conditions: temperature and duration
- what are the steps to take: rostering, rest breaks, stop work, hydrating
- what specific equipment and facilities must be used.

As there are many different sorts of outdoor workplaces and outdoor activities, safe working conditions will vary. Professional health care providers such as occupational physicians are your best source of advice as they can assess the specific conditions workers find themselves in and prescribe proper controls. Industrial agreements may give some additional guidance, provided they are based on sound medical advice.[2] The following is extracted from Sports Medicine Australia's policy.

STRATEGIES FOR REDUCING THE RISK OF HEAT ILLNESS (GENERAL POPULATION)

Heat exhaustion

- Characterised by a high heart rate, dizziness, headache, loss of endurance/skill/confusion and nausea.
- The skin may still be cool/sweating, but there will be signs of developing vasoconstriction (eg, pale colour).
- The rectal temperature may be up to 40°C and the athlete may collapse on stopping activity. Rectal temperature should only bne measured by a doctor or nurse.

To avoid heat exhaustion, if people feel unwell during exercise they should immediately cease activity and rest. Further benefit comes if the rest is in a shaded area with some passing breeze (from a fan if necessary) and the person takes extra hydration. Misting or spraying with water can also help.

Heat stroke

- Characteristics are similar to heat exhaustion but with a dry skin, confusion and collapse.
- Heat stroke may arise in an athlete who has not been identified as suffering from heat exhaustion and has persisted in further activity.
- Core temperature measured in the rectum is the only reliable diagnosis of a collapsed athlete to determine heat stroke.

    This is a potentially fatal condition and must be treated immediately. It should be assumed that any collapsed athlete is at danger of heat stroke. The best first aid measures are "Strip/Soak/Fan":
    - strip off any excess clothing;
    - soak with water;
    - fan;
    - ice placed in groin and armpits is also helpful.

    The aim is to reduce body temperature as quickly as possible. The athlete should immediately be referred for treatment by a medical professional.

    Important: heat exhaustion/stroke can still occur even in the presence of good hydration.

Dehydration

Dehydration is fluid loss which occurs during exercise, mainly due to perspiration and respiration. It makes an athlete more susceptible to fatigue and muscle cramps. Inadequate fluid replacement before, during and after exercise will lead to excessive dehydration and may lead to heat exhaustion and heat stroke.

To avoid dehydration, SMA recommends that:

- athletes drink approximately 500 mls (2 glasses) in the 2 hours prior to exercise;
- during exercise longer than 60 minutes, 2-3 cups (500-700ml) of cool water or sports drink are sufficient for most sports.
- after exercise replenish your fluid deficit to ensure that you are fully rehydrated, but not over-hydrated.
- refer to SMA's free DRINK UP brochure available as a web download at http://www.smartplay.com.au or from your local National Pharmacies store.

Points to consider:

- Will your players and officials be able to consume enough water during the event?
- Even a small degree of dehydration will cause a decrease in performance.
- Take care not to over-hydrate. Drinking too much fluid can lead to a dangerous condition known as hyponatraemia (low blood sodium). Aim to drink enough to replace lost fluids, but not more than that.

Source: Sports Medicine Australia, Hot Weather Guidelines, pp. 2–3, http://sma.org.au/wp-content/uploads/2009/05/hotweather-guidelines-web-download-doc-2007.pdf. © 2009 Copyright of Sports Medicine Australia, http://sma.org.au.

Green jobs

Climate change also brings with it so-called 'green jobs' and industries, none of which are without risk to workers and others. This was shown with the federal government's home insulation program. Designed to make homes more energy efficient, the program resulted in fires and four fatalities due to shonky installation practices and light regulation.

Industries such as waste management and recycling will be affected by efforts to make the economy sustainable. They are also some of the most dangerous industries as garbage collectors and scrapyard workers well know.

Recycling can involve electronic waste ('e-waste'), which is a hazard in itself. Lead, cadmium, beryllium, mercury and brominated flame retardants are known hazards and can increase risk with the recycling or dumping of computers and older technology.

Efforts to make our buildings more energy efficient by retrofitting also exposes workers to asbestos and lead. Installing solar panels on rooftops comes with the risk of falls and UV radiation. Energy-efficient compact fluorescent lamps contain mercury, posing a potential danger to workers as well as the environment. There is risk of contact allergies and dermatitis at plants manufacturing wind-turbine blades using epoxy-resin-based plastics. New cleaner sources of energy such as tidal, biomass and geothermal will bring with them a range of workplace hazards that we are just beginning to appreciate.

Of course, we need to stem and reverse climate change – urgently. We have no other option. Rather, this is a reminder that in the rush to put the planet on a sound environmental footing, we should not neglect the precautionary principle that lies at the heart of health and safety. In short, a green job should be a safe and healthy job.

NANOTECHNOLOGY[3]

Health and safety are directly affected by developments in technology and nanotechnology is a good example of where WHS has to play catch-up.

Nanotechnology is the precision engineering of materials at the scale of 10^{-9} metres (one billionth of a metre), at which point unique properties occur. Carbon nanotubes are a modern-day 'miracle' material. Frequently described as '100 times stronger than steel and six times lighter', carbon nanotubes are also incredibly good conductors of electricity. They are used in growing numbers of electronics, reinforced plastics, specialty building materials and sports goods manufactured internationally. They are touted for future use in capacitors, pharmaceuticals, solar cells and in defence applications. They are already in use in sunscreens, cosmetics and some food products.

AREAS OF INCREASED RISK

Manufactured nanomaterial has also led to concerns about the health and safety of people exposed to it, such as workers in the industry and consumers. There are reports of links between products containing manufactured nanomaterial and damage to DNA and chromosomes, as well as lung diseases. There is increasing alarm that such tiny particles could one way or another 'cross over' into the human body with toxic effects, making it comparable to asbestos. While we've always been exposed to naturally occurring nanoparticles, we have never been exposed to specifically manufactured nanoparticles; for example, to influence food properties.[4]

Many groups have raised concerns here in Australia where nanotechnology is already established. Nanotubes are handled in laboratories across Australia, where research, administrative, cleaning and maintenance staff face potential exposure.[5]

The debate over the safety of nanotechnology is carried out with contending sets of values: roughly, those that prize innovation and productivity over social responsibility and those that prize the safety of workers and the community first. The precautionary principle favoured by the latter would restrict the nanotechnology industry to further research until we can be assured that it could work to our benefit and not endanger our lives. This would appear to be supported by the WHS Act.

DUTY OF CARE

Section 19 of the Act says that 'a person conducting a business or undertaking must ensure, so far as is reasonably practicable, the health and safety of … workers … [and] other persons is not put at risk from work carried out as part of the conduct of the business or undertaking … [including] … the safe use, handling, storage and transport of plant, structures and *substances*' (our emphasis).

Sections 22–25 of the Act, which deals with the duties of designers, manufacturers, importers and suppliers of substances, state that they must ensure, so far as is reasonably practicable, that the substance is without risks to the health and safety of persons at a workplace. Further the '[designer, manufacturer, importer, supplier] must carry out, or arrange the carrying out of, any calculations, analysis, testing or examination that may be necessary for the performance of the duty … and … the [designer, manufacturer, importer, supplier] must give adequate information to each person to whom the [designer, manufacturer, importer, supplier] provides the … substance'.

In light of these comprehensive duties and the concerns raised about nanotechnology, two questions should be asked: what is being done to assist duty-holders in respect to nanotechnology products and what are duty-holders doing themselves to fulfil their responsibilities?

What is being done to assist duty-holders?

Safe Work Australia is supporting development of a nationally coordinated approach to promoting workplace safety in the use of nanotechnology. There are five focus areas in the Nanotechnology Work Health and Safety Program:

* ensuring that the Australian WHS regulatory framework can effectively protect workers from the potential health and safety impacts of nanotechnologies
* improving understanding of the hazardous properties of engineered nanomaterials
* developing nanoparticle measurement capability
* understanding the effectiveness of workplace controls
* providing support for nanotechnology organisations.[6]

It has been noted that labels and MSDSs do not provide sufficient information on the presence and potential danger of products containing nanomaterials.

NICNAS has prepared a *Guidance for Notifiers Handbook* detailing the requirements for the notification of new industrial nanomaterials.[7]

The Australian Government has also developed a National Enabling Technologies Strategy (NETS) to provide a 'framework for the responsible development of enabling technologies such as nanotechnology and other new technologies as they emerge in Australia'.[8] Australia is also closely involved in the international effort to develop reliable techniques and benchmarks for exposure measurement.

Such initiatives sound reassuring, but so far the picture is unclear about what, if anything, is dangerous about the nanotechnology industry and, if dangerous, what we should do about it.

What are duty-holders doing about nanotechnology?

Has the nanotechnology industry carried out any calculations, analysis, testing or examination necessary to ensure that it provides substances without risks to the health and safety of persons at a workplace and gives adequate information to each person to whom it provides the substance?

Readers can judge for themselves, and if they find the answer in the negative, ask themselves if any legal proceedings have been initiated. The picture is less reassuring.

For those not in the nanotechnology industry, what are employers (PCBUs) doing to ensure their primary duty of care to workers is being met? Are supplied products or substances being checked for nanotechnology content? This is admittedly difficult without suppliers being able to give you this information. Nevertheless, the duty of ensuring a safe workplace as far as reasonably practicable does not go away.

What the case of nanotechnology, and others such as asbestos, show is that the precautionary principle requires law but also strong institutions, not just defensive groups such as activists, unions and regulators but businesses that have the strength to take their social responsibilities seriously. Until then, workplace safety is not assured.

BEHAVIOUR-BASED SAFETY PROGRAMS

WHS is influenced by psychological research into behaviour, and this can be seen in the development and spread of behaviour-based safety programs.

Behavioural safety, or behaviour-based safety (BBS), is the name given to programs that aim to improve safety by changing the behaviour of workers. BBS programs focus on the unsafe act that immediately led to an accident. They enlist frontline staff trained in techniques to look for 'critical behaviours' and ensure our workplace behaviour is safe, and then provide feedback. A set of 'model behaviours' is constructed by workers and they, in turn, measure their current and past behaviour by these models.

This is a clear application of behavioural psychology, using the notion of positive and negative feedback, or conditioning, to explain actions or behaviours.

Supporters of BBS claim that it has reduced accident rates significantly and go on to provide statistical evidence for this. The famous DuPont safety program (STOP™, Safety Training Observation Program) is a BBS program and finds support among many firms in Australia – Qantas, Queensland Rail and BlueScope, for example – although its application can take slightly different forms.

BBS programs are attractive on a number of other scores:

- The language the programs use – like 'watch', 'talk', 'do' – is not overly technical, when terms like 'risk assessment' and the 'hierarchy of controls' can appear abstract.
- Not only the wording but also the explanation is straightforward. Unsafe acts are indeed part of the causal chain leading to many accidents. Stop them and you stop the accident. What could be simpler?
- The programs fit with the common understanding that safety is everyone's responsibility and all of us must play a part. And so, the programs appear to empower workers auditing themselves.

- The programs use important motivators such as peer recognition and reward as ways to promote safe behaviour.
- The programs claim to fit in with other programs such as hazard identification and risk assessment and control. They are seen to be part of the package.

DID YOU KNOW?

In its March 2004 research report titled *Irresponsible Care*, the US Public Interest Research Group, a non-profit, non-partisan public-interest advocacy group, analysed data compiled by the National Response Centre (NRC), the sole national point of contact for reporting oil or chemical discharges into the environment. The NRC database includes every accident and incident reported to the agency. For the time period of 1990–2003, DuPont ranked third overall in accidents with 2115 – nearly 150 a year.[9]

CRITICISM OF BBS PROGRAMS

For the reasons outlined above and others, many employers are attracted to WHS behaviour-based programs. However, the programs have been criticised by WHS professionals, managers and unions for the following reasons.

- The statistics showing success have been challenged for their accuracy and the baseline used to compare any improvements. What other programs were organisations using at the time of introducing BBS? A simple before-and-after analysis has to take into account other factors that may have changed. Secondly, were any improvements sustained or have they plateaued? Why have the programs been dropped on some occasions?
- BBS focuses firstly on accidents and breakdowns – usually repeatable events not complex events with multiple causes. One of the main proponents of behavioural safety is oil company BP (think Texas City oil-refinery explosion in which 15 were killed). BBS also doesn't include the contraction of illnesses, both physical (for example, occupational cancer) or psychological (stress resulting from workload).
- BBS focuses downstream on the unsafe event preceding the accident. The spotlight is limited and can crowd out the standard approach to risk management, using the hierarchy of control. Why is the worker acting unsafely? What is the situation in the workplace? Is it inherently dangerous? What about the actions of management?
- BBS is time-consuming and costly to develop, implement and maintain. A lot of ongoing training, supervision and auditing is needed, the costs of which may be used more profitably elsewhere in your WHS budget.

In short, BBS has firm supporters and critics. The debate is ongoing as there are different schemes.

Changing safety behaviour

Should we stop trying to change safety behaviour? Certainly not. Reinforcing safe ways of working is absolutely critical and helps build a safety culture. Proper supervision, training and information for workers are key parts of any attempt to management of health and safety. We can also change behaviour with a strong HS culture, having management show commitment, introducing a just culture and through consultation with workers and their representatives.

However, changing behaviour is not a substitute for removing or controlling the risk. That must be the priority, and hazard control must be based on risk assessment.

If you are approached by a company offering behaviour-based WHS programs – they can come in many shapes and sizes – show them your policy, describe your system, ask lots of questions and research the supplier. Learn more about such programs.[10] If the company can demonstrate that what they are offering fits your needs and is independently capable of being shown to be value for money, then maybe it is worth a closer look by management and the health and safety committee, if you have one.

CORPORATE REPORTING[11]

WHS has been affected by the development of community standards and the requirement of organisations to act as socially responsible corporate citizens. Internationally, this is represented by the Global Reporting Initiative, a network-based organisation that supports disclosure on environmental, social and governance performance.[12] Sustainability reporting is an important feature of many company reports these days, though it is often practised in a wide variety of forms, good and bad, and can include a lot of 'greenwash'.

The other factor at play is socially responsible investing (SRI) and the growth of SRI funds looking to invest in and support private companies doing the right thing by the environment, the community and workers. Individuals and funds look to corporate reporting to tell them where to find such companies. People do not want to invest when the information is inadequate, unclear or not there at all. One of the things they want to see are annual reports in which such information, including WHS performance, can be found readily. For this purpose, WHS reporting must be relevant, valid, comparable and reliable.

RELEVANCE OF WHS REPORTING

Information is relevant when it is useful to the intended recipients. Surveys of stakeholders show that they want information on governance, processes and outcomes.

WHS governance

Management commitments can sound like motherhood statements unless it comes up with detail such as:

* oversight by a board of directors (for example, operation of a HS subcommittee)
* the integration of WHS in corporate strategy

- the role and enforcement of WHS policy
- identification of the major HS risks or hazards
- structures for employee consultation.

WHS processes

WHS processes are the programs and activities used to manage risk and promote wellbeing. They include positive or process indicators (lead indicators), reflecting the hierarchy of control, such as:

- worker consultation – meetings held, membership
- WHS risk assessment – numbers carried out
- monitoring of health exposures to chemical, environmental and medical risks, as well as results
- WHS training – numbers trained
- WHS audit non-conformances
- incident analysis.

WHS outcomes

Severity-based measures of WHS outcomes are wanted by most stakeholders. These include the:

- number of work-related fatalities
- number of permanent disabilities (medical discharge)
- number and rate of permanent disability (return to work)
- number and rate of long-term (more than 6 months) temporary disability
- rate of medium-term temporary disability (2 weeks to 6 months)
- rate of short-term temporary disability (up to 2 weeks).
  Other outcome measure should include:
- *productivity-based measures* of HS outcomes; that is, lost-time and recordable injury rates, accident costs
- *expenditure measures*, such as compensation costs and fines
- *contravention statistics.*

  HS outcomes such as fatality numbers, injury rates and cost data should be presented using a scorecard, tables or precise and unambiguous graphs that can clearly communicate key performance data.

VALIDITY OF WHS REPORTING

When presenting relevant information in WHS reports, ensure that the information can be understood by report users. This requires metrics to be valid in that they must measure what they purport to measure. A glossary in the report is a useful tool for achieving valid and understandable data. An example of a glossary term is 'total recordable case frequency rate (TRCFR)' and the definition might be 'calculated as the total number of recordable cases (medical treatment injuries and lost-time injuries) per million hours worked'.

COMPARABILITY OF WHS REPORTING

WHS data must be comparable across both time and entities. Comparability over time requires that firms report on consistent indicators from one period to another. Comparability across entities requires that different firms measure outcomes in a consistent manner and present a shared set of accepted performance indicators.

RELIABILITY OF WHS REPORTING

For information to be reliable it must be accurate (free from error) and presented in a balanced and impartial manner (free from bias). This means data must be complete, with KPIs consistently presented from year to year and not only in those years when results are most favourable.

The following is an example of a checklist for WHS reporting in annual reports, taken from the WHS Reporting Award section of the Australasian Reporting Awards scheme.

CHECKLIST FOR WHS REPORTING IN ANNUAL REPORTS

The overall purpose of the Australasian Reporting Awards is to improve the business practices of organisations and foster the development of organisational cultures that will support them – by way of open and honest reporting in all areas about what has happened, good and bad, and what the organisation has done, or plans to do, to avoid any repetition of negative outcomes in the future.

OH&S Management

The annual report should:

- Express a clear commitment by the organisation to OH&S
- Demonstrate that OH&S is embedded in general management systems
- Outline key OH&S objectives and/or specific strategies
- Record future OH&S targets
- Record the resources allocated to OH&S
- Address, where appropriate, specific OH&S issues
- Provide evidence of consultation with employees regarding OH&S
- Address, where appropriate, the OH&S management of contractors.

OH&S Performance

The annual report should:

- Provide both negative and positive OH&S key performance indicators
- Where a fatality is recorded, the company's response and preventive actions should be detailed
- Compare the current year's OH&S performance with that of previous years and/or against industry benchmarks
- Record details of OH&S training
- Where appropriate, record the outcomes of any OH&S audits and follow-up actions
- Where appropriate, record any regulatory interventions, including prosecutions and subsequent actions taken by the organisation.

Independent Verification

The annual report should:

• Record the results, where appropriate, of any internal audits and the follow-up by the corporation

• Record any OH&S awards or certificates the organisation has received

• Provide details, where appropriate, of the organisation's contribution to improving OH&S within its industry.

Continuous Improvement

The annual report should:

• Provide details of any OH&S innovations

• Where appropriate, give examples of a problem-solving, consultative approach to creating solutions for identified OH&S issues

• Demonstrate that the organisation has kept abreast of OH&S best practice in its industry.

Presentation

The annual report should:

• Be written in clear, succinct and user-friendly language

• Be easy to navigate

• Highlight the importance of health and safety in its structure and content.

Source: Australasian Reporting Awards, Occupational Health & Safety Reporting Award, http://www.arawards.com.au/index.php/eng/Criteria/Criteria-Applicable-to-Special-Awards-for-Excellence/Occupational-Health-Safety-Reporting-Award.

The following case study focuses on the workplace health and safety section of the Australian Electoral Commission's 2008–09 annual report.

CASE STUDY

AEC ANNUAL REPORT 2008–09

The AEC is committed to promoting, maintaining and ensuring the health, safety and welfare at work of its employees. The AEC provides an annual report on its occupational health and safety (OHS) performance in accordance with s. 74 of the *Occupational Health and Safety Act 1991* (OHS Act).

POLICIES

In 2008–09, the AEC developed and implemented the following policies:

• Managing Attendance Policy

• Workplace Bullying Policy and Guidelines

• Working in Remote Localities Policy and Guidelines.

The OHS and Injury Management Plan 2008–10 was also implemented to guide and monitor the AEC's OHS performance.

HEALTH AND SAFETY ACTIVITIES

The OHS and Injury Management Plan 2008–10 sets out the AEC's OHS objectives and responsibilities. The plan allows the AEC to track its performance in OHS and injury prevention and management across the organisation.

The AEC remains focused on timely and effective injury management, including early intervention strategies to return AEC employees to work, in accordance with Comcare legislation and AEC policies and guidelines. The AEC also continues to implement health promotion strategies to improve the health and wellbeing of staff.

In 2008–09, to ensure the health, safety and welfare of employees:

- The National OHS Committee met three times, to provide reports and recommendations to consultative forums and strategic committees on health and safety matters of national relevance.
- State OHS committees met regularly to discuss and manage local health and safety issues. Minutes of the OHS committees were made available to all employees through the AEC intranet.
- AEC employees in the Organisational Health area attended Comcare client network meetings and conferences to keep up to date with developments in OHS and rehabilitation case management.
- Under its preventive health strategy, the AEC provided a national influenza vaccination program for staff in April and May 2009.
- The AEC provided current advice to staff on the H1N1 Influenza virus and took appropriate measures to minimise the risk of the virus spreading.
- The AEC provided an Employee Assistance Program for all staff.
- The AEC engaged a service provider to deliver ergonomic workstation assessment services. The service provider is available to conduct specified assessments at any AEC location in Australia, for new employees or those who are experiencing injury or discomfort.
- The AEC participated in Safe Work Week 2008, promoted by the Australian Safety and Compensation Council, and arranged for a hazard inspection to be undertaken in all AEC offices.

HEALTH AND SAFETY OUTCOMES

As a result of the AEC's ongoing commitment and 2008–09 initiatives:

- Incident reports were managed in a timely manner, allowing early intervention support for staff with injuries.
- Early intervention resulted in reduced time off work for new claims during 2008–09 and contributed to a significant reduction in the AEC's estimated Comcare premium for 2009–10.

COMCARE PREMIUMS

Table 1. Comcare premiums, 2006–07 to 2009–10

	2006–07 (actual)	2007–08 (actual)	2008–09 (actual)	2009–10 (actual)
Annual premium ($)	714 102	1 009 573	1 001 648	360 260

The AEC's actual and estimated Comcare premiums for four financial years are included in Table 1.

The Comcare premium for 2009–10 is estimated to be $360 260. This represents a decrease in the premium rate from 1.49 per cent of payroll in 2008–09 to 0.95 per cent of payroll in 2009–10.

CLAIMS MANAGEMENT

The Human Resources Strategy and Development Section manages compensation and non-compensable claims. An external provider performs rehabilitation and case management services for approximately 15–20 hours per week.

COMPENSATION CLAIMS

In 2008–09, the AEC managed 55 compensation claims, of which nine were new claims. This is a significant reduction in the number of claims managed in 2007–08, as shown in Table 2. Mental stress and body stressing claims resulted in the highest levels of lost time.

Table 2. New Comcare claims, 2005–06 to 2008–09

	2005–06	2006–07	2007–08	2008–09
New claims	14	27	28	9

NON-COMPENSABLE CASES

In 2008–09, the AEC managed 30 non-compensable cases, including fitness for continued duty assessments, invalidity retirement, and rehabilitation and counselling support. This number was significantly higher than in 2007–08, when 12 non-compensable cases were managed by the AEC.

INCIDENT STATISTICS

As shown in Table 3, the number of incident reports in 2008–09 was considerably lower than in 2007–08.

Table 3. Accident and incident reports, 2005–06 to 2008–09

	2005–06	2006–07	2007–08	2008–09
Accidents/incidents reported	41	86	140	45
Dangerous occurrences	36	85	126	39

INVESTIGATIONS, DIRECTIONS AND NOTICES

There were no investigations under s. 41 of the OHS Act. No notices or directions were issued pursuant to sections 29, 46 or 47 of the OHS Act.

Questions

1 Which features of this report would you consider key?
2 Are there any features missing from this report?

Source: Australian Electoral Commission, Appendix C – Occupational health and safety, *AEC Annual Report 2008–09*, http://www.aec.gov.au/About_AEC/Publications/Annual_Reports/2009/append_c.htm. © Commonwealth of Australia 2009.

Summary

- Health and safety in your workplace is affected by new developments such as climate change, technological development (nanotechnology), psychological research (behaviour-based safety) and changing community standards (corporate reporting).
- The health and safety manager needs to be aware of such developments, the issues they pose and what steps to take.
- Climate change requires a review of emergency procedures, working in hot conditions and the recognition that green jobs will raise old and new problems for health and safety.
- The risks posed by nanotechnology have not been properly assessed and duty-holders must exercise the precautionary principle.
- Behaviour-based safety programs can undermine proper risk assessment and the hierarchy of controls. They should only be used when that threat to WHS is eliminated.
- Modern-day WHS corporate reporting must be significantly improved if it is to meet heightened community standards for greater corporate accountability.

In your workplace

The boss has heard that behavioural safety is the way to go with WHS. At a recent conference she went to a lecture from someone promoting the DuPont STOP program and how it had led to a dramatic drop in the accident rate. Your boss wants you to investigate a number of companies that supply BBS programs to see if they can help improve your company's health and safety performance.

1 How would you approach this task?
2 What steps would you take?
3 How would you assess the proposed solutions?

Questions

1 The issue of environmental sustainability is broader than greenhouse gas emissions and climate change. What other issues does it raise for HS in the workplace?
2 How does the precautionary principle apply to nanotechnology?
3 Many unions complain that BBS is an attempt to shift the responsibility for WHS from management to the worker. Is this fair?
4 Assuming you are (or would like to be) a socially responsible investor, what key WHS data would you look for in a company annual report?

Activities

1 Examine your organisation's or company's heat stress and emergency procedures to see whether they need to be changed. Prepare a set of recommended improvements.
2 Check if your organisation or company uses nanomaterials and what its policy is. If this is too difficult, find out whether you or your family uses nanotechnology products. (Use the website http://www.nanotechproject.org/inventories/consumer/.)
3 If your organisation uses a BBS program, find out how successful it has been and how any success was measured. Alternatively, find a supplier of BBS programs and ask them for details about how they have measured success.
4 Read the section of the BHP Sustainability Report that discusses worker safety and assess it against the recommendations set out in this chapter. For 2010, see page 9, http://www.bhpbilliton.com/bbContentRepository/docs/bhpBillitonSustainabilityReport2010.pdf.

Search me!

Explore **Search me! management** for relevant articles on emerging issues in health and safety. Search me! is an online library of world-class journals, ebooks and newspapers, including *The Australian* and the *New York Times*, and is updated daily. Log in to Search me! through www.cengage.com/sso using the access card in the front of this book.

KEYWORDS

Try searching for the following terms:
▶ work and climate change ▶ behaviour-based safety programs
▶ nanotechnology ▶ health and safety annual reporting

Search tip: **Search me! management** contains information from both local and international sources. To get the greatest number of search results, try using both Australian and American spellings in your searches, e.g. 'globalisation' and 'globalization'; 'organisation' and 'organization'.

Additional resources

• A useful background paper on the warming climate can be found at http://www.australasianscience.com.au/article/issue-december-2010/heat-stress-warming-world.html.
• WorkSafe Victoria's *Guidance Note: Working in Heat* is available at http://www.worksafe.vic.gov.au/wps/wcm/connect/2c0293804071f64baf35ffe1fb554c40/guidance+working+in+heat4b.pdf?MOD=AJPERES.
• At the time of writing, SWA was preparing material on nanotechnology. Many websites deal with nanotechnology. The Queensland Government has a good website at www.deir.qld.gov.au/workplace/subjects/nanotechnology/index.htm. See also the Health and Safety

Executive (UK) at http://www.hse.gov.uk/nanotechnology/index.htm?ebul=hsegen&cr=8/31-jan-11.

- For one side of the debate on nanotechnology, go to the Australia Institute's website at https://www.tai.org.au/index.php?q=node%2F19&act=display&type=1&pubid=703.
- For those concerned about nanotechnology-based consumer products, the Nanotechnology Project website has information. See http://www.nanotechproject.org/inventories/consumer/.
- See the article by Andrew Hopkins 'What are we to make of safe behaviour programs?' at http://www.efcog.org/wg/ism_pmi/docs/Safety_Culture/Hopkins_what_are_we_to_make_of_safe_behavior_programs.pdf.
- The checklist for WHS reporting can be found at http://www.arawards.com.au/index.php/eng/Criteria/Criteria-Applicable-to-Special-Awards-for-Excellence/Occupational-Health-Safety-Reporting-Award.

Endnotes

1 At the time of writing, early 2011, Safe Work Australia said, 'A State of the Science and Policy Discussion Paper is being prepared that outlines the work health and safety policy issues associated with climate change. Based on the work health and safety policy challenges and gaps in research regarding climate change, this research will in particular focus on extreme weather events as well as exposure to heat and how it will impact on workers. This includes identifying the policy and regulatory implications for this emerging hazard.'

2 See WorkSafe Victoria's *Guidance Note: Working in Heat* at http://www.worksafe.vic.gov.au/wps/wcm/connect/2c0293804071f64baf35ffe1fb554c40/guidance+working+in+heat4b.pdf?MOD=AJPERES.

3 Many websites deal with nanotechnology. The Queensland Government has a good website at http://www.deir.qld.gov.au/workplace/subjects/nanotechnology/index.htm. See also the Health and Safety Executive (UK) at http://www.hse.gov.uk/nanotechnology/index.htm?ebul=hsegen&cr=8/31-jan-11.

4 Those concerned about nanotechnology-based consumer products should go to the website http://www.nanotechproject.org/inventories/consumer/.

5 For one side of the debate on nanotechnology, go to https://www.tai.org.au/index.php?q=node%2F19&act=display&type=1&pubid=703.

6 For details go to http://www.safeworkaustralia.gov.au/aboutsafeworkaustralia/WhatWeDo/Research/Nanotechnology/Pages/Nanotechnology.aspx.

7 'Guidance on new chemical requirements for notification of industrial nanomaterials' at http://www.nicnas.gov.au/Current_Issues/Nanotechnology/Guidance%20on%20New%20Chemical%20Requirements%20for%20Notification%20of%20Industrial%20Nanomaterials.pdf.

8 For further details, go to www.nanotechnology.gov.au.

9 Purvis, M. & Bauler, J., 2004, *Irresponsible Care: The Failure of the Chemical Industry to Protect the Public from Chemical Accidents*, US Public Interest Research Group Education Fund, p. 1, http://cdn.publicinterestnetwork.org/assets/w5zgDsAv4kL_kJejmVQczg/IrresponsibleCare2004.pdf.

10 See the article by Andrew Hopkins 'What are we to make of safe behaviour programs?' at http://www.efcog.org/wg/ism_pmi/docs/Safety_Culture/Hopkins_what_are_we_to_make_of_safe_behavior_programs.pdf.

11 This section is based on Sharron O'Neill's paper 'Best Practice OHS Reporting', given to the SIA Conference, Sydney, in October 2009. Go to http://www.onlineohs.com.au/News/SIA_best_practice.pdf.

12 http://www.globalreporting.org/AboutGRI/WhatIsGRI/.

FURTHER REFERENCES

Anyone with health and safety management responsibilities will need to know what the employer's legal requirements are and how best to develop health and safety in the workplace. At the same time, you need to be able to restrict information to that which is relevant, accurate and timely. This guide is set out with these objectives in mind.

WEBSITES

1   **WHS regulator websites.** Go to the websites of the regulators in your employer's jurisdiction. The sitemap will list the information and advice on employer obligations and workplace hazards. The regulators also provide links to related organisations in Australia and overseas. Many provide an update service through which you will be sent emails on recent developments. Note that workers' compensation and injury management matters may be dealt with by a different government agency (and website).

JURISDICTION	REGULATOR	WEBSITE
NSW	WorkCover NSW	www.workcover.nsw.gov.au
Victoria	WorkSafe Victoria	www.worksafe.vic.gov.au
Queensland	Workplace Health and Safety Queensland	www.deir.qld.gov.au/workplace/index.htm
South Australia	SafeWork SA	www.safework.sa.gov.au
Tasmania	Workplace Standards Tasmania	www.wst.tas.gov.au
Western Australia	WorkSafe Western Australia	www.commerce.wa.gov.au/WorkSafe
Northern Territory	NT WorkSafe	www.worksafe.nt.gov.au
ACT	WorkSafe ACT	www.worksafety.act.gov.au/health_safety
Commonwealth	Comcare	www.comcare.gov.ua

2   **Safe Work Australia website** (www.swa.gov.au). This website provides information on national issues covered by SWA such as the National OHS Strategy, national standards and codes of practice, as well as national compensation data. It also has links with the main organisations in Australia and overseas.

3   **Standards Australia website** (www.standards.com.au). There are some 400 Australian standards relevant to WHS.

4   **Industry or employer association websites.** Your industry or employer association website may contain information on WHS issues and developments. From time to time, the Australian Chamber of Commerce and Industry website (www.acci.asn.au) offers policy and advice on WHS from an employer perspective.

5 **Union or professional association websites.** Many of the unions or professional associations representing employees in your organisation maintain information on WHS issues relating to their members:

- The Victorian Trades Hall Council OHS Unit produces an online OHS Reps@Work SafetyNet Journal. This is provided free at www.ohsrep.org.au/safetynet-journal.

- The ACTU website (www.actu.asn.au) keeps members abreast of developments and campaigns as well as information on employee rights in WHS.

6 **International Labour Office of the ILO.** The ILO produces the comprehensive *Encyclopaedia of Occupational Health and Safety*, now in its fourth edition, and the CISILO Database. However, the subscription is expensive. Go to www.ilocis.org/en/default.html.

WHS BLOGS

The blogosphere has ballooned to include many useful sites on WHS, as well as others that are strange. Kevin Jones runs a blog called SafetyatWork (http://safetyatworkblog.wordpress.com/), which has received recognition.

UPDATE SERVICES

WHS authority websites offer a free update service. However, some managers find that they need a more regular and comprehensive service covering the issues and developments in OHS. WorkplaceOHS and CCH Australia provide subscription services.

BOOKS

Australian Master OHS and Environment Guide 2007, 2nd edn, CCH: Sydney. This is a collection of important articles covering the main topics in WHS and the environment. It is slightly biased towards issues of legal compliance.

Quinlan, M., Bohle, P. & Lamm, F., 2010, *Managing Occupational Health Safety in Australia: A Multidisciplinary Approach*, 3rd edn, Macmillan: Melbourne.

CCH, 2009, *Planning Occupational Health and Safety*, 8th edn, CCH: Sydney.

Reason, J., 1997, *Managing the Risks of Organizational Accidents*, Ashgate: London.

VIDEOS, CDS AND DVDS

There are hundreds of WHS videos and DVDs, many of which are found at state and territory WHS Authority libraries. While they are useful for training purposes, they can get out of date quickly and vary dramatically in quality. Professional WHS trainers may be able to provide advice on the best ones to hire or purchase.

CCH produces a CD entitled *Managing Occupational Health & Safety*. This is a very useful – and expensive – package suitable for the WHS manager.

YouTube also has some short videos on WHS, some of which are harrowing.

JOURNALS

The *Australian Journal of Health, Safety and Environment*, published by CCH, provides interpretations of current legislation as well as analyses of various safety management strategies. While it is the 'most respected peer-reviewed safety journal' in Australia, it is expensive, restricting it to library or corporate purchases.

The Safety Institute of Australia produces the *Journal of Health & Safety, Research & Practice*, available only to members of the SIA.

PROFESSIONAL ASSOCIATIONS

The main professional associations dealing with WHS are:

- Human Factors and Ergonomics Society of Australia: www.ergonomics.org.au
- Australasian Faculty of Occupational and Environmental Medicine: http://afoem.racp.edu.au/
- Australian Institute of Occupational Hygienists: www.aioh.org.au
- Australian College of Occupational Health Nurses: www.acohn.com.au
- Safety Institute of Australia: www.sia.org.au

PROVIDERS

Among the largest WHS providers in Australia is the National Safety Council of Australia: www.nsca.org.au.

APPENDIX

Material Safety Data Sheet

---

1. IDENTIFICATION OF THE MATERIAL AND SUPPLIER

Product Name: **HYDROCHLORIC ACID - 20% OR GREATER**

Other name(s): Hydrogen chloride solution; Spirits of salts; Chlorohydric acid; Muriatic acid; Hydrochloric acid solution; Hydrochloric acid 20%; Hydrochloric acid 33%; Hydrochloric acid 42%; Hydrochloric acid Concentrate.

Recommended Use: Precursor for generation of chlorine dioxide gas used in water treatment.

Supplier: Orica Australia Pty Ltd
ABN: 004 117 828
Street Address: 1 Nicholson Street,
Melbourne 3000
Australia
Telephone Number: +61 3 9665 7111
Facsimile: +61 3 9665 7937

Emergency Telephone: **1 800 033 111 (ALL HOURS)**

---

2. HAZARDS IDENTIFICATION

This material is hazardous according to criteria of ASCC; HAZARDOUS SUBSTANCE.

Classified as Dangerous Goods by the criteria of the Australian Dangerous Goods Code (ADG Code) for Transport by Road and Rail; DANGEROUS GOODS.

Risk Phrases: Causes burns. Irritating to respiratory system. Risk of serious damage to eyes.

Safety Phrases: Keep container in a well ventilated place. Do not breathe vapour. Avoid contact with skin and eyes. In case of contact with eyes, rinse immediately with plenty of water and seek medical advice. Wear suitable protective clothing, gloves and eye/face protection. In case of accident or if you feel unwell, seek medical advice immediately (show the label whenever possible).

Poisons Schedule: S6 Poison.

---

3. COMPOSITION/INFORMATION ON INGREDIENTS

Components / CAS Number	Proportion	Risk Phrases
Hydrochloric acid -	>=20%	R34 R37 R41
Water 7732-18-5	to 100%	-

Product Name: *HYDROCHLORIC ACID - 20% OR GREATER*
Substance No: *000031061101*   *Issued:* *01/08/2008*   *Version:* *4*

Material Safety Data Sheet

Water   to 100%   -
7732-18-5

---

4. FIRST AID MEASURES

For advice, contact a Poisons Information Centre (Phone eg. Australia 131 126; New Zealand 0 800 764766) or a doctor.

Inhalation: Remove victim from area of exposure - avoid becoming a casualty. Remove contaminated clothing and loosen remaining clothing. Allow patient to assume most comfortable position and keep warm. Keep at rest until fully recovered. If patient finds breathing difficult and develops a bluish discolouration of the skin (which suggests a lack of oxygen in the blood - cyanosis), ensure airways are clear of any obstruction and have a qualified person give oxygen through a face mask. Apply artificial respiration if patient is not breathing. Seek immediate medical advice.

Skin Contact: If spilt on large areas of skin or hair, immediately drench with running water and remove clothing. Continue to wash skin and hair with plenty of water (and soap if material is insoluble) until advised to stop by the Poisons Information Centre or a doctor.

Eye Contact: If in eyes, hold eyelids apart and flush the eye continuously with running water. Continue flushing until advised to stop by the Poisons Information Centre or a doctor, or for at least 15 minutes. Continue to wash with large amounts of water until medical help is available.

Ingestion: Immediately rinse mouth with water. If swallowed, do NOT induce vomiting. Give a glass of water. Seek immediate medical assistance.

Medical attention and special treatment: Treat symptomatically. Can cause corneal burns.

---

5. FIRE FIGHTING MEASURES

Hazards from combustion products: Non-combustible material.

Precautions for fire fighters and special protective equipment: Decomposes on heating emitting toxic fumes. If safe to do so, remove containers from path of fire. Fire fighters to wear self-contained breathing apparatus and suitable protective clothing if risk of exposure to products of decomposition.

Suitable Extinguishing Media: Not combustible, however, if material is involved in a fire use: Fine water spray, normal foam, dry agent (carbon dioxide, dry chemical powder).

Hazchem Code: 2R

Product Name: *HYDROCHLORIC ACID - 20% OR GREATER*
Substance No: *000031061101*   *Issued:*   *01/08/2008*   *Version:*   *4*

Material Safety Data Sheet

6. ACCIDENTAL RELEASE MEASURES

Emergency procedures: Clear area of all unprotected personnel. If contamination of sewers or waterways has occurred advise local emergency services.

Methods and materials for containment and clean up: Slippery when spilt. Avoid accidents, clean up immediately. Wear protective equipment to prevent skin and eye contact and breathing in vapours. Work up wind or increase ventilation. Contain - prevent run off into drains and waterways. Use absorbent (soil, sand or other inert material). Neutralise with lime or soda ash. Collect and seal in properly labelled containers or drums for disposal. Wash area down with excess water.

7. HANDLING AND STORAGE

This material is a Scheduled Poison S6 and must be stored, maintained and used in accordance with the relevant regulations.

Conditions for safe storage: Store in cool place and out of direct sunlight. Store away from incompatible materials described in Section 10. Store away from foodstuffs. Keep containers closed when not in use - check regularly for leaks.

Precautions for safe handling: Avoid skin and eye contact and breathing in vapour, mists and aerosols. Keep out of reach of children.

8. EXPOSURE CONTROLS/PERSONAL PROTECTION

Occupational Exposure Limits:
No value assigned for this specific material by the National Occupational Health and Safety Commission. However, Exposure Standard(s) for constituent(s):

Hydrogen chloride: Peak Limitation = 7.5 mg/m3 (5 ppm)

As published by the National Occupational Health and Safety Commission.

Peak Limitation - a ceiling concentration which should not be exceeded over a measurement period which should be as short as possible but not exceeding 15 minutes.

These Exposure Standards are guides to be used in the control of occupational health hazards. All atmospheric contamination should be kept to as low a level as is workable. These exposure standards should not be used as fine dividing lines between safe and dangerous concentrations of chemicals. They are not a measure of relative toxicity.

Engineering controls:
Ensure ventilation is adequate and that air concentrations of components are controlled below quoted Exposure Standards. If inhalation risk exists: Use with local exhaust ventilation or while wearing suitable mist respirator. Keep containers closed when not in use.

Product Name:	*HYDROCHLORIC ACID - 20% OR GREATER*				
Substance No:	*000031061101*	*Issued:*	*01/08/2008*	*Version:*	*4*

Material Safety Data Sheet

Personal Protective Equipment:
The selection of PPE is dependant on a detailed risk assessment. The risk assessment should consider the work situation, the physical form of the chemical, the handling methods, and environmental factors.

Orica Personal Protection Guide No. 1, 1998: J - OVERALLS, RUBBER BOOTS, AIR MASK , GLOVES (Long), APRON.
* Not required if wearing air supplied mask.

Wear overalls, full face shield, elbow-length impervious gloves, splash apron and rubber boots. Use with adequate ventilation. If inhalation risk exists, wear air-supplied mask meeting the requirements of AS/NZS 1715 and AS/NZS 1716. Always wash hands before smoking, eating, drinking or using the toilet. Wash contaminated clothing and other protective equipment before storage or re-use.

9. PHYSICAL AND CHEMICAL PROPERTIES

Physical state:	Clear Liquid
Colour:	Colourless to Slightly Yellow
Odour:	Pungent
Solubility:	Miscible with water.
Specific Gravity:	1.14 @ 20°C (for 28% concentration)
Relative Vapour Density (air=1):	Not available
Vapour Pressure (20 °C):	Not available
Flash Point (°C):	Not applicable
Flammability Limits (%):	Not applicable
Autoignition Temperature (°C):	Not applicable
Boiling Point/Range (°C):	98 (for 28% concentration)
pH:	ca. 1

10. STABILITY AND REACTIVITY

Chemical stability:	Corrosive to many metals with the liberation of extremely flammable hydrogen gas.
Conditions to avoid:	Avoid contact with foodstuffs.
Incompatible materials:	Incompatible with alkalis , oxidising agents , sodium hypochlorite , cyanides , and many metals .
Hazardous decomposition products:	Hydrogen chloride.
Hazardous reactions:	Reacts violently with alkalis . Reacts with oxidising agents and sodium hypochlorite liberating toxic chlorine gas.

Material Safety Data Sheet

---

11. TOXICOLOGICAL INFORMATION

No adverse health effects expected if the product is handled in accordance with this Safety Data Sheet and the product label. Symptoms or effects that may arise if the product is mishandled and overexposure occurs are:

Ingestion: Swallowing can result in nausea, vomiting, diarrhoea, abdominal pain and chemical burns to the gastrointestinal tract.

Eye contact: A severe eye irritant. Corrosive to eyes; contact can cause corneal burns. Contamination of eyes can result in permanent injury.

Skin contact: Contact with skin will result in severe irritation. Corrosive to skin - may cause skin burns.

Inhalation: Breathing in mists or aerosols will produce respiratory irritation.

Long Term Effects:
Repeated exposure to low levels of hydrochloric acid may produce discolouration and erosion of teeth and ulceration of the nasal passages.

Toxicological Data:
No LD50 data available for the product. However, for constituent(s) HYDROGEN CHLORIDE:
Oral LD50 (rat):   >900 mg/kg.
Inhalation LC50 (rat):   3124 ppm/1h.

12. ECOLOGICAL INFORMATION

Ecotoxicity   Avoid contaminating waterways.

13. DISPOSAL CONSIDERATIONS

Disposal methods: Refer to Waste Management Authority. Dispose of material through a licensed waste contractor. Decontamination and destruction of containers should be considered.

14. TRANSPORT INFORMATION

Road and Rail Transport
Classified as Dangerous Goods by the criteria of the Australian Dangerous Goods Code (ADG Code) for Transport by Road and Rail; DANGEROUS GOODS.

UN No: 1789
Class-primary   8 Corrosive
Packing Group: II
Proper Shipping Name: HYDROCHLORIC ACID

Product Name: *HYDROCHLORIC ACID - 20% OR GREATER*
Substance No: *000031061101*   *Issued:*   *01/08/2008*   *Version:*   *4*

Material Safety Data Sheet

Hazchem Code: 2R

Marine Transport

Classified as Dangerous Goods by the criteria of the International Maritime Dangerous Goods Code (IMDG Code) for transport by sea; DANGEROUS GOODS.

UN No:	1789
Class-primary:	8 Corrosive
Packing Group:	II
Proper Shipping Name:	HYDROCHLORIC ACID

Air Transport

Classified as Dangerous Goods by the criteria of the International Air Transport Association (IATA) Dangerous Goods Regulations for transport by air; DANGEROUS GOODS.

UN No:	1789
Class-primary:	8 Corrosive
Packing Group:	II
Proper Shipping Name:	HYDROCHLORIC ACID

15. REGULATORY INFORMATION

Classification: This material is hazardous according to criteria of ASCC; HAZARDOUS SUBSTANCE.

Hazard Category: C: Corrosive

Risk Phrase(s):
R34: Causes burns.
R37: Irritating to respiratory system.
R41: Risk of serious damage to eyes.

Safety Phrase(s):
S9: Keep container in a well ventilated place.
S23: Do not breathe vapour/mist/aerosol.
S24/25: Avoid contact with skin and eyes.
S26: In case of contact with eyes, rinse immediately with plenty of water and seek medical advice.
S36/37/39: Wear suitable protective clothing, gloves and eye/face protection.
S45: In case of accident or if you feel unwell, seek medical advice immediately (show the label whenever possible).

Poisons Schedule: S6 Poison.

All the constituents of this material are listed on the Australian Inventory of Chemical Substances (AICS).

Product Name:	*HYDROCHLORIC ACID - 20% OR GREATER*						
Substance No:	*000031061101*		*Issued:*	*01/08/2008*	*Version:*		*4*

Material Safety Data Sheet

16. OTHER INFORMATION

'Registry of Toxic Effects of Chemical Substances'. Ed. D. Sweet, US Dept. of Health & Human Services: Cincinatti, 2008.

This material safety data sheet has been prepared by SH&E Shared Services, Orica.

Reason(s) for Issue:
5 Yearly Revised Primary MSDS

This MSDS summarises to our best knowledge at the date of issue, the chemical health and safety hazards of the material and general guidance on how to safely handle the material in the workplace. Since Orica Limited cannot anticipate or control the conditions under which the product may be used, each user must, prior to usage, assess and control the risks arising from its use of the material.

If clarification or further information is needed, the user should contact their Orica representative or Orica Limited at the contact details on page 1.

Orica Limited's responsibility for the material as sold is subject to the terms and conditions of sale, a copy of which is available upon request.

Product Name:	*HYDROCHLORIC ACID - 20% OR GREATER*					
Substance No:	*000031061101*	*Issued:*	*01/08/2008*	*Version:*	*4*	

GLOSSARY

The following is a brief glossary of some of the main terms and initials used in this book. It is also important to become familiar with the definitions used in WHS law; for example, 'PCBU' and 'workplace'. These can be found on the jurisdiction websites where legal definitions are set out.

ACCI
Australian Chamber of Commerce and Industry

ACTU
Australian Council of Trade Unions

ALARA
as low as reasonably achievable; the principle used to identify the level of acceptable risk (sometimes known as ALARP, as low as reasonably practicable)

ALARP
as low as reasonably practicable; the principle used to identify the level of acceptable risk (sometimes known as ALARA)

anthropometry
the technique of measuring the human body in terms of dimensions, proportions and ratios

ASCC
Australian Safety and Compensation Council, formerly the National Occupational Health and Safety Commission (NOHSC), has now been replaced by Safe Work Australia (SWA)

Australian standard
a standard developed by Standards Australia

average lost time rate (ALTR)

$$\frac{\text{number of working days lost in the period}}{\text{number of lost time injuries or illnesses in the period}}$$

biomechanics
the study of the mechanics of muscular activity

carcinogen
an agent capable of producing cancer in humans or animals

code of practice
a technical document on a health and safety issue approved by a government minister, providing practical guidance on ways to achieve compliance with WHS legislation

common law
law deriving from judges' decisions based on established legal principles

dangerous goods
any material listed in the Australian Dangerous Goods Code

disease
damage to the body that shows up only after a period of time from first exposure to a hazard

duty of care
a principle that requires each person or organisation to take care not to cause harm to other persons

engineering control
changing the physical characteristics of machinery or the workplace in order to remove or reduce the risk associated with it

ergonomics
the study of the characteristics of people and their work systems with the object of achieving optimal interaction in terms of comfort, health, safety and performance

guidance note
document prepared by a government agency to provide information or technical guidance on a WHS issue

hazard
a source or situation with a potential for harm or damage

hazard identification
the process of identifying potential causes of injury or illness, sometimes known as risk identification

hazardous substance
a material classified as hazardous under hazardous substances legislation or other WHS legislation

hierarchy of control
: the descending order of effectiveness of different types of control measures; for example, elimination, substitution, engineering control, isolation, administrative control and personal protective equipment

HSE
: Health and Safety Executive; UK government body responsible for administering WHS

ILO
: International Labour Office

injury management
: treatment of a workplace injury, rehabilitation back to work, retraining into a new skill or new job, management of the workers' compensation claim, and the employment practices of the employer

JSA
: job safety analysis

jurisdiction
: a realm of governance and law; there are 9 major (WHS) jurisdictions: New South Wales, Victoria, Queensland, South Australia, Western Australia, Tasmania, the Northern Territory, the Australian Capital Territory, Commonwealth (APS employment)

lost time injury (LTI)
: an occupational injury whereby the injured person is not able to work for at least one full work day (or shift) any time after the day the injury occurred

lost time injury frequency rate (LTIFR)

$$\frac{\text{number of lost time injuries or illnesses in the period} \times 1\,000\,000}{\text{number of hours worked in the period}}$$

lost time injury incidence rate (LTIIR)

$$\frac{\text{number of lost time injuries or illnesses in the period} \times 1000}{\text{number of workers employed}}$$

lump sum
: a single payment to compensate for an injury, disease or death, as opposed to regular payments

material safety data sheet (MSDS)
: a summary of relevant properties of a hazardous substance with information on safety, health, storage, handling and emergency information; now also known as safety data sheets (SDSs)

MSDS
: material safety data sheet

musculoskeletal disorders
: physical injuries caused by performing unsafe manual handling tasks, such as muscle sprains and strains; injuries to muscles, ligaments and discs in the back; injuries to nerves, ligaments and tendons in the hands, wrists, arms, shoulders, neck or legs; abdominal hernias; long-term pain

NICNAS
: National Industrial Chemicals Notification and Assessment Scheme; the Australian Government's industrial chemical safety regulator

NIOSH
: National Institute for Occupational Safety and Health; US federal government body responsible for research into WHS

NOHSC
: National Occupational Health and Safety Commission, now Safe Work Australia

NOSI
: National Online Statistics Interactive system

occupational hygiene
: evaluation and control of exposure from chemical, physical, biological and psychosocial hazards

OOS
: occupational overuse syndrome; refers to musculoskeletal disorders, primarily those affecting the hands, wrists, arms and shoulders; previously also known as repetitive strain injury (RSI)

OSHA
: Occupational Safety and Health Administration; US government authority for the administration of workplace health and safety

personal protective equipment (PPE)
equipment worn by workers to reduce risk from WHS hazards

physiology
the study of the functioning of living organisms

plant
any machinery, equipment, appliance, implement or tool, including their components, fittings or accessories

reasonably practicable
a term used to describe the standards expected in order to comply with the law

regulation
subordinate legislation passed by parliament to amplify or make explicit the requirements of an Act

repetitive strain injury (RSI)
see OOS

residual risk
risk that remains after the application of controls

return to work
the process of restoring an injured worker to the fullest physical, psychological, social, vocational and economic function of which they are capable

risk (WHS)
the probability and consequences of injury, illness or damage arising from exposure to a hazard(s)

risk analysis
the process of analysing the potential risk of injury or illness from exposure to hazards; risk analysis forms part of risk assessment

risk assessment
the process of analysing the probability and consequences of injury or illness arising from exposure to hazards

risk control
controlling the risk of exposure to hazards; see 'hierarchy of control'

risk evaluation
evaluating whether the risk is acceptable or not

risk management
the process of recognising situations that have the potential to cause harm to people or property, and the act of doing something to prevent the hazardous situation occurring or the person being harmed

safe design
the design process that eliminates hazards or minimises potential risk throughout the life cycle of the designed product

safe working procedures
a set of written instructions that identifies the health and safety issues that may arise from the jobs and tasks that make up a system of work

statute law
law passed by parliament

stress
an individual's negative response, physical or mental, to challenging situations

systems of work
work methods and processes (including the tools, machines and furnishings) used in a business enterprise

WHO
World Health Organization

WHS audit
systematic check of the WHS management system

WHS management
the design, implementation and maintenance of work activities to promote health and safety

WHSMS
workplace health and safety management system: a system of linked management practices designed to meet WHS legal and policy requirements and achieve continuous improvement

workplace rehabilitation
restoration of the functional effectiveness and health of an injured worker

INDEX